29. 99

THE CAMBRIDGE COMPANION TO
THE JESUITS

Ignatius of Loyola (1491–1556) obtained papal approval in 1540 for a new international religious order called the Society of Jesus. Until the mid-1700s the 'Jesuits' were active in many parts of Europe and far beyond. Gaining both friends and enemies in response to their work as teachers, scholars, writers, preachers, missionaries, and spiritual directors, the Jesuits were formally suppressed by Pope Clement XIV in 1773 and restored by Pope Pius VII in 1814. The Society of Jesus then grew until the 1960s; it has more recently experienced declining membership in Europe and North America, but expansion in other parts of the world.

This *Companion* examines the religious and cultural significance of the Jesuits. The first four parts treat the period prior to the Suppression, while part V examines the Suppression and some of the challenges and opportunities of the restored Society of Jesus up to the present.

Thomas Worcester, S.J., is Associate Professor of History at the College of the Holy Cross, Massachusetts. He is the author of *Seventeenth-Century Cultural Discourse: France and the Preaching of Bishop Camus*, and co-editor (with Pamela Jones) of *From Rome to Eternity: Catholicism and the Arts in Italy, ca. 1550–1650*. He is also co-editor (with Franco Mormando) of *Piety and Plague: From Byzantium to the Baroque*, and he is a member of the editorial board for *Studies in the Spirituality of Jesuits*.

CAMBRIDGE COMPANIONS TO RELIGION

A series of companions to major topics and key figures in theology and religious studies. Each volume contains specially commissioned chapters by international scholars which provide an accessible and stimulating introduction to the subject for new readers and non-specialists.

Other titles in the series

THE CAMBRIDGE COMPANION TO CHRISTIAN DOCTRINE
edited by Colin Gunton (1997)
ISBN 0 521 47118 4 hardback   ISBN 0 521 47695 8 paperback

THE CAMBRIDGE COMPANION TO BIBLICAL INTERPRETATION
edited by John Barton (1998)
ISBN 0 521 48144 9 hardback   ISBN 0 521 48593 2 paperback

THE CAMBRIDGE COMPANION TO DIETRICH BONHOEFFER
edited by John de Gruchy (1999)
ISBN 0 521 58258 x hardback   ISBN 0 521 58751 6 paperback

THE CAMBRIDGE COMPANION TO LIBERATION THEOLOGY, FIRST EDITION
edited by Christopher Rowland (1999)
ISBN 0 521 46144 8 hardback   ISBN 0 521 46707 1 paperback

THE CAMBRIDGE COMPANION TO KARL BARTH
edited by John Webster (2000)
ISBN 0 521 58476 0 hardback   ISBN 0 521 58560 0 paperback

THE CAMBRIDGE COMPANION TO CHRISTIAN ETHICS
edited by Robin Gill (2001)
ISBN 0 521 77070 x hardback   ISBN 0 521 77918 9 paperback

THE CAMBRIDGE COMPANION TO JESUS
edited by Markus Bockmuehl (2001)
ISBN 0 521 79261 4 hardback   ISBN 0 521 79678 4 paperback

THE CAMBRIDGE COMPANION TO FEMINIST THEOLOGY
edited by Susan Frank Parsons (2002)
ISBN 0 521 66327 x hardback   ISBN 0 521 66380 6 paperback

THE CAMBRIDGE COMPANION TO MARTIN LUTHER
edited by Donald K. McKim (2003)
ISBN 0 521 81648 3 hardback   ISBN 0 521 01673 8 paperback

THE CAMBRIDGE COMPANION TO ST. PAUL
edited by James D. G. Dunn (2003)
ISBN 0 521 78155 8 hardback   ISBN 0 521 78694 0 paperback

THE CAMBRIDGE COMPANION TO POSTMODERN THEOLOGY
edited by Kevin J. Vanhoozer (2003)
ISBN 0 521 79062 x hardback   ISBN 0 521 79395 5 paperback

THE CAMBRIDGE COMPANION TO JOHN CALVIN
edited by Donald K. McKim (2004)
ISBN 0 521 81647 5 hardback   ISBN 0 521 01672 x paperback

THE CAMBRIDGE COMPANION TO HANS URS VON BALTHASAR
edited by Edward T. Oakes, S. J. and David Moss (2004)
ISBN 0 521 81467 7 hardback   ISBN 0 521 89147 7 paperback

THE CAMBRIDGE COMPANION TO REFORMATION THEOLOGY
edited by David Bagchi and David Steinmetz (2004)
ISBN 0 521 77224 9 hardback   ISBN 0 521 77662 7 paperback

THE CAMBRIDGE COMPANION TO AMERICAN JUDAISM
edited by Dana Evan Kaplan (2005)
ISBN 0 521 82204 1 hardback   ISBN 0 521 52951 4 paperback

THE CAMBRIDGE COMPANION TO KARL RAHNER
edited by Declan Marmion and Mary E. Hines (2005)
ISBN 0 521 83288 8 hardback   ISBN 0 521 54045 3 paperback

THE CAMBRIDGE COMPANION TO FRIEDRICH SCHLEIERMACHER
edited by Jacqueline Mariña (2005)
ISBN 0 521 81448 0 hardback   ISBN 0 521 89137 x paperback

THE CAMBRIDGE COMPANION TO THE GOSPELS
edited by Stephen C. Barton (2006)
ISBN 0 521 80766 2 hardback   ISBN 0 521 00261 3 paperback

THE CAMBRIDGE COMPANION TO THE QUR'AN
edited by Jane Dammen McAuliffe (2006)
ISBN 0 521 83160 1 hardback   ISBN 0 521 53934 x paperback

THE CAMBRIDGE COMPANION TO JONATHAN EDWARDS
edited by Stephen J. Stein (2007)
ISBN 0 521 85290 0 hardback   ISBN 0 521 61805 3 paperback

THE CAMBRIDGE COMPANION TO EVANGELICAL THEOLOGY
edited by Timothy Larsen and Daniel J. Trier (2007)
ISBN 0 521 84698 6 hardback   ISBN 0 521 60974 7 paperback

THE CAMBRIDGE COMPANION TO MODERN JEWISH PHILOSOPHY
edited by Michael L. Morgan and Peter Eli Gordon (2007)
ISBN 0 521 81312 3 hardback   ISBN 0 521 01255 4 paperback

THE CAMBRIDGE COMPANION TO THE TALMUD AND RABBINIC
LITERATURE
edited by Charlotte E. Fonrobert and Martin S. Jaffee (2007)
ISBN 0 521 84390 1 hardback   ISBN 0 521 60508 3 paperback

THE CAMBRIDGE COMPANION TO LIBERATION THEOLOGY, SECOND
EDITION
edited by Christopher Rowland (2008)
ISBN 9780521868839 hardback   ISBN 9780521688932 paperback

Forthcoming

THE CAMBRIDGE COMPANION TO ISLAMIC THEOLOGY
edited by Tim Winter

THE CAMBRIDGE COMPANION TO THE VIRGIN MARY
edited by Sarah Boss

THE CAMBRIDGE COMPANION TO ANCIENT CHRISTIANITY
edited by Rebecca Lyman

THE CAMBRIDGE COMPANION TO

THE JESUITS

edited by Thomas Worcester

CAMBRIDGE
UNIVERSITY PRESS

CAMBRIDGE UNIVERSITY PRESS
Cambridge, New York, Melbourne, Madrid, Cape Town, Singapore, São Paulo, Delhi

Cambridge University Press
The Edinburgh Building, Cambridge CB2 8RU, UK

Published in the United States of America by Cambridge University Press, New York

www.cambridge.org
Information on this title: www.cambridge.org/9780521673969

First published 2008

Printed in the United Kingdom at the University Press, Cambridge

A catalogue record for this publication is available from the British Library

ISBN 978-0-521-85731-4 hardback
ISBN 978-0-521-67396-9 paperback

Contents

Illustrations

Notes on contributors

Thomas Worcester, S. J., is Associate Professor of History at the College of the Holy Cross, Massachusetts. He is the author of *Seventeenth-Century Cultural Discourse: France and the Preaching of Bishop Camus*, and co-editor (with Pamela Jones) of *From Rome to Eternity: Catholicism and the Arts in Italy, ca. 1550–1650*. He is also co-editor (with Franco Mormando) of *Piety and Plague: From Byzantium to the Baroque*, and he is a member of the editorial board for *Studies in the Spirituality of Jesuits*.

Gauvin Alexander Bailey is Senior Lecturer in Art History at the University of Aberdeen. His books include *Art on the Jesuit Missions in Asia and Latin America, 1542–1773*, *Between Renaissance and Baroque: Jesuit Art in Rome, 1565–1610*, and *Art of Colonial Latin America*.

Louis Caruana, S. J., is Senior Lecturer in Philosophy at Heythrop College, London, and Adjunct Scholar at the Vatican Observatory. He is the author of *Holism and the Understanding of Science*, and of *Science and Virtue: An Essay on the Impact of the Scientific Mentality on Moral Character*.

Thomas M. Cohen is curator of the Oliveira Lima Library and Associate Professor of History at The Catholic University of America, Washington, DC. He is the author of *The Fire of Tongues: António Vieira and the Missionary Church in Brazil and Portugal*.

J. Carlos Coupeau, S. J., is a resident professor at the Istituto di Spiritualità, Pontifical Gregorian University, Rome. He is secretary of the *Manresa* journal (Madrid), and co-editor of the *Diccionario de Espiritualidad Ignaciana*.

Philip Endean, S. J., is Tutor in Theology at Campion Hall, Oxford, and Editor of *The Way*, a journal of spirituality published by the British Jesuits. He is the author of *Karl Rahner and Ignatian Spirituality*, and co-editor (with Joseph Munitiz) of *Saint Ignatius of Loyola: Personal Writings*.

Mary Ann Hinsdale, I. H. M., is Associate Professor of Theology at Boston College, Massachusetts. She the author of *Women Shaping Theology*, and co-author of *It Comes from the People: Community Development and Local Theology*.

Lu Ann Homza   is the Class of 2009 Professor of History at the College of William and Mary, Virginia. She has published *Religious Authority in the Spanish Renaissance* and *The Spanish Inquisition, 1478–1614* (an anthology of sources).

Thomas M. McCoog, S. J.,   divides his time between London where he is archivist of the British Province of the Society of Jesus, and Rome where he is editor of the publications of the Jesuit Historical Institute. Most recently he has edited *The Mercurian Project: Forming Jesuit Culture, 1573–1580*, and an enlarged second edition of *The Reckoned Expense: Edmund Campion and the Early English Jesuits*.

Gerald McKevitt, S. J.,   is Ignacio Ellacuría Professor for Jesuit Studies at Santa Clara University, California. His focus is on Jesuit history in the USA, and his most recent book is *Brokers of Culture: Italian Jesuits in the American West, 1848–1919*.

Jacques Monet, S. J.,   is Director of the Canadian Institute of Jesuit Studies, Toronto, and past president of Regis College, Toronto. He is the author of many writings on religious and national identity in Canada, including *The Last Cannon Shot: A Study of French Canadian Nationalism*.

Paul V. Murphy   is Director of the Institute of Catholic Studies and Associate Professor of History at John Carroll University, Ohio. He is the author of *Ruling Peacefully: Cardinal Ercole Gonzaga and Patrician Reform in Sixteenth-Century Italy*.

Stanisław Obirek,   a former Jesuit priest, is currently Professor of Philosophy and Theology at the University of Łódź, Poland. His many publications in Polish include a book on Piotr Skarga (1536–1612), a well-known Jesuit preacher, and a study of Jesuits in Poland and Lithuania, 1564–1668. Obirek is also active in contemporary interreligious dialogue and in efforts to promote understanding and reconciliation between Polish Catholics and Jews.

Gemma Simmonds   is a sister of the Congregation of Jesus (C.J.), formerly known as the Institute of the Blessed Virgin Mary. Simmonds lectures on ecclesiology and spirituality at Heythrop College, London; she has published articles on the history of spirituality, and has published a translation of Henri de Lubac's *Corpus Mysticum*.

Nicolas Standaert, S. J.,   is Professor of Sinology at K. U. Leuven (Catholic University of Leuven, Belgium). He is the author of *Tingyun, Confucian and Christian in Late Ming China: His Life and Thought*, and the editor of *Handbook of Christianity in China: Volume One (635–1800)*.

M. Antoni J. Üçerler, S. J., is a Lecturer in modern languages and comparative history at Campion Hall, Oxford. He previously taught at Sophia University in Japan, where he co-edited the online *Laures Rare Book Database* of early Japanese Christian sources. Üçerler has also published works on Alessandro Valignano, S. J. (1532–1606), and the Jesuit missions in Japan.

Jonathan Wright is an independent scholar. He is a former Thouron Fellow at the University of Pennsylvania and a former fellow at the Institute for European History, University of Mainz. He is the author of *God's Soldiers: Adventure, Politics, Intrigue, and Power – A History of the Jesuits*, and of *Shapers of the Great Debate on Freedom of Religion*.

Introduction

THOMAS WORCESTER

The Society of Jesus is a Catholic religious order of men, whose members are known as Jesuits. It is often recognized by a monogram, IHS, and a motto, AMDG. The former honors the name of Jesus, Jesus who is the savior of the world (*Iesus Hominum Salvator*).[1] The latter points to the raison d'être of the Jesuits, "For the greater glory of God" (*Ad maiorem Dei gloriam*). In this introduction and eighteen essays that follow, *The Cambridge Companion to the Jesuits* focuses principally on the early modern period, from Ignatius of Loyola (1491–1556), founder of the Jesuits, to the suppression of the Society of Jesus in the eighteenth century by Pope Clement XIV. Four of the five parts of the book treat this period: I. Ignatius of Loyola; II. European Foundations of the Jesuits; III. Geographic and Ethnic Frontiers; IV. Arts and Sciences. The last part, Jesuits in the Modern World, examines some key aspects of the Society of Jesus, from its suppression in 1773 and subsequent restoration in 1814, to the present.

Ignatius of Loyola was born at the end of the fifteenth century, at Loyola, in the Basque country of Spain.[2] He grew up at a time when Spain was rapidly becoming the dominant power of Europe and indeed of the world. It was also a time of religious change and tension, an age when Spain's monarchs expelled Jews and Muslims, and sought to enforce a kind of uniformity in belief and practice among Catholics. Yet diverse movements, ideas, and practices, old and new, prospered among Spanish Catholics. Lu Ann Homza's essay, the first in this *Companion*, examines the complexity of the religious culture Ignatius would have experienced in early sixteenth-century Spain.

Injured in battle at Pamplona in 1521, Ignatius recovered slowly and painfully, but as he did so he began to read about the lives of the saints and the life of Christ. Setting out on a pilgrimage to Jerusalem, he crossed northern Spain to the shrine of Our Lady of Montserrat, where he prayed for guidance in his desire to follow Christ. He then spent some months in prayer, as a kind of hermit, at nearby Manresa. In

Figure 0.1. Sunrise at Bellarmine House (Jesuit residence), Cohasset, Massachusetts, 2006. Photo by Thomas Worcester.

1523 he journeyed to the Holy Land, but was not permitted to remain there by its Franciscan guardians. In 1524, after returning to Spain, Ignatius began to study at the universities of Alcalá and Salamanca, trying to get an education, even well into adulthood, in Latin, and in philosophy and theology, matters he knew little about. Ignatius believed that he was called to "help souls" live more authentically Christian lives, and he sought to do this by various means, but especially by helping them to do certain "spiritual exercises." These exercises in prayer and discernment would help people to know themselves and to know Christ better, and help them to make good decisions about how best to serve God and neighbor. Philip Endean's essay considers in detail the Spiritual Exercises of Ignatius. Refined by Ignatius through much of his life, and first published in the 1540s, they became the heart and soul of the spiritual "formation" of Jesuits themselves, and a central focus of much of their ministry to others.

In 1528 Ignatius began studies at the University of Paris, where he remained until 1535. In Paris, Ignatius succeeded in gaining the education he wanted and needed in order to "help souls," by earning a Master's degree. He also gained a small group of companions and followers from among his fellow students. With Ignatius, in 1534, six others made a vow to go to Jerusalem, or, should that be impossible, to offer their services to the pope. In the event, after travel to Venice and ordination as priests for those who were not yet ordained, they were unable to obtain passage to the Holy Land, and instead went to Rome. They presented a proposal for a new religious order, the Society of Jesus, to Pope Paul III in 1539, a proposal accepted by the pope in 1540, over the objections of some cardinals. The following year Ignatius was elected Superior General of the new order, and he devoted the rest of his life to governance of what became known as the Jesuits, and to writing constitutions for this religious order. Ignatius died in Rome in 1556, and was canonized as a saint by Pope Gregory XV in 1622. J. Carlos Coupeau's essay in this book explores five different *personae* or roles of Ignatius, as they have been imagined and propagated since the sixteenth century.

Europe was where the Society of Jesus was born, and Rome was where its central government was based. Part II of the *Companion* examines the ways in which the Society grew rapidly in Europe after 1540, but also some of the principal challenges and limitations it faced. Paul Murphy's essay explores what Jesuits did in Rome and in Italy, and gives some particular attention to the origins of Jesuit schools. Ignatius had not initially imagined his "company" as taking on the responsibility of running schools; Jesuits were to be pilgrims, itinerant ministers of the word of God, mobile and ready to go anywhere, not resident schoolmasters. But by the late 1540s Jesuits began to found schools and take over existing educational institutions when invited to do so by princes, town officials, bishops, and other authorities. Schools became a central locus of Jesuit ministries that also went beyond the classroom, with Jesuit communities attached to schools serving as a kind of base of operations for a broad range of pastoral and other ministries.[3]

In the 1540s and 1550s, with the help of other Jesuits, Ignatius wrote Constitutions for the Society of Jesus.[4] Detailed norms for admission of new members and their formation are one of the main topics treated. One does not become a Jesuit quickly. With some adaptations, Jesuit formation today is what Ignatius envisioned, and it lasts many years. It begins with a two-year novitiate, in which novices are introduced to Jesuit life, by learning about its history, but especially by participating in Jesuit prayer, Jesuit community, and Jesuit work of various kinds. Most importantly, novices make the full, thirty-day version of the Spiritual Exercises. At the end of the novitiate, if approved by the provincial superior, novices may pronounce vows of poverty, chastity, and obedience. If seeking ordination as a priest, the newly vowed Jesuit becomes a scholastic (a Jesuit student). A brother is a Jesuit who, though not seeking ordination, may undertake studies in various fields; he will then take a full share in the Society's work, according to his talents. For a scholastic, his studies normally include a broad exposure to the humanities and to sciences; this is followed by two years of philosophy, after which he becomes a regent for a year or two or three, or occasionally longer. Regency is a period of full-time work in a Jesuit ministry, and it could be anywhere in the world. Four years of theology study follow before a scholastic is ordained to the priesthood. Some time after ordination – often several years later – a Jesuit does tertianship, a period of some months, providing time for extended reflection on what one's experience of Jesuit life has been, in view of the possibility of taking final vows as a Jesuit. Like the novitiate, details of tertianship vary, but they always include a thirty-day retreat. Final vows may include the fourth vow, a vow of obedience to the pope, in the sense of availability to be missioned anywhere in the world, for the greater glory of God.[5]

The Constitutions also outlined a system of governance in which a Superior General, elected for life, would oversee implementation of, and fidelity to, the Constitutions and related documents. Father General would also appoint provincial superiors. These superiors would govern Jesuit provinces, and the provinces were to correspond to geographic areas, such as a city and its environs, or sometimes an entire country, or several countries together. As the number of provinces grew, these were grouped together in several "assistancies" and for each of these there was an assistant to Father General in Rome. There were also local superiors who would govern individual communities of Jesuits. But it was not a simplistic top-down pyramid, for individual Jesuits were encouraged to "represent" their views, including when they differed from those of superiors. Mere commands from above could be relatively rare, and often much was left to individual initiative. In an age before rapid transportation and electronic communication, letters from Rome could be slow in coming, and action could not always await their arrival.[6] Though exempt in various ways from episcopal authority, Jesuits did at times depend on financial and other support from local bishops. Jesuits looked to Rome for authorization for what they did, but also to local situations and needs for how to deal with day-to-day work and life. Jesuits were not exempt from various forms of oversight by civil powers, and the management of good relations with emperors, monarchs, princes, parliaments, law courts, city councilors, and other government authorities could require much diplomacy, tact, flattery, and protracted negotiations.

There can be no question in this volume of a comprehensive survey of every country in Europe where Jesuits went – several large volumes would be required – but rather of a sampling of several important contexts and issues that shed light on Jesuit priorities, and the opportunities and difficulties their implementation faced.

England and France had strong, centralized monarchies. Post-Reformation England was a difficult place for Jesuits, and a Protestant monarch who claimed supremacy over a national church was unlikely to view favorably a group of Catholic priests committed to an international vision of Christianity, and to the upholding of papal authority. Thomas McCoog's essay considers how Jesuits fared in England, Scotland, Ireland, and in the English Jesuit mission to Maryland. My essay, on France, focuses specifically on how French Jesuits used the printing press, *c.* 1600–50, in an effort to obtain and retain royal favor. Though France's monarchs were Catholic, their support for Jesuit endeavors, and the support of other French Catholics for the Society of Jesus, was often fragile, at best. While not a few in England and France wanted to have the Jesuits expelled, others, especially some female Catholics, wanted to become Jesuits, or at least something very much like them. Gemma Simmonds' essay considers such efforts by Mary Ward and other women.

In central and eastern Europe Jesuits worked in a complex religious and political context, where Lutherans, Calvinists, Anabaptists, and other Protestant groups fought against each other as well as against Catholics. Peter Canisius (1521–97) was a Jesuit who devoted his energies to preaching, teaching, and founding educational institutions in places such as Cologne, Vienna, and Prague. His publications included several catechisms, reprinted many times.[7] Canisius and other Jesuits sought to "counter" Protestant inroads of various kinds, but they also sought to promote internal reform of the Catholic Church, especially through conversion of individuals from a lukewarm religion to an active, heartfelt, well-educated Catholic piety. Stanisław Obirek's essay in this volume focuses principally on Jesuit successes and failures in early modern Poland.

Many in the first generation of Jesuits were Portuguese or Spanish, and their homelands were the leaders in European exploration, conquest, and evangelization of the Pacific and Atlantic worlds. Part III, Geographic and Ethnic Frontiers, considers some of the ways in which Jesuits made "missions" outside Europe a priority. Francis Xavier (1506–52), a Basque like Ignatius, and a roommate of Ignatius at the University of Paris, became the first Jesuit missionary to Asia. John III, King of Portugal, wanted more missionaries for India, and Xavier was chosen by Ignatius for this task. Francis Xavier left Lisbon in 1541, never to return to Europe. He labored in India, in Indonesia, in Japan; he died while seeking to enter China. He was canonized as a saint in 1622. The cover image of this volume shows the Jesuit Church of St. Francis Xavier, built in the late seventeenth century, in Lucerne, Switzerland. By that period, St. Francis Xavier had become not only the premier exemplar of a missionary saint, but a very popular intercessory saint to whom Catholics prayed in time of plague and other illness, and at the hour of death. M. Antoni J. Üçerler's essay considers Jesuit efforts in India, and especially in Japan, in the aftermath of Xavier's work. Nicolas Standaert's essay examines Jesuits in China, and how they were learners as well as teachers. European Jesuits in Asia, perhaps especially those in China, sought to separate Christianity from European culture, and to accept and adopt many local customs and traditions. Such a way of proceeding did not always please authorities in Rome, and some popes intervened to put a stop to Jesuit acceptance of what some Europeans considered to be pagan practices.

Jesuits pushed outward the boundaries of European knowledge and understanding of the rest of the world. For example, by the early seventeenth century, French Jesuits in Canada were sending back to

France detailed reports of what they experienced. Published in Paris beginning in 1632, these *Jesuit Relations* stimulated and fascinated their European readers' imaginations, though they could also give ammunition to Eurocentric enemies who sought to discredit the Society of Jesus as soft on paganism, as too willing to accommodate non-Christian practices.[8] Jacques Monet's essay examines the complexity of the Jesuit mission to New France. Whether or not converts among Native peoples could or should be admitted to Catholic religious orders or to the priesthood was a controversial question in the early modern era, and it paralleled a question within Europe, especially on the Iberian Peninsula. Should New Christians, that is, Jewish converts to Catholicism, be admitted to the Society of Jesus? Thomas Cohen's essay examines how this issue was handled (and/or mishandled) in the sixteenth and seventeenth centuries.

Recent scholarship has shown how, in Europe and elsewhere, Jesuits played a major role not only in a religious context or sphere of influence, but also more broadly, in culture, arts, and sciences.[9] John O'Malley has argued that the deepening Jesuit commitment to schools went hand-in-hand with commitment to civic education, to the arts, including painting and architecture, theater, music, ballet and opera, as well as to scientific knowledge and discovery.[10] Part IV of this *Companion*, Arts and Sciences, focuses on two examples: Jesuit architecture in Latin America, with an essay by Gauvin Bailey, and Jesuit contributions to the scientific revolution, with an essay by Louis Caruana.

But by the mid-eighteenth century, appreciation of Jesuit contributions was increasingly outweighed by the venom of those seeking destruction of the Society founded by Ignatius. Succumbing to pressure from several European monarchs, Pope Clement XIV suppressed the Order in 1773, in what Eamon Duffy has described as "the papacy's most shameful hour."[11] And yet the Jesuits did not disappear altogether, and they were eventually formally restored by Pius VII; Jonathan Wright's essay examines both how the Suppression came about and how it came to an end.

An explanation for the greater attention this *Cambridge Companion to the Jesuits* pays to the earlier period than to the last two centuries is in order. Much is known about certain exceptional Jesuits of the restored Society, though many of these men were considered marginal or misfits in their own time, to be honored postmortem. Prominent examples include the poet Gerard Manley Hopkins (1844–89) and the scientist Pierre Teilhard de Chardin (1881–1955).[12] But there are relatively few good studies of the Jesuits since 1814 – in any part of the world – at least compared with the abundance of excellent work done on the history of the "old" Society and its "corporate" culture. In general, the Society of Jesus, for much of the century and a half from its restoration until Vatican II, was conservative and even reactionary. In Europe, nostalgia for the close relationship between Church and State (altar and throne) that existed before the French Revolution was strong in Jesuit circles. By the midtwentieth century, a growing number of Jesuits in Europe, and elsewhere, began to break new ground in theology and in biblical studies, in other scholarly fields, and in promotion of Catholic social teaching that called for just wages for workers, and for support of their right to organize and defend their dignity.[13]

The USA is one of the parts of the world where the nineteenth and twentieth centuries saw dramatic growth in Jesuit numbers and institutions. There had been but a few Jesuits before the Suppression in what became the new American republic. After 1814, Jesuits in the USA struggled to balance fidelity to Old World traditions with openness to the realities and opportunities of the New World. Not altogether unlike earlier generations of Jesuits elsewhere, Jesuits in the USA faced a myriad of questions about how to accommodate and adapt to unfamiliar contexts and cultures. Gerald McKevitt's essay in this volume, on Jesuit schools in the United States to *c.* 1970, examines some ways in which such questions were answered.

By the 1970s Jesuit numbers were declining in western Europe and North America, but growing in many other places. In recent times, the Society of Jesus has become far more multi-cultural and multi-racial than ever before. In the post-colonial era, and in the post-Vatican II decades, Jesuits have put increasing emphasis on promotion of justice for the poor and the oppressed, this emphasis being not a substitute for earlier works, but a constitutive, central element of all Jesuit ministries, including teaching, scholarship, preaching and pastoral work, and Ignatian spirituality. It has also meant a critique of ways in which Jesuits have, at times in their history, too easily "accommodated" oppressive practices.[14] Mary Ann Hinsdale's essay considers how Jesuits have done theology in the past four decades. Finally, my essay on "Jesuits today" surveys some of the challenges and possibilities for the Society of Jesus at the early stages of the twenty-first century.

I owe a debt of gratitude to many people for their assistance with this book. The College of the Holy Cross provided a semester's faculty fellowship; the Jesuit community at Holy Cross provided the resources for an additional semester of leave essential for completion of this project. Several people read drafts of one or more essays and provided critical and/or technical comments: Hanna Buczynska-Garewicz, James Corkery, S. J., Mary Morrisard-Larkin, Danielle Bacon, Simon Smith, S.J., Jacqueline Diot, librarian for the Jesuit libraries in Paris, facilitated my research there. Conversations with many other colleagues and fellow Jesuits have also been important for refining the structure and content of this *Companion*.

Notes

1 The IHS monogram had been promoted in the late medieval period by Franciscans, Bernardino of Siena in particular. It was not original to the Jesuits.

2 Among biographies of Ignatius is the very readable one by John Patrick Donnelly, *Ignatius of Loyola: Founder of the Jesuits* (New York: Pearson Longman, 2004). See also Cándido de Dalmases, *Ignatius of Loyola, Founder of the Jesuits: His Life and Work*, trans. Jerome Aixalá (St. Louis: Institute of Jesuit Sources, 1985).

3 On the first Jesuit schools, see John O'Malley, *The First Jesuits* (Cambridge, MA: Harvard University Press, 1993), 200–42.

4 See *The Constitutions of the Society of Jesus and Their Complementary Norms*, ed. John Padberg (St. Louis: Institute of Jesuit Sources, 1996).

5 See John O'Malley, "The Fourth Vow in Its Ignatian Context: A Historical Study," *Studies in the Spirituality of Jesuits* 15 (January 1983), 1–59; John Padberg, "Ignatius, the Popes, and Realistic Reverence," *Studies in the Spirituality of Jesuits* 25 (May 1993), 1–38.

6 On Rome as a communication center in the early modern era, see Peter Burke, "Rome as Center of Information and Communication for the Catholic World, 1550–1650," in Pamela M. Jones and Thomas Worcester, eds., *From Rome to Eternity: Catholicism and the Arts in Italy, ca. 1550–1650* (Leiden: Brill, 2002), 253–69.

7 See John Patrick Donnelly, "Peter Canisius," in Jill Raitt, ed., *Shapers of Religious Traditions in Germany, Switzerland, and Poland, 1560–1600* (New Haven: Yale University Press, 1981), 141–56. On Jesuits and politics in the Holy Roman Empire, see Robert Bireley, *The Jesuits and the Thirty Years War: Kings, Courts, and Confessors* (New York and Cambridge: Cambridge University Press, 2003).

8 For an excellent introduction to, and excerpts from, the *Jesuit Relations*, see Allan Greer, ed., *The Jesuit Relations: Natives and Missionaries in Seventeenth-Century North America* (New York: Bedford/St. Martin's, 2000).

9 See especially the published versions of major international conferences held at Boston College, in 1997 and 2002, organized by the same four scholars: John O'Malley, Gauvin Bailey, Steven J. Harris, and

T. Frank Kennedy, eds., *The Jesuits: Cultures, Sciences, and the Arts, 1540–1773* (Toronto: University of Toronto Press, 1999), and *The Jesuits II: Cultures, Sciences, and the Arts, 1540–1773* (Toronto: University of Toronto Press, 2006).

10 John O'Malley, Introduction to *The Jesuits II*, xxiii–xxxvi.

11 Eamon Duffy, *Saints and Sinners: A History of the Popes* (New Haven: Yale University Press, 1997), 194.

12 See *The Poetical Works of Gerard Manley Hopkins*, ed. Norman Mackenzie (Oxford: Clarendon Press, 1992); Robert Martin, *Gerard Manley Hopkins: A Very Private Life* (New York: Putnam, 1991); on Teilhard, see Christopher Mooney, *Teilhard de Chardin and the Mystery of Christ* (New York: Harper & Row, 1966); Ursula King, *Spirit of Fire: The Life and Vision of Teilhard de Chardin* (Maryknoll, NY: Orbis, 1996).

13 An excellent example is the German Jesuit Oswald von Nell-Breuning, who played a major role in the writing of Pius XI's social encyclical, *Quadragesimo Anno*. See Oswald von Nell-Breuning, *Reorganization of Social Economy: The Social Encyclical Developed and Explained*, trans. Bernard Dempsey (Milwaukee, WI: Bruce, 1936).

14 One example is slavery; see Thomas Murphy, *Jesuit Slaveholding in Maryland, 1717–1838* (New York: Routledge, 2001).

Part I

Ignatius of Loyola

1 The religious milieu of the young Ignatius

LU ANN HOMZA

The Spanish Christianity that Ignatius of Loyola experienced between his birth in 1491 and his departure from Spain in 1527 was often unexpectedly flexible, even when authorities of Church and State tried to make Christians conform to new religious standards. Despite the formal powers of kings, inquisitors, and bishops, it was one thing to pronounce a change, but quite another to carry it out; and modern historians are unanimous in emphasizing the degree to which local environments in Spain routinely outflanked or complicated centralizing mandates. Those local milieux also exhibited a range of religious commitments and achievements. The Spanish laity frequently was deeply involved in religious life, and men and women often demanded better clergy, better sermons, and the more frequent reception of the sacraments. At the same time, a substantial proportion of the laity voiced doubt about some theological truths, such as the Immaculate Conception of the Virgin Mary, and failed to know basic Catholic prayers.[1] Competent clergy could be hard to find, but energetic ecclesiastics also could galvanize a diocese. This variation was enhanced by a printing boom that made religious texts in Spanish accessible to everyone with the ability to read or desire to listen, and yet persons could attend to the divine through revelations from God as well as written catechisms: in fact, heavenly messages propelled accountants and wives, as well as nuns, into roles as spiritual advisors, and such individuals counseled their followers for years without arousing substantial mistrust. Thus for the first three decades of his life, Ignatius saw variety in his religious world as well as standardization. As a result, there very often remained a space for individual religious initiatives, even if total religious freedom was unthinkable.

There is remarkably little scholarship on the religious setting of Ignatius' childhood.[2] He was born in 1491 in the province of Guipúzcoa in the Kingdom of Navarre, which was conquered by King Ferdinand of Aragón in 1512, and which answered to the bishopric of Pamplona. The

Loyola family belonged to one of the two *parientes mayores*, the major kinship groups that dominated the social, economic, and military life of the province.[3] Ignatius' family had controlled the church of San Sebastián de Soreasu and its district, with occasional challenges, since 1387; Pope Benedict XIII formally conceded its patronage to them in 1415. According to this papal concession, the Loyola would receive three-quarters of the tithes and an annual rent of 1,000 ducats, confer all the benefices, and hand down reform measures for the clergy and people (*pueblo*). The Loyola also controlled the chapels (*ermitas*) and abbeys that fell under the church's jurisdiction. For the chapels, they were to arrange open-air sermons to convey sacred doctrine, and keep the eucharist for administration to the sick; for the abbeys, they would provide masses for the populace on specific days.[4] After 1509, when one of Ignatius' older brothers, Martín García de Loyola, had inherited the family estates, the Loyola were responsible for six abbeys and ten chapels in the valley of Urola. They put their bastard daughters into positions of authority in those chapels with some regularity.[5]

Ignatius, then, was certainly exposed to one of the ironies of Catholicism in early modern Europe:[6] that church offices were as valuable for their income and privileges as for any spiritual vocation. Most clerics tried to accumulate as many ecclesiastical positions as possible and to preserve those benefices within their families.[7] In 1556, for example, Cardinal Alessandro Farnese controlled posts involving ten cathedrals, twenty-six monasteries, and 133 lesser church positions, and it was routine for clergymen like Farnese to resign particular posts to their nephews.[8] This amassing of church offices occurred irrespective of whether the positions entailed the care of souls, or *cura animarum*, which dictated the administration of the sacraments. There is no evidence that ecclesiastics shied away from collecting such parish pastorates along with deaconries, cathedral canonries, and the like; moreover, priests felt little or no obligation to reside in the parish for which they were nominally responsible.[9] Instead, an ecclesiastic who held a benefice with the *cura animarum* would provide for the sacraments by employing a *mercenario*, or priest-for-hire, and *mercenarios* in turn presumably felt little obligation toward such parishes. There also was no guarantee that anyone ordained to the priesthood had the requisite grasp of theology and Latin to administer the sacraments properly and to know exactly what he was supposed to be doing.

As Ignatius moved throughout Spain (and Italy and France), absentee, ignorant priests were everywhere, and they tended to live with their concubines and children: such, at least, is the portrait drawn by concerned ecclesiastics. For example, in 1500–1, Bishop Alonso Manrique called a synod in his new diocese of Badajoz: among that synod's constitutions, one read, "Because priests and rectors of churches and benefices do not reside [there], and [neither do] other persons whose benefices require it, there consequently follows a great diminution in public religious worship, and damage to souls"; another cautioned, "No cleric may be present at the baptism, weddings, or funerals of his children," whereby someone added "and grandchildren" in the margin.[10] Twenty years later, after Manrique became bishop of Córdoba, his synod adjured "rectors, their substitutes, [or] the person who says High Mass" to explain the Gospel to the village every Sunday in its literal, historical sense, or find someone else to do it. The priests in Córdoba were also supposed to know the articles of the faith in Latin and Spanish, the sacraments, the Ten Commandments, the seven deadly sins, the spiritual and corporal works of mercy, and the gifts of the Holy Spirit. Nevertheless, Manrique wanted more than the parroting of formulas, since he also specified that priests "should know what the words and ceremonies of the Mass mean."[11] And secular clerics were not the only object of his synod, for he also targeted the misdeeds of friars and monks, who could administer the sacraments if they were ordained. One constitution chastised friars for tricking people into funding cycles of masses for dead relatives on the promise that it would be revealed whether the dead were in heaven, hell, or purgatory.

While reproaches against clerical families tended to disappear in synodal constitutions after 1510, admonitions about preaching, prayers, and the sacraments continued to crop up. In fact, because synodal constitutions across Spain treated such consistent themes – for instance, ones from the same diocese often repeated the same prescriptions in the same language – scholars have debated whether their directions reveal anything about religious life, or simply amount to literary clichés.[12] Still, if bishops tended to reiterate their predecessors' mandates, they were under no obligation to do so. For our purposes, synods demonstrate a concern with clerical standards, while also revealing a range of clerical aptitude.

Ignatius undoubtedly witnessed first-hand the sort of clerical flaws and gifts outlined in synodal constitutions, but he also could have learned about them in print, namely through a genre called the confessors' manual.[13] The confessors' manual in late fifteenth- and sixteenth-century Europe had a long genealogy. It was indebted to the *summae de casibus* of the thirteenth century, which were Latin guides to cases of conscience, written to help priests and friars hear confessions and impose penances. The *summae* were created after 1215, when the Fourth Lateran Council, called by Pope Innocent III, decreed that every Christian should confess and do penance once a year upon reaching the age of discretion, or six to seven years of age. By Ignatius' time period, Christians well knew that they were supposed to receive the sacrament of penance at least once a year, before Easter. And beginning about 1500, clerical authors in Spain began to try to deepen the process of confession by writing about it in the vernacular.

The confessors' manual was prominent in the wave of devotional publishing that swept Spain between 1490 and 1530.[14] Manuals in Spanish were newly composed and older, Latin ones were translated; large numbers of copies were offered for sale in bookstores, at prices that could accommodate even rural laborers. In 1514, a well-known theologian named Pedro Ciruelo wrote a Spanish treatise entitled "The Art of Confessing Well," which became the most reprinted confessors' manual in Spain in the first half of the sixteenth century. In the 1550s, Ciruelo's manual was carried in bookstores in hundreds of copies, priced at 10 maravedís for an unbound version. Circulating as well were hundreds of anonymous "Brief confessors' manuals," a "Memorandum on sin" by the Dominican Pedro de Covarrubias, and a "Brief form of confessing" by the first archbishop of Granada, Hernando de Talavera.[15] Because day laborers in Castile in the middle of the sixteenth century earned 34 maravedís a day, buying one of these manuals was conceivable. Moreover, individuals might read a copy of Ciruelo's manual, but they also might hear it, since reading aloud, especially to groups of women, was routine.[16] Reading aloud was the common way to learn prayers such as the *Our Father* and the *Hail Mary*. There is no reason to think that a confessors' manual *per se* involved an essentially private process of reading.[17]

At the same time, literacy rates in early modern Spain were higher than modern scholars ever anticipated.[18] Vernacular confessors' manuals were written in the expectation that they would sell, and not just to the clerical class: in every vernacular manual, the laity was presumed to be part of the audience. Significantly, because these works addressed clerical sins as energetically as secular ones, ordinary people would have become aware of minimum standards of clerical behavior. If the laity was instructed to avoid pride and avarice, and to practice loving their neighbors as much as themselves, then clerics were admonished to be kind to penitents,[19] to preserve the secrecy of the confession, to stay sober during baptisms, and to observe the Seventh Commandment against theft.[20]

These manuals also promoted certain values. They reinforced the place of catechisms, because they organized misdeeds according to Christian formulas such as the Ten Commandments and the seven deadly sins.[21] They stressed concepts such as the Trinity through their repetition of sacred numbers, such as three; indeed, they were suffused with number symbolism, so that they might contain three questions on the First Commandment, seven on pride, and so forth. The manuals also asked penitents to ponder their internal spiritual condition: each began by adjuring penitents to look into their hearts, to think carefully about the circumstances surrounding each misdeed, to ponder the motive behind the sin, and to express a true sorrow that had nothing to do with fear of punishment. Finally, though all the manuals highlighted the Ten Commandments, they routinely phrased the first one according to its recapitulation in Matthew 22:37–39, which stressed love for God and neighbor. Matthew's version of this commandment contrasted sharply with Exodus 22:2–6, where God was mighty, jealous, and willing to visit the iniquity of fathers upon children, though He showed "manifold mercy to those who loved Him and kept His Commandments." The Spaniards wrote the First Commandment, then, in terms of love rather than judgment. They also stressed community when they explained the seven deadly sins.[22] Throughout, they treated their readers as "rational sheep," a phrase that was highly illuminative: though priests directed the flock, the individuals who composed it had to be reasoned with and persuaded. The road to salvation was a cooperative enterprise.[23]

Notably, Ignatius and his peers could read more than just confessors' manuals in the vernacular. An even more prevalent component of Spanish publishing in this time period was the devotional treatise, whose printing formed one of the special projects of Cardinal Francisco Jiménez de Cisneros (1436–1517).[24] Cisneros was a Franciscan friar who became the Archbishop of Toledo in 1495, the Inquisitor-General of Castile in 1507, and twice the Regent of Spain. Cisneros wished to revive theological studies on a very high level: to that end, he founded the University of Alcalá in approximately 1508, and asked the faculty to teach a range of theological approaches, to instruct students in Greek and Hebrew, and, beginning in 1510, to collaborate on a multi-lingual edition of the Old and New Testaments. This last project became the Complutensian Polyglot Bible, a six-volume publication in Hebrew, Greek, and Latin. Ignatius took some classes at the University of Alcalá, and even if he never handled the Complutensian Old and New Testaments, given their price, the atmosphere there was one in which languages and scholarly inquiry were valued.[25]

More accessible were biblical excerpts, saints' lives, and medita-
tional texts in the vernacular, many of which were translated and
published through Cardinal Cisneros' sponsorship. The medieval compilation called the *Vita Christi* by Ludolf of Saxony was translated into
Spanish verse in 1501 by the Spanish Franciscan Ambrosio Montesino
and printed in Alcalá in 1502–3. The *Vita Christi* merged the four
Gospels into a single life of Christ, and surrounded it with quotations
from the Latin Fathers of the Church.[26] This work was a potential
conduit to the biblical text and the learned apparatus that theologians
had constructed around it. Later, Montesino was asked by King
Ferdinand to improve an earlier Spanish translation of the Gospels
and epistles: the revision appeared in 1512 as *Epístolas y Evangelios*
and went through at least six more editions.[27] Another key text was
Thomas à Kempis' *Imitatio Christi*, which was known in Spain as the
Contemptus mundi and was commonly attributed to Jean Gerson: this
tremendously Christocentric guide, which Ignatius read, urged readers
to forsake pride, embrace humility, and distrust human knowledge. It
also strongly recommended the frequent reception of the eucharist.
The *Imitatio* appeared in Catalan in 1482 and 1518, and in Spanish
editions in 1490, 1493, 1495, 1513 and 1523.[28]

When it came to Cardinal Cisneros' particular contributions to print
culture, historians are unanimous in highlighting his taste for mystical
and hagiographical works.[29] He strongly endorsed a piety based on divine
revelations. He sponsored at least two and perhaps three to four editions
of Angela of Foligno's *Book* and *Life* in both Latin and Spanish: born in
Umbria, Italy, Angela pursued a prayerful life after being widowed and
became a Franciscan tertiary.[30] She received frequent visions, especially
of the Lord's Passion, and died in 1309.[31] In 1504, Cisneros mandated the
publication of St. John Climacus' *La escalera espiritual* [*The Ladder of
Divine Ascent*]: Climacus withdrew to a life of silence, prayer, and mortification, became the abbot of the monastery at Sinai, and died *c*. 649.
The third part of his *Escalera espiritual* describes how a monk who
follows a program of penance and self-abnegation progresses to a tranquil
life of solitude.

Cisneros' devotional sympathies also found an outlet in works by
members of the Dominican Order. To that end, he printed Raymond of
Capua's *Life* of St. Catherine of Siena in 1511, and Catherine's own
letters and prayers in 1512.[32] Catherine of Siena became a Dominican
tertiary after refusing to accede to her parents' wishes and marry;
she died in 1380 and was canonized in 1461. She practiced self-
mortification and mental prayer; she also fasted and received the

eucharist so constantly that it looked as if she lived on that sacrament.[33] God frequently rewarded her for her humility by giving her visions, including spiritual marriage with Jesus, as well as the stigmata, or the reproduction of Christ's wounds on her own body.[34] Catherine's pursuit of prayer and mortification did not prevent her from pursuing an active apostolate, notably in her efforts to persuade Popes Gregory XI and Urban VI to return to Rome and end the Great Schism, when multiple popes claimed Christians' obedience. In Raymond of Capua's version of her life, spiritual progress came with the growth of humility and supernatural rewards.

Thus the Latin and vernacular works printed under Cardinal Cisneros' aegis elevated Scripture, mysticism, the reception of the eucharist, and the interaction of a "profoundly penitent conscience" with "the direct exercise of God's grace."[35] Notably, the works that Cisneros sponsored frequently featured women as the recipients of divine favors,[36] and he clearly was willing to endorse women in the same role in his own time period. For example, he visited the Franciscan Juana de la Cruz, whose mystical raptures between 1505 and 1518 convinced her audience "that the Holy Spirit spoke through her mouth in the person of Christ."[37] He also championed María de Santo Domingo, who became a Dominican tertiary around 1502 in Piedrahita.[38] María was a *beata* who had not taken formal vows as a nun: the term *beata* signified a woman who attempted to live a holy life outside of convents by taking personal vows of chastity and often of poverty, and who frequently joined the "third orders" of the Franciscans or Dominicans.[39] María experienced visions, endorsed a harsh asceticism, and worked for the reform of the Dominican Order. When complaints about her surfaced, King Ferdinand invited her to court, and Cardinal Cisneros met with her personally.[40] María was investigated four times between 1508 and 1509 and enjoyed Ferdinand's and Cisneros' support throughout; she ultimately was exonerated and ended up as the prioress of a convent founded expressly for her by the Duke of Alba.[41]

If we survey the values in print and the examples of practice which Ignatius and his peers could have noticed or heard about in their childhood and adolescence, we end up with a replete set of messages. We find plenty of evidence that secular people were encouraged to examine their consciences, ponder their sinfulness, seek the eucharist, practice humility and self-mortification, and hope for heavenly revelations. Catechisms abounded, but so did "charismatic spirituality, ultra-asceticism, and the authority of direct, mystical experience."[42] Relationships with the ecclesiastical hierarchy were a given, but prayerful conversations with God were also encouraged. Conversion could be highlighted, either on an individual, personal level, or via efforts with Muslims in Granada and North Africa or natives in the Americas; Jerusalem was the touchstone for Christian millenarianism.[43] As for works – or the notion that physical actions could affect the soul and help it to progress toward salvation – the stress on self-denial, practical charity, and the reception of the sacraments implied that acts mattered.

Nevertheless, neither treatises nor court favorites can tell us everything about Catholicism in this epoch, especially how it was practiced by ordinary men and women, literate though they might have been. Lived religion is challenging because of the difficulty of the sources: we do not possess diaries in which religious obligations and observances were laid out, and if we turn to documents that address liminal or heterodox experiences, such as inquisition trials, we run into problems of exceptionalism. Still, we can come to some conclusions about religious experience from literary sources and studies of later time periods. Such materials reveal that Spanish Christians found saintly intercessors supremely important, imposed no firm boundary between the earthly and the heavenly realms, and acted as if the local environment mattered most.

Between 1575 and 1578, King Philip II sent questionnaires to the cities and settlements of New Castile, the region in central Spain bounded by the towns of Sigüenza, Cuenca, Almagro, and Talavera. The royal survey inquired into urban history, legal jurisdictions, social composition, and religious institutions and rituals.[44] Two of the questions asked about the place's notable relics, chapels, and oratories, and again about special holy days that inhabitants had vowed to observe, in addition to feast days dictated by the Church. Scholars have used the answers to great effect. From the perspective of early modern Castilians, when God was angry, He intervened in human affairs: He communicated his displeasure through natural disasters such as hail, pestilence, lightning, floods, and fires.[45] At the same time, the *absence* of hail or lightning when it was expected could be read as a sign of God's benignity. And villagers chose to beg God's forgiveness or to thank Him by appealing to intercessors, namely, saints who would intervene on their behalf: the saints were explicitly described as *abogados*, or lawyers or advocates.

Thanking or appeasing a saint might take various forms. A village could vow to observe a particular saint's feast day if the inhabitants were threatened or saved from a particular misfortune on that specific date; the vow was a corporate act that explicitly involved every citizen. Chapels and shrines also served as a focus for community spirituality, and they were most often dedicated to the Virgin Mary, especially local, specific incarnations of her, when she was denoted as Our Lady of a particular place or a particular quality. Such shrines were founded differently from vows, because Mary herself initiated the relationship, either through apparitions that indicated where the shrine should be built, or by allowing a statue of herself to be found: when the statue was moved, it always managed to return to the place where Mary wanted the shrine to be. Thus "the apparitions and the statues told the people not only who would help them, but also where to go for grace."[46] Devotion to Marian shrines was profound in early modern Spain.

Philip II's questionnaire asked nothing about sacramental life, but we know that children were baptized in Ignatius' epoch, because clerical writers bemoaned the dangerous proliferation of godparents and the incompetent liturgical skills of parish priests. We know that prayers such as the *Our Father* and the *Hail Mary* were learned and recited, as was the Creed, because they were reproduced in confessors' manuals and synodal constitutions. The sacraments of penance, the eucharist, and extreme unction were received, because defendants in inquisition trials highlighted them; mass was attended, because fights broke out over who would be the first to receive the peace of Christ. At the same time, such universal rituals and signs of Catholic Christianity gained their fullest significance for ordinary Spaniards when they took place in a specific locale: thus an archbishop of Toledo could tell parish priests to give sermons, but that mandate only became meaningful when one's *local* priest stumbled through a homily; in the same way, the Virgin Mary in general might have been an abstraction, but Our Lady of Montserrat was not.[47]

Still, even if lived religion was local religion for ordinary Spaniards, central authorities in Spain often cared deeply about religious matters and tried to influence them. Besides taking an interest in mystical *beatas*, King Ferdinand and Queen Isabella attempted to assert control over renegade ecclesiastics and to reform corrupt ones. After ending the civil war over the succession to the Castilian throne, Isabella and Ferdinand called a congregation of clergy to Seville in 1478: that assembly decided on a number of measures to improve the clergy, including:

- making Latin obligatory for men seeking a benefice in a parish or a cathedral chapter;
- requiring that ten clerics from each cathedral or collegiate church have at least three years' training in theology, canon law, or the liberal arts;

- ordering ordained priests to celebrate mass at least four times a year, and bishops, three;
- prohibiting clerics from carrying arms, entering the service of temporal overlords, or having concubines;
- ascertaining whether misbehaving ecclesiastics had a right to ecclesiastical immunity;
- finally, adjuring all clergy with benefices involving the *cura animarum* to reside in their parishes and sees.[48]

These measures were in response to real issues, as the synodal constitutions attest. There were no seminaries or examinations for the clerical office, and episcopal visitations of dioceses between 1491 and 1527 were practically non-existent. Once an ecclesiastic was in place, especially a bishop, he became the indisputable lord of the diocese, and he had vassals, lands, and rents at his disposal; such men could become helpful allies or damaging opponents.[49] As a result, Ferdinand and Isabella sought above all to control appointments to major ecclesiastical benefices, and to convince the papacy that they had the right of presentation because it flowed logically from other rights of patronage, namely, foundation, endowment, and conquest.[50] They also argued that, because they protected the common good (*bien común*), they were obliged to reject the election of suspicious candidates. Such responsibilities were that much weightier because of their frequent bad relations with France and Portugal, and their eventual conquest of Granada. Having reliable and loyal ecclesiastics on the frontiers was crucial.[51]

Ferdinand and Isabella tried for thirty years to convince various popes of this right of presentation. In 1486, Pope Innocent VIII gave them the right to establish churches, control appointments, and levy taxes in the Canary Islands and in Granada when it was conquered; that agreement was extended to the New World in 1508. By the time the papacy amplified the *patronato* agreements, as they were called, to all the churches in all the kingdoms of the Spanish monarchy, Ferdinand and Isabella were dead: in 1523, Pope Adrian VI gave this concession to their grandson, Holy Roman Emperor and King of Spain Charles V, not because he wanted to, but because the same right had been given to the French king Francis I in 1516.[52] Yet having some control over ecclesiastical candidates did not necessarily result in control over churches. For instance, in the early sixteenth century the bishop of Calahorra tried for some fifteen years to establish his authority over the churches in the Basque provinces of Vizcaya and Alava, but the clergy there followed the lead of their secular lords and would have none of it.[53] In the 1490s, the bishop of Barcelona could not visit the governing body of his cathedral, because the cathedral chapter refused to acknowledge him. Ferdinand and Isabella had to request a papal bull from Pope Alexander VI in 1496 to clarify that cathedral chapters *were* in fact liable to episcopal visitations, and then had to repeatedly exhort the Barcelona bishop to be steadfast in his efforts.[54]

A similar pattern occurred when the monarchs attempted to correct monasteries. In 1493, two papal bulls from Alexander VI authorized them to appoint "prelates and certain holy men" to conduct visitations of monastic houses, to assess the rules those houses were allegedly following, and to reform them in "head and members." But jurisdictional conflicts, apathetic officials, and opposition from abbesses in particular meant that the visitors had their work cut out for them and, once they left, monastic institutions tended to return to their former ways.[55] In short, local religious environments usually displayed a conservative reaction when change was imposed by outsiders.[56] The same dynamic occurred when Cardinal Cisneros tried to pressure his fellow Franciscans into a greater observance of their Rule.[57] Of course, for modern readers, the central authority most associated with early modern Spain is the Inquisition, an institution that fused state and religious power in a peculiar way. When Pope Sixtus IV granted Ferdinand and Isabella the right to name inquisitors in 1478, he created a situation in which Spanish inquisitors received their jurisdiction from the papacy, but were politically subservient to the monarchy; in terms of loyalties, Spanish inquisitors tended in practice to follow kings rather than popes, which was what Ferdinand and Isabella intended.[58] As a child in Guipúzcoa, Ignatius would not have encountered inquisitors or perhaps even known about the Inquisition, since the tribunal that handled that territory was only founded in the city of Calahorra in 1513, after Navarre had been conquered in 1512. By his late twenties, inquisitors would have entered his worldview as he moved through Catalonia and Castile, and he would have been aware of their persecuting mission; yet their targets were so specific until 1521 that Ignatius himself had no reason to fear.

The Inquisition was founded to prosecute judaizing *conversos*, namely individuals of Jewish ancestry who were baptized as Christians but who continued to practice aspects of Mosaic Law, such as dietary rules and rituals associated with the Sabbath. To Christian religious authorities, *conversos* who followed Jewish ceremonies were heretics because they appeared to be practicing two religions simultaneously and hence were betraying their baptismal vows. The Inquisition was supposed to find these judaizing heretics and, if at all possible, enclose them again in the Christian community after eliciting from them an expression of repentance. If the suspected heretic refused to confess her error and had sufficient eyewitness testimony against her, she would be "relaxed to the secular arm," a phrase that meant released to the secular authorities and burned at the stake. (Most of the *conversos* arrested for judaizing were women, due to the link between aspects of Mosaic Law and the domestic sphere.[59]) Suspects also could be executed if they had previously confessed and repented, and subsequently relapsed. Because most of the trial records for the period 1480–1530 have been lost, it is impossible to say how many *conversos* were tried and what percentage was sent to the stake, though historians presume that this earliest period of Spanish Inquisition history was also the most violent. When it came to judaizing, the Inquisition did not usually suspect Old Christians, that is, Spaniards who lacked Jewish ancestry; since Ignatius belonged to the Basque, Old Christian nobility, it may be presumed that he was safe from suspicion.

This position could have changed, however, after 1521, when a different kind of heresy was catalogued: that year, Martin Luther was excommunicated from the Catholic Church by Pope Leo X and put under the ban of Empire by Charles V. The Spanish Inquisition immediately ordered its officials to confiscate Lutheran writings, and prohibited the population from reading, selling, or preaching Lutheran works and ideas.[60] Spanish inquisitors had few specific ideas about what, exactly, Luther had written, but they widened their field of interest: in 1524, they arrested Isabel de la Cruz, a Franciscan tertiary, and Pedro Ruiz de Alcaraz, an accountant and employee of the Marquis of Villena in Escalona. Isabel and Pedro were called *alumbrados*, or "the illuminated ones." They conceived of themselves as illuminated because they abandoned themselves to the love of God, focused on the reception of direct spiritual impulses, spurned priests as intermediaries, and discarded the external rituals of Catholicism.[61] There is no evidence that the *alumbrados*, who were endemic to Castile, used the writings of Luther or even Desiderius Erasmus for inspiration, because they had been voicing their religious ideas to a wide circle of followers since approximately 1512. Still, their comments on the uselessness of saints, the non-scriptural origin of the sacrament of penance, and the futility of papal indulgences "matched" what inquisitors knew about Lutheran teachings. A year after Isabel and Pedro's arrests, the

Inquisition issued an edict against *alumbradismo*: by mandate of the Inquisitor-General, that document was read aloud in churches on Sundays and feast days, in order that Christians should "flee and withdraw from [such] errors and deceptions."[62]

Such measures might lead us to assume that Spanish Christians after 1521 immediately and drastically curtailed any actions to deepen their spiritual lives which fell outside the channels of church, priest, and sacraments. But what is truly remarkable about Spanish religious culture in the 1520s is the degree to which Christians kept experimenting with their devotional practices.[63] The evidence suggests that religious life in Spain was pliant enough to allow debate about belief, hierarchy, and ritual, even as inquisitors were amplifying their range of suspects.[64] For instance, the same Isabel de la Cruz who was arrested for *alumbradismo* had been acting as a spiritual advisor to dozens of individuals for at least twelve years before her arrest; a disgruntled competitor even reported her to the Inquisition in 1519, but to no effect. Isabel's trial in 1524 also had no apparent effect on other women who not only knew her, but were also acting as religious advisors. For example, Francisca Hernández – who was not affiliated with any religious order – received revelations from God throughout the 1520s. Her visions told her who was in heaven, hell, and purgatory, and who was receiving the eucharist in a state of sin; she attracted numerous male disciples who viewed her as another saint.[65] Though inquisitors and episcopal vicars tried to break up her circle by banishing her most faithful male admirer from her company in 1519, 1522, 1523, and 1524, she was only arrested in 1529 for *alumbradismo*.[66]

Most significant of all is María de Cazalla, who began to direct the *alumbrados* after Isabel de la Cruz's arrest.[67] Cazalla was a wife and mother, and not connected to the tertiary orders in any way. Nevertheless, she routinely read and commented on Scripture to groups of women, whom she referred to as *mis señoras*. When she arrived in a village and began to speak to a group of people in a private home, people left the road to hear her. She openly criticized confessors for a lack of thoroughness and preachers for a want of affect, and no one thought her presumptuous: on the contrary, her defense witnesses indicated that they did the same. María even told clerics to try reading the words of consecration when handling the eucharist, rather than relying on memorization. Cazalla was arrested by the Inquisition in 1532 on charges of Erasmianism, Lutheranism, and *alumbradismo* – she had been implicated by Francisca Hernández – but her example is nonetheless useful for what it can tell us about religion in the 1520s. Clearly the laity had ideas about ways to heighten their devotion, and they were not afraid to act on them; moreover, the authorities did not necessarily suspect groups of men and women who spoke about Scripture and prayer, or criticized the clergy. What Ignatius and his followers attempted to do in Alcalá between 1526 and 1527 was not extraordinary for that time and place.

The Christianity experienced by Ignatius in Spain was complex. It emphasized a variety of elements – such as Jesus, saints, works, revelations, and catechisms – that may strike us as contradictory. Its tolerance and even encouragement of a range of religious actors may also surprise us. Yet the Spanish religious environment offers an essential, provocative context for pondering Ignatius' spiritual preferences and choices. There is no doubt that his vision of what the clergy and laity could be was profoundly indebted to it.

Notes

1   See John Edwards, "Religious Faith and Doubt in Late Medieval Spain: Soria *circa* 1450–1500," *Past and Present* 120 (1988), 3–25; Sara T. Nalle, *God in La Mancha* (Baltimore: Johns Hopkins University Press, 1992), 8–23, 41–45; Henry Kamen, *The Phoenix and the Flame: Catalonia and the Counter Reformation* (New Haven: Yale University Press, 1993), 1–43, 82–93.

2   Ironically, the lack of investigation into religion in Guipúzcoa in this period means that I will be treating Ignatius as if he were a Castilian or a Catalan, not a Basque, for the duration of this essay, despite the importance of the local in Spanish Christianity.

3   The Loyola family occupied the valley of Urola and belonged to the Lazcano lineage, which was contrasted with the lineage of Gamboa-Olaso. Both lineages practiced endogamy and maintained their bands of followers via treaties. José Luis Orella Unzue, *Instituciones de Gipuzkoa y oficiales reales en la provincia (1491–1530)* (Gipuzkoa: Juntas Generales de Gipuzkoa/Diputación Foral de Gipuzkoa, 1995), 75. For the Loyola clan, ibid., 102–8.

4   Ibid., 102–3.

5   Martín García was the second eldest son of the Loyola's eleven children; ibid., 105–6, 108–9.

6   Not even the Tridentine decrees, promulgated in Spain in 1564, instantly rectified pluralism. See Barbara McClung Hallman, *Italian Cardinals, Reform, and the Church as Property* (Berkeley: University of California Press, 1985); Nalle, *God in La Mancha*, 70–74 (see especially Table 3.2).

7   Because men could be ordained but have no guarantee of an ecclesiastical position, and because income was not tied to a benefice in any standard way, clerics' incomes could vary tremendously, and many were destitute. For an example, see Nalle, *God in La Mancha*, 73.

8 Hallman, *Italian Cardinals*, 36, and Lu Ann Homza, *Religious Authority in the Spanish Renaissance* (Baltimore: Johns Hopkins University Press, 2000), 114–16.

9 Though some Spanish ecclesiastics in the early sixteenth century did adjure priests to reside: for example, Juan Bernal Díaz de Luco, *Instrucción de perlados* (Alcalá, 1530).

10 *Constituciones synodales* (Badajoz, 1501), f. D6r–v.

11 *Constituciones synodales* (Córdoba, 1521), ff. 29r–v, 41r–v.

12 On clerical abuses, Nalle, *God in La Mancha*, 70–87. For an inventory of synodal proceedings, see María Milagros Cárcel Ortí, *Las visitas pastorales de España (Siglos XVI–XX): Propuesta de inventario y bibliografía* (Oviedo: Asociación de Archiveros de la Iglesia en España, 2000).

13 Homza, *Religious Authority*, ch. 5.

14 Ibid., 168–71.

15 William Pettas, *A Sixteenth-Century Spanish Bookstore: The Inventory of Juan de Junta*, Transactions of the American Philosophical Society, 85/1 (Philadelphia: American Philosophical Society, 1995), and Antonio Blanco Sánchez, "Inventario de Juan de Ayala, gran impresor toledano (1556)," *Boletín de la Real Academia Española* 67 (1987), 207–50. Pamphlets and broadsheets numbered in the thousands in such bookshops: Nalle, *God in La Mancha*, 114–18.

16 "It is important to note that illiteracy did not necessarily block access to written culture, for reading almost always meant reading aloud and thereby sharing the contents of a book with a circle of listeners." Ronald Surtz, *Writing Women in Late Medieval and Early Modern Spain: The Mothers of Saint Teresa of Ávila* (Philadelphia: University of Pennsylvania Press, 1995), 13.

17 Confessionals had not yet been invented, and the sacrament of penance was conducted in public spaces inside churches. For further developments, see Wietse de Boer, *The Conquest of the Soul: Confession, Discipline, and Public Order in Counter-Reformation Milan* (Leiden: Brill, 2001).

18 Sara T. Nalle, "Literacy and Culture in Early Modern Castile," *Past and Present* 125 (1989), 65–96. On book culture and literacy, see, as a sample, Antonio Castillo Gómez, ed., *Escribir y leer en el siglo de Cervantes* (Barcelona: Gedisa, 1999); Pedro M. Cátedra, *Invención, difusión, y recepción de la literatura popular impresa, siglo XVI* (Mérida: Junta de Extremadura, 2002).

19 For the deep personal relationships between confessors and especially female penitents, see Jodi Bilinkoff, *Related Lives: Confessors and their Female Penitents, 1450–1750* (Ithaca, NY: Cornell University Press, 2005).

20 For example, Hernando de Talavera, *Breve forma de confesar*, in vol. 1 of Nueva Biblioteca de Autores Españoles, ed. Miguel Mir (Madrid: Casa Editorial Bailly, 1911), 10.

21 The seven deadly sins were almost always expressed in Spain in this time period through the formula *saligia*, with each letter standing for one of the sins. See Morton W. Bloomfield, *The Seven Deadly Sins* (East Lansing: Michigan State University Press, 1967).

22   For contrasting arguments about the potential effect of the Ten
     Commandments on Christian spirituality, see John Bossy, "Moral
     Arithmetic: Seven Sins into Ten Commandments," in Edmund
     Leites, ed., *Conscience and Casuistry in Early Modern Europe*
     (Cambridge: Cambridge University Press, 1988), 214–31, and Homza,
     Religious Authority, ch. 5.

23   Homza, *Religious Authority*, 141.

24   For Cisneros and print culture, see Felipe Fernández-Armesto, "Cardinal
     Cisneros as a Patron of Printing," in Derek W. Lomax and David
     Mackenzie, eds., *God and Man in Medieval Spain: Essays in Honour of
     J. R. L. Highfield* (Warminster: Aris & Phillips, 1989), 149–68.

25   See Jerry Bentley, *Humanists and Holy Writ* (Princeton: Princeton
     University Press, 1983), for ways in which the Complutensian
     Polyglot project was less innovative than we once believed. The atmo-
     sphere in Alcalá was just as energetic intellectually in the 1520s as it
     was before Cisneros' death in 1517.

26   For a description, see Marcel Bataillon, *Erasmo y España* (Mexico City:
     Fondo de Cultura Económica, 1950), 44–45, and Surtz, *Writing
     Women*, 14.

27   Montesino was revising the 1493 work of Gonzalo García de Santa
     María, who had originally translated the *Postilla super epístolas et
     evangelia* (1437) of the Dominican William of Paris: Bataillon, *Erasmo
     y España*, 45.

28   Bataillon, *Erasmo y España*, 48.

29   Notably, it looks as if Cisneros was deliberately attempting to recreate
     a typical library of Observant Franciscan readings, and make it avail-
     able to a wider public: Fernández-Armesto, "Cardinal Cisneros as a
     Patron of Printing," 158–59.

30   A tertiary is a member of the "Third Order" of the Dominican,
     Franciscan, or Carmelite religious orders. Members of third orders
     typically took vows of poverty and often chastity, and continued to
     live in the world while pursuing holiness. Members of third orders who
     lived in monastic-style communities and followed a rule were called
     "regular tertiaries."

31   Cisneros' 1505 Latin edition of Angela's *Book* was bound with two
     more Latin texts, the Franciscan Rule, and the *Liber Spiritualis
     Gratiae Sanctae Melchiadis*, an account of the visions experienced
     by St. Mechtild of Hackeborn (c. 1241–98) in the community of
     Benedictine nuns in Helfta.

32   Bataillon, *Erasmo y España*, 49; Surtz, *Writing Women*, 11. For
     Catherine of Siena as a model for women, see Gillian T. W. Ahlgren,
     "Ecstasy, Prophecy, and Reform: Catherine of Siena as a Model for
     Holy Women of Sixteenth-Century Spain," in Robert Boenig, ed., *The
     Mystical Gesture: Essays on Medieval and Early Modern Spiritual
     Culture in Honor of Mary E. Giles* (Burlington, VT: Ashgate, 2000),
     53–66.

33   For the profound relationship between medieval female spirituality
     and food, see Caroline Walker Bynum, *Holy Feast and Holy Fast: The*

Religious Significance of Food to Medieval Women (Berkeley: University of California Press, 1987).

34 Ahlgren, "Ecstasy, Prophecy, and Reform," 55–57.

35 Fernández-Armesto, "Cardinal Cisneros as a Patron of Printing," 167.

36 The Cisneros-backed edition of St. Vincent Ferrer's Tractatus de Vita Spirituali omitted crucial chapters that might have linked women's revelations and raptures to demonic deception: Surtz, Writing Women, 11.

37 Surtz, Writing Women, 105. Juana de la Cruz was a member of the Regular Franciscan Tertiaries and lived according to a rule in a convent in Cubas. Her followers called her locutions "sermons," and in 1508–9, one of her companions wrote them down: they make up the book called El libro del conorte. See Surtz, Writing Women, 104–26, for a treatment of part of this text, as well as Ronald Surtz, The Guitar of God: Gender, Power, and Authority in the Visionary World of Mother Juana de la Cruz (1481–1534) (Philadelphia: University of Pennsylvania Press, 1990).

38 Jodi Bilinkoff, "A Spanish Prophetess and Her Patrons: The Case of María de Santo Domingo," Sixteenth-Century Journal 23 (1992), 21–34.

39 See n. 30 above.

40 Both men were deeply impressed with her revelations, which happened to correspond to their political needs: when María prophesied that Ferdinand would conquer Jerusalem, or that God would help Cisneros to victory against the Moors of North Africa, she was lending them charismatic authority: Bilinkoff, "A Spanish Prophetess," 28–29, 31–34. It should be noted here that the court chroniclers of Ferdinand trumpeted his connections to Jerusalem and promoted millenarian expectations, an outlook that found a parallel in the messianism of the Franciscan Order and Christopher Columbus. Ignatius' pilgrimage to Jerusalem thus fit into a larger cultural obsession. See Alain Milhou, Colón y su mentalidad mesiánica en el ambiente franciscanista española, in vol. 11 of Cuadernos colombinos (Valladolid: Casa-Museo de Colón, 1983), especially 348–403, 435–49.

41 Bilinkoff, "A Spanish Prophetess," 24. See Mary E. Giles, The Book of Prayer of Sor María de Santo Domingo: A Study and Translation (Albany: State University of New York Press, 1990), for María's extant writings. For the positions of the beata's supporters and detractors, see Jodi Bilinkoff, "Charisma and Controversy: The Case of María de Santo Domingo," in Magdalena S. Sánchez and Alain Saint-Saëns, eds., Spanish Women of the Golden Age: Images and Realities (Westport, CT: Greenwood Press, 1996), 23–37.

42 Bilinkoff, "Charisma and Controversy," 30.

43 Milhou, Colón y su mentalidad mesiánica.

44 William A. Christian, Local Religion in Sixteenth-Century Spain (Princeton: Princeton University Press, 1981), 3–6. For complements to Christian's work, see Nalle, God in La Mancha; Kamen, The Phoenix and the Flame; and Benjamin Ehlers, Between Christians

and Moriscos: Juan de Ribera and Religious Reform in Valencia, *1568–1614* (Baltimore: Johns Hopkins University Press, 2006).

45 Christian, *Local Religion*, 33–35.

46 Ibid., 75, and William Christian, *Apparitions in Late Medieval and Renaissance Spain* (Princeton: Princeton University Press, 1981).

47 Christian, *Local Religion*, 84–87, 178.

48 Helen Rawlings, *Church, Religion and Society in Early Modern Spain* (New York: Palgrave, 2002), 50–53; and José García Oro, O. F. M., *Cisneros y la reforma del clero español en tiempo de los reyes católicos* (Madrid: CSIC, 1971).

49 García Oro, *Cisneros y la reforma*, 32.

50 Ibid., 33.

51 To put their reasoning in context, it is helpful to note that Italian cardinals and papal relatives controlled the bishopric of Cádiz between 1495 and 1525, the dioceses of Osma (1483–93) and Cuenca (1479–82, 1493–1518), and were entrenched in the See of Pamplona, too. Rawlings, *Church, Religion, and Society*, 52. Not surprisingly, such ecclesiastics were frequently absent. When it came to native Spanish bishops, Ferdinand and Isabella themselves were responsible for most of their non-residence before 1492, when they required bishops at court or used them as ambassadors: García Oro, *Cisneros y la reforma*, 38–39.

52 García Oro, *Cisneros y la reforma*, 34.

53 Ibid., 140–42.

54 Ibid., 117. For Ferdinand's efforts to make his own nephews reside after he himself had given them bishoprics, see 125–26.

55 Ibid., 40–49, 98–117. Castilian nuns were even imported into convents in Barcelona in an attempt to get those institutions on the right track: ibid., 106.

56 That insight comes from Christian, *Local Religion*, 178.

57 See García Oro, *Cisneros y la reforma*, 184–90, 193–201 for some summary statements on Cisneros' reform efforts with the Franciscan Order.

58 Lu Ann Homza, *The Spanish Inquisition, 1478–1614: An Anthology of Sources* (Indianapolis: Hackett Publishing, 2006), xvi–xvii.

59 Renée Levine Melammed, *Heretics or Daughters of Israel? The Crypto-Jewish Women of Castile* (New York: Oxford University Press, 1998).

60 See Augustín Redondo, "Luther et l'Espagne de 1520–1536," *Mélanges de la Casa de Velázquez* 1 (1965), 109–65, and Werner Thomas, *La represión del protestantismo en España, 1517–1648* (Leuven: Leuven University Press, 2001).

61 Antonio Márquez, *Los alumbrados* (Madrid: Taurus, 1972), and Melquiades Andrés Martín, *La teología española en el siglo XVI*, vol. 1 (Madrid: Editorial Católica, 1976).

62 Homza, *The Spanish Inquisition*, 91.

63 Despite the ban on Lutheran works, no index of prohibited books was created in the 1520s, and the publishing boom continued unabated.

Vernacular devotional works did not spurn interiority. See, for instance, the "spiritual alphabets" composed by the Franciscan friar Francisco de Osuna: *The Third Spiritual Alphabet*, trans. Mary E. Giles (New York: Paulist Press, 1981).

64 A point I have made previously in *Religious Authority*, 11.

65 Mary E. Giles, "Francisca Hernández and the Sexuality of Religious Dissent," in Mary E. Giles, ed., *Women in the Inquisition* (Baltimore: Johns Hopkins University Press, 1998), 75–97.

66 The record of Francisca's trial is no longer extant. For the trials of Antonio de Medrano, her most fervent follower, see Javier Pérez Escohotado, *Proceso inquisitorial contra el Bachiller Antonio de Medrano (Logroño 1526–Calahorra 1527)* (Logroño: Gobierno de La Rioja, 1988), and Javier Pérez Escohotado, *Antonio Medrano, alumbrado epicúreo: Proceso inquisitorial, Toledo 1530* (Madrid: Editorial Verbum, 2003).

67 Cazalla's Inquisition trial has been transcribed in its entirety by Milagros Ortega-Costa, *Proceso de la Inquisición contra María de Cazalla* (Madrid: Fundación Universitaria Española, 1978), and excerpts translated in Homza, *The Spanish Inquisition*, 112–52.

2 Five *personae* of Ignatius of Loyola

J. CARLOS COUPEAU

During the last sixteen years of his life, Ignatius of Loyola founded the Society of Jesus, served as its Superior General (from 25 April 1541), and wrote Constitutions for this new religious order. Access to Ignatius of Loyola, however, cannot be direct but has to pass through his various *personae*. This essay examines in turn five titles, representative of these *personae*, titles that originated with his companions, followers, biographers, and historians and are indicative of five different strata that make up his figure: "Iñigo" (the Christian in his relationship with the Absolute), "our Father Master Ignatius" (the friend for the group of his intimate and close colleagues), the "Founder" (the leader for the Society of Jesus), "Saint Ignatius" (the point of departure for a new spirituality), "Loyola" (as known by the Encyclopaedists and "Counter-Reformation" historians).

IÑIGO THE PILGRIM

This first section will attempt to present some human aspects of the man, Iñigo. "Iñigo" is the name fitting here because such was the Christian name he received at baptism. Iñigo is the man in relation to the God of Jesus Christ, and, as it were, a pilgrim between Loyola and Rome. Recovered from a war wound to his leg (1521), Iñigo set about treading roads, sailing across the Mediterranean (1523–24), and studying in the universities of Alcalá, Salamanca and Paris (1526–35).[1] Then he succeeded in gathering extraordinary friends and colleagues to share in his pilgrimage to Jerusalem, which proved impossible. Iñigo would settle definitively in Rome for the final quarter of his life. He was fifty years of age.

Biographers of Loyola have sought to describe Iñigo's character. Some looked for its genesis in the circumstances of his infancy, others looked for it in the world of chivalry of his adolescence and early manhood. These authors approached this man's makeup from the viewpoint of race, family, language, and culture.[2] They emphasized

the courtly training he received in Arevalo, where his natural gifts
were complemented with that education in the virtues of a gentleman
through which Iñigo fostered the distinguished ease that people would
later note.[3] The influence of the Basque language and the paucity of his
initial education nonetheless left their mark on his particular use of
Castilian to the end of his days, especially when writing.[4]

However, more important than inherited or learned traits, it was a
religious transformation that proved decisive for the mature Iñigo. No
interpretation of the second half of his life should overlook this fact.
Iñigo admonishes the heir of the Loyola patrimony: "If he [God] has
given you an abundance of this world's goods it is to help you to earn
those of heaven";[5] here is the Basque-born man who would later affirm
that he would rather belong to the same race as Jesus Christ. A sense of
gratitude for having been created and redeemed moved Iñigo at his
conversion in 1521. After that religious conversion, intellectual,
moral, affective, and social transformations followed.[6]

After he had served feudal lords, Iñigo resolved to "serve God." The
source that witnesses to this self-determination is improperly titled
"Autobiography."[7] It transcribes accounts heard from Iñigo and spells
out his conversion, his consequent religious endeavor and some prayer
experiences he had (*Autobiography* §§27–31, 99–100). The same religious quality reappears consistently in other sources. The most exceptional one, the *Spiritual Diary*, is a compilation of the prayer notes
written by Iñigo between February 1544 and March 1545.[8]

Iñigo has to be understood in relationship with God. When his
companions pressed him to narrate "how the Lord had guided him,"
Iñigo chose to refer to himself as a "pilgrim" in relation to the will of
his "Creator and Redeemer," "the Divine Majesty," and "Our Lord."
Iñigo ardently desired to find out and fulfill God's plan for himself.[9]
The *Spiritual Diary* shows that Iñigo used his liberty as a way to
respond to God, perceiving himself as an "instrument" in God's providential hands.[10] Iñigo's social commitment integrated the moral and
affective dimensions of his conversion.

Iñigo's religious quest is echoed by his academic pilgrimage. In his
thirties, Iñigo uprooted himself from his culture, journeying through
Spain, Italy, Palestine, and France, and crafted for himself a new religious subject, "becoming a spiritual individual and recognizing himself as such."[11] Once in Rome, Iñigo's pilgrimage continued: his
changes of residence reveal his option for the urban setting and his
steady approach from its outskirts to its populated heart, where he
could serve more people.[12]

Pilgrimage wore Iñigo's health out. Severe abstinences and privations undermined his vigor, and the Roman weather, the stress of work, and the lack of physical exercise, along with the administration of an inexperienced physician, worsened his condition. Iñigo himself described his situation: "I go on falling and rising." His correspondence suffered from such an instable condition, and he delegated much of it to his secretary, who manifested his anxiety: "[Iñigo] is not accustomed to promise himself one more day of life" (*FN* I: 358) and apologized for replying to some letters: "It is a trial for him even to sign a letter" (*Epp.* VIII: 284). Some aides were in favor of lightening his load of all but the indispensable, but as Iñigo's health improved their fears diminished, even a few months before his death. Iñigo went into terminal decline in July 1556 and died at dawn, 31 July, a victim of severe stomach pains.

FROM PARISIAN "MASTER" TO ROMAN "PADRE"

The focus shifts now to seeing the person of Iñigo in relation to those who joined him. Iñigo's companions and aides perceived him through friendship and institutional concerns. They were the early "companions" at the University of Paris, and the "first-wave Jesuits" who joined them after 1541. Those who had addressed him as "Iñigo" then addressed him as "Master" and "Father," once he had graduated (1534) and was ordained (1537). The contemporaneous use of "Master" and of "Father" in written sources indicates a period of transition. The very formal "*our Father* Master Ignatius" evokes the person in so far as he engendered the Society at a later stage of development.[13]

The early companions (Pierre Favre, Francis Xavier, Diego Laínez, Simão Rodrigues, etc.) had dealt with Iñigo more informally.[14] Gonçalves da Câmara remembers in his *Memoriale* that someone described how Francis Xavier had announced: "Iñigo! Here's Araoz wanting to speak to you!"[15] Da Câmara emphasizes, "in the same way [i.e., as "Iñigo"] Father Pierre Favre would refer to *our Father Ignatius*" [my italics]. Favre too writes of him often as "Ignatius" and so does Laínez.[16]

This passage makes a point of the greater intimacy distinctive of the first companions. As the companions continued to write to Iñigo from their distant mission stations, their letters reveal an increasingly formal tone, aware as they were the letters could be read in public. Therefore while Bobadilla, a Paris companion, continues to call him "Master" in 1589,[17] reverence in addressing or referring to Iñigo is more prominent with Polanco, Nadal, Gonçalves da Câmara, Pedro de Ribadeneira, and other first-wave Jesuits, acknowledging paternal authority and institutionalized relationships.

As the pilgrimage to Jerusalem had proved impossible, Iñigo and his companions tried to relive the apostolic way of life in the West. They sought out the pope, "Vicar of Christ," that he might send them on missions. Paul III (Farnese) accepted their offer, and consequently they decided to constitute themselves into a religious order, submitting a canonical description of their way of life (*Formula vitae*), required before ecclesiastical approval. This was granted by the bull *Regimini militantis* (1540) and the group proceeded to the election of its first Superior. All the votes cast elected Iñigo, who only agreed on the insistence of his companions and confessor. One of his responsibilities before the group was to develop the *Formula* into detailed regulations. Over the writing of such constitutions, however, Ignatius gave precedence to his priestly ministries.

As a priest he took on a second sort of paternity. This spiritual fatherhood found scope in guiding others through the Spiritual Exercises, in teaching the catechism to children and simple folk, and in preaching in the squares. Such were the ministries contemplated in the *Formula*. Father Ignatius also undertook what the *Formula* calls "works of charity." Thanks to his example and leadership, he quickly achieved the Roman citizens' collaboration.[18] By 1541, the Father had founded a confraternity to help orphans and gathered financial support for several other projects on behalf of the poor, in particular the impoverished noble families,[19] and the prostitutes.

Rome was the European capital for prostitution. Public alarm at the spread of *le mal français* was not met with decisive initiatives. In contrast, Father Ignatius sought prostitutes out, did not mind dealing with them in public, and requested help to support them. Unable to raise all the funds needed, he had to draw on the Society's own resources and thus provided the initial capital for a house where ex-prostitutes could lodge and distance themselves from their clients. Iñigo made arrangements for them to marry or return to their families; for those who so wished, he founded a convent.

Iñigo's commitment to this ministry won over the active support and cooperation of the powerful. Such support proved invaluable when he next turned to forestall the dangers that threatened daughters of prostitutes and poverty-stricken young girls. On their behalf, he set up the "House of St Catherine," and organized a confraternity for its support (1546).

THE SUPERIOR GENERAL AT THE HEAD
OF THE BODY

The epitaph on Iñigo's tomb summed up our next *persona* as "Founder and First Superior General."[20] Hagiographers and historians saw Ignatius primarily as the Superior General and head of a missionary order, or as the founder of a religious order, from the viewpoint both of his mandate and of his sanctity.[21]

The *Formula* had chosen the term "placed before" (*praepositus*) to designate the Superior and head of the Society. The *praepositus*, in turn, liked to refer to the Society of Jesus as the "smallest" of religious congregations. That companionship of ten in 1539 counted one thousand by the end of his life, becoming a missionary enterprise spread over four continents, eleven administrative provinces and about one hundred Jesuit schools and residences.[22]

The figure of the first Superior General of that powerful order had overshadowed the poor "pilgrim" by 1572, when the *Vita Ignatii Loyolae* by P. de Ribadeneira appeared. It was the first biography of the General. Francis Borja (or Borgia, 1510–72) encouraged it and transformed Ribadeneira's biography into the official account about Ignatius. Borgia had all copies of the *Autobiography* withdrawn from circulation. Now, Ribadeneira's *Vita* informs his reader that by 1549 Ignatius' followers had reached "both the outside and the inside of Africa" (*FN* IV: 467) plus seven other countries across four continents (*FN* IV: 381).[23] Ribadeneira's triumphalistic presentation did not take into account that the Jesuit presence was so uneven in Congo, Brazil, and India compared with Italy, where Rome alone counted some seventy members, or the fact that Francis Xavier was the only fully rightful member outside Europe.

Before 1549, the work of the Superior on behalf of the Society had relied on his persuasive example, letters, and fame during the first half of his mandate. The General attracted followers, gave them spiritual formation and saw to it that they got solid academic training, selected them with his gift of insight into human character, and ingeniously assigned them to missions suggested by Christian kings and offered to the Society by the pope. One cannot hesitate to emphasize here the General's "leadership."[24]

Ribadeneira contributed to developing the figure of "our *Padre*" into that of the Superior General using the text of the *Constitutions*. Laínez' and Polanco's early descriptions of Iñigo (*FN* I: 136; 154–61) are echoed by the description that the *Constitutions* give of absolutely *any*

Superior General (*Const.* §§723–35).[25] These paragraphs became the backbone of Ribadeneira's concluding presentation of Ignatius: the Superior General (*FN* IV:734).

Following on Ribadeneira, many biographers have analyzed the relations of the General to the Church at large and to the Society in particular. The General established a model of fidelity to the Church through service to the See of Rome. Also pertinent are his relations with the popes, his attitude against allowing professed Jesuits to accept episcopal offices, his missionary policies, and his detailed instruction to Jesuits sent "on mission," such as to the Council of Trent. With regard to his ministry to the Society, his relations with his curia, his care for the distant companions, and his concern with new recruits are noteworthy.

As well as for his relations with the papacy, although secondary to them, the General was known for his dealings with the European royal houses. The General incarnated the reverential attitude towards the Holy See that inspired the Fourth Vow, which made Jesuits available for missions from the pope. This primary activity on behalf of the whole Society is not adequately reflected by the General's correspondence, but the General held annual audiences with the pope and mediated on the occasion of the Inquisition being established in Portugal, and in the reconciliation between the King of Portugal and Paul III. The General kept good relations with the next popes: Julius III (del Monte), Marcellus II (Cervini), and Paul IV (Carafa), as can be deduced from eleven papal bulls,[26] seven papal briefs,[27] and other documents that the Holy See extended during his mandate. These documents reflect a growing trust of the Holy See in the General.

Even more frequently, the General had contacts with influential persons who sought his advice, or whom he would visit. Occasionally he would invite guests and size them up in the intimacy of his frugal midday meals. The General held written correspondence with kings and princes, cardinals and bishops and their respective curiae,[28] covering up to one third of his correspondence sent to non-Jesuits.[29] The General diligently consolidated the identity of the Society of Jesus before these authorities, but he opposed them no less tenaciously at times. Conflict situations reveal much about the General's firm way of governing when faced with either spiritual or temporal powers. For instance, he opposed with all his might the appointment of three members of the Society to bishoprics, and the granting of a cardinal's hat to a fourth one. These early appointments threatened the Society for they represented the loss of one out of every nine of its professed members by 1553. The General wanted to dispel suspicions that ambition could be a motive for joining the Society. He intervened to block the appointments, requesting masses and prayers from all his colleagues, writing to dissuade the authorities promoting the ordinations, and even arguing with the pope in the case of Francis Borja.

In dealings with religious and laypeople, the General watched over the independence of the Society. He freed Jesuits from "spiritual responsibility" (*cura animarum*) over religious and lay congregations and turned down a proposed integration of the Society with other regular clerics (Theatines [1545] and Somascans [1547]).

The flagship for the Society's work *ad extra* was to be education. "Master Ignatius" had opposed the idea of running colleges, for colleges entailed admitting regular incomes. Laínez, favorable to that possibility, suggested a solution to the problem. Once a General, Ignatius resolved to launch the Society fully into this ministry.[30] Soon, the first schools developed in an unforeseeable way.[31] Colleges became centers for the formation of would-be Jesuits only in 1540, like the one at the University of Paris, where several candidates moved to study. The King of Portugal founded the first college in Coimbra (1541); the General staffed it with Jesuits, sent from Rome and Paris. Some other experiments in Spain (Valencia, Valladolid, Gandía), and especially the new school in Messina (Italy) from 1547, taught the General how to take up new challenges like a center of studies for the clergy (the Roman College, 1551), a residence for seminarians attending that center (the German College, 1552), and a series of secondary schools.[32]

The General ran the Society through his curia and correspondence. The inflow and outflow of correspondence kept the General connected and informed. He repeatedly laid down norms for the writing of letters, moved by considerations of size and storage, but also by the desire that some might be publishable. The General had written his first 250 letters before the twentieth month of his mandate, increasing this output constantly in the following years. The standard edition of his correspondence contains more than 5,300 letters to Jesuits, especially superiors outside Rome. Juan de Polanco, the last and most competent of the secretaries assisting the General, set up a professional central office in the curia from 1547. It allowed the flow of letters to almost quadruple by 1548. Polanco found himself overwhelmed sometimes, but from 1553 he had transformed an amateur system into a sophisticated bureaucratic machine.[33]

This brings us to the curia of the General. Part of his genius consisted in selecting collaborators, integrating them into his method of government, and winning their support. The General "coached many first generation Jesuits" and, most importantly, all his collaborators.[34] The General *minimized* the contents of formation while he *maximized* each one's will to serve and love. According to a pedagogy that can be traced to the Spiritual Exercises, the General showed a genuine appreciation of them and, on the presupposition that they were dignified and talented, sought their training in virtues like abnegation, in order to maximize their ability for self-donation. Contrary to what happened in Portugal or Sicily, no proper novitiate existed in Rome. The professed house (for those in final vows) and General's residence *was* the novitiate.

The General's government rested on processes of consultation, experimentation, decision and implementation. He used various types of councils to take decisions, either delegating to them or asking advice. The "consultation" proved to be the most helpful one. It comprised the secretary, a procurator and, from 1555 on, the vicar general and assistants. Two other consultants residing elsewhere in the city and three of his first companions (Laínez, Salmerón, and Bobadilla) when they passed through Rome were eventually called on. The consultation functioned on the basis of "trust and on the need to research in common".[35] An initial discussion to gain information was followed by a test period, finally reaching some decision concerning the course to be followed, and its implementation (usually entailing its handing on to a subordinate and setting up a body capable of carrying out the task). It appeared to be the General who took the decision (the *determinación*), but, once he had proof of and could rely on the self-denial of his men, he was ready to empower "co-responsibility" on their part and would delegate his authority. The General struck a good balance between centralized and delegated authority.[36]

SAINT IGNATIUS, THE FOUNDER OF THE SOCIETY OF JESUS

Câmara recorded Ignatius' confessor as saying "[Ignatius is] not simply Father Ignatius, but a saint and more than a saint" (*Memoriale* §162). This remark of Fr. Eguía serves to introduce a fourth *persona*: the "saint" that the hagiographic tradition has handed down to us. "Saint Ignatius" has been the canonical definition for many devotees of his spirituality. They treasure holiness as the quality that liberates our figure for a community beyond chronological and geographical limits. This section draws a distinction between the "first

General" and the "founder raised to the altars" on account of the fact that, although Iñigo became Superior General through a unanimous election, no papal bulls founding the Society mention *a* founder.[37] The recognition of Saint Ignatius as *the* founder constitutes an interpretation.

The life of the founder bore an exemplary value for his followers. Writing it down triggered a process of "classicalization." If the *Autobiography* reflects a life in constant flux, as typified by its main character, "the Pilgrim," that aspect loses its appeal from 1538 on, and when the Society of Jesus was given official approval. Likewise, Polanco's *Summaries* (*FN* I: 256–98) and Nadal's exhortations on the Institute retell the story of "how the Society was truly founded" (*FN* I: 360), aiming to capture the essence and making the life of Saint Ignatius appear "classical."

Câmara, Polanco, and Nadal regarded the General as a founder. They uncovered the narrative of events that led him to found the Society, "[s]ince I knew," Nadal wrote, "that the holy Fathers, the founders of any monastic institute, *normally* gave those coming after them, in place of a last will and testament, such pieces of advice . . ." (my stress; *FN* I: 355–57; cf. *EN* V: 36–48). Subsequent generations would perceive him through an analogy, the one established between the great religious orders of the past and the Society, between their great founders and Ignatius. Moreover, Nadal's analogical imagination interpreted the life of the first companions along the line of contemporary understanding of apostolic life: just as the post-apostolic Church was the successor to the apostolic community, and the writing of the Gospels followed on after the preaching of the apostles, so the expansion and growth of the Society followed on after the founder and the first companions. And finally, just as the four Gospels, the Acts and the Pauline letters made possible the transmission once the eyewitnesses of the salvific events had died, so the *Constitutions*, the *Autobiography* (its real title being *Acta Quaedam*), and the *Letters* and *Instructions* would also lay the corresponding foundations for the Society.[38]

A providentialist theology lay beneath these analogies. Central to its rationale was the idea of a divine mission. For example, Nadal would speak of the founder thus: "our most holy Father ended his life after having accomplished with exactness the task that God had commended to him" (*FN* II: 8), thus elevating *the* mission to a spiritual status; something more complicated than the "missions" entrusted by the Holy See. So Saint Ignatius appeared as the one faithfully carrying out a divine commission, a view resulting from contemporary preconceptions and expectations.[39] As someone sent by divine Providence, Iñigo ended up transformed into the chosen one to fight Luther's Reform (*EN* v: 314).

If prayer and heroic virtue are the mark of many saints, the same is true of Saint Ignatius. Persecutions test the saint's degree of virtue and orthodoxy. Nadal, Ribadeneira, etc. explain how Saint Ignatius was shown to be innocent before civil tribunals and those of the Inquisition on at least sixteen occasions.[40] His Spiritual Exercises endured the criticism of the famous Dominicans Melchor Cano and Thomas Pedroche. Other attacks were those of Mattia della Posta (1546) and Giovanni di Torano (1552).[41]

Powerful intercessory prayer was another characteristic of the saint. His followers entrusted themselves to his prayers,[42] and it was in prayer that the saint composed the foundation-texts of the Society. Besides the *Constitutions*, Nadal attributed to Saint Ignatius the authorship of the *Formula*. The *Formula*, however, appears to be rather the end product of the discussions that Master Ignatius held with his companions. For the definitive text approved by the bull *Exposcit Debitum* (1550), the saint counted on Polanco's, Nadal's, and other specialists' opinions. A spiritualizing understanding of holiness was oblivious to the concrete means by which the saint's heritage has come to us (*FN* III: 637), for it is evident that this second major legislative text is the product of secretarial editing, corporate experience, and collaboration.[43] When Ribadeneira referred to the inspiration tradition in his *Vita* and in his *Tratado* on the Institute, no new evidence was brought forward.[44] Joannes Dirckinck (1641–1716), a century later, presented the saint as a divinely inspired founder, to whom even the *Rules* had been revealed by means of an angel.[45] Contemporary to the Baroque style of Fr. Dirckinck, the Bollandists published a critical biography of the saint for the *Acta Sanctorum*.[46] It constituted the first carefully academic presentation of the person of the saint.

In short, whereas the previous section dwelt on the decisions taken by the General, this section has dealt with the writings the Jesuits received as from a saint, the figure who authorized the legislative basis of the Order. The *Spiritual Exercises*, the *Formula*, the *Constitutions* and the *Rules* reflect the talent of the man who knew how to harmonize and integrate others' cooperation. The *Constitutions*, instead, became the canonized expression of a charism reified out of the saintliness of a founder recognized by the Church.

LOYOLA, THE COUNTER-REFORMATION LEADER

The Enlightenment generated a fifth image of Ignatius, contrary to the one generated by the Baroque saint in many regards.[47] This *persona* appeared during a period marked by confessional conflicts, in the writings of some of the French *philosophes*, and some nineteenth-century historians. It developed further with the start of the twentieth century, thanks to a better knowledge of the sources.

Up against "Saint Ignatius" appears the "Loyola" of the Encyclopaedists. The appellation "Loyola" flourished as expressed by these authors. They used "Loyola" as a key figure to explain "Jesuitism," the driving force of the Counter-Reformation.[48] This is not the place to study the implicit hermeneutic principles that led these authors to interpret Ignatius the way they did, but on the whole their account of "Loyola" was very distant from the *persona* of "Iñigo."[49]

Some *philosophes* encouraged the use of the term "Jesuit" as a historical cliché. They focused on the man who invented the method of the Exercises and organized the *Constitutions*, as if the Exercises served to train people in discipline and will-power, to serve those in control, and the *Constitutions* were an expression of the Machiavellian form of government that had gained power over European courts and princes.[50] The *philosophes* exaggerated the transcendence of Jesuit obedience, and thought of Loyola as some super spy-trainer intent on infiltrating society.[51]

Some German historians made Loyola the leading champion *against* Luther.[52] The famous Leopold von Ranke began this approach among Protestant historians, according to whom Loyola had died just at the threshold of his *Gegenreformation*.[53] Wilhelm Maurenbrecher, along with Eberhard Gothein and Martin Phillippson, continued to propagate von Ranke's opinion of the founder of the Jesuits.[54] No obvious signs at the start of his generalate, however, allow us to think of Loyola as a Counter-Reformer. The idea of Loyola founding an army against the Reformation is misleading. Two of Loyola's first companions set off for Ireland, and three others left Rome for Germany. They were on papal, not Loyola's, missions. True, Loyola sent Peter Canisius to Germany (1549), but only after first sending him to Sicily. Loyola's seven Instructions to accompany missions to central Europe show him mainly concerned with the overall Jesuit presence that he desired. Loyola considered interior reform the prerequisite for any Reformation, and edification through virtuous life to be more powerful than theological disputes.[55] Thus Loyola writes to the first Jesuits sent to Germany:

> Your first and greatest asset will be a distrust of self together with a great and magnanimous trust in God ... The second means is a good life, and therefore an exemplary life ... For as Germany is in great need of good example, she will derive much help from it ... You should cherish a genuine affection and show it for all.[56]

Loyola's encouragement for the foundation of colleges followed the advice of Nadal.[57] Loyola intended to provide the youth with a Christian education, and to regenerate the local clergy by means of a rigorous intellectual formation. Loyola searched for financial help to set up and maintain the German College (1552), invested men of high quality and every other means at his disposal into this enterprise, and approved the foundation of colleges in Cologne (1544), Vienna (1551), Prague and Ingolstadt (1556). The foundation of the German College was secondary to the general policy of ensuring a good formation for the members of the Order along with the proper formation of the clergy, irrespective of their origin.[58] As for the colleges, those in central Europe were only a fraction of those already established in other parts of Europe by 1556. Loyola had sent ten Jesuits to start the college in Messina and twelve Jesuits to the college of Palermo before he sent three to the University of Ingolstadt. Sicily was hardly being rocked by the seismic shock of the Reformation! Above all, historians were oblivious to the fact that Loyola had offered his resignation as General in 1551, hoping to be sent to Ethiopia, rather than to Germany.

John O'Malley has shown that the categories of "Reform" and "Counter-Reformation" became obstacles for historians to a proper understanding of Loyola and his achievements, these being in fact less Eurocentric.[59] Only in the light of actual facts have contemporary historians recognized that such views were a projection of later ideas: "opposing Protestantism was peripheral and occasional to them [the Jesuits] for their first ten or fifteen years."[60]

"Loyola" was used almost as a "buzz word." Confessional motives, critical attitudes, nationalist sentiments, and a historiography primarily interested in the history of ideas approached "Loyola" from an interest in Jesuitism. It was opportune, therefore, for the Society of Jesus to make the sources contained in its Archives available also for the wider public. The series known as the *Monumenta Historica Societatis Iesu* published all that had been preserved on St Ignatius of Loyola (*Monumenta Ignatiana*, 1909–77).[61] At present, there are 23

Ignatian volumes, divided into four sub-series: these include the letters and instructions written or authorized by him, *Epistolae Ignatianae* (12 vols.), a critical edition of the *Spiritual Exercises* (2 vols.), the foundational texts *Constitutiones et Regulae* (4 vols.), and source materials for his life, *Fontes Narrativi* and *Fontes Documentales* (5 vols.). This tremendous work consists of more than twenty thousand pages of critically presented manuscript evidence from the sixteenth century: a valuable resource to better appreciate the figure of Loyola.

In conclusion, although "Loyola" emphasizes the genius who organized the Society of Jesus, it should not be forgotten that he also knew how to "breathe into it a certain spirit and open for it the doors to a world-wide apostolate."[62] Thus, as historians within the Order sought the saint, other historians fixed their attention on the psychology that Loyola could have transmitted to his followers. The latter tended to disregard the role that faith and trust in God's providence had played. Ignatius' spirituality resulted from his faith, mysticism, love for the Church, and theology.[63] The critical and rational approach of the nineteenth century put the accent on suspicion and lacked the empathy to understand Loyola's motivation, without which the most accurate portrait of Loyola remains "an enigmatic and cold death-mask."[64]

AT THE SOURCE OF THE *CONSTITUTIONS*

Spelling out these five *personae* could bear on further studies on Ignatius Loyola. In the last section, I will reflect on some consequences in connection with the *Constitutions*. The composition of the *Constitutions* spans the whole period considered here. Each of these *personae*, in fact, is at the source of today's approach to the *Constitutions*. My concluding remarks will try to illustrate that following the reverse sequence of the essay.

Loyola. As late as the 1960s, the ideas of power, obedience, and organization attracted a fine commentator's attention to the *Constitutions*. David Knowles considered the *Constitutions* the "state-of-the-art" of religious rules. Knowles affirmed that their structure, arrangement, and form of government were all geared towards the achievement of a single aim. Therefore: "In intent and by constitution [the Society of Jesus] is a *corps d'élite* in the hands of a single commander." In other words, the acorn of religious legislation became an oak in the *Constitutions*, and, sure enough, Loyola was that commander and creator of such a powerful and influential religious order.[65]

Saint Ignatius. More than any other foundational text, however, the *Constitutions* appropriate the content of the saint's mature mystical experience. During prayer time, Saint Ignatius pondered aspects of the *Constitutions*, struggling to efface himself and tune into God's own design for the followers of the Institute. The *Autobiography* gives witness to this and the *Spiritual Diary* provides hand-written evidence for at least one passage of the *Constitutions* (*Const.* §555). These prayer notes helped the saint to bring his thoughts into line with what he perceived as the thoughts of God between February and March, 1544. We may surmise that the saint used a similar method to decide other key-points, simply lacking the time to apply himself to all 826 paragraphs equally.

The General. Besides the saint's mystical experiences, the curia of the General assisted him with composition. Research, correspondence, and planned visitations enriched the draft. The General had his secretary investigate most of the religious rules of the past, the outcome of which is traceable in many paragraphs. Letters and visitors to the provinces advised the General of the situation of this international Order, to facilitate adaptation. Regulations were adapted to times, places, and peoples. The General made his immediate subordinates responsible for that adjustment in a series of declarations by which he implemented the *Constitutions*. His diminutive staff illustrates a process of modernization for which the General deserves credit: the bureaucratic efficiency of a central curial office, communal discipline based on mutual confidence, obedience and manifestation of conscience, and overall functioning rationalized by frequent correspondence.[66]

The Master. Consultation for the *Constitutions* unveils new dimensions of their author. Master Ignatius was true to the content of deliberations and agreements reached with his companions from 1539 on, but most notably in 1550. He submitted drafts and explained resolutions to them. In the most prominent place, the text exhibits a fourfold theological justification in support of the need to write constitutions.[67] The scholastic principle that grace presupposes nature and brings it to perfection, for example, presides over the concluding section of the *Constitutions*. Although the structure of other rules shows a beginning, middle, and end, no religious rule has combined so neatly with a theological principle.

Iñigo. Finally, the *Constitutions* capture and interpret the essence of the pilgrim's experience as an individual and as the member of a companionship. He who had learnt "on the go" what human growth and spiritual maturation meant for an apostle outlined a formation process through four stages: initial commitment (Parts I–II), formation of the virtues (Part III), academic formation (Part IV) and the school of the affections (Part V). This training leads from courageous determination to mature surrender, through the appreciation and practice of the virtues (poverty, humility, self-denial, and obedience) and through the study and practice of the humanities and theology. Each stage resonates with Iñigo's own process: conversion, asceticism, higher studies, and surrender of all the previous in the profession of religious vows. Structure, therefore, unfolds the process by which an individual grows into a member of a body. Next, Part VI through to Part IX deal with regulations pertaining to that body, following on the Pauline metaphor. Themes proper to this second half are the maturing of those virtues when regulated by charity (Part VI), and the bonds keeping the union among the members (Part VIII) and with the head (the Superior General, Part IX). Central here are the criteria for choosing among missions and the regulations pertaining to who may send whom, how, and for what assignment (Part VII). This small treatise on service attempts to reconcile what is good with what is better, the ideal with the reality.

In conclusion, it is clear that the interpretive trajectories that are traceable in the *Constitutions* are also operative in the definition of Ignatius of Loyola between 1540 and 1556. This essay reflects on his personal relations with God, contemporaries, and many others ever since. The myth-like figure Modernity left us with, far from the concrete individual at the origins of the Society of Jesus, can tempt us to stay with the pilgrim Iñigo, yet this essay offers a multi-layered account and a written text as a way to empower the reader for a more dynamic relationship with Ignatius; a critical relation with five *personae*, aware of the complexity involved, sensitive to value and relevance. Each *persona* started with a community of readers. For each community, that *persona* treasured dominant values, like subjectivity, companionship, international leadership, spirituality, cultural agency, and transformation. Each *persona* may help to moderate and balance the others.

Abbreviations

Autobiography	Ignatius Loyola, *Saint Ignatius of Loyola: Personal Writings*, ed. and trans. Joseph Munitiz and Philip Endean (London and New York: Penguin, 1996), 1–64.
Const.	*The Constitutions of the Society of Jesus*, trans. with an Introduction and Commentary by George E. Ganss (St. Louis: Institute of Jesuit Sources, 1970).

DHCJ	*Diccionario Histórico de la Compañía de Jesús*, ed. E. O'Neill and J. M. Domínguez, 4 vols. (Rome: Institutum Historicum Societatis Iesu, 2001).
EN	Jerónimo Nadal, *Epistolae P. Hieronimi Nadal Societatis Jesu*, 5 vols. (Madrid: Augustini Avrial and Monumenta Historica Societatis Iesu, 1898–1962).
Epp.	Ignatius Loyola, *Sancti Ignatii de Loyola Societatis Jesu Fundatoris Epistolae et Instructiones*, 12 vols. (Madrid: G. Lopez del Horno, 1903–11).
Exx.	*The Spiritual Exercises* in *Saint Ignatius of Loyola: Personal Writings*, ed. and trans. J. Munitiz and P. Endean (London: Penguin, 1996), 281–358.
FN	*Fontes Narrativi de S. Ignatio de Loyola*, ed. Cándido de Dalmases *et al.*, 4 vols. (Rome: Monumenta Historica Societatis Iesu, 1943–65).
Memoriale	Luís Gonçalves da Câmara, *Remembering Iñigo: Glimpses of the Life of Saint Ignatius of Loyola: The Memoriale of Luís Gonçalves da Câmara*, trans. A. Eaglestone and J. Munitiz (Leominster, UK: Gracewing Publishing; St. Louis: Institute of Jesuit Sources, 2004).

Notes

1   José Ignacio Tellechea Idígoras, *Ignatius of Loyola: The Pilgrim Saint* (Chicago: Loyola University Press, 1994).
2   He is the valiant and sincere Basque nobleman in José María Salaverría, *Iñigo de Loyola* (Madrid: Nuestra Raza, 1935); the descendant of the feudal lords of the valley in Pedro de Leturia, *Iñigo de Loyola* (Chicago: Loyola University Press, 1965).
3   A balanced summary is in William W. Meissner, *Ignatius of Loyola: The Psychology of a Saint* (New Haven: Yale University Press, 1992), 18–28. Meissner has broken new ground with his approach to Iñigo's self-development.
4   Sabino Sola, "En torno al castellano de san Ignacio," *Razón y Fe* 153 (1956), 45–70; *Diccionario de Espiritualidad Ignaciana*, s.v. "Lenguaje Ignaciano."

5 William J. Young, *Letters of St Ignatius of Loyola* (Chicago: Loyola University Press, 1959), 8; *Epp.* 1: 81.
6 Donald L. Gelpi, *Adult Conversion and Initiation* (Collegeville, MN: Michael Glazier, 1993).
7 *Autobiography*, 1–64.
8 Ibid., 65–109.
9 Manuel Ruiz Jurado, *El peregrino de la voluntad de Dios: Biografía espiritual de San Ignacio de Loyola* (Madrid: BAC, 2005).
10 Iñigo wrote the *Spiritual Exercises* as a method of prayer to guide others towards God. In the "principle and foundation" of the *Exercises* he declares: "The human person is created to praise, reverence and serve God our Lord" (*Exx.* §23). *Exx.*, 281–358; Const. §814.
11 Peter Burke, "Representations of the Self between Petrarch and Descartes," in Roy Porter, ed., *Rewriting the Self: Histories from the Renaissance to the Present* (London: Routledge, 1997), 17.
12 Thomas M. Lucas, *Landmarking: City, Church, and Jesuit Urban Strategy* (Chicago: Loyola Press, 1997). Young, *Letters of St. Ignatius*, 245.
13 See this sequence in Polanco's *Summary of the Origin and Progress of the Society* (1547–48), where he refers to "Iñigo de Loyola," "Master Iñigo," and "Father Master Ignatius" (*FN* I: 153, 192, 204).
14 For example, see Simão Rodrigues, *"A Brief and Exact Account": The Recollections of Simão Rodrigues*, trans. J. F. Conwell (St. Louis: Institute of Jesuit Sources, 2004).
15 Araoz, a relative of Ignatius, was to join the Society (*c.* 1538), *FN* I: 613. *Memoriale*, 86–87.
16 An account of Iñigo through the writings of these and the first companions is in Ignacio Cacho Nazabal, *Iñigo de Loyola ese enigma* (Bilbao: Mensajero, 2003).
17 *FN* III: 325–31.
18 Pietro Tacchi-Venturi and Mario Scaduto, *Storia della Compagnia di Gesù in Italia*, 5 vols. (Roma: Civiltà Cattolica, 1951), II/2, 147–209.
19 Ibid., 141.
20 *FN* I: 776.
21 More recently: John P. Donnelly, *Ignatius of Loyola: Founder of the Jesuits* (New York: Pearson Longman, 2004).
22 The provinces and their foundation years are the following: Portugal (1546), Spain (later divided) (1547), India (1549), Italy (1551), Sicily and Brazil (1553), Castile, Aragon and Andalucia (1554), France (1555), Upper and Lower Germany (1556). Fifteen Jesuits had been appointed to Ethiopia, at least on paper.
23 However, these incursions were mainly failures: Jesuits were able to remain in Ceuta and Tetuán for only a short period, and the four Jesuits sent to the Congo were unable to establish a mission. In both cases, the incentive came from John III of Portugal, and these missions cannot be considered the fruit of a strategic missionary plan by the Superior General exclusively.
24 Chris Lowney, *Heroic Leadership: Best Practices from a 450-Year-Old Company that Changed the World* (Chicago: Loyola Press, 2003), 163–64, 289–90.

25 J. W. O'Malley has suggested that in this description one can find the influence of the *humanist* ideal of the "good man" (Cicero, *De officiis* 1.20.66); see O'Malley, "Jesuit Spirituality: The Civic and Cultural Dimensions," *Review of Ignatian Spirituality* 105 (2004), 37–44. I am inclined to think, however, that it is more easily connected to the description in Laínez' letter to Polanco of 1547.

26 Two bulls deal with the approval of the Society of Jesus. Others deal with the foundation of a confraternity for the care of prostitutes (1543), the setting up of a center for catechumens (1543), the foundation of a university of the Society in Gandía (Spain) (1547), approval for the grant of important privileges to the Society (1549), and the foundation of the German College (1552).

27 Some of the briefs deal with the appointment of two apostolic nuncios in Scotland (1541), the setting up of a confraternity to help catechumens (1543), and the approval of the text of the *Spiritual Exercises* (1548).

28 Listed among the personalities, one finds cardinals such as Cervini (the future Marcellus II), Contarini, Alvarez de Toledo, Farnese, Morone, Pole, etc., also the ambassadors of Spain, Portugal, and Siena, aristocrats, and professors: cf. Ricardo García-Villoslada, *San Ignacio de Loyola Nueva Biografía* (Madrid: BAC, 1986), 601–3.

29 Cf. Dominique Bertrand, *La politique de Saint Ignace de Loyola: L'analyse sociale* (Paris: Cerf, 1985), 42.

30 John O'Malley, "How the First Jesuits Became Involved in Education," in Vincent J. Duminuco, ed., *The Jesuit Ratio Studiorum: 400th Anniversary Perspectives* (New York: Fordham University Press, 2000), 58–74.

31 For a concise exposition of all this, cf. *DHCJ*, s.v. "Casas."

32 *Epp.* 4: 5–9, 9–11, 18–19, 23, 24–25, 33, etc. By the end of his days, the General had agreed on the creation of these schools: Collegio Romano, Collegio Germanico (Rome); Bologna, Florence, Genoa, Loreto, Modena, Naples, Padua, Palermo, Tivoli, Venice (Italy); Alcalá, Toledo, Valladolid, Amelia, Medina del Campo, Valencia, Gandía (Spain); Coimbra, Evora, St. Antony in Lisbon (Portugal), Paris, Billom (France), and Prague.

33 See J. A. de Polanco, *Polanci Complementa* (Madrid: Typis G. Lopez and Monumenta Historica Societatis Jesu, 1916), 1: 87–88. Bertrand, *La politique*, 34–57.

34 Lowney, *Heroic Leadership*, 290.

35 Bertrand, *La politique*, 50.

36 Lowney, *Heroic Leadership*, 163–64.

37 *Const.*, 64.

38 *EN*, v: 45, 123–27; and cf. notes, 262–64.

39 Even recent studies of the saint have been inspired by the theological notion of "mission", e.g., J. M. Granero, *San Ignacio de Loyola: La misión de su vida* (Madrid: Razón y Fe, 1984).

40 Cacho Nazábal, *Iñigo de Loyola ese enigma*, 407.

41 *EN* v: 251, 253, and *passim*; *FN* iv: 431ff.

42 Francis Xavier, *The Letters and Instructions of Francis Xavier*, ed. and trans. M. J. Costelloe (St. Louis: Institute of Jesuit Sources, 1992), 344–45; P. Favre, *Fabri Monumenta*, ed. F. Lirola (Madrid: Lopez del Horno and Monumenta Historica Societatis Iesu, 1914), 397; A. Salmerón, *Epistolae*, 2 vols. (Madrid: López del Horno and Monumenta Historica Societatis Iesu, 1906–7), 1: 38; *FN* IV: 457; J. Nadal, *Orationis Observationes*, ed. M. Nicolau (Rome: Institutum Historicum Societatis Iesu, 1964), 137.

43 *Constitutiones Societatis Iesu*, ed. Dionysius Zapico, 4 vols. (Rome: Monumenta Historica Societatis Iesu, 1934–48), 1: cxcvii–cxcix, 268, n. 1; see Antonio M. de Aldama, "La composición de las Constituciones de la Compañía de Jesús," *Archivum Historicum Societatis Iesu* 84 (1973), 201–45. See Ignacio Iparraguirre, "Desmitificación de San Ignacio," *Archivum Historicum Societatis Iesu* 41 (1972), 357–73.

44 Pedro de Ribadeneira, *Tratado en el qual se da razón del Instituto de la Compañía de Jesús* (Madrid: Colegio de la Compañía de Jesús, 1605).

45 "St Ignatius therefore was a sun, blazing with heavenly brightness and illuminating the whole Society, indeed even the world," Johannes Dirckinck, *Exhortationes ad Religiosos*, 3 vols. (London, 1913); first published in 1730 and frequently republished during the next two centuries, one edition appearing immediately after the restoration of the Society.

46 Ioannes Pinius (Pien), *Acta S. Ignatii Loyolae, Fundatoris Clericorum Regularium S.I.* (= *Acta Sanctorum Iulii*, vol. VII) (Antwerp, 1731 and Venice, 1749).

47 Iparraguirre, "Desmitificación de San Ignacio," 358–60.

48 John O'Malley, "The Historiography of the Society of Jesus: Where Does It Stand Today?" in John W. O'Malley, Gauvin Bailey, Steven J. Harris, and T. Frank Kennedy, eds., *The Jesuits: Cultures, Sciences, and the Arts, 1540–1773* (Toronto: University of Toronto Press, 1999), 3–37; see "Antijesuitismo" (various authors), in *DHCJ*.

49 Joaquín Iriarte, "Loyola ante la intelectualidad no-católica," *Razón y Fe* 153 (1956), 71–96.

50 For instance, René Fülöp-Miller, *The Power and Secret of the Jesuits* (London: G. P. Putnam, 1930).

51 Geoffrey Cubitt, *The Jesuit Myth: Conspiracy, Theory and Politics in Nineteenth-Century France* (Oxford: Clarendon Press, 1993).

52 Ricardo García-Villoslada, "La figura histórica de San Ignacio de Loyola a través de cuatro siglos," *Razón y Fe* 153 (1956), 65.

53 Leopold von Ranke, *Deutsche Geschichte im Zeitalter der Reformation* (Berlin, 1842–47), V: 501; quoted in O'Malley, "The Historiography of the Society of Jesus," 19.

54 Maurenbrecher, Wilhelm, *Geschichte der katholischen Reformation* (Nördlingen: Beck, 1880); Martin Phillippson, *Les origines du catholicisme moderne: La Contre-révolution religieuse au XVIe siècle* (Brussels and Paris: Félix Alcan, 1884); Eberhard Gothein, *Ignatius von Loyola und die Gegenreformation* (Halle: Max Niemeyer, 1895).

55 For example, *Epp.* 1: 387–88, *Autobiography*, 165.
56 Young, *Letters of St Ignatius*, 212.
57 The oldest presentation of Loyola as an "anti-Lutheran" is to be found in the writings of Nadal and Canisius: see Miquel Batllori, "El mito contrarreformista de San Ignacio anti-Lutero," in Julio Caro Baroja, ed., *Ignacio de Loyola, Magister Artium en París 1528–1535* (Donostia–San Sebastián: Sociedad Guipuzkoana de ediciones y publicaciones, 1991), 88–93.
58 Tacchi-Venturi, *Storia della Compagnia di Gesù in Italia*, II/2, 127.
59 O'Malley, "The Historiography of the Society of Jesus," 18–24.
60 John O'Malley, *Trent and All That: Renaming Catholicism in the Early Modern Era* (Cambridge, MA: Harvard University Press, 2000), 127.
61 http://xoomer.alice.it/mmorales/catalogo.htm (31 January 2007).
62 Cándido de Dalmases, "Generales de la Compañía de Jesús: 1. Ignacio de Loyola," *DHCJ* II: 1600; the date (1544) given here for Loyola's letters to Peter Canisius and the King of the Romans is incorrect, it should say (1554); see Rogelio García Mateo, *Ignacio de Loyola* (Bilbao: Universidad de Deusto, 2000), 413–18.
63 For a fine vision of Ignatius by a Lutheran see Gottfried Maron, *Ignatius von Loyola: Mystik, Theologie, Kirche* (Göttingen: Vanderhoeck & Ruprecht, 2001).
64 Hugo Rahner, "Iñigo López de Loyola: Ein Überblick über die neueste Ignatius-Literatur," *Stimmen der Zeit* 138 (1940), 97.
65 D. Knowles concluded his book on the history of constitutional development of religious orders with a commentary on the *Constitutions* of the Society of Jesus. David Knowles, *From Pachomius to Ignatius* (Oxford: Clarendon Press, 1966), 62.
66 Wolfgang Reinhard, "Gegenreformation als Modernisierung? Prolegomena zu einer Theorie des Konfessionellen Zeitalters," *Archive for Reformation History* 68 (1977), 226–52; see O'Malley, *Trent and All That*, 111.
67 Arguably, the opening paragraph of the *Preamble* meets the objections presented by the malcontent Bobadilla.

3 The Spiritual Exercises

PHILIP ENDEAN

Pierre Favre (1506–46) was the first of Ignatius' companions to have stayed with him, and hence the second Jesuit. After the Society was founded in 1540, he was sent on mission to Germany, and in 1542 he began to keep a spiritual journal. He begins by recalling the events of his life, and notably his encounter with Ignatius in Paris. Though Pierre helped Ignatius with his studies, the roles of master and pupil were soon reversed:

> As time passed he became my master in spiritual things and gave me a method of raising myself to a knowledge of the divine will and of myself. In the end we became one in desire and will and one in a firm resolve to take up that life we lead today – we, the present or future members of this Society of which I am unworthy.[1]

This quotation expresses two important truths about the Ignatian Spiritual Exercises. First, the common life of the Society of Jesus is closely connected to the experience of the Exercises. Favre and the other Jesuit companions share a "firm resolve to take up that life we lead today" – a resolve that proceeds from the goal of the Exercises: "a knowledge of the divine will and of myself." For Ignatius, both the Exercises and the Society were key means through which he realized his life-project of "the progress of souls in Christian life and doctrine."[2] Jesuits became Jesuits through the Exercises – "most of the good people who are today in the Society have left the world to come to it by using this way." Conversely, the Exercises were seen, right from the beginning, as the Society's own characteristic ministry – "among the means which our Society uses, this one is very proper to her, and God has used it in large measure among countless souls."[3]

Second, it is significant that Favre's account evokes the text of the Exercises only secondarily and indirectly, while stressing far more the quite personal and particular process of growth that he undergoes at Ignatius' hands. This passage of his journal tells us far more about

Favre himself than about what Ignatius had written. Typically expressive is the following paragraph:

> Before that – I mean before having settled upon the course of my life through the help given me by God through Iñigo – I was always very unsure of myself and blown about by many winds: sometimes wishing to be married, sometimes to be a doctor, sometimes a lawyer, sometimes a lecturer, sometimes a professor of theology, sometimes a cleric without a degree – at times wishing to be a monk. I was being borne about previously by these winds, according as the greater or the lesser heavenly body was dominant, that is, according as one or other attraction reigned. Delivering me, as I have said, from these attractions by the consolations of his Spirit, our Lord led me to make a firm decision to become a priest completely dedicated to his service.[4]

Spiritual Exercises is not a book to be read; Ignatius is quite explicit that the person making the Exercises should not have the full text to hand, and not know what is coming (*Exx.* 11). Rather, Ignatius' book is a collection of resources that "the one who gives to another the way and order of meditating and contemplating" (*Exx.* 2) should have in mind when seeking to help the particular individual who is undergoing the process. The fundamental principle is that they be applied to the dispositions of the person who wishes to receive them: "to each one it should be given in accord with however they might want to dispose themselves, so that there can be greater help and profit (*según que se quisieren disponer, se debe de dar a cada uno, porque más se pueda ayudar y aprovechar*)" (*Exx.* 18). When Ignatius writes about how the Exercises might help a potential Jesuit recruit, the stress is on the exercitant's distinctive experience, shaped as it is by a particular history. The candidate is to be occupied in,

> making spiritual exercises for one month or a little more or less; that is to say, in examining his consciousness, turning over his whole past life and making a general confession, meditating upon his sins, and contemplating the steps and mysteries of the life, death, resurrection and ascension of Christ our Lord, exercising himself in praying vocally and mentally according to the capacity of the person, as will be taught him in our Lord *etc.*[5]

Ignatius does not directly prescribe the use of his own book – he simply says "spiritual exercises." The candidate's personal history should somehow come into contact with the story of Christ, but always in a way that respects his personal capacities.

In what follows, I want first to explore how this sensitivity to God's ongoing action in human history informs Ignatius' general approach to prayer and spiritual growth in *Spiritual Exercises*. Then I shall offer – in a disconnected fashion befitting the content – some basic information on key elements in Ignatius' text. Finally, I shall present some reflections for historians on how the Ignatian Exercises have functioned in Jesuit life.

IGNATIAN PRAYER

Central to *Spiritual Exercises* is a particular approach to prayer around a Gospel text, illustrated most fully – and by way of example – in connection with the Incarnation and birth of Christ (*Exx.* 101–17). Ignatius begins with three preambles, or preludes. The first is the recall of the story:

> The first Prelude is the narrative and it will be here how Our Lady went forth from Nazareth, about nine months with child, as can be piously meditated, seated on an ass, and accompanied by Joseph and a maid, taking an ox, to go to Bethlehem to pay the tribute which Caesar imposed on all those lands.

The jargon for the second is "composition of place": a setting oneself within the scene. In the case of the birth of Christ:

> to see with the sight of the imagination the road from Nazareth to Bethlehem; considering the length and the breadth, and whether such road is level or through valleys or over hills; likewise looking at the place or cave of the Nativity, how large, how small, how low, how high, and how it was prepared.

The third "prelude" is a prayer, "for what I want: it will be to ask for knowledge of the Lord from inside, Who for me has become human that I may more love and follow Him".

After this prayer for knowledge, love, and dedication to service, there follow the three main "points." Typically, an Ignatian contemplation has just three of them: you begin by focusing on what the scene looks like; then you consider what the characters are saying; finally, you ponder what the characters might be doing. After each point, you are expected to "reflect and draw profit." In the contemplation on Christ's birth, Ignatius spells the process out a little further – perhaps at the beginning he is a little clearer than he otherwise might be: "I making myself a poor creature and a wretch of an unworthy slave, looking at them and serving them in their needs, with all possible respect and reverence, as if I found myself present." The prayer ends with a "colloquy," an imaginative conversation. It is in the contemplation on the Incarnation that this is most clearly set out:

> At the end a Colloquy is to be made, thinking what I ought to say to the Three Divine Persons, or to the Eternal Word incarnate, or to our Mother and Lady, asking according to what I feel in me, in order more to follow and imitate our Lord, so lately incarnate.

Ignatius encourages us imaginatively to engage one of the figures in the scene, and to develop a conversation that might somehow lead us closer to the goal desired.

The key text for interpreting this method of prayer is the second of the so-called Annotations (Ignatius' indicative notes at the beginning of the book):

> the person who gives to another the way and order in which to meditate or contemplate, ought to relate faithfully the events of such Contemplation or Meditation, going over the Points with only a short or summary development: for if the person who is contemplating takes the true foundation which is the story, working on it and thinking about it on their own, and finds something which makes them understand or feel for the story a little more ... (it is better) ... than if the one who gives the Exercises had explained and expanded the meaning of the story a great deal – for it is not the knowing of much that contents and satisfies the soul, but the feeling and relish for things from inside.   (*Exx.* 2)

The energy is meant to come not from the creativity or eloquence of the retreat-giver, but from the person's own prayer – and hence the presentation of the exercise should be minimalist, no more (though also no less) than what will enable the person's own process to start. Crucial to the prayer is the retreatant's own reflection and drawing profit – an idea that recurs at the end of every "point." Ignatius' own conversion on his sickbed in Loyola had begun with his reflections on chivalric romances and on religious texts; he expects the retreatant to do the same. Ignatius had recognized a difference, perhaps quite a subtle one, in the *quality* of his reactions. The delight from "that worldly stuff" would vanish, and leave him feeling "dry and discontented"; by contrast, when he thought about the heroic exploits of the saints, he was left "content and happy" even after he had left the actual thoughts aside. As he reflected on "this difference in kind" of reaction he assigned it to a "difference in kind of spirits that were stirring: the one from the devil and the other from God." Luis Gonçalves da Câmara, the Jesuit to whom Ignatius was dictating his life story, added a note that included the claim: "later, when he produced the Exercises, it was from here that he began to get clarity regarding the difference in kind of spirits."[6]

Ignatius is far too respectful of the retreatant's individuality to suggest that the content of his own reactions should be normative. But it is nevertheless clear that he expects the retreatant to get in touch with the diversity of his or her reactions to the Gospel story, and gradually to become aware of which of these are more authentic, leading the person towards a fuller kind of life. The clear indication of this connection in the text comes in Ignatius' expectation that the exercitant should make *repeticiones* of the prayer – "re-seekings" or "re-petitions" ("repetition," the transliteration that has become standard in the jargon, is clearly misleading). A *repetición* depends on the noting of "some more crucial (*principales*) parts ... where the person has felt some knowledge, consolation or desolation" (*Exx.* 118). Ignatius wants the process to be driven by the exercitant's responses to the text, and he rather expects that these will be conflicting (to the point of suggesting in *Exx.* 6 that where conflict is absent the director should be worried). The hope is that cumulative reflection on responses will gradually lead to clarity regarding the overall shape of God's invitation to the exercitant.

Another crucial element in Ignatian prayer is the so-called colloquy, or imaginative conversation, that Ignatius suggests should happen at the end of the prayer. The phrase "asking according to what I feel in me" is another indication that it is the person's responses and desires which determine the process. An early text of the Exercises, probably to be attributed to Jean Codure, one of the first ten companions, expands on Ignatius' terse indications in a way that confirms the point:

> And here describe what you want, not so as to teach God, who knows what you desire before you turn to prayer, but that you may set your own mind alight with a greater desire of the same good as you are naming it and explaining it in words.[7]

The whole process is aimed at the clarification of desire.

Themes and ideas

The basic principle, then, for reading *Spiritual Exercises* is that the book is only a means to an end: the free interplay of the Creator with the creature (*Exx.* 15), leading to the disposition of the creature's life in such a way as to promote the soul's salvation (*Exx.* 21). It is this open-ended goal that governs Ignatius' bitty, otherwise seemingly random, text.

Near the beginning, Ignatius presents us with a structure:

> ... the following exercises are divided into four parts:
> first, the consideration and contemplation on sins;
> second, the life of Christ our Lord up to Palm Sunday inclusively;
> third, the passion of Christ our Lord;
> fourth, the resurrection and ascension, with the three methods of
> prayer.   (*Exx.* 4)

Because Ignatius envisages his process taking about a month, he calls each of these parts "weeks." It is not the case, however, that each of these "weeks" lasts "seven or eight days," because people will attain the goals of each "week" at different speeds. These four main parts, or "weeks," are supplemented with other material. There is a set of introductory observations – Annotations – placed before the First Week; some rules about eating are placed, perhaps anomalously, at the end of the Third Week; and finally we have an extensive set of appendices – Gospel scenes set out in "points" for prayer, together with guidelines about the discernment of spirits, about the giving of alms, about scruples, and about allegiance to the Church. The next sections begin with looking at how the different weeks present God's action in Christ, before moving on to what Ignatius says and implies about our response.

The "weeks" of the Exercises

Ignatius' purpose is to provide support in order that "the Creator and Lord Himself should communicate Himself to His devout soul" (*Exx.* 15). A modern Jesuit theologian, Karl Rahner (1904–84), wrote a piece in which he imagined Ignatius speaking to a contemporary Jesuit, and justly commented on this claim: "Such a conviction perhaps sounds innocuous in your pious trade, working as it does with the most elevated words available. But fundamentally it is outrageous ..."[8] The pattern of the Incarnation, of God united substantially with the creature, persists in human experience at large; hence the creature's task is to discover and cooperate with this divine initiative. But it remains a mystery, a matter of wonder and improvised discovery. How can it be that the infinite unites itself to the finite? Still more, how can the divine *goodness* be united with the creation's manifest *imperfection*? Christianity, properly understood, does not answer these questions. Its proper mode of expression is question and exclamation rather than statement; it bespeaks a mystery beckoning our committed participation, rather than a state of affairs that we can neutrally describe.

Ignatius' *First Week* initiates us into the interplay, the sheerly incomprehensible contrast, between divine goodness and creaturely sinfulness. The text certainly presupposes an encouragement of repentance, sacramental confession, and contrition, and it recommends us to think of hell "in order that, if, through my faults, I should forget the love of the Eternal Lord, at least the fear of the pains may help me not to come into sin" (*Exx.* 65). But its central concern is deeper.[9] Central to the grace of the First Week is an awed sense of how creaturely perversity fails to frustrate divine love:

> to consider what God is, against Whom I have sinned, according to His attributes; comparing them with their contraries in me – His Wisdom with my ignorance; His Omnipotence with my weakness; His Justice with my iniquity; His Goodness with my malice.
>
> (*Exx.* 59)

> … an exclamation wonderingly with increased feeling, going through all creatures, how they have left me in life and preserved me in it; the Angels, how they are the sword of the Divine Justice, how yet they have endured me, and guarded me, and prayed for me; the Saints, how they have been engaged in interceding and praying for me; and the heavens, sun, moon, stars, and elements, fruits, birds, fishes and animals – and the earth, how it has not opened to swallow me up, creating new Hells for me to suffer in them forever!
>
> (*Exx.* 60)

Ignatius does not present us with an extended treatise on the nature of sin. Central to the First Week are two key exercises, one about how sin has been at work in the creation at large (typified by the fallen angels, by Adam and Eve, and by one hypothetical damned sinner), and one about the individual's history of complicity in this rejection of God's plan. The genre of a prayer exercise enables Ignatius to avoid the insoluble problems about whether sin is a matter of conditioning or free consent, or indeed about its origin within the providence of God. Instead, the focus is on how the individual responds; the third and fourth of the First Week Exercises specifically direct the exercitant to work with what the evocation of sin summons forth from his or her own memory (*Exx.* 62, 64). The tone is constantly one of awed exploration, of imaginative dialogue or "colloquy," with a focus on what all this means for me.

> Imagining Christ our Lord present and placed on the Cross, to make a Colloquy; how from Creator He has come to make Himself a human being, and from life eternal has come to temporal death, and thus to die for my sins. Likewise, looking at myself: what I have done for Christ, what I am doing for Christ, what I ought to do for Christ. And so, seeing Him in this state, and nailed thus on the Cross, to go over that which might present itself.   (*Exx.* 53)

As the process deepens, Ignatius encourages us to place ourselves imaginatively within a community of those who are not tainted by this history of non-response to God: Christ Himself, Mary His mother, and the Father, and to ask for three key gifts:

> first, that I may feel an interior knowledge of my sins, and hatred of them; second, that I may feel the disorder of my actions, so that, hating them, I may correct myself and put myself in order; third, to ask knowledge of the world, in order that, hating it, I may put away from me worldly and vain things.   (*Exx.* 63)

The point of the Ignatian First Week is to learn to cope realistically with sin: to recognize its reality, but also to learn to read the world in a way that is not simply controlled by it. It is an important preparatory step for the processes of choice and discernment regarding the form of one's discipleship of Jesus which come in the Second Week.

The *Second Week* centers on the life of Christ, from conception to Palm Sunday; a major part of it is taken up with the Gospel-centered prayer described earlier in this essay. During this time, Ignatius envisages that people should make an "election," an option about the state of life they are to adopt or a reorientation within one that has already been chosen (*Exx.* 189). What needs to be noted here is the frame within which Ignatius sets his Gospel contemplation. The Week begins with a consideration of Christ the King. There follow three "days" when the prayer centers on the infancy narratives in the Gospels, and from the fifth day onwards Ignatius suggests various scenes from Jesus' ministry (though the director is free to reduce or add to these – *Exx.* 162).

On day four, Ignatius begins explicitly to prepare for the Election, and he seems to envisage this process occurring in parallel with the Gospel prayer through the rest of the Second Week. Central here are a meditation on "Two Standards" (*Exx.* 136–47), aimed at enabling the exercitant to become sensitive to the subtler strategies by which he or she might be tempted (*Exx.* 10); a consideration of three classes of person, whose respective responses to God's call are indefinite procrastination, an attempt at manipulative bargaining, and complete acceptance (*Exx.* 149–56); and a pondering of "Three Kinds of Humility" (*Exx.* 164–68).

Both the Kingdom meditation and these exercises prior to the Election center on a desire to follow Christ in his suffering that is nevertheless significantly qualified. Here is the version that comes in the Two Standards:

> that I may be received under His standard; and first in the highest spiritual poverty, and – if His Divine Majesty would be served and would want to choose and receive me – not less in actual poverty; second, in suffering contumely and injuries, to imitate Him more in them, if only I can suffer them without the sin of any person, or displeasure of His Divine Majesty. (*Exx.* 147)

The complexity here is puzzling, and the temptation is to oversimplify it, most obviously by commending devotion to the crucified Christ without facing the issues about masochism and the fact that Ignatius does introduce qualifications, admittedly rather obscurely. Perhaps once again it is the dynamics of the divine engagement with creaturely evil that are central here. Without wanting to condone or justify evil in any way, Ignatius is reminding us of a conviction that is surely central to Christianity: a belief in Christ's power, and ours in Him, mysteriously to overcome evil, the power of Christ that in itself – in abstraction from the evil – is supremely desirable.

About the *Third Week* and the *Fourth Week* rather less can be said. The prayer centers first on Christ's Passion and death, and then on his resurrection appearances. Ignatius' language here is brief and elliptical, and commentators are tempted to fill it out with whatever is their own preferred theology of the cross and resurrection. The graces he encourages us to pray for are suggestively formulated. In the second exercise of the Third Week, we are told: "It belongs to the Passion to ask for grief with Christ in grief, shatteredness with Christ shattered, tears, interior pain at such great pain that Christ suffered for me" (*Exx.* 203). For its part, the prayer of desire governing the Fourth Week is more than simple joy because Christ has risen; Ignatius seems to be hinting at a sharing in Christ's *own* joy at the experience of having risen: "to ask for what I want, and it will be here to ask for grace to rejoice and be glad intensely at so great glory and joy of Christ our Lord" (*Exx.* 221). The sheer length of the experience – in conventional contemporary practice generally nine or ten days for the two Weeks together – gives it a distinctive character. For whatever reason, the official commentary on the Exercises finally published in 1599 – and arguably the official Latin translation of 1548 – significantly down-played passages such as these. What Ignatius intended here arguably was not received in the mainstream Jesuit tradition.[10]

Movements and decisions

What can we say in general terms about how the individual retreatant might respond to this material? First, and most straightforwardly, we as retreatants should be *open to whatever God might want* to bring about within us, or ask of us (*Exx.* 5) – or, to use Ignatius' own word "indifferent,"[11] with the result that "we do not want health more than sickness, riches than poverty, honor than dishonor, a long life than a short one," but desire and choose only "what is more conducive for us in view of the end for which we are created" (*Exx.* 23).

At the end of the process, in the so-called "Contemplation to Attain Love," Ignatius envisages the relationship between Creator and creature more fully. The creature is to respond in kind to the Creator's self-giving generosity in creation, redemption, and particular gifts, "pondering with much feeling how ... the same Lord desires to give me Himself as much as He can":

> And with this to reflect on myself, considering with much reason and justice, what I ought on my side to offer and give to His Divine Majesty, that is to say, everything that is mine, and myself with it, as one who makes an offering with much feeling: Take, Lord, and receive all my liberty, my memory, my understanding, and all my will, all that I have and possess. You gave it to me: to you, Lord, I return it; it is all yours; dispose it entirely to your will; give me your love and grace – that is enough for me.   (*Exx.* 234)

Second, Ignatius positively expects that the retreatant should experience movements both of attraction towards God and repulsion away from God – or, to use the technical terms, *consolation* and *desolation*. One of Ignatius' reasons for stressing indifference is precisely that we become the more sensitive to the patterns of God's working in our experience; should such movements not be occurring, Ignatius suggests that the retreat-giver needs to become suspicious (*Exx.* 6). The retreat-giver's central task is to help the exercitant "perceive and know in some manner the different movements which are caused in the soul, the good to receive them and the bad to reject them" (*Exx.* 313). There are two sets of "rules" (one to be used generally, the other for use only when the exercitant is being tempted subtly, by an apparent good) that are designed to help in this regard (*Exx.* 313–36).

Third, a full engagement with the Exercises should lead the retreatant to make some form of *election* or *decision*. Ignatius sets out three ways – his word is "times" – in which this can occur. The second of these, which many commentators take to be normative, is rooted in the reflection on consolations and desolations: "when enough light and knowledge is received by experience of consolations and desolations, and by the experience of the discernment of various spirits" (*Exx.* 176). But Ignatius' own heading for this passage suggests that the other two ways are equally valid: one that evokes a sense of irresistible conviction (*Exx.* 175), and one rooted in objective consideration of the pros and cons of a particular option (*Exx.* 178–88).[12]

Fourth, the fruit of the process should be *within the life of the Church*:

> It is necessary that everything about which we want to make an election should be indifferent, or good, in itself, and should be allowed within our Holy Mother the hierarchical Church, and not bad nor opposed to her. (*Exx.* 170)

The Exercises were written at the time of a Reformation schism, generated by an experienced conviction of justification by faith, independent of church practice. In Spain particularly, many who claimed insight into divine matters on the basis of experience were regarded as suspect, and indeed condemned as *alumbrados*. Ignatius himself in Spain, and subsequently the first Jesuits as a group, came frequently under suspicion.[13]

The underlying issue here is that the conviction of God's working directly with the creature (*Exx.* 15) raises at least the logical possibility that what the individual discovers in this way may go beyond what is ecclesiastically sanctioned. It is clear that the early Jesuits, through the Exercises, sought to promote life within the Church, but they had no solution to this theological problem, and addressed the issues diplomatically rather than theoretically. Ignatius merely made the fundamental intention explicit by developing a set of rules "in the interests of the true sense that we should have in the Church militant" (*Exx.* 352–70). The Jesuit tradition lives with the tension between a missionary commitment to life at the Church's boundaries and an allegiance to the visible, hierarchical institution.

THE SPIRITUAL EXERCISES AND THE SOCIETY
OF JESUS

It remains to make a few observations about the Spiritual Exercises in historical context. It was a commonplace in early Jesuit writing about the Exercises to speak of how Ignatius had learned the wisdom of the Exercises "not so much by books as by the unction of the Holy Spirit and from experience."[14] However much such a statement raises the contemporary historian's suspicions, it is plausible to suggest an independence of Ignatius' text from earlier literary sources. Parallels may be drawn with other documents in Christian tradition, and Ignatius himself points us to what he read on his sickbed in Loyola as a stimulus, but no significant and substantial intellectual dependency on Ignatius' part has been established.[15] Whatever he had read, he gave his material a structure and slant that was both decisive and original. Moreover, though Jesuit tradition has regularly traced the text of the Exercises back to intense personal experiences of Ignatius at Loyola in 1521 and Manresa in 1523, the early biographical material echoes only some elements from the rules about discernment and about scruples. Between those experiences and the appearance of something close to the present text in the mid-1530s, Ignatius accomplished a feat of literary organization, and above all of abstraction.[16] From his more personal writings, we know that he himself had intense spiritual experiences; remarkably, however, both in *Spiritual Exercises* and in the *Constitutions*, he keeps his own history rigorously out of the text, and encourages each reader to undergo his or her own process of growth. The achievement, however, remained largely unrecognized in the hagiography written by his followers.

Because the gestation of the text is so hidden from us, it is also hazardous to situate it against the historiographical categories now used in accounts of sixteenth-century Catholicism. It makes sense to see *Spiritual Exercises* as a work of early modernity, and responding to the changes in religious sensibility provoked by the invention of printing. In this respect, there are indeed striking parallels between Ignatius' account of the relief of scruples at Manresa and Luther's discovery of justification by faith; at the same time, however, Luther's marginalization of moral action and performance from religious identity in *The Freedom of a Christian* contrasts markedly with the formulation of the prayer with which Ignatius would have us begin each exercise: "that all my intentions, *actions* and *operations* may be directed purely in the service and praise of His Divine Majesty" (*Exx.* 46). Even at this level,

Ignatius can be read as a figure of both Catholic Reform and Counter-Reformation. There seems to have been Jesuit participation in the whole range of spiritual and intellectual currents within early modern Catholicism short of outright schism.

Neither of Ignatius' major works, *Spiritual Exercises* and the *Constitutions*, is a prescriptive text; the concern, rather, is to offer a "way of proceeding," a way of handling realities as yet unforeseen. Hence the history of how those texts have been interpreted virtually coincides with the history of the Society of Jesus itself as it has interacted with different ages and cultures. One foundational shift, however, should be highlighted. It is an unanswered question of Jesuit history why the small group round Ignatius, once it arrived in Rome and was constituted as a Society of Jesus in 1540, grew to 1,000 members in the sixteen years up till Ignatius' death in 1556, but it is clear that this institutional expansion outpaced the ability of the new membership to absorb and pass on the spirituality of the Exercises, and indeed to develop that spirituality in such a way that it could nourish the corporate identity of a relatively large international organization. The disparity gave rise to confusion and conflict that was resolved only in the generalate of Claudio Acquaviva (1580–1615). Ignatius seems to have presupposed that people would make the Exercises only once, as a life-changing experience. The *Constitutions* seems to envisage a relatively small group of itinerant apostles, resourced by a network of helpers – or "coadjutors" – who would maintain a support network of houses. Only later did it become normal for Jesuits to think of the Society as a new, alternative kind of religious order in the full sense, paralleling the Dominicans or Franciscans. A seminal secondary work speaks of "the definitive systematization of *Jesuit* spirituality in the light of the Exercises";[17] it was in Acquaviva's generalate that the Society of Jesus finally settled as a large and distinctive group of consecrated religious. The process required that the Society's distinctive spiritual resource, the Exercises, become a basis for daily life; Jesuits came to make a week's retreat on an annual basis, and normally to draw on the Exercises also for their daily prayer. There were significant arguments about the regulation of prayer, and about the balance between the cognitive and the affective, and these played themselves out in the discussions leading to the publication of the Official Directory, a supplementary handbook for retreat-givers.[18]

Historians need to be cautious about linking Jesuit behavior to particular ideas within the spirituality of the Exercises. It is indeed true that Ignatius' *Spiritual Exercises* has shaped the corporate rhetoric of the Jesuits, and served as an important element in their foundational myth. But the text has served these functions only because its inter-active character encourages a variety of possible responses. Its most suggestive language evokes and stimulates rather than describes: the first "time" of election (*Exx.* 175), the "prayer of the senses" with which the Ignatian day culminates (*Exx.* 121–25), or the idea of a consolation "without preceding cause" (*Exx.* 330). Ignatius' hope for the "Contemplation to Attain Love is" that the exercitant will be given

> knowledge from within of such great good received, so that
> recognizing this entirely, I may be able in all to love and serve
> His Divine Majesty.   (*Exx.* 233)

But both the good and the response are particular; the wise interpreter of this text is cautious about making generalizations.

Notes

"*Exx.*" throughout the text refers by paragraph number to *Spiritual Exercises*. Many translations exist, and the question of translation may sometimes be contentious; in this essay I offer versions based on the 1909 "literal translation" by Elder Mullan, reproduced in D. Fleming, *Draw Me into Your Friendship: The Spiritual Exercises – a Literal Translation and a Contemporary Reading* (St. Louis: Institute of Jesuit Sources, 1996). The standard critical editions of Ignatian sources are to be found in the more than 150 volumes of the *Monumenta Historica Societatis Iesu* (*MHSI*), begun in Madrid in the 1890s, and now published from the Jesuit Historical Institute in Rome. This essay uses the 12 volumes of Ignatius' letters (*EI*), and the second *MHSI* edition of *Spiritual Exercises* (*MI* [1969]).

1   *The Spiritual Writings of Pierre Favre*, ed. and trans. E. Murphy, J. Padberg, and M. Palmer (St. Louis: Institute of Jesuit Sources, 1996), 64–65.
2   *The Constitutions of the Society of Jesus*, trans. G. Ganss (St. Louis: Institute of Jesuit Sources, 1970) – Formula of the Institute, n. 3.
3   Both quotations come from Polanco (on Ignatius' behalf) to Philipp Faber (Leernus), 3 February 1554 (*MHSI EI* 6, 280–82). A convenient collection of passages from Ignatian letters dealing with the Exercises can be found in *Texte autographe des Exercices Spirituels et docu-ments contemporains (1526–1615)*, ed. E. Gueydan *et al.* (Paris: Desclée, 1985), 214–27. This passage occurs on p. 217.
4   *The Spiritual Writings of Pierre Favre*, 67.
5   *Constitutions, Examen* 4.9 [64], my translation. Ignatius' detachment from his own program here echoes the beginning of *Spiritual Exercises*. The first note "to give some understanding of the Spiritual Exercises which follow" begins by stating that "spiritual exercises" denotes

"*every* way" – not just, therefore, the ways in the book – of examining consciousness, of meditation, contemplation, and the like (*Exx.* 1).

6   *Autobiography*, n. 8, cited from *Saint Ignatius of Loyola: Personal Writings*, ed. and trans. J. Munitiz and P. Endean (London and New York: Penguin, 1996).

7   "The Exercises of Master John," *The Way* 44/1 (January 2005), 117–32, here 125.

8   *Karl Rahner: Spiritual Writings*, ed. and trans. P. Endean (Maryknoll, NY: Orbis, 2005), 37.

9   Thus the famous and extensive Hell sermon in James Joyce's *A Portrait of the Artist as a Young Man* rather misses the Ignatian point, not only because of its content, but also because of the very genre in which it is written.

10 See *On Giving the Spiritual Exercises: The Early Jesuit Manuscript Directories and the Official Directory of 1599*, ed. and trans. M. Palmer (St. Louis: Institute of Jesuit Sources, 1996), 340–43; B. O'Leary, "Third and Fourth Weeks: What the Directories Say," *The Way Supplement* 58 (Spring 1987), 3–20; P. Endean, "'Our Lady' and the Graces of the Fourth Week," *The Way Supplement* 99 (Autumn 2000), 44–60.

11 It may be significant that Ignatius avoids the noun form "indifference." The literature reflects a more general uncertainty in Christian spirituality as to whether the goal should be escape from the material order or right engagement with it.

12 See, in reaction to Karl Rahner and many who have followed him in prioritizing the second "time," J. Toner, *Discerning God's Will: Ignatius of Loyola's Teaching on Christian Decision Making* (St. Louis: Institute of Jesuit Sources, 1991).

13 See Ignatius to John III of Portugal, 15 March 1545 (*Letters of St Ignatius of Loyola*, selected and translated by W. Young [Chicago: Loyola University Press, 1959], 79–91), in which, as a means of preventing rumor, Ignatius catalogues the various processes in which he had been involved.

14 From the preface to the authorized Latin version (Vulgate) produced in 1548: ... *quae non tam a libris, quam ab unctione Sancti Spiritus et ab interna experientia et usu tractandorum animorum edoctus*: *MHSI MI* (1969), *Exx.* 79. For a sense of the controversies that such claims raised with the Inquisition, see J. Nadal, E. Mercurian, and C. Acquaviva, "Spirit, Contemplation and Ministry: Three Early Jesuit Texts," *The Way*, 42/4 (October 2003), 89–104.

15 By way of example, see the collection of essays *Las fuentes de los Ejercicios Espirituales de San Ignacio*, ed. J. Plazaola (Bilbao: Mensajero, 1998), and J. Melloni, *The Exercises of St Ignatius Loyola in the Western Tradition*, trans. M. Ivens (Leominster: Gracewing, 2000 [1998]).

16 See P. de Leturia, "Génesis de los ejercicios de San Ignacio y su influjo en la fundación de la Compañía de Jesús (1521–1540)," in *Estudios ignacianos*, ed. I. Iparraguirre, 2 vols. (Rome: Jesuit Historical Institute, 1957), 3–55. In English, see R. García Mateo, "The

'Accommodated Texts' and the Interpretation of the *Spiritual Exercises*," *The Way* 44/1 (January 2005 [1994]), 101–16. On the basis of different styles in the earliest Latin translation of the text, it may be possible to differentiate between material available when Ignatius first arrived in Paris in 1528 and what was added later: see J. Calveras, "Estudios sobre la redacción de los textos latinos de los Ejercicios anteriores a la Vulgata," *Archivum Historicum Societatis Jesu* 31 (1962), 3–99.

17 I. Iparraguirre, *Historia de los Ejercicios de San Ignacio Vol 2: Desde la muerte de San Ignacio hasta la promulgación del Directorio oficial. 1556–1599* (Rome: Jesuit Historical Institute, 1955), 495.

18 The texts are conveniently collected in *On Giving the Spiritual Exercises*.

Part II

European Foundations of the Jesuits

4 Jesuit Rome and Italy

PAUL V. MURPHY

The Jesuits of early modern Italy exercised as broad an array of ministries as would be found in any region of the world. While in the past they were viewed almost solely in terms of teaching in the many colleges they founded there, recent research has emphasized other works including the organization of lay confraternities, domestic missions in urban and rural areas, and the arts.[1] These works, moreover, reflect an interdependence on one another that underlines the complexities of Jesuit ministries.

No city in Italy experienced the presence of the Jesuits more strongly than Rome. From the arrival of Ignatius to the suppression of the Society, the Jesuits left a strong imprint on the city. No religious order prior to them was as centered on Rome as were the Jesuits. This was largely due to the authority of the Superior General in the administration of the Order and its central administration in the city. Moreover, the Jesuits consciously sought out the patronage of popes and powerful cardinals as a means to support their works. With such support, the Jesuits in Rome avoided many of the conflicts that they found in other cities of Italy such as Milan and Venice.

Rome's centrality in Jesuit undertakings in Italy also arose from Ignatius Loyola's preference for placing his men and their works where they would have the greatest impact. In placing a Jesuit community or apostolate he sought out a *commodo luogo*, or convenient location for the establishment of a church, residence, or school. He wrote of how to do this:

> Presupposing the equal service of God that is to be hoped for, it seems that three things should be considered. First, with all things being equal, to settle in that location where, with the passage of time, you think it would be useful to establish some works; secondly, where there might be found greater readiness and openness toward the service of God after the manner of our Institute;

thirdly where the good accomplished might receive good repute, such that those who govern would hear of the work of the Society for divine service. If there were a ready opportunity, it would be good to see to it that the residence was near the court.[2]

The location of the original Jesuit headquarters itself reflects this preference. The church of Santa Maria della Strada, later to be replaced by the monumental church of the Gesù, fit these criteria. It was located near the center of the city and virtually around the corner from the Palazzo Venezia which, at the time of the foundation of the Jesuits, was the residence of Pope Paul III. Thus, it was convenient for the ministries of the Society, easily reached by those who came to hear Jesuit preaching and other ministries, and was located very near to the court *par excellence* of early modern Italy.

Soon Rome was dotted with other Jesuit sites. By 1622, the year of the canonization of Ignatius, the Jesuits boasted of thirteen different houses and works in Rome. For artistic grandeur the most outstanding of these were the churches of the Gesù and Sant'Ignazio. These became ever more ornamented by major art commissions between the late sixteenth century and the suppression of the Society in the late eighteenth century. The ceiling frescoes in Sant'Ignazio by the Jesuit Andrea Pozzo (1642–1709) are a primary example of this. The art itself came to reflect the concern of Ignatius that "those who govern would hear of the work of the Society."[3]

THE COLLEGES

Italy saw the birth of Jesuit involvement in education on a large scale. The first of these colleges opened its doors in Messina in the spring of 1548. The example of this college is in many respects emblematic both of how the Jesuits became involved in schools and of how they proceeded pedagogically. Ignatius sent seven Jesuits there in response to a request from the Spanish Viceroy of Sicily and with the understanding that the city of Messina would provide financial subsidies. Such political and social support was critical to Jesuit success. The school offered classes from elementary literacy to studies of philosophy and theology, with the lower-level studies predominating. The number of Jesuits and the building that they used allowed for a dramatic increase in the number of students at the school in comparison to previous Italian experience. Earlier in the Renaissance, most students in the cities of Italy gained access to primary and secondary education via the smaller schools of independent humanist school-masters or schoolmasters employed by communal governments. Education was therefore decentralized and on a small scale.[4] In contrast, by 1549 the College of Messina enrolled more than two hundred students in the lower school in courses in grammar, humanities, and rhetoric. Approximately sixty students enrolled in upper-level courses in dialectic, philosophy, scholastic theology, mathematics, Greek, and Hebrew. The school would maintain an average enrollment of nearly three hundred students.[5] The insistence of Ignatius that these schools not charge tuition in order to maintain a Jesuit commitment to the "gratuity of ministry," linked with the public subsidies from both the Viceroy and the city government of Messina, made the school particularly attractive to prospective students.

The Jesuits inherited the literary curriculum itself from earlier humanists but institutionalized their schools on a previously unknown scale. The need for this arose in part from the rapid growth of this area of Jesuit efforts. The success of the experiment at Messina led Ignatius to invest his men in a growing number of schools. Not all of the foundations were successful. Several closed after only a few years as a result of insufficient local support or the inability of the Jesuits to provide a dependable faculty. Nevertheless, at the death of Ignatius Loyola in 1556 the Society of Jesus already supervised eighteen colleges in Italy and Sicily.[6] By 1600 the Jesuits operated forty-nine colleges in Italy. By the end of the seventeenth century that figure had risen to over one hundred. By the time of the suppression of the Society of Jesus in 1773 the Jesuits operated more than 120 colleges throughout the peninsula and Sicily.[7] Where they were successful the colleges enrolled on average more than two hundred students. This growth was facilitated by the growth in the number of Jesuits themselves. At the death of Ignatius the Jesuits in Italy numbered 428, nearly half of the entire membership in the Society of Jesus. By the last quarter of the sixteenth century that number had risen to over a thousand.[8] Nevertheless, the pressure that local governments brought to bear on the Society to open more colleges seems to have created an excessive burden upon the Society to maintain these schools and the Jesuits turned down many such requests.

With the foundation of these schools there began to appear treatises on Jesuit education itself. In the year of the foundation of the College of Messina, 1548, Jeronimo Nadal wrote his *Constitutiones Collegii Messanensis*. By 1551 Annibal Coudret had penned the *De Ratione Studiorum Messanae*.[9] From these early Italian colleges of the

Society therefore arose the first efforts to outline what a Jesuit education might entail, efforts that came to completion in the *Ratio
Studiorum* in 1599. [This establishment of a school system based on
humanist rhetorical and literary principles and the method of teaching
philosophy that the early Jesuits encountered at Paris transformed the
delivery of secondary and tertiary education.]

In time the Roman College stood out as the paradigmatic Jesuit
educational enterprise. Opened in 1551, it enrolled almost three hundred students in its first year of operation. As elsewhere, the Society in
Rome depended upon the support of the Roman elites for the success of
this enterprise. The renaming of the school in 1584 as the Gregorian
University in honor of its greatest patron, Pope Gregory XIII, is an
example of this. In many respects the significance of the Roman
College transcends the borders of Italy. From the beginning the
college exemplified the international character of the Society in its
multi-national community and faculty that included Roberto
Bellarmino, Francisco Suárez, Manuel de Sá, Christopher Clavius,
and Athanasius Kircher. This was consistent with the desires of
Ignatius to make it the premier scholarly institution of the Society of
Jesus and continued to be the case throughout the early modern period.
The Roman College became a center of learning that was in many ways
the heart of early modern Catholic intellectual life.

The relationship of many of these scholars to early modern science
may not have been as polarized as once believed. While the ability of
Jesuits to embrace fully the new scientific method was limited by their
commitment to Thomism, they nevertheless contributed to these
developments via their mathematical treatises, their astronomical
observations, and their relationships with other scientists. It was at
the Roman College that the Jesuit mathematician and astronomer
Christopher Clavius calculated the new Gregorian Calendar established in 1582. There too Athanasius Kircher, described recently by
one author as the "last man to know everything," established a
museum that held an enormous collection of scientific, anthropological, and archaeological artifacts.[10]

In addition to the Gregorian University, the Jesuits directed a
number of colleges in Rome established for the education of clergy
from other parts of Europe. The work they undertook at the German
College, the Hungarian College, the Greek College, the Roman
Seminary, and the English College, in particular, is an example of
Jesuit activity in Rome that found direction in the international missions of the Society of Jesus. These colleges played a major role in

preparing clergy who would return to their homelands in the context of the religious conflicts of early modern Europe. The case of the English College and its training of English clergy was perhaps the most outstanding example.

CONFRATERNITIES

An area of Jesuit activity that has in recent years become the subject of much interest is that of the confraternities that they organized, especially among the students at their colleges. The confraternities, or sodalities, allowed the Jesuits to continue their early work of spiritual conversation and to continue to offer the Spiritual Exercises among the students. These organizations also allowed Jesuits to influence others including nobles, professionals, and artisans. It was the laity, under Jesuit supervision, who largely carried out the ongoing charitable works of the confraternities. Thus, Jesuit organization of confraternities and sodalities and lay staffing of them became a practical solution to instituting permanent arrangements for works the Jesuits themselves would not have been able to maintain on their own.

These confraternities manifest three primary characteristics. First, they focused on a piety typical of Ignatius and his early companions, including a deep personal devotion to Christ and rules that called for regular meditation, the examination of conscience, and frequent communion. Pierre Favre articulated this emphasis in 1540 when he urged those who had gathered around him in Parma to "even aim at not missing confession and Holy Communion at least once a week."[11]

Second, the confraternities served as a means to mobilize laymen in Jesuit missions and in charitable activities. An early notable example of this work was the Casa di Santa Marta, founded by Ignatius Loyola in Rome in 1542. Essentially, this was a shelter for prostitutes and women who had suffered abuse. There they could initiate a change in their lives that might include either, in the case of the prostitutes, leaving their customary trade behind to become a nun or enter into a marriage or, in the case of battered women, to determine whether and how to return to their husbands. Ignatius effectively established this institution as a place of temporary residence where women in difficult circumstances could discern a change in their future path. This is consistent with the goal of the Spiritual Exercises of assisting an individual in making a choice about a vocation.[12]

Ignatius entrusted the care of the Casa di Santa Marta to a confraternity called the Compagnia della Grazia. The Jesuits encouraged a

similar work in the Conservatorio di Santa Caterina delle vergini mis-
erabili, which supported the daughters of prostitutes in order to direct
them into activities different from their mothers'. Other Jesuit confraternities in Rome addressed the needs of Jewish converts, who confronted serious financial challenges on account of their conversions,
and the establishment of the first hospital for the mentally insane in
Rome and a confraternity to oversee it at Santa Maria della Pietà dei
Pazzarelli.[13]

The most successful of the Jesuit confraternities was the Sodality
of the Blessed Virgin Mary, established at the Roman College in 1563
by the Belgian Jesuit Jean de Leunis. Initially Leunis gathered groups of
students to participate in organized prayer, participation in the sacraments, and works of charity. The rules of the congregation required
weekly confession, monthly communion, daily presence at mass, and
praying of the rosary or the Office of the Madonna. Charitable works
included visiting prisons and providing assistance in hospitals. In this
organization Leunis synthesized practices he had witnessed elsewhere
in Italy and established them in a particularly effective way.[14] This
congregation of lay students at the Roman College soon became the
model for similar congregations in other Jesuit schools and in other
cities. Its success was such that by 1576 there were chapters of this
Marian Congregation spread through the Jesuit school system enrolling nearly 30,000 members.[15] The founding chapter of this association
at the Roman College received the title of the *Prima primaria* to highlight its preeminence in this movement of lay activity. The works that
the members of these confraternities undertook included a broad array
of social welfare initiatives generally representative of charitable
undertakings by confraternities and cities throughout early modern
Europe.

Third, these sodalities included a rather broad social range of
members. Jesuit schools drew their students from the aristocracy and
the middle class, and even included some sons of artisans. The confraternities likewise included members from each of these sections of
Italian society. The Jesuits' work of confraternal organization therefore
reflects the stratification of Italian society. For example, Ignatius
Loyola organized the Arciconfraternità de' Santissimi Dodici
Apostoli in the 1540s as an organization of nobles who distributed
relief to the *poveri vergognosi*, or shame-faced poor, that is, down-at-
the-heels members of their own social class.[16] In Rome alone the
Jesuits supervised more than two dozen confraternities of these
various types.

In Naples, Jesuit work with confraternities was among their earliest undertakings. Initially the Jesuits sought out already existing organizations and used these confraternities to further their own purposes. In particular this meant introducing the most active of the members to Ignatian spirituality, especially more frequent confession and communion. In 1552 Alfonso Salmerón arrived in Naples and joined the Compagnia dei Bianchi della Giustizia, an organization that had as its principal work accompanying condemned prisoners to their executions. This allowed Salmerón to engage an already active group of laity for purposes both of supporting them and winning their support for future Jesuit undertakings. Jesuits remained members of the organization as a means to maintain those bonds of mutual support. Members of the Bianchi della Giustizia became major benefactors of the Jesuits as they opened their college there.[17]

Not long after their arrival, the Jesuits in Naples began to establish confraternities of their own. As early as 1552 a Jesuit scholastic named Giovanni Francesco Araldo founded the Compagnia della Venerazione del Santissimo Sacramento. As its name indicates the confraternity took special interest in inculcating Jesuit spirituality and frequency of communion. Apart from the devotions of the confraternity members these groups engaged in Naples, as elsewhere, in charitable activities. These included the teaching of catechism to children and uneducated adults in keeping with the demands of the *Constitutions of the Society of Jesus*. Such interest in sound doctrine could also lead the confraternity members to be attentive to the possibility of heresy in the local population, thus illustrating a degree of participation in efforts at social control of religion. In the case of Araldo's foundations there was also great emphasis on doing these acts secretly, hence the nickname for them, the *Zitti*, or silent ones. This confraternity was only the first of what would become dozens of Jesuit-sponsored confraternities scattered throughout the Kingdom of Naples.[18]

By 1577 the congregations of the Society in Naples began to be drawn into the orbit of the Marian Congregations and the *Prima primaria* in Rome. Students in this new lay organization under Jesuit auspices carried out works that paralleled those of other Jesuit confraternities and supported the works of the Jesuits themselves. In particular the lay members of these congregations carried out promotional activities for Jesuit ministries. The Jesuits sent laity "fishing" in the piazzas for likely individuals who would come for Jesuit preaching and confessional practice. Further, the Jesuits supported communities of piety among lay students that effectively fostered vocations to their own Order as well as to other religious communities.[19]

DOMESTIC MISSIONS

The Jesuits focused most of their works in Italy on the urban centers. Nevertheless, even in Italy the Jesuits engaged in a longstanding effort to evangelize the countryside. These domestic missions had not only a religious end but a distinctly secular one as well. The Jesuits engaged in a "civilizing mission" that sought not only a more thorough understanding of Christian doctrine but a fuller integration of the individual into the body politic. The colleges where Jesuit teachers trained the future administrators of Italy's governments is an obvious example. But urban and rural missions directed towards a less sophisticated audience of peasants, residents of small towns, and the rural nobility also represent this civilizing mission.[20] And this work could present challenges every bit as great as those Jesuit missionaries encountered in Latin America or Asia.

In the Kingdom of Naples the Jesuits had a significant impact via domestic missions. Some of Ignatius' earliest companions initiated the work there. Nicholas Bobadilla, Diego Laínez, and Alfonso Salmerón all took up the usual ministries of the first generation of Jesuits: preaching, hearing confessions, and directing the Spiritual Exercises. These works prepared the way for the establishment of the College of Naples in 1552. But they also served as the foundation for the domestic missions.[21] In both cities and countryside Jesuits continued to act to a certain extent as itinerant preachers who sought the conversion of sinners and the inculcation of social virtues. Noteworthy among the Neapolitan Jesuits who maintained this practice was Pierantonio Spinelli (1555–1615). In addition to practicing this ministry, Spinelli served as provincial of Naples and saw to the establishment of formal methods of carrying out urban missions in the Kingdom of Naples.

Activity among the poor residents of Naples placed Jesuits in a delicate position at times of social unrest. The Neapolitan Revolt of 1585 required of them exceptional negotiating skills and impressed upon them the need to respond adequately to the social conditions that they met. The revolt began, at least in part, as a reaction to rising bread prices. The Jesuits of Naples went into the streets to pacify the population and bring an end to the violence. This public act of peacemaking was a prominent display of Jesuit influence in the social life of the city. It also displays the attachment of the Jesuits to maintaining good order in an early modern society. As an aspect of their "civilizing mission," the work of Neapolitan Jesuits in urban missions presents a prime example of preaching virtues that sought social concord and

served to promote obedience to both ecclesiastical and civil authority.[22] This required expending energy among the poor in a departure
from an earlier tradition that had emphasized the cultivation of powerful patrons.[23] It is clear however that the Jesuits in their urban missions participated in a process of social disciplining that would not
displease their customary patrons.[24]

The work of pacifying the poor was often accompanied by the work of
bringing peace among the more powerful. "Reconciling the estranged"
had been an explicit work of the Jesuits since the life of Ignatius and was
specifically mentioned in the founding document of the Society, the
Formula of the Institute.[25] Reconciliation through the work of a Jesuit
often seemed to require dramatic practices such as that seen in a conflict
between a local parish priest and his parishioners in which the priest
placed a noose around his neck in an act of penitence while the people of
the parish ritually and exuberantly kissed his feet.[26] In another case a
Jesuit missionary transformed a local chapel into a scene fit to move
hearts and minds: it was darkened with black curtains and strewn with
mourning cloths and bones. All of this was calculated to engender a fear of
death. It also, as one scholar has effectively demonstrated, drew upon the
dramatic traditions of the *commedia dell' arte* that were so prevalent in
the culture of southern Italy.[27] Adaptation to the local culture was a
missionary strategy taken up not only by Jesuits such as Matteo Ricci in
China but by Jesuits on urban and rural missions in Italy.

The efforts to work in urban and rural missions increased during the
generalate of Claudio Acquaviva, who issued his first directions on how
Jesuits were to conduct these domestic missions in 1590. The purpose, in
Acquaviva's mind, was to equip Jesuits to bring about the conversion of
the poor from the vices in which, he assumed, they were mired. A Jesuit
awareness of the need for method in this missionary field continued to
grow. By the middle of the seventeenth century the Superior General
Vincenzo Carafa took the further step of establishing an official in each
province to oversee domestic missionary activity. The seventeenth century witnessed a growth in the publication of missionary manuals that
served to train potential missionaries on how to go about their work.[28] It
is clear also that the Jesuits were conscious that their work in southern
Italy was not entirely separate from the more global purposes of the
Society in missions in Asia and Latin America. The desire of many
Jesuits to be sent abroad, as expressed in letters to the Superior General
called *Indipetae*, illustrates the missionary frame of mind that could lead
one Italian Jesuit to refer to his field of activity in the Kingdom of Naples
as the "Indies down here."[29]

In Milan the Jesuits encountered the political situation of a Spanish dominion governed in ecclesiastical terms by some of the most prominent prelates of early modern Italy. Cardinal Carlo Borromeo facilitated their entrance into Milan in order that they might operate his local seminary and a college of their own. Thus, as elsewhere, they began work with the assistance of the powerful. However, the relationship of the Society of Jesus to Borromeo was anything but tranquil. For a time the Jesuits did operate the Milanese seminary. Nevertheless, Borromeo sought to impose certain restrictions on the Jesuits teaching there, in particular the prohibition on any seminarian choosing to enter the Society of Jesus rather than the diocesan clergy. In one respect this reflects the perennial tensions that can exist between a diocesan bishop and exempt religious orders. It was heightened in this case by differences between the Jesuits and Borromeo over how to educate the students at the seminary. Borromeo seems to have been concerned for a formation of the seminarians that gave primacy to moral and disciplinary education over academic training. While this was not necessarily opposed to what the Jesuits sought in their own schools he remarked of them that they favored those "who have some talent for letters."[30] The work of the Jesuits with Milanese seminarians did not last long. But their contributions at the College of Brera were longstanding. Here Borromeo saw the opening of a college that was to have an enduring influence in Milanese intellectual life into the eighteenth century. The College of Brera remained the flagship educational institution of the Milanese Jesuits where they educated the future administrators of Habsburg Milan.

The Jesuits throughout Italy used drama to achieve their pastoral goals. In Milan they promoted theater as a vehicle for achieving these goals as well as serving the interests of the Habsburg monarchy. The Jesuit Emmanuele Tesauro, for example, worked both in the organization of student dramas at the Brera and in the organization of ceremonies marking the death of King Philip III in 1621. The latter included designing the catafalque, statues, and paintings temporarily installed in the *duomo* for that occasion. In the student dramatic presentations as well as in the funerary celebrations, Tesauro expressed the cardinal virtues of Christianity as pertinent especially in the life of a ruler and his servants. This use of drama and spectacle to teach was typical of the Jesuits in many places. That is, for more than two centuries Jesuit drama in Milan and elsewhere acted as a school of virtue and a method of teaching how to live actively in the world. The civilizing mission of the Jesuits was as evident and as dramatic in Milan as it was in Naples.[31]

Jesuit activities in the Republic of Venice were particularly complex. At their origins the Jesuits had benefited from the support of the most prominent Venetian cardinal of the sixteenth century, Gasparo Contarini. By 1542, on the request of the doge, Ignatius sent Diego Laínez to Venice. It appears that the Venetian government originally saw the Jesuits as capable of putting order into charitable organizations similar to those that Jesuits were reorganizing elsewhere in Italy. In the short run, however, Jesuit activity conformed to their earliest practice of preaching, offering lectures, and teaching catechism to children. Jesuits carried out these ministries not only in Venice itself but in other dioceses of the Veneto such as Verona and Belluno.[32]

Padua became the site of the earliest institutional arrangements of the Jesuits in the Republic of Venice. As a result of the benefactions of Andrea Lippomani a college of the Society of Jesus was founded there. As early as 1542 he had provided shelter for the Jesuit scholastics sent to Padua for studies at the university. By 1546 Pope Paul III issued a bull permitting the transfer of Lippomani's benefices to the Society of Jesus for the purpose of supporting the college in Padua. After lengthy negotiations the government of Venice agreed to this transfer of property.[33] The delay of the Venetian government in approving the transfer and assisting in the establishment of the Society of Jesus arose from a traditional Venetian desire to supervise the Church within the boundaries of the Republic. Within a generation, however, the Jesuits operated colleges at Padua, Verona, Brescia, and Forlì.

Tensions between the Jesuits and the Venetian government increased after 1578 when the Society of Jesus divided its Lombard province, erecting the eastern portion of it as the Venetian province. Soon, the Jesuits of Venice sought to enhance the quality of their colleges, especially that at Padua, in order to compete with the schools in Milan and Rome. Pope Julius III had offered the College of Padua the privilege of issuing university degrees in 1550. In 1579 the Jesuits opened their philosophy classes to lay students and almost immediately enrolled eighty extern students. In 1582 they opened a residential college for nobles. By 1589 the Jesuits at Padua were educating over 450 lay students.[34] They offered university-level courses in their *studium* in a way that challenged the privileges of the neighboring University of Padua itself. In 1591 the University of Padua formally protested the practices of the Jesuits to the Venetian Senate. The complaint touched upon an issue of concern to the Venetian government: that in granting degrees on the authority of the pope, the Jesuits in Padua essentially circumvented the authority of the Venetian Senate.[35]

The concerns over the success of the College of Padua touched on broader issues of contention between the papacy and Venice. These often related either to lay acquisition of ecclesiastical lands, which the government supported, or to the increase in transfers of land from laity to religious orders with a concomitant reduction in the tax base, which the government opposed. A series of legislative acts by the Venetian government to retain traditional controls over the Church, combined with the papacy's willingness to resist, brought conflict between Venice and Rome to a head. In 1603 the Venetian government forbad the construction of new churches in the Venetian Republic without the permission of the government, a decision that especially affected newer religious orders such as the Jesuits. In 1605 the government placed limits on laymen who sought to transfer land to the Church. These early years of the seventeenth century also saw a Venetian effort to reassert the right of the government to try clergy accused of serious crimes. To a large extent these acts constituted the application to the whole of the Venetian state of legal arrangements that had applied, or at least been asserted, in the city of Venice for centuries. The Church saw them as novelties that impinged on its rights.[36]

By the end of 1605 the papacy chose to take action against Venice. Pope Paul V called upon the government of Venice to revoke these laws or undergo excommunication and the imposition of an interdict. During the negotiations that ensued, the Venetian government employed the Servite priest Paolo Sarpi as its theological advisor. Negotiations to end the conflict failed and the ecclesiastical penalties went into effect. The Venetian government remained under excommunication and its territories under interdict from May of 1606 to April of 1607. In order to maintain public support for its resistance to the pope, the government of Venice ordered that all clergy continue to offer their pastoral services despite the interdict. Along with the Theatines and Capuchins, the Jesuits of Venice supported the actions of the pope. The government then expelled the Jesuits, along with other religious, from the Venetian state and issued a decree of permanent banishment.[37]

As negotiations to resolve the crisis crept forward it became clear that the Jesuits were themselves a stumbling block to a resolution. In the end, with the support of the Jesuit General, Claudio Acquaviva, a solution was reached that excluded the Jesuits from Venetian territories. The pope lifted the interdict but Venice did not permit the Jesuits to return. The primary reason for this was the formal attachment of the Society of Jesus to the papacy. It has also been argued recently that a stern morality expressed by the Jesuits in the face of a

city that enjoyed its carnival and its emerging tradition in opera was ✓
also a reason for hostility towards the Jesuits that contributed to their
expulsion.[38] The Jesuits would not return to Venice until 1657.]

A location of Jesuit work that combined many of the characteristics seen throughout Italy was that at Loreto. The shrine of Loreto was
said to contain the house from Nazareth where the Angel Gabriel
appeared to Mary and announced to her that she would give birth to the
Messiah. Thus by tradition the house was considered the place of
the Incarnation. According to legend the angels carried this house to
the Marche region of Italy, not far from Ancona, arriving there in 1294.
For some time it remained a marginal cult center. During the
Renaissance, however, its prominence grew dramatically. It received
benefits, both spiritual and temporal, from the popes. Pilgrims to
Loreto, for example, received the same indulgences as those who
went to Rome. By the sixteenth century it became the most visited
pilgrimage site in western Europe after Rome. For this it was both
praised and blamed. Erasmus composed a mass in honor of Our Lady
of Loreto and the Litanies of Loreto came into wide use. Protestant
writers looked upon the shrine in a negative light, seeing in it many of
the problems that they identified with Roman Catholicism. The tradition of the house having been saved from the Saracens in the Middle
Ages provided the shrine with an anti-Turkish tone for Christians in
the sixteenth and seventeenth centuries.

[This shrine took on special meaning to Ignatius Loyola and he
maintained a strong devotion to it. In 1552 he sent a small group of
priests and brothers under the leadership of Olivier Manaerts to serve
as confessors at the shrine. As a holy site translated from one of the
places that Ignatius himself had visited in the Holy Land, and one that
was closely associated with the life of Christ, the Santa Casa provided
Jesuits with the opportunity to work at one of those holy places but in
Italy itself. It is reported that in the Jubilee year of 1575, 60,000 pilgrims availed themselves of these confessors. In addition to hearing
confessions the Jesuits there maintained their customary practice of
giving the Spiritual Exercises. The Santa Casa provided a concrete, if
somewhat idiosyncratic, location for Jesuit spiritual directors to
work.[39] Additionally the Jesuits in Loreto operated a college for their
own scholastics as well as local students, the Collegio di Loreto. For a
time they also operated the Collegio Illirico for the education of priests
from the Balkans who would return to minister to Catholics under
Turkish rule. And they also carried out missions to the surrounding
villages. Thus, for over two hundred years the Jesuits at Loreto

maintained a tradition that reflected their commitment to the *consueta ministeria* of the Society: preaching, hearing confessions, giving the Spiritual Exercises, education, and an awareness of global missions as exemplified by the region of the Turks in a setting that recalled the desire of Ignatius himself and the early Jesuits to work in the Holy Land. A more complex example of the multiplicity of Jesuit works would be difficult to identify.[40] They remained there until the suppression of the Society.

SUPPRESSION

With the growth of absolutist monarchies throughout Europe and the emergence of the Enlightenment, Jesuits of the eighteenth century had to contend with new forces that often stood in opposition to them. It is true that they adapted themselves to the changing intellectual climate of the Enlightenment.[41] Nevertheless they became tangled in an almost unavoidable set of conflicts with the great powers of Europe. The desires of kings and their chief ministers in Catholic Europe to centralize control of their states as much as possible made the power and relative autonomy of the Jesuits seem an anomaly that needed to be eliminated. The well-known tale of the royal suppressions of the Society in the various kingdoms and overseas territories of Europe did not at first involve Italy. The Jesuits underwent expulsion from Portugal in 1759, from France in 1764, from Spain in 1766, and then from Naples in 1767. Also, many of the Jesuit exiles of these regions were unceremoniously deposited on the shores of the Papal States and swelled the population of Jesuits in Italy in the years immediately prior to the papal suppression.

The final act in the drama of the suppression of the Society of Jesus was played out on the Roman stage. The Superior General who presided over the Society in this crisis was Lorenzo Ricci. He had been elected in 1758 at the last General Congregation of the Society prior to its suppression despite a lack of significant experience as a superior. By the death of Pope Clement XIII in 1769 it had become clear that the final determination of the question of the Society's existence was close at hand. The conclave that elected his successor turned on the attitude of candidates to the Jesuits. The cardinals selected Cardinal Lorenzo Ganganelli who took the name Clement XIV. Although he did not explicitly indicate that he wanted to suppress the Society, he did express the opinion that it could be done if carried out in a canonical manner. For four years he avoided the pressures of the royal ambassadors at the papal court to carry out a general suppression. Of his hesitancy to act against the Jesuits the French ambassador commented that Clement XIV "had looked too long at the deep chasm over which he had to jump."[42] But he was not a man capable of resisting the combined pressures of the great Catholic powers of Europe indefinitely. Finally, on 16 August 1773, Clement issued the papal brief *Dominus ac Redemptor.* That night soldiers appeared at the Jesuit generalate, read the papal decree, and imprisoned Ricci. The last Jesuit General of the pre-Suppression Society of Jesus remained imprisoned in the Castel Sant'Angelo until his death in 1775.

After the early experiences of Ignatius Loyola in Spain and Paris there is no region more closely associated with the pre-Suppression Society of Jesus than Italy. The history of the Jesuits in Italy in the early modern period shares in the particular complexity of the history of Italy as a whole during that same period: how to construct a coherent account in a context of political and social disunity. Nevertheless, the Jesuits did bring to their work there a unity of purpose and a way of proceeding that allow for analysis on a regional basis. As diverse as the locations and challenges of Jesuits in Venice, Sicily, Milan, or Rome, the common works of the Society in education, confraternities, rural and urban missions, and the arts, and the Jesuits' way of dealing with powerful patrons, demonstrate a unity that extended throughout *Italia*.

Notes

1 William V. Bangert, S.J., *A History of the Society of Jesus* (St. Louis: Institute of Jesuit Sources, 1972), 55.
2 Ignatius of Loyola to Bernard Olivier, 23 May 1554. *Monumenta Historica Societatis Iesu, Epistolae Ignatii*, VII: 48.
3 On this urban strategy see Thomas M. Lucas, S.J., *Landmarking: City, Church, and Jesuit Urban Strategy* (Chicago: Loyola Press, 1997).
4 Paul F. Grendler, *Schooling in Renaissance Italy: Literacy and Learning, 1300–1600* (Baltimore: Johns Hopkins University Press, 1989), ch. 1.
5 Ibid., 364–65.
6 Bangert, *A History*, 55.
7 Grendler, *Schooling*, 371.
8 Ibid.
9 Bangert, *A History*, 27–28.
10 On Kircher see Paula Findlen, ed., *Athanasius Kircher: The Last Man to Know Everything* (London: Routledge, 2004) and "Scientific Spectacle in Baroque Rome: Athanasius Kircher and the Roman College Museum," in Mordechai Feingold, ed., *Jesuit Science and the Republic of Letters* (Cambridge, MA: MIT Press, 2003), 225–84.

11   Bangert, *A History*, 57.
12   Lance Gabriel Lazar, *Working in the Vineyard of the Lord: Jesuit Confraternities in Early Modern Italy* (Toronto: University of Toronto Press, 2005), 52–56.
13   Lance Gabriel Lazar, "The First Jesuit Confraternities and Marginalized Groups in Sixteenth-Century Rome," in Nicholas Terpstra, ed., *The Politics of Ritual Kingship: Confraternities and Social Order in Early Modern Italy* (Cambridge: Cambridge University Press, 2000), 132; John W. O'Malley, S.J., *The First Jesuits* (Cambridge, MA: Harvard University Press, 1993), 165–99.
14   Mario Scaduto, S.J., *Storia della Compagnia di Gesù in Italia*, vol. IV, *L'Epoca di Giacomo Lainez, 1556–1565. L'Azione* (Rome: Edizioni "La Civiltà Cattolica," 1974), 466–67.
15   Bangert, *A History*, 57.
16   Lazar, "First Jesuit Confraternities," 137.
17   Mark A. Lewis, S.J., "The Development of Jesuit Confraternity Activity in the Kingdom of Naples in the Sixteenth and Seventeenth Centuries," in Terpstra, *Politics of Ritual Kingship*, 213–14.
18   Ibid., 216–17.
19   Ibid., 221–22.
20   On this "civilizing mission" see Jennifer D. Selwyn, *A Paradise Inhabited by Devils: The Jesuits' Civilizing Mission in Early Modern Naples* (Aldershot: Ashgate; Rome: Institutum Historicum Societatis Iesu, 2004).
21   Mark A. Lewis, S.J. and Jennifer D. Selwyn, "Jesuit Activity in Southern Italy During the Generalate of Everard Mercurian," in Thomas M. McCoog, S.J., *The Mercurian Project: Forming Jesuit Culture, 1573–1580* (St. Louis: Institute of Jesuit Sources; Rome: Institutum Historicum Societatis Iesu, 2004), 525–26.
22   Selwyn, *A Paradise*, 73–75.
23   Ibid., 76.
24   Giovanni Romeo, *Aspettando il Boia. Condannati a morte, confortatori, e inquisitori nella Napoli della Contrariforma* (Florence: Sansoni, 1993).
25   Ignatius of Loyola, *The Constitutions of the Society of Jesus*, ed. and trans. George M. Ganss, S.J. (St. Louis: Institute of Jesuit Sources, 1970), 67.
26   Selwyn, *A Paradise*, 204.
27   Ibid., ch. 6.
28   Ibid., 144.
29   Ibid., 136–37.
30   Cited in Adriano Prosperi, "Clerics and Laymen in the Work of Carlo Borromeo," in John M. Headley and John B. Tomaro, eds., *San Carlo Borromeo: Catholic Reform and Ecclesiastical Politics in the Second Half of the Sixteenth Century* (London and Toronto: Associated University Presses; Washington, DC: The Folger Shakespeare Library, 1988), 125.
31   Giovanna Zanlonghi, *Teatri di formazione. Actio, parola, e imagine nella scena del Sei–Settecento a Milano* (Milan: V & P Università, 2002).

32 Pietro Tacchi-Venturi, *Storia della Compagnia di Gesù in Italia* (Rome: Civiltà Cattolica, 1922), II/2, 211–21.

33 Ibid., 305–24.

34 Paul F. Grendler, "Italian Schools and University Dreams during Mercurian's Generalate," in *The Mercurian Project: Forming Jesuit Culture, 1573–1580* (Rome: Institutum Historicum Societatis Iesu, 2004), 513.

35 William J. Bouwsma, *Venice and the Defense of Republican Liberty: Renaissance Values in the Age of the Counter Reformation* (Berkeley: University of California Press, 1968), 254.

36 Ibid., 344–45.

37 Ibid., 386.

38 Edward Muir, "Why Venice? Venetian Society and the Success of Early Opera," *Journal of Interdisciplinary History* 36/3 (2005), 331–53.

39 On this use of the Santa Casa for giving the Spiritual Exercises at Loreto see Paul V. Murphy, "The Jesuits and the Santa Casa di Loreto: Orazio Torsellini's *Lauretanae historiae libri quinque*," in Thomas M. Lucas, S.J., ed., *Spirit, Style, Story: Essays Honoring John W. Padberg, SJ* (Chicago: Jesuit Way, 2002), 269–81.

40 Ibid., 275.

41 See Zanlonghi, *Teatri di formazione, passim*.

42 Marcus Cheke, *The Cardinal de Bernis* (New York: Norton, 1959), 243.

5 The Society of Jesus in the Three Kingdoms[1]
THOMAS M. McCOOG

INTRODUCTION[2]

Despite subsequent hagiographical embellishment, we know very little about Ignatius Loyola's sojourn in England in 1531 when, as a student at the University of Paris, he visited the island to beg money from Spanish merchants.[3] We know more about the diplomatic mission of Alfonso Salmerón and Paschase Broët, two of Loyola's first companions, to Irish ecclesiastical and secular leaders in rebellion against King Henry VIII in 1541–42, and the activities of two Jesuits sent to Scotland and Ireland by Pope Pius V in the 1560s. The Dutch Jesuit Nicolas da Gouda concluded that only Mary Stuart's marriage to a strong Catholic prince could save orthodoxy. Henry Stuart, Lord Darnley, may not have been the strong Catholic prince that da Gouda recommended but Catholic hopes blossomed after his marriage to Mary. Until Mary had secured Catholicism's position in Scotland, there would be no Jesuit mission. But by May 1568 Mary was under house arrest in England and her infant son James under the protection of a staunch Protestant regent.[4]

David Wolfe carried papal letters of introduction to Irish leaders contesting Elizabeth's authority. As Wolfe nominated suitable candidates for Irish bishoprics, two Jesuits operated a small school in and around Limerick. The Englishman William Good was never happy: his continual complaints about the impossibility of religious life in these circumstances, along with increased enforcement of anti-Catholic legislation, prompted his religious superiors to recall the Jesuits in 1570. After a period in prison, Wolfe was on the continent in 1573, seeking Spanish aid for the FitzGerald revolt, which led to his departure from the Society circa 1577.[5]

During the first twenty years of Elizabeth's reign (1559–79), Jesuit contact with England was intermittent: the Spanish Jesuit Pedro de Ribadeneira observed the transition from Mary's to Elizabeth's reign;

William Good passed through England; Thomas Woodhouse, a secular priest, professed himself a Jesuit on the eve of his execution. Thomas King, the only Jesuit actually sent to England, went for reasons of health. The Society remained on the fringe of Catholic activity within the three kingdoms until the administration of the English College, Rome, was entrusted to it in 1579.[6]

PERMANENT MISSIONS

Everard Mercurian, the fourth Superior General of the Society of Jesus, was by temperament cautious. Good's lament about the impossibility of living the religious life in Ireland, and Wolfe's pro-active remedies for the plight of Irish Catholics, reinforced Mercurian's hesitancy during his administration as Superior General (1573–80). He replied to periodic petitions for assistance from the diocesan priest William Allen, the founder of the English College at Douai and later a cardinal, and generally recognized as the leader of the English Catholic refugees, with prayers not men. He opposed further Jesuit involvement for three reasons: fear that the English government (perhaps in light of Wolfe's activities) would portray the mission as a political enterprise; apprehension that conditions in England would prevent Jesuits from living according to their proper, religious style; anxiety that the absence of an ecclesiastical hierarchy (unlike in Ireland, Rome did not nominate Catholic successors for English sees) would occasion tension between Jesuits and the secular clergy. In late 1578 Allen finally persuaded Mercurian to authorize the fabled Jesuit mission, perhaps in the expectation that modified religious tolerance would follow the proposed match between Queen Elizabeth and François, Duke of Anjou. Among others, three Jesuits (Robert Parsons, Edmund Campion, and Ralph Emerson) left for England in April 1580. As negotiations for the match collapsed and news of a Spanish-papal military expedition to Ireland spread, the government legislated stronger measures against recusants, Jesuits, and seminary priests. Protests that their mission was spiritual were dismissed as specious: what in Catholic eyes was religious reconciliation to the Roman Church was alienation of loyalty from the crown's perspective. Campion was captured in July 1581 and executed on 1 December 1581. Parsons, meanwhile, escaped to the continent. Mercurian most likely would have aborted the mission, but he had died in August 1580. His successor as Superior General, Claudio Acquaviva, an advisor who spoke in favor of the mission, permitted it to continue despite periodic misgivings.

A series of laws dating back to the first acts of Elizabeth's reign coerced Catholics to accept the church recently established. The Act of Supremacy (1559) forbad recognition of the spiritual and ecclesiastical authority of the pope with graduated penalties culminating in a charge of high treason for the third offense. The Act of Uniformity (1559) imposed a new prayer book to be used in every church and chapel. In 1571 Parliament reacted to Elizabeth's excommunication in 1570 by making it high treason to claim that Elizabeth was either a heretic, a schismatic, or not the rightful sovereign. Another law forbad reconciliation with the Roman Catholic Church: rejection of the religious authority of the queen was tantamount to political disloyalty. *Post hoc* and most likely *propter hoc*, the Jesuit mission to England and the collapse of marital negotiations, Parliament in 1581 demanded that all recusants conform (that is, attend Protestant services) at least once a month and proclaimed guilty of high treason anyone reconciled to the Church of Rome along with the reconciler. In 1585 a new law threatened anyone ordained in the Roman Church after 1559 with a charge of high treason unless he left the kingdom within forty days.

Throughout the Elizabethan era, there were rarely more than a dozen Jesuits in England. Some, such as William Weston and Thomas Pounde, spent years in prison; others, such as Robert Southwell and Henry Walpole, were singled out for execution. Campion and Parsons had successfully constructed a network of country houses, complemented by rented residences in London, through which priests could pass with relative safety. By assuming disguises and multiple identities as they traveled from house to house, the Jesuits provided ammunition for the "myth of the evil Jesuit." To prevent such concessions to secular life from eroding their religious fervor and identity, the Jesuits, along with some secular clergy, met twice a year, often at considerable risk, for prayer, discussion, and the regular daily rhythm of religious life.

After his escape to the continent in 1581, Parsons played a major role in the formation of different unsuccessful coalitions and alliances directed towards the liberation of Mary, Queen of Scots, imprisoned in England since 1568, and her proclamation as Elizabeth's successor or replacement. Spain finally launched the famous Armada in 1588, more than a year after the judicial execution of Mary. Subsequent armadas in the 1590s never posed much of a real threat. Suspicions and fears within England that something was afoot in foreign courts rendered more credible stories about plots to assassinate Elizabeth, and thus further marginalized Catholics and villainized Jesuits. Despite their protest that they were faithful subjects, their loyalty was doubted.

Many might have echoed Viscount Montague's insistence that he would receive the pope on his knees if he landed in England with a cross but would resist him unfailingly if he came with a sword. But could they be believed? Catholic acceptance of such pernicious practices as mental reservation and equivocation, Protestants argued, subverted the value of any oaths of allegiance or sworn testament of Catholics. Nonetheless, attempts were made to formulate an oath that would not disturb the religious sensitivities of Catholics and at the same time would quell any apprehensions of the government, but without success.

The Society of Jesus provided whatever ecclesiastical structure existed within the kingdom: Jesuits welcomed secular priests into England and directed them to specific missions. Moreover the wider international Jesuit network provided the principal means of contact with ecclesiastical authorities in Rome and the transfer of needed funds to security on the continent. Critics believed that Jesuits diverted secular clergy into the poorer areas, and diverted the mission's funds into Jesuit enterprises. Jesuits already controlled the English College in Rome (1579) and the newer seminaries in Valladolid (1588) and Seville (1592). Now they were perceived as having designs for the mission itself. Secular clergy's resentment of the role the Society played in the running of the English mission increased after the death of Allen in 1594. The Society revealed its true intentions, they claimed, in an attempt by a few Jesuit prisoners in Wisbech to subject imprisoned secular clergy to their style and rule. Only the restoration of a Catholic hierarchy could prevent total Jesuit domination. Their request for a bishop resulted in the appointment of an archpriest whose jurisdiction over the secular clergy was exercised in consultation with the Jesuit superior. This new ecclesiastical order, instead of liberating secular clergy from the Jesuits, seemed to many to have strengthened the latter's control over the mission. The group, known as the appellants because of their appeal to Rome, successfully separated in 1602 the two ecclesiastical structures, the archpresbyterate of the secular clergy and the mission of the Jesuits.

Disagreements between secular clergy and Jesuits extended beyond ecclesiastical governance. Suspicions, at times justified, that Jesuit involvement in international diplomatic activity was initially concerned with the overthrow of Elizabeth and later with the selection of a Catholic candidate in the anticipated contest over her successor resulted only in more strict enforcement of the penal laws. Generally speaking, opponents of the Jesuits saw them as overly Hispanized zealots whose high-profile antics only goaded the government into more extreme measures. They themselves not only preferred the more native Scottish successor James to the foreign Spanish princess Isabella Eugenia but sought a *modus vivendi* with the government. To demonstrate their loyalty to the crown in all things but religion, some secular clergy were more than eager to acquire some type of religious tolerance at the expense of the Society of Jesus' continuation in England. Attempts to sacrifice the Jesuits failed in the final years of Elizabeth's reign.

Relations between English and foreign Jesuits were often as tense as those between English Jesuits and secular clergy. The foundation of English colleges in Spain and Belgium introduced anomalous administrative units into the Society's ordinary mode of governance. Robert Parsons was the superior of the English Jesuits but what was his authority vis-à-vis provincials and rectors? In 1598 Acquaviva promulgated *Officium et Regulae* at the same time that the pope established the archpriest. English Jesuits were henceforth governed by a prefect (Robert Parsons who returned to Rome in 1597 as rector of the English College), assisted by vice-prefects in Belgium and Spain, and a superior for the Jesuits in England. *Officium et Regulae* did not resolve all difficulties despite subsequent revisions and modifications.

THE SEVENTEENTH CENTURY[7]

Despite fears of a contested succession, James Stuart ascended the English throne with remarkable ease, facilitated no doubt by the absence of a viable Catholic candidate. To retain and augment his support among Catholics, he dangled before them the prospect of tolerance if not his complete acceptance of the Roman Church. Catholics presented James with petitions as he progressed south from Edinburgh to possess his inheritance in the spring of 1603. But James did not, indeed could not, deliver all his alleged promises. Discontent replaced hope as a relaxation of the penal laws did not materialize. The infamous Gunpowder Plot on 5 November 1605, perhaps instigated but at least exploited by Robert Cecil, Earl of Salisbury, climaxed a series of riots and disturbances. Jesuits were quickly accused of being the masterminds of the plot. Their popular identification with treachery and treason fueled the demand that they be expelled from the mission. A clear consequence of the Plot was a new oath of allegiance which required Catholics to deny the papal power to depose monarchs. The previous intra-Catholic debate on the lawfulness of occasional conformity (to avoid temporal punishment) and church popery (attendance at Protestant services despite Catholic beliefs) segued into a debate over the oath of allegiance.

From the foundation of the mission, Jesuits met two or three times a year to discuss strategy, missionary problems, and moral issues. Despite the obvious danger that one surprise attack could destroy the entire mission (as nearly happened at Baddesley Clinton in 1591), the meetings were considered an integral part of their religious identity. As Jesuits on the mission increased, it became impossible to gather them together and for one man to serve as their religious superior. By 1609, so-called spiritual prefects assisted the superior of the mission, each with delegated authority. Prefects were responsible for a specific number of Jesuits within a certain geographical area. They visited each, supervised their finances and religious life in general, and arranged for periodic meetings. Periodic exhortations and guidelines for religious life within a country manor testify to a persistent concern that this unorthodox style of life not corrode religious zeal.

Because of periodic complaints from Spanish provincials, the future of the prefecture was *sub iudice* (under review) when Acquaviva died in January 1615. The consequent General Congregation investigated the impact of nationalism on Jesuit life. The Society of Jesus, the congregation argued, was composed of many nationalities working together for the greater good. Insistence of independent missions that they have novitiates exclusively for their own countrymen, and that their rectors be of the same nationality, threatened the very nature of the Society. Thus these national entities could be brought under the ordinary jurisdiction of a provincial. Because England was not a province within the Society, it was not represented at the congregation. With no one to speak in the mission's defense, the congregation condemned the practice and insisted that the newly elected Father General Muzio Vitelleschi restore proper governance. Aware that the full implementation of the congregational decree would destroy the English mission, Vitelleschi resolved the dilemma by elevating the English mission to vice-provincial status in the summer of 1619. To quell the anger of the Flemish provincial, Vitelleschi directed that English Jesuit institutions within his province be moved into the southern Belgian province. In 1623, once Vitelleschi had been assured that the English Jesuits could open religious residences within England with relative impunity, have regular income from secured investments, and convene a congregation, he transformed the vice-province into a full province.

The mission's progress benefited from James' relative tolerance. In 1606, forty Jesuits operated in England and Wales; by the late 1610s, there were approximately a hundred. In the early 1620s three Jesuit residences opened: a retreat house/school/apostolic center at Cwm in the Welsh marches; a novitiate/retreat house in London; and an apostolic center/school somewhere in Staffordshire. From hints in the correspondence there may have been others. The Cwm community thrived under the protection of the Earls of Worcester until the Popish Plot in 1678/79. The London novitiate migrated from Blackfriars to Edmonton, Camberwell, and eventually Clerkenwell where it was raided and closed in March of 1628.

As Jesuits agitated for full provincial status and the establishment of the normal style of government within the Society, secular priests pushed for the re-establishment of episcopal government. In February 1623, Pope Gregory XV appointed William Bishop bishop of Chalcedon. He died within a year. His successor was Richard Smith. Almost immediately Smith and his supporters clashed with Jesuits and Benedictines over the nature of his authority and his relationship to the recently established Sacred Congregation of the Propagation of the Faith. Clearly he was a bishop; the issue was the nature of his authority. Did he have the ordinary authority proper to his office as he asserted? Or was he a vicar whose authority was simply delegated to him by a higher power, the pope, as the Jesuits and Benedictines claimed? In *Britannia* (May 1631) Pope Urban VIII decided in favor of Smith's opponents. A few months later Smith fled England to his patron Armand-Jean Du Plessis, Cardinal Richelieu. Once more England lacked a Catholic bishop.

During the final years of James' reign and during the personal rule of his son Charles, the province's growth was spectacular. Wealthy benefactors endowed Jesuit works in East Anglia and Derbyshire. Besides the spiritual center in Cwm, the province operated schools in Holywell, Stanley Grange, and near Wolverhampton. Foreign patrons, specifically the Habsburgs and the Wittelsbachs, increased their gifts from the profits of the Thirty Years' War. In 1634 the province established its first mission: the English colony of Maryland founded by George Calvert, Lord Baltimore, with unprecedented religious liberty. In 1639 the English province numbered approximately 350 members, nearly 200 of whom worked in England. With papal agents at the English court, prospects for the continued growth of the province were good. But these papal agents, rumors of more Irish Catholic insurrectionists murdering good Protestants, and suspicions about

Charles' intentions fueled rumors of popish plots aimed at the destruction of Church and State.

The English Civil War and a reversal of Catholic fortunes in the Thirty Years' War triggered a downward spiral for the English province. A dramatic decline in income restricted the number of novices it could accept, and forced it to rely on the generosity of other provinces to accommodate and support nearly forty members. This difficult situation made the Society more dependent on nobles and gentry, some of whom interfered too much in the affairs of the Society while some Jesuits were criticized for interfering too much in the affairs of the gentry. Especially disturbing to the authorities in Rome was the insistence of Catholic nobles that they have Jesuit chaplains/tutors as they traveled around the continent.

The Society's reputation for political involvement prompted some to blame it for all the ills of the era. The "Grand Remonstrance" of 1641, a list of grievances drawn up by angry members of Parliament, asserted that the subtle practices introduced into the kingdom by Jesuits fomented friction between king and Parliament. After the execution of King Charles I in 1649, Jesuits returned to a more familiar role of regicides. Jesuits had cleverly infiltrated the army and were responsible for the king's death. Jesuits along with other Catholics had attempted a *modus vivendi* with the Independents in 1647 but Rome rejected the propositions. By the restoration of the monarchy in 1660, the size of the province had fallen by 70 members to 287; the number of Jesuits within England and Wales had fallen by nearly 40 to 147.

English Catholics, clothing themselves as staunch royalists who suffered during the Commonwealth, expected leniency with the restoration of the monarchy. In the Declaration of Breda (1660), Charles II promised religious toleration but was twice forced to rescind declarations in favor of it by a recalcitrant House of Commons (1662 and 1672). The first attempt revealed yet again a division among English Catholics regarding the Jesuits. The dean and chapter of the secular clergy (the so-called Old Chapter), vestiges of the hierarchical structures established by the bishops Bishop and Smith but with questionable authority, argued in favor of religious toleration for Catholics and the exclusion and exile of the Jesuits, known troublemakers and intriguers. Tension between the chapter and the Jesuits persisted after this failed bid for toleration.

Rumors regarding the conversion of James, Duke of York, Charles' brother and heir, to Catholicism circulated widely in the 1670s. Anti-Catholic sentiment was aroused to alert the nation to the dreadful consequences of a Catholic monarch. Into this volatile situation Titus Oates provided the match with his outrageous claims of a Jesuit plot to assassinate Charles and install his brother. The Popish Plot unleashed a furor throughout the kingdom. Charles' hands were tied. He personally did not believe in any plot but the hysteria was so cleverly managed by James' opponents that any intervention could result in his brother's exclusion. Six Jesuits were executed in 1679; others died in prison; many fled to the continent. In 1678, there were 128 Jesuits in England; the following year, there were 87. But the Stuarts and the Jesuits weathered the storm, the latter albeit with reduced numbers and lost income and property. James was proclaimed king on 16 February 1685. Jesuits served as royal confessors and preachers and one served on the Privy Council. The province opened at least eight colleges (Wigan, Wolverhampton, Bury St Edmunds, Lincoln, Durham, Pontefract, and two in London) and numerous chapels. The arrival of William of Orange and his overthrow of James in 1688 ended Catholic and Jesuit prospects. The Jesuit schools were attacked and plundered; the chapels were destroyed. Many Jesuits again fled to the continent: there were only 94 in England in 1690. Anti-Jacobite propaganda blamed the forward policy of the Jesuits for James' defeat. Despite the turmoil surrounding the overthrow of James, the fortunes of the province continued to improve. In 1700, there were 337 members of the province with 131 in England. Throughout the eighteenth century, numbers hovered around 300 and 130. Because of suspected and real association with the Jacobite uprisings of 1715 and 1745, Catholics were marginalized even more from English public life. Catholic nobles and gentry withdrew to their country homes; their chaplains followed.[8]

The nomination of Catholic bishops for England did not immediately follow James' accession, partly as the result of a disagreement over whether the bishops would be ordinaries or vicars apostolic. In late 1685, John Leyburn was appointed Vicar Apostolic for England and Wales; three years later, there were four for the London, Midland, Northern, and Western Districts. Relations between the English province and the vicars apostolic were periodically disturbed by the same issues that had troubled their antecedents. Vicars apostolic insisted that religious orders obtain proper faculties from them. Jesuits retorted that their faculties came from the pope and thus did not require specific faculties from bishops who were not in fact ordinaries but vicars of the pope. Appeals to Rome were answered by decisions generally favorable to the regulars until the mid-1700s. Pope Benedict XIV's bull

Apostolicum Ministerium or *Regulae Observandae in Anglicanis Missionibus* (1753) resolved the matter in favor of the vicars apostolic but one clause irritated the regulars:

> some regulars in England dwell outside monasteries, in private houses, wear secular dress and enjoy a liberty which they would not have in their monasteries . . . . Therefore it is enjoined on all missioners that after six years they shall return to a Catholic country, and there resume their religious habit and dwell for three months in a monastery of their Order . . . . Wherefore the vicars apostolic ought not to prolong them [faculties] beyond a period of six years but grant them at the utmost for six years, and even then during that time at their discretion.

Around the same time there were unsuccessful attempts by some vicars to remove the Society of Jesus from the administration of the English College, Rome, or failing that to entrust its administration to Italian Jesuits.

With the expulsion of Jesuits from France in 1762, the English Jesuits lost their college at St-Omer and moved the students to Bruges. With the universal suppression of the Society in 1773, former Jesuits moved the college to Liège. In Rome secular clergy finally assumed control of the English College. Within England, former Jesuits remained united along their previous institutional lines and carefully protected their financial assets against episcopal attempts at confiscation. These former Jesuits may have had a nebulous canonical existence but, with funds and a seminary at Liège to provide their replacements, they could weather the storm. Better times arrived with the restoration of the English province in 1803.

IRELAND[9]

James Archer returned to Ireland in 1596, the first Jesuit in the kingdom for nearly a decade, to seek funds to support and endow colleges on the continent. Irish colleges had opened in Lisbon in 1590 and in Salamanca in 1592. Archer eventually fled to Ulster where he allied himself with Hugh O'Neill, the Earl of Tyrone, then in rebellion against English rule. The burning issue was Catholic support for O'Neill. Was he a crusader for the Catholic faith? Should all Catholics be obliged to support him? O'Neill requested a papal nuncio. Instead of his preferred candidate, Clement named an Italian Jesuit, Ludovico Mansoni, who never left Spain. After the defeat of the

Spanish force at Kinsale in January 1602, Archer remained in exile and his companion, the Jesuit brother Dominic Collins, was executed at Youghal.

In the early seventeenth century, only six Jesuits operated in Ireland. With the defeat of O'Neill, the mission became less concerned with military ventures and more with Christian renewal. Catholicism could be practiced openly beyond the pale and the fathers embarked on popular missions. By 1629, there were fifty-five Jesuits in Ireland and fifty Jesuits on the continent, primarily at the Irish Colleges in Lisbon, Salamanca, and newer ones in Santiago de Compostella (1613), Seville (1619), Rome (1635), and Poitiers (1674). In May 1642, a Catholic Confederacy of bishops, some clergy, Gaelic chieftains and Old English gentry united under the motto "Pro Deo, Pro Rege, Pro Patria" to resist Parliament. Despite Father General Vitelleschi's reservations, Jesuits aided the confederacy as the Irish struggle became intertwined with the English Civil War. As in England, the Irish Jesuits suffered financially because of the war, and their numbers declined. The restoration of the Stuart monarchy in 1660 led to the revival of Jesuit residences and missions throughout the island, a revival short-lived because of the Orange Revolt and the subsequent war in Ireland. Despite promises of toleration in the Treaty of Limerick (1691), a series of penal laws passed between 1695 and 1728 made the practice of Catholicism much more difficult. As the military threat diminished, conditions for Catholics improved. Dressed as laymen, Jesuits mingled with all social levels but concentrated on the foundation of schools. As the Bourbon monarchs turned against the Jesuits and expelled them from their kingdoms, the Irish Jesuits lost their colleges in France (1764) and Spain (1767). In 1772, a year before the universal suppression of the Society, the Irish Jesuits were removed from the college in Rome. In 1773 there were fewer than twenty Jesuits in Ireland. Having secured the mission's finances, the former Jesuits, especially in Dublin, remained in contact as they hoped for better days.

SCOTLAND [10]

Robert Parsons' investigations into the possibility of Scotland offering occasional sanctuary to persecuted English Catholic lay persons and Jesuits resulted not only in a series of diplomatic intrigues and alliances but also in the foundation of a Jesuit mission. Claudio Acquaviva approved its establishment by late December of 1581. Despite some early apprehensions, the mission survived, although there were rarely more than five Jesuits, usually residing as chaplains with Catholic nobles. Others worked on the continent, often in colleges administered by the Society for the Scottish Church: Douai (1612 after various migrations for thirty years); Rome (1600 but administered by Jesuits from 1615); Madrid (1627). In the early seventeenth century, the Society decided to concentrate on the colleges instead of the mission itself. Although the penal laws promulgated by Parliament were severe and the Jesuits endured numerous deprivations, only one, John Ogilvie (died 1615), was executed. The accession of the Catholic James II inaugurated a brief revival of Catholicism. Two Jesuits were named royal chaplains and a small interconfessional school was opened in the Palace of Holyrood. But all ended with the Orange rebellion of 1688. Catholics tended to support the Jacobite uprisings of 1715 and 1745; one Jesuit was captured during the first and five in the second. Two died during their captivity and two were exiled.

Like England, Scotland lacked a Catholic bishop. In 1694, Scotland was created a vicariate apostolic; in 1727 it was divided into two. There were periodic tensions as the Society adjusted to the new ecclesiastical order. The Scots College in Madrid passed to the diocesan clergy with the expulsion of the Jesuits from Spain in 1767 and was moved to Valladolid in 1771. With the expulsion of the Society from France in 1764, the Scots College moved from Douai to Dinant until the universal suppression. The Scots College, Rome, passed to the administration of the secular clergy. The few Jesuits in Scotland remained *in situ* with the Society's suppression and administered the mission's funds. One member of the old mission joined the English province at its restoration in 1803.

MARYLAND[11]

Early in the reign of King James I, a "Mr. Winslade" proposed the foundation of a colony in the New World where Catholics could migrate for religious freedom. Robert Parsons dismissed the project as not only unfeasible but dishonorable. Sir George Calvert was granted a charter to establish the colony of Avalon in Newfoundland in 1621. After its failure, he tried again with the colony of Maryland, which promised a separation of church and state, and general religious freedom. His son Cecil Calvert negotiated for Jesuit involvement. The first colonists and Jesuits arrived in March 1634. The Jesuits ministered to the Catholic colonists and among the Amerindians. Having been granted large farms, Jesuits purchased slaves to work them.

Although they did not always run the plantations well, the mission was a significant property-owner. The mission's estates became a canonical problem because Jesuit law forbad regular income to any institutions but colleges and houses of formation. Eventually the portfolio was entrusted to a college in England. During the Civil War, Protestant colonists from Virginia destroyed the Jesuit church and forced the Jesuits into hiding. After the restoration, the Jesuits opened small schools in Newton Manor (1677–c. 1688) and Bohemia Manor (c. 1742–50), and a college in New York (1683–89). Public practice of Catholicism was forbidden in Maryland after the Glorious Revolution. Some Catholic families emigrated to the more tolerant atmosphere of Pennsylvania. The Jesuits followed, extending the mission into Philadelphia, New Jersey, and the Hudson valley. In 1773, twenty-one Jesuits in the mission submitted to the brief of suppression. However, they remained united spiritually and financially as the Corporation of Roman Catholic Clergymen. A former Jesuit, John Carroll, was approved as bishop of Baltimore in 1789; two other former Jesuits, Leonard Neale and Lorenz Grässel, were his coadjutors. Petitions from surviving members of the mission to rejoin the restored English province were denied because Maryland was no longer part of the British Empire. Instead the Mission of the United States was formally established in 1805. It opened a novitiate at the Georgetown Academy (later University, founded by Carroll in 1789) in 1806.

CONCLUSION

Mercurian's initial concerns reverberate through the pre-Suppression history of the Society in the British Isles. Frequent acrimonious clashes between Jesuits and secular clergy, primarily in England, continued. Indeed, former Jesuits threatened to denounce English bishops to the government on the charge of *praemunire*[12] if they persisted in their attempt to confiscate the province's financial assets. Ironically the first bishops in the thirteen American original colonies were former members of the Society of Jesus. Because of unique conditions, religious life required constant monitoring. If Jesuit superiors were unable to ensure that their men lived properly and piously, bishops were increasingly willing to do it for them. Last but definitely not least, the Society of Jesus quickly and justifiably acquired a reputation for political involvement. Jesuits were suspected of trampling underfoot the fragile border separating the reign of Caesar from the kingdom of Christ. So persistent and universal were the accusations that the Fifth General Congregation (1593–94) legislated against Jesuit involvement with princes. Worried that he violated these decrees by working for the restoration of Catholicism in England, Parsons sought a dispensation. Acquaviva's reply is important: Parsons did not need a dispensation because the decree did not forbid Jesuits providing secular rulers with advice on matters pertinent to the service of the Lord even if these matters were intermingled with state affairs. The shrewd Acquaviva had succeeded the cautious Mercurian. Instead of repeating his predecessor's fear that Jesuits would become politically engaged to the detriment of their religious institute, Acquaviva redefined the question.

Notes

1   "Three Kingdoms" is a now conventional designation for the kingdoms of England, Scotland, and Ireland. Important archives for the history of the Society of Jesus in these kingdoms are: Archivum Romanum Societatis Iesu (ARSI); Archivum Britannicum Societatis Iesu (ABSI) (London); Irish Jesuit Archives (IJA) (Dublin); Stonyhurst College (Lancashire, England); and the Archivio segreto Vaticano and Biblioteca Apostolica Vaticana. Other important depositories are the Bodleian Library (Oxford); Venerable English College (Rome); National Archives (Kew, England); and the British Library (London). Both ABSI and IJA hold large collections of transcripts of pertinent documents from various archives. Many of the codices traditionally listed as being at Stonyhurst College, e.g. the Anglia and Collectanea series, have been transferred to the ABSI. Many documents, generally concerned with English martyrs, have been published in the Catholic Record Society series. The third volume of *Monumenta Angliae*, ed. Thomas M. McCoog, S.J., and László Lukács, S.J. (Rome: Institutum Historicum Societatis Iesu, 2000), contains all pertinent documents from ARSI (and some from the Vatican Archives) from 1541 to 1562.

2   There are two quasi-complete historical accounts of Jesuit activity in England: Bernard Basset, S.J., *The English Jesuits from Campion to Martindale* (London: Burns and Oates, 1967), and Francis Edwards, S.J., *The Jesuits in England from 1580 to the Present Day* (London: Burns and Oates, 1985).

3   For a more complete treatment of Jesuit activities in the Three Kingdoms, see Thomas M. McCoog, S.J., *The Society of Jesus in Ireland, Scotland, and England 1541–1588: "Our Way of Proceeding"?* (Leiden: Brill, 1996).

4   See John Hungerford Pollen, S.J., ed., *Papal Negotiations with Mary Queen of Scots* (Edinburgh: Edinburgh University Press, 1901).

5   Edmund Hogan, S.J., planned a multi-volume edition of documents pertinent to the Jesuit mission. Unfortunately only the first volume, containing documents from 1540 to 1607, appeared: *Ibernia Ignatiana*

(Dublin: Excudebat Societas Typographica Dubliniensis, 1880). For the most recent analysis of David Wolfe see Thomas J. Morrissey, S. J., "'Almost Hated and Detested by All'?: The Problem of David Wolfe," in *The Mercurian Project: Forming Jesuit Culture, 1573–1580* (Rome/St. Louis: Institutum Historicum Societatis Iesu/ Institute of Jesuit Sources, 2004), 675–703.

6 For biographical information on English, Welsh, Irish, and Scottish Jesuits, see (in chronological order) George Oliver, *Collections towards Illustrating the Biography of the Scotch, English, and Irish Members SJ* (Exeter: W. C. Featherstone, 1838); Henry Foley, S. J., *Records of the English Province of the Society of Jesus*, 7 vols. in 8 (Roehampton/London: Manresa Press/ Burns and Oates, 1875–83); Geoffrey Holt, S. J., *The English Jesuits 1650–1829: A Biographical Dictionary*, Catholic Record Society (= CRS) 69 (London: Catholic Record Society, 1979); Thomas M. McCoog, S. J., *Monumenta Angliae*, 2 vols. (Rome: Institutum Historicum Societatis Iesu, 1992); Thomas M. McCoog, S. J., *English and Welsh Jesuits 1555–1650*, 2 parts, CRS 74, 75 (London: Catholic Record Society, 1994–95); Thomas M. McCoog, S. J., "The Society of Jesus in Wales; The Welsh in the Society of Jesus: 1561–1625," *The Journal of Welsh Religious History* 5 (1997), 1–29; Thomas M. McCoog, S. J., "'Pray to the Lord of the Harvest': Jesuit Missions to Scotland in the Sixteenth Century," *Innes Review* 53 (2002), 127–88. Nothing has been published recently on the Irish.

7 There is no thorough study of the English Jesuits in the seventeenth century. For background information see Thomas H. Clancy, S. J., *A Literary History of the English Jesuits: A Century of Books 1615–1714* (San Francisco: Catholic Scholars Press, 1996); Michael C. Questier, ed., *Newsletters from the Archpresbyterate of George Birkhead*, Camden Society, 5th series, XII (Cambridge: Cambridge University Press, 1998); Michael C. Questier, ed., *Newsletters from the Caroline Court, 1631–1638*, Camden Society, 5th series, XXVI (Cambridge: Cambridge University Press, 2005); Caroline Hibbard, *Charles I and the Popish Plot* (Chapel Hill: University of North Carolina Press, 1983); John Miller, *Popery and Politics in England, 1660–1688* (Cambridge: Cambridge University Press, 1973).

8 For the eighteenth century see Geoffrey Holt, S. J., *William Strickland and the Suppressed Jesuits* (London: British Province of the Society of Jesus, 1988); Geoffrey Holt, S. J., *The English Jesuits in the Age of Reason* (London: Burns and Oates, 1993); Eamon Duffy, ed., *Challoner and His Church: A Catholic Bishop in Georgian England* (London: Darton, Longman & Todd, 1981); Thomas M. McCoog, S. J., *Promising Hope: Essays on the Suppression and Restoration of the English Province of the Society of Jesus* (Rome: Institutum Historicum Societatis Iesu, 2003).

9 The only general history is Louis McRedmond, *To the Greater Glory: A History of the Irish Jesuits* (Dublin: Gill and Macmillan, 1991).

10 See William Forbes-Leith, S. J., ed., *Narratives of Scottish Catholics under Mary Stuart and James VI* (Edinburgh: William Patterson, 1885);

William Forbes-Leith, S. J., ed., *Memoirs of Scottish Catholics during the XVIIth and XVIIIth Centuries*, 2 vols. (London: Longmans, Green, and Co., 1909); Brian Halloran, "Jesuits in 18th-century Scotland," *Innes Review* 52 (2001), 80–100; Christine Johnson, *Developments in the Roman Catholic Church in Scotland, 1789–1829* (Edinburgh: John Donald, 1983); McCoog, "'Pray to the Lord of the Harvest'"; Michael J. Yellowlees, *"So strange a monster as a Jesuite": The Society of Jesus in Sixteenth-Century Scotland* (Isle of Colonsay: House of Lochar, 2003).

11 Important for the history of the Maryland mission are the Archives of the Maryland Province located at Georgetown University, Washington, DC, and the archives of the Archdiocese of Baltimore. Secondary sources include Luca Codignola, *The Coldest Harbour of the Land* (Kingston and Montreal: McGill-Queen's University Press, 1988); Robert Emmett Curran, ed., *American Jesuit Spirituality: The Maryland Tradition, 1634–1900* (New York: Paulist Press, 1988); Thomas Hughes, S. J., *History of the Society of Jesus in North America*, 4 vols. (New York: Longmans, Green, and Co., 1908–17).

12 A series of fourteenth-century statutes designed to protect English prerogatives against perceived papal encroachments. Recognition of papal authority could lead to an accusation of treason. The statutes were finally repealed in 1967.

6 Jesuit dependence on the French monarchy

THOMAS WORCESTER

Jesuit history in France begins with the arrival of Ignatius of Loyola, as a student at the University of Paris, in 1528. His seven years in Paris were the time and place that gave birth to a small group of companions that became the Society of Jesus.[1] It would be hard to exaggerate the place of Paris and France in the life of Ignatius and in the origins of the Jesuits. The University of Paris, with its international student body, its highly structured curriculum, and its strengths in classical languages, rhetoric, philosophy, and theology, would strongly influence both the education or "formation" that Jesuits themselves would receive, and the education offered to others in Jesuit schools throughout the world.[2] Yet France, albeit Catholic, and albeit the birthplace of the Jesuit Order, was often a very difficult place for Jesuits to function. Gallican traditions of ecclesiastical independence from Rome, and of royal patronage of the French church, helped to ground deep hostility to a new religious order founded by a Spaniard and under a vow of obedience to the pope.[3]

Still, Jesuits also overcame opposition, and were able to establish themselves in France. Some Jesuit colleges were founded in France in the 1550s and 1560s, laying the groundwork for the later proliferation of Jesuit institutions.[4] The late sixteenth century was a period of phenomenal growth for Jesuit numbers and institutions in much of Europe and indeed elsewhere; in France, even in the midst of the Wars of Religion, Jesuit numbers grew and several colleges were founded.[5] The late sixteenth and early seventeenth centuries were also a time of political assassinations in France, and Jesuits were used as scapegoats for such violence. In this essay I will focus on how Jesuits nevertheless succeeded, in the first half of the seventeenth century, in adapting to the French political context, and prospered and grew in close collaboration with the French monarchy, a collaboration that would last until the 1760s. I will pay particular attention to how several Jesuit writers used the printing press to defend the Society of Jesus against various

Figure 6.1. Church of Saint-Paul–Saint-Louis, Paris (formerly the Jesuit church of Saint-Louis), 2000. Photo by Thomas Worcester.

enemies and accusations, and how these writers used print to gain and retain royal support.[6]

In an age when many European monarchs and their apologists made growing claims to absolute power – kings would answer to God alone, not to popes, parliaments, or the people – some political theorists saw assassination as potentially a legitimate way to deal with a monarch become a tyrant. In France, speculation turned to reality on 1 August 1589, when King Henry III was assassinated, by Jacques Clément.[7] Clément represented radical Catholic groups that saw Henry as too soft on Protestant heretics; ironically, Henry's death opened the succession to Henry of Navarre (or Henry IV), a Calvinist. By 1593, Henry IV had converted to Catholicism, and in the wake of that change managed to bring the most violent periods of the Wars of Religion to an end. Yet some Catholics still did not trust the king. On 27 December 1594, Jean Châtel, a former student at the Jesuit college in Paris, attempted to kill Henry IV. Opponents of the Jesuits took full advantage of the situation; in January 1595 began the first – certainly not the last – expulsion of Jesuits from France.

Regional French law courts – the *parlements* – played the central role in expelling the Jesuits, though Henry acquiesced in this action. The *parlement* of Paris led the way against the Society of Jesus, and some other *parlements* followed, though not all. In much of western France, Jesuits were not expelled.

But on 1 September 1603, Henry IV signed the Edict of Rouen readmitting the Jesuits throughout his kingdom. Eric Nelson's recent book on the period of Jesuit exile following Châtel's assassination attempt, and on the royal decision to readmit the Jesuits, makes clear how King Henry IV used the Edict of Rouen as a way to assert his authority both over the *parlements* and over the Jesuits.[8] In the years after 1603 Henry not only permitted Jesuits and Jesuit institutions in his kingdom but became a generous patron of them, perhaps most visibly as the founder of the Jesuit college at La Flèche.[9] Henry also took a Jesuit, Pierre Coton (1564–1626), as his confessor, and the tradition of a Jesuit father as the king's confessor would last in France all the way to the mid-1700s.[10]

Coton was not only a confessor, but also a prolific preacher and writer. In 1598 Henry IV extended a measure of toleration to Protestants in France; this did not mean, however, that controversy between Catholics and Protestants disappeared. Indeed, Coton devoted several works to refutation of what he saw as Huguenot heresy. A prominent example is his *Institution catholique* – a work in four books deliberately reminiscent of the four books of John Calvin's *Institutes* – first published in 1610.[11] That was also the year in which François Ravaillac succeeded where Jean Châtel had failed; Henry IV was assassinated on 14 May 1610. Henry's widow, Marie de' Medici, became Queen Regent, and Coton dedicated his *Institution catholique* to her.

As regent, Marie lost no time in appointing Coton as confessor to the young Louis XIII (born in 1601), and in making clear in other ways her support of the Jesuits, though some of their opponents would have liked to find a way to implicate the Society of Jesus in the regicide.[12] Jesuit writers such as Coton were particularly active in the period after

Henry's death, going to great lengths to demonstrate their devotion and loyalty to Henry, to Louis XIII, and to his mother. Coton published a fourteen-page letter in 1610, addressed to the Queen Regent, in which he argued that Jesuits rejected arguments in favor of the possibility of legitimate regicide, and that Jesuits held Henry in the highest regard.[13] Henry's life, Coton asserted, far from in any way being a tyranny, was the model of piety, justice, clemency, valor, and paternal affection for his subjects, a model for other monarchs of the earth to follow.[14]

Juan de Mariana (1535–1624), a Spanish Jesuit, had published *De Rege et Regis Institutione* in 1599, a work that seemed to justify regicide in certain circumstances.[15] In his letter, Coton sought to isolate Mariana's work as exceptional, insisting that French Jesuits and many other Jesuits, including the theologian Robert Bellarmine and the Jesuit Father General Claudio Acquaviva, rejected Mariana. Coton even asserts that it is the Protestants in France who read Mariana.[16] Protesting that "the body of our Company cannot be infected by one person's opinion," Coton declares that an attack on the person of the king is an execrable parricide and a detestable sacrilege. He also points out that the assassin of Henry IV could not have been inspired by Mariana, for Ravaillac was not intelligent enough to read the language (Latin) in which Mariana's book was written.[17]

In the concluding sections of his letter, Coton addresses (apostrophizes) the Queen Regent, France, the French Jesuits, and Henry IV. The Queen Regent he praises as gifted by God with sublime understanding and clear vision. France, "eye of Christendom, rose of Empires, the pearl of the world," Coton deplores as having lost the "mantle of glory" with which Henry covered it. The Society of Jesus in France, he laments, is "lowered" and "afflicted," for it has existed but by the good will of this monarch. To Henry, "the marvel of kings" and "the ornament of the century," Coton bids adieu, calling him "the second founder and first benefactor of our Company."[18]

Coton's exaltation of the French monarchy is prominent in many of his writings, not solely those concerned with management of the aftermath of the 1610 assassination. For example, in a book of daily prayers "for all Catholics," Coton includes lengthy prayers for the king and royal family. One is to ask God that nothing may disturb "peaceful subordination" to the monarchy, and that the days of the king and his house be like the days of heaven, unalterable, incorruptible, and blessed. And one is to pray that the king, God's image, and who represents God on earth, be the "organ" of God's will and the "instrument" of God's glory.[19]

Of the same generation as Coton, Louis Richeome, S.J. (1544–1625) was no less articulate than Coton as a published author. Richeome's writings included a 1598 treatise, addressed to Henry IV, in which he laid out arguments for readmission of the Society of Jesus throughout France. He explains that false reports have been sent to Henry regarding this Company, and that false accusations have been made. Falsely, French Jesuits have been called enemies of the French state, enemies of Henry IV, and corrupters of youth.[20] Seeking to defend "the cause of our innocence," Richeome argues that Jesuits teach students to honor kings, and he recalls that Jean Châtel, under torture, denied that Jesuits were in any way involved in his effort to assassinate Henry.[21] As for the claim that Jesuits "seduce" young men into joining the Society of Jesus, Richeome protests that this is not so, and – he suggests that this is unlike the practices of some other religious orders – the Jesuits require no money from those who do join.[22]

Richeome also responds to claims that Jesuits are proud, ambitious, and rich, and he insists French Jesuits do not seek vengeance against those who engage in calumny against them. While their libraries may be excellent, Richeome argues, Jesuits themselves live in poverty, and take no salary for their labors and actions. Though some criticize the name of the Society of Jesus as evidence of Jesuit pride, Richeome points to approval of the name by the Holy See. Even though those who persecute the Society of Jesus are like the devil in their calumnies, all that Jesuits seek from His Majesty is "the freedom to work" for the salvation of both their friends and their enemies.[23]

When such freedom, granted to the French Jesuits in 1603 by Henry IV, was endangered by his assassination in 1610, Richeome was quick to seek support for the Society of Jesus from the Queen Regent. In a published work entitled a *Consolation* for the Regent, Richeome declares that the entire Jesuit Order wishes to console Her Majesty, by means of "loyal service," and by giving witness to its desire to cherish with "eternal affection" the "sacred memory" of the recently deceased king. For the Jesuits remember having been "honored and cherished" by his royal and paternal friendship, and gratified by thousands of favors.[24] Richeome enumerates Henry's many qualities: prudent and courageous, Henry was a true king in war, and a true king in peace, "an Augustus in one, an Alexander in the other." In his clemency, Henry was the "living image of God," and he was a most magnanimous prince in pardoning his enemies. Humble and modest in conversation, Henry called his soldiers companions, and he treated his subjects as companions. His clothing was so modest that he was barely recognized as king.[25]

Machiavelli's treatise *The Prince* was hotly contested in Richeome's era for its praise of rulers who act in immoral ways when they deem it "necessary" for the sake of their hold on power.[26] An example of such "necessity" was the breaking of promises; moreover, rulers would at times need to "disregard the precepts of religion."[27] But Richeome praises Henry for keeping his promises, and for his conversion to Catholicism, a conversion accompanied by a charity that "engendered in him a truly most Christian zeal," for promoting the good of Catholicism, for combating error, and for bringing the erring back to the "fold of Jesus Christ."[28] Some Catholics had questioned the sincerity of Henry's 1593 conversion to the Catholic faith;[29] Richeome affirms Henry's sincerity, pointing to the king's tears that were seen when he received communion, and when he attended sermons. According to Richeome, Henry was like his holy ancestor Saint Louis (= Louis IX, reigned 1226–70): Henry even died at the same age – fifty-seven – as Saint Louis.[30]

While Richeome likens Henry IV to the devout Saint Louis, he contrasts him sharply with slanderers of the Society of Jesus. By "false discourses" Jesuits were slandered as enemies of kings, as haughty and ambitious men, as avaricious and opulent, as spoilers of youth.[31] But Henry, Richeome asserts, even thought of why he might have wanted to be a Jesuit: Richeome had heard it reported that Henry said that, had he wanted to be a member of a religious order, he would either have been a Jesuit, in order to help souls, or a Carthusian, for solitude and complete retreat from the world. Richeome adds that Henry "sent" Jesuits on mission to Constantinople in 1609, and in 1610, shortly before his death, he decided on a Jesuit mission to Canada, "in order to bring the light of faith to this poor people, still wandering in the shadows of paganism."[32]

Jesuit publication of works in praise of Henry did not cease in the months just after his death. One example is Etienne Binet, S.J. (1569–1639), who preached a funeral oration on 14 May 1611, in the cathedral of Troyes, on the first anniversary of Henry's death. This oration was reprinted as late as 1627 in a second edition of a collection of Binet's works.[33] Like Coton and Richeome, Binet was a prolific author. Binet published some fifty books, and these included lives of the saints, works on rhetoric, works on consolation in time of plague and other illness, and a work on gentle and rigorous styles of ecclesiastical governance.[34] A contemporary and acquaintance of Francis de Sales (1567–1622), Binet and the future bishop of Geneva were students together, in the 1580s, at the Jesuit college in Paris.[35]

Binet begins his oration on Henry by criticizing other preachers and writers who have sought to honor Henry by comparing him to Alexander the Great and to Caesar. Such comparisons are mistaken, Binet insists, for King Henry was without equal (*sans pair*). God wished to make a beautiful Idea of Kings, and so he assembled all royal perfections and called this miracle Henry IV.[36] Extending such hyperbole, Binet declares that there is no "good Frenchman" who does not wish to die, for – on account of the death of Henry – "half of our life" is dead. For Henry was the "diamond of the human race," and he shone as the sun on the throne of Majesty; he was our "incomparable" prince and the father of his people.[37] Referring to Henry's assassin as "this Judas" and "this viper," Binet questions God as to why He did not send an angel to stop "this Antichrist" who was seeking to assassinate His (God's) "Christ," lieutenant general, and image on earth. Yet such questioning of God's action, or inaction, does not prevent Binet from asserting that it was by a "singular divine providence" that Henry had come back to the Roman Church.[38]

Machiavelli had warned a prince against too much generosity, lest he impoverish himself and come to be held in little regard; thus for Machiavelli it was better to be miserly than generous.[39] But Binet praises Henry for his almsgiving and especially for his generosity to widows. Many are the widows, from all provinces of France, who would storm heaven to bring Henry back to life, for he gave to them "peace, happiness, and rest," and he made of France a promised land, and a paradise of delights.[40] Yet Binet is quick to make clear that widows are by no means the only people in France with such sentiments for Henry. Using a musical analogy, Binet imagines a motet to be sung in four parts: the clergy will sing of Henry's piety, in the churches; the nobility will sing of his courage, in battles; the magistrates will sing of his equity, in justice; and the people will sing of his "paternal providence," in all corners of the kingdom. And these voices may be joined by others, from outside France, for Henry was the "Arbiter of Europe," and he sent Jesuits to Turkey, and is also the "founder of the faith in the new world."[41]

Binet's exaltation of Henry's Catholicism includes the presentation of his death as a good death. Here Binet echoes a tradition of writings on what constitutes an exemplary death, or the "art" of dying well.[42] Writing in an era when the Catholic Church strongly emphasized the importance of sacramental preparation for a good death, Binet seeks to show how Henry's sudden death, without benefit of sacraments or attending priests, was nevertheless exemplary. Like

Richeome, Binet highlights Henry's tears as evidence of his authentic piety: Henry often wept while praying, and "they say" (*on dit*) that at the moment of death he shed some tears; the tear made "in this case" a general confession, and the tear never deceives, for it is the "mistress of hearts" and the golden key of heaven. Thus Henry raised his eyes and his heart to God in a "kind of confession" in these last extremities. Moreover, his death was a kind of martyrdom (*une espece de martyre*), for he shed his blood in innocence. And the suddenness of his death was a "mark of predestination," for it spared him death by a long illness, or by rotting in the filth of a bed.[43]

To praise of Henry as a martyr, as innocent, as a Christ, Binet adds sainthood. Preaching not long after the regicide, Binet exhorts his audience to "hold as canonized" one who after his death is lauded even by those who had hated him. Further accenting the positive, Binet states that in losing a king "we gain a saint" whose memory is an image of all virtues and whose death an example to everyone. We may console ourselves by turning to heaven "to contemplate his glory."[44]

Of his mortal body, Henry had bequeathed his heart to the Jesuits, to the Jesuit college at La Flèche, founded by Henry.[45] Binet finds in Henry's gift evidence of his love for the Jesuits. This monarch had "engraved upon his heart a paternal love for this small Company," and he had ordered that this heart fall into Jesuit hands, and Jesuits have "planted" his heart in the midst of their hearts. For Henry knew well the oracle that says "where your treasure is there is your heart," and in giving his heart to the poor Jesuits he gave his heart to God, for what is given to the poor is given to God.[46] Addressing Henry's son and successor, Louis XIII, Binet insists that in fact the king never dies in France; for "you marry in yourself the four of your father, and the nine of your ancestor Saint Louis IX, to make thirteen, which will be the golden number that will make us relive the golden age in France."[47]

Louis XIII reigned from 1610 to 1643. In that time France did prosper in many ways, especially under Cardinal Richelieu as the king's minister (1624–42). This was also a time of prosperity and growth for Jesuits in France. Binet's 1611 funeral oration for Henry IV was reprinted in 1626 in his *Recueil des oeuvres spirituelles*; that same year saw completion and approval of plans for a large Jesuit church in Paris, the church of Saint-Louis, in what was becoming the very fashionable district of the Marais. Louis XIII laid the foundation stone in 1627, and in 1642 Richelieu celebrated the first mass in the church.[48] This church would become a place where many famous preachers preached, Louis Bourdaloue, S.J. (1632–1704) among them, and for which leading musicians, such as Marc Antoine Charpentier (1634–1704), composed masses and other music.[49]

Yet after 1640 French Jesuits faced relentless opposition from a new source: Jansenists. Inspired at least in part by the writings of Cornelius Jansen (1585–1638), and especially by his work *Augustinus*, published in 1640, these critics of the Society of Jesus lambasted Jesuits for understating the ravages of sin and the breadth and depth of human depravity. Jesuits were portrayed as soft on sin, as overstating the role of human free will in salvation, and as too lax in absolving penitents and in encouraging them to receive communion. These and other disputed points were a source of enduring polemic through the end of the seventeenth century and well into the eighteenth century. Both Jansenists and Jesuits relied heavily on the printing press to advance their positions and to refute the arguments of their opponents. Jansenists tended to seek ways to minimize central authority, whether royal or papal, while Jesuits tended to appeal to kings and popes for support against the Jansenists.[50]

Nicolas Caussin (1583–1651) was a French Jesuit who knew well the monarchy and court. For a time he was confessor to Louis XIII, until dismissed by Richelieu, at least in part because Richelieu feared that Caussin would dissuade the king from continued French involvement in (what we now call) the Thirty Years' War. Caussin was also a well-known preacher and prolific writer; his books include a life of Blessed Isabelle, the sister of Saint Louis.[51] This work was published in 1644, the same year as Caussin's *Apologie pour les religieux de la Compagnie de Iesus*, a work Caussin dedicated to the Queen Mother and Regent, Anne of Austria (1601–66).[52] At his father's death in 1643, Louis XIV was but five years old; his mother would serve as regent until his majority at the age of thirteen, in 1651.

Caussin explains to Anne that "prudence" obliges him to render to her an exact account of what Jesuits do, and of the troubles, sufferings, outrages, injuries, and persecutions they undergo.[53] Among calumnies were claims, in 1643, that French Jesuits were sending wheat to Spain at a time of shortage in France, and that Jesuits in Canada were making profits from the trade in beaver furs.[54] But the principal attacks on the Jesuits to which Caussin responds in this apology concern the Jansenists and their teachings on grace, free will, and related theological topics. Against accusations of Jesuit heresy on the doctrine of grace, Caussin cites the 1547 decree of the Council of Trent on justification by faith, in which the Council declared anathema those who deny the existence of free will after the fall of Adam and Eve. Like Trent, the Jesuits teach that God's free gift of grace in Jesus Christ is necessary for salvation, but though this grace "pushes" us to do good works, it does not "constrain" or "force" an individual's free will.[55]

Jansenists argued that they were only teaching what Saint Augustine had taught, and that Jesuits rejected Augustine in favor of Pelagianism, a heretical theology of grace that minimizes the role of grace and maximizes the possibility for human beings to earn salvation through their own meritorious works. But Caussin's approach to these questions is one that insists that Jesuits do teach what Saint Augustine taught. Jesuits "say with Saint Augustine" that "God who made us without us, does not wish to save us without us," because God wanted our salvation to be both from Him and from us, "from him in calling us, from us in consenting."[56]

Antoine Arnauld (1612–94), a leading Jansenist, published a book on "frequent communion" in 1643; it was a work that cautioned against frequent reception of communion, and lauded confessors who insisted that their penitents undergo rigorous penance before approaching the eucharist. Arnauld argued that he was only calling for fidelity to the practices of the Early Church, and he excoriated the Jesuits for their failure to prescribe rigor, and for their encouragement of excessive and easy access to the sacrament.[57] In his 1644 *Apologie*, Caussin acknowledged that Arnauld could indeed cite some support from the early centuries of the Church for his ideal of rigorous sacramental practice. But Caussin responds by arguing that, in its practices and customs, the Church had long since changed; while in its belief the Church was unchanging, in its discipline it could and did change, under the guidance of the Holy Spirit. And thus for some five hundred years councils, popes, prelates, priests, and preachers had promoted the practice of frequent communion.[58] Leaving behind a partly conciliatory tone, Caussin states that Arnauld, if followed, would destroy the reception of communion. The "exactitude" Arnauld requires of communicants, with its insistence on prior purification from every stain of even venial sins, would exclude from the sacrament James, John, and the other apostles. And Arnauld's principles will leave even "good souls" discouraged.[59]

Moving beyond Arnauld, Caussin responds to other critics of the Jesuits, including those whose "custom" it is to use the occasion of the king's death to make false accusations against the Society of Jesus. Caussin recalls and praises Père Coton for his defense of the Jesuits at the death of Henry IV, and says that he now takes up the "same commission" as Coton did, of addressing a Queen Mother shortly after the death of her most dear spouse. Caussin points out to Queen Anne of Austria that, like Henry IV, Louis XIII "protected" the Jesuits against attacks; he "will not abandon us" now that he has reached eternal life.[60] Caussin also seeks to persuade Anne that the people who attack the Jesuits in so doing also attack royal authority, including hers. The choice made by "your father-in-law" Henry IV (to support the Jesuits), and "your authority which maintains us," are challenged.[61] Some fault the Jesuits for a lavish church of Saint-Louis, as if they were in some way guilty in its building, yet this church was something that it "pleased" the recently deceased king (Louis XIII) to build in honor of Saint Louis, and to entrust to the Jesuits.[62] While we Jesuits "do not seek vengeance" against our adversaries, we desire that it please Your Majesty "to stop the evil" (*arrester le mal*) that troubles your subjects and creates scandal.[63]

Caussin brings his *Apologie* to a conclusion with praise of Anne as regent and as mother of Louis XIV. Evils would be without remedy, Caussin declares, if God had not elicited, in her person, an excellent Queen, gifted with celestial wisdom and a magnanimous heart. Addressing Anne, Caussin urges her to "shine like the dawn" that gave birth to the Sun, that is, to Louis XIV, "the highest hope that ever was in nature."[64] Eight years later Louis reached the age of thirteen, the age of majority for kings in France, and thus the age at which a young monarch could rule directly, without a regent. For the occasion of the king's majority, Caussin again dedicated a printed work to Anne of Austria, his *Eloge du Roy Louis XIV, Dieu-Donné.*

Published just months after Caussin's death, his *Eloge* of Louis XIV appeared in the era of the *Fronde*, a revolt, or more accurately a series of revolts, against the authority of the Queen Regent, and more specifically against her first minister Jules Cardinal Mazarin.[65] In the political context of 1651 in France, Caussin's publication of abundant praise of Anne and her son would surely have been seen as an effort to distance the Jesuits from any possible suspicion of involvement in or sympathy for the *Fronde*. In the event, Caussin opted for the winning side; the *Fronde* was a failure, and Louis XIV retained Mazarin as his first minister all the way to the Cardinal's death in 1661.

The term *Dieu-Donné* (God-Given) for Louis XIV points to the central theme of Caussin's *Eloge*: how God's providence is at work in the birth and life of Louis. Thus the bosom of Anne has produced "a great and divine light," a monarch who should be received as a gift from heaven.[66] Louis XIII and Anne of Austria were married in 1615; Anne gave birth to the future Louis XIV in 1638. In these many years Anne waited to give birth to a prince, Caussin finds "proof" of a divine plan. Louis XIV was for a time "hidden" in the sanctuary of divine ideas, for God "takes pleasure" in making us wait for great things so that we appreciate them. Ordinary things happen easily and right away; Adam, God's "masterpiece," came into the world after all other creatures; the patriarch Noah was born to a father over one hundred years old, and Noah brought peace to the world. And so Louis is "another Noah," for he will bring peace and heal hearts.[67]

Caussin, like Coton, Binet, and Richeome, used the printing press to promote and publicize close association of the Society of Jesus with the French monarchy. They worked hard to retain royal support, and to disseminate a public image of close alliance between the Jesuits and the monarch that could counter and discourage a broad range of attacks by opponents of the Society. Through the long reign of Louis XIV the French Jesuits did continue to prosper and to depend, in various ways, on royal support. Jesuits continued to serve as royal confessors, and royal policies in opposition to the Jansenists reflected Jesuit priorities. There was surely also a kind of Jesuit subservience to the French monarchy – the writings of a Coton or a Caussin make that clear – and a linking, for good times and bad, of monarch and Jesuits. But in the reign of Louis XV royal support would weaken, eventually giving way altogether under pressure from various factions in France, the Jansenists among them.[68] Functioning in the kingdom of France at the king's pleasure, the Jesuits could just as well be expelled if that pleasure were withdrawn. And thus the Jesuits were expelled from Louis XV's France, in the 1760s, approximately a decade before the suppression of the Society by Pope Clement XIV.

Notes

1 For an excellent study of Paris in the time of Ignatius, see Philippe Lécrivain, *Paris au temps d'Ignace de Loyola (1528–1535)* (Paris: Editions facultés jésuites de Paris, 2006).

2 On how the Parisian model (*modus parisiensis*) of education was adopted and adapted in Jesuit schools, see John O'Malley, *The First Jesuits* (Cambridge, MA : Harvard University Press, 1993), 215–25.

3 On religion and national consciousness in sixteenth-century France, see Alain Tallon, *Conscience nationale et sentiment religieux en France au XVIe siècle* (Paris: Presses Universitaires de France, 2002).

4 On the history of Jesuit schools and other Jesuit institutions in France, see Pierre Delattre, *Les établissements des jésuites en France depuis quatre siècles*, 5 vols. (Enghien: Institut supérieur de théologie,

1940–57). On Jesuit education as a part of Renaissance culture, see Luce Giard, ed., *Les jésuites à la Renaissance: Système éducatif et production du savoir* (Paris: Presses Universitaires de France, 1995).

5 On these wars, see Mack Holt, *The French Wars of Religion, 1562–1629*, 2nd edn (Cambridge: Cambridge University Press, 2005). For a general work on Jesuits in France, see Henri Fouqueray, *Histoire de la Compagnie de Jésus en France des origines à la Suppression*, 4 vols. (Paris: Bureaux des Etudes, 1910–25). The volumes completed deal with the period 1575–1645. On Jesuit institutions in France up to 1580, see A. Lynn Martin, "The Jesuit Mission to France," in Thomas McCoog, ed., *The Mercurian Project: Forming Jesuit Culture 1573–1580* (St. Louis: Institute of Jesuit Sources; Rome: Institutum Historicum Societatis Iesu, 2004), 249–93.

6 On the broader context of print and polemic in France, see Jeffrey Sawyer, *Printed Poison: Pamphlet Propaganda, Faction Politics, and the Public Sphere in Early Seventeenth-Century France* (Berkeley: University of California Press, 1990).

7 On this assassination see Nicolas Le Roux, *Un régicide au nom de Dieu: L'assassinat d'Henri III* (Paris: Gallimard, 2006). On Jesuits and tyrannicide theory, see Harro Höpfl, *Jesuit Political Thought: The Society of Jesus and the State, c. 1540–1630* (Cambridge: Cambridge University Press, 2004), 314–38; Georges Minois, *Le couteau et le poison: L'assassinat politique en Europe (1400–1800)* (Paris: Fayard, 1997), 134–41.

8 Eric Nelson, *The Jesuits and the Monarchy: Catholic Reform and Political Authority in France (1590–1615)* (Aldershot: Ashgate; Rome: Institutum Historicum Societatis Iesu, 2005).

9 Ibid., 97–99.

10 See Georges Minois, *Le confesseur du roi: Les directeurs de conscience sous la monarchie française* (Paris: Fayard, 1988).

11 Pierre Coton, *Institution catholique où est declarée et confirmée la vérité de la foy contre les hérésies et superstitions de ce temps* (Paris: Claude Chappelet, 1610). For examples of Coton as preacher, see his *Sermons sur les principales et plus difficiles matieres de la foy* (Rouen: Besongne, 1626).

12 See Nelson, *The Jesuits and the Monarchy*, 164–67.

13 Pierre Coton, *Lettre déclaratoire de la doctrine des Pères Iesuites* (Paris: Claude Chappelet, 1610).

14 Ibid., 3.

15 See discussion of Mariana in Höpfl, *Jesuit Political Thought*, 318–21; H. E. Braun, *Juan de Mariana and Early Modern Spanish Political Thought* (Aldershot: Ashgate, 2007).

16 Coton, *Lettre déclaratoire*, 3–7.

17 Ibid., 9–10. All translations of this and other works are my own unless otherwise indicated.

18 Ibid., 10–12.

19 Coton, *Oraisons devotes pour tous chrestiens et tous catholiques pour chaque iour de la sepmaine* (Paris: Eustache Foucault, 1615), 101–2, 85–86.

20 Louis Richeome, *Tres-Humble Remonstrance, et Requeste des Religieux de la Compagnie de Iesus* (Bordeaux: Millanges, 1598), 10–15.
21 Ibid., 50–60.
22 Ibid., 72–73.
23 Ibid., 97–103, 109–12, 142–47.
24 Louis Richeome, *Consolation envoyee a la Royne mere du Roy, et Regente en France* (Paris: Claude Rigaud, 1610), 2.
25 Ibid., 7–17. Even if it were true for Henry, what Richeome recounts about the king's clothing would not have applied to Henry's successor, Louis XIII, and even less to Louis XIV. See Philip Mansel, *Dressed to Rule: Royal and Court Costume from Louis XIV to Elizabeth II* (New Haven: Yale University Press, 2005).
26 On early modern Catholic critiques of Machiavelli, see Robert Bireley, *The Counter-Reformation Prince: Anti-Machiavellianism or Catholic Statecraft in Early Modern Europe* (Chapel Hill: University of North Carolina Press, 1990).
27 Machiavelli, *The Prince*, ed. Quentin Skinner and Russell Price (Cambridge: Cambridge University Press, 1988), 61–63.
28 Richeome, *Consolation*, 18–27.
29 See Michael Wolfe, *The Conversion of Henri IV: Politics, Power, and Religious Belief in Early Modern France* (Cambridge, MA: Harvard University Press, 1993), 12–21.
30 Richeome, *Consolation*, 50, 71. On the meaning of tears in the seventeenth century, see Sheila Bayne, *Tears and Weeping: An Aspect of Emotional Climate Reflected in Seventeenth-Century French Literature* (Tübingen: Narr; Paris: Editions Jean-Michel Place, 1981).
31 Richeome, *Consolation*, 35–41.
32 Ibid., 47–49. On Jesuits in Canada, see the essay by Jacques Monet in this volume.
33 Etienne Binet, *Recueil des oeuvres spirituelles du R. P. Estienne Binet*, 2nd edn (Rouen: Richard L'Allemant, 1627), 787–809. On funeral orations for Henry, see Jacques Hennequin, *Henri IV dans ses oraisons funèbres* (Paris: Klincksieck, 1977).
34 See Carlos Sommervogel, *Bibliothèque de la Compagnie de Jésus*, 9 vols. (Brussels: Schepens, 1890–1900), I: 1488–1505.
35 See René Champagne, *François de Sales ou la passion de l'autre* (Montreal and Paris: Médiaspaul, 1998), 155–56.
36 Binet, *Recueil*, 789.
37 Ibid., 790–91.
38 Ibid., 793–94.
39 Machiavelli, *The Prince*, 55–58.
40 Binet, *Recueil*, 795.
41 Ibid., 796–97.
42 On the printing press and this genre of literature in France, see Roger Chartier, *The Cultural Uses of Print in Early Modern France*, trans. Lydia Cochrane (Princeton: Princeton University Press, 1987), 32–70.
43 Binet, *Recueil*, 798–801.

44 Ibid., 802–4. Binet seems altogether unconcerned with the (slim) prospects for actual canonization of Henry by a pope. On the few canonizations in Binet's era, see Peter Burke's essay "How to Be a Counter-Reformation Saint," in his *The Historical Anthropology of Early Modern Italy: Essays on Perception and Communication* (Cambridge: Cambridge University Press, 1987), 48–62.

45 Nelson, *The Jesuits and the Monarchy*, 168.

46 Binet, *Recueil*, 806–7.

47 Ibid., 808.

48 *Saint-Paul – Saint-Louis: Les jésuites à Paris* (Paris: Musées de la Ville de Paris, 1985). After the French Revolution, what had been the Jesuit church of Saint-Louis became a parish church, adding the name of the local parish church that had been destroyed in the Revolution. For a detailed account of Jesuit history in the era of Richelieu, see Fouqueray, *Histoire de la Compagnie de Jésus en France*, vols. IV–V.

49 On Bourdaloue, see Thomas Worcester, "The Classical Sermon," in Joris van Eijnatten, *Preacher, Sermon, and Audience in the Long Eighteenth Century* (Leiden: Brill, 2008 forthcoming); on Charpentier, see C. Jane Lowe, "Charpentier and the Jesuits at St Louis," *Seventeenth-Century French Studies* 15 (1993), 297–314.

50 Cornelius Jansen, *Augustinus* (Leuven: Zegeri, 1640). The literature on Jansenism is enormous; for a good introduction, see William Doyle, *Jansenism: Catholic Resistance to Authority* (New York: St. Martin's Press, 2000).

51 On Caussin as royal confessor, see Minois, *Le confesseur du roi*, 363–74. On Caussin's life of Isabelle, see Thomas Worcester, "Neither Married nor Cloistered: Blessed Isabelle in Catholic Reformation France," *Sixteenth Century Journal* 30 (1999), 457–72.

52 There was a Paris edition as well as a Lyons edition; my citations are from the latter, *Apologie pour les religieux de la Compagnie de Iesus*, 2nd edn (Lyons, 1644).

53 Ibid., 5–9.

54 Ibid., 9–17.

55 Ibid., 23–32.

56 Ibid., 40.

57 Antoine Arnauld, *De la fréquente communion* (Paris: Vitré, 1643). On Antoine Arnauld and other prominent Jansenists in his family, see Alexander Sedgwick, *The Travails of Conscience: The Arnauld Family and the Ancien Régime* (Cambridge, MA: Harvard University Press, 1998). By the mid-1650s, Blaise Pascal emerged as the most eloquent of the Jansenist opponents of the Jesuits. On Pascal see Nicholas Hammond, ed., *The Cambridge Companion to Pascal* (Cambridge: Cambridge University Press, 2003).

58 Caussin, *Apologie*, 45–49.

59 Ibid., 50–51.

60 Ibid., 106–8.

61 Ibid., 133.

62 Ibid., 164.

63 Ibid., 147.
64 Ibid., 178–79. On the various ways in which Louis XIV's image was constructed during his long reign (1643–1715), see Peter Burke, *The Fabrication of Louis XIV* (New Haven: Yale University Press, 1992).
65 For an excellent study of this complex period, see Orest Ranum, *The Fronde: A French Revolution 1648–1652* (New York: Norton, 1993).
66 Nicolas Caussin, *Eloge du Roy Louis XIV, Dieu-Donné* (Paris: Denis Bechet, 1651), 5–7.
67 Ibid., 7–14.
68 See Dale Van Kley, *The Jansenists and the Expulsion of the Jesuits from France, 1757–1765* (New Haven: Yale University Press, 1975). See also the essay in this volume, by Jonathan Wright, on the suppression of the Society of Jesus.

7 Women Jesuits?

GEMMA SIMMONDS

WOMEN OUTSIDE THE ENCLOSURE

Attempts by women to live religious life on the Jesuit model have been fraught with difficulty since the time of Ignatius himself. The reform of female communities was a major project proceeding from the Council of Trent, involving Ignatius and his early companions in a Herculean task. The question arose of taking some of these convents under Jesuit jurisdiction. While the nuns and several of their Jesuit confessors were enthusiastic, Ignatius resisted. Of supreme importance to him was the principle of universal mission and mobility for his fledgling Society of Jesus. To tie his men down to the service of monastic houses was to act in contradiction to this identifying principle.[1] The freedom and flexibility in Ignatius' new concept of religious life for men had already given rise to substantial controversy. Given prevailing views on the place of women in society, and scandals, real or imagined, involving breaches of nuns' enclosure, he was strongly averse to violating social and moral codes with a branch of women Jesuits.

While the Jesuits were not exempt from the social prejudices and misogynistic assumptions of their time, Ignatius himself had a wide spiritual correspondence with prominent women and never hesitated to enlist their support in promoting the welfare and apostolic ministries of his nascent order.[2] The establishment of an order of "Jesuitesses" was, however, an entirely different matter. The early generation of Jesuits offered the Spiritual Exercises to women and trained them in turn to be spiritual guides to other women, and there are many instances of fruitful apostolic collaboration between Jesuits and female friends and companions.[3] In advance of their contemporaries, some gave serious consideration to a third alternative to the two options, *aut maritus aut murus*, which offered women a choice of enclosures, either monastic or domestic.[4] The outstanding personal piety and zeal of many early Jesuits inspired numerous women with a desire to imitate them. This and the dream of doing great deeds for God without retiring behind monastic walls gave rise to several attempts by women to live as Jesuits, but they could not have come at a less encouraging time in the history of the Church.

So problematic were the founder's own relations with those women who persisted in their desire to live as Jesuits that he petitioned the pope to render it impossible.[5] Despite this, both in Ignatius' lifetime and in the centuries following, attempts were made to overcome opposition within the Society of Jesus and the wider Church to the institution of a Jesuit-style order for women. The dual impediments of Tridentine legislation on the enclosure of religious women and deepseated Jesuit opposition to any kind of female "Second Order" under their jurisdiction bedeviled the desire of women to become Jesuits in the same way that others had become Benedictines, Dominicans, or Carmelites. The idea of Mary Ward (1585–1645), that women might live in the manner of Jesuits while remaining entirely autonomous, went so far beyond the imagination of her male contemporaries as to beggar their understanding.

Strict enclosure was imposed on all nuns in the Western Church from the time of Boniface VIII's (1294–1303) constitution *Periculoso*, which was confirmed at Trent. This rendered it impossible for female religious to undertake works of charity outside the monastic enclosure, with the limited exception of the education of girls. Nor was it permitted for women religious to organize themselves under a superior general or in a province of several houses. These restrictions could be avoided by sisters living as tertiaries under simple vows, but Pius V's constitution *Circa Pastoralis* (1566) confirmed Boniface and Trent and obliged tertiaries to take solemn vows and observe pontifical enclosure. Full approbation was not given to women attempting to live an apostolic life under simple vows for nearly three centuries. Further attempts to circumvent this were made by establishing lay pious associations without perpetual vows, where a common life for the effective practice of charity and the sanctification of their members was permitted.[6] While several congregations gained a measure of commendation from the Holy See in this way, none of them was granted approbation as such until Benedict XIV's constitution *Quamvis Justo* (1749), in response to a controversy concerning Mary Ward's "English Ladies."[7] This was eventually followed by Leo XIII's *Conditae* (1900), which legislated for congregations of simple vows under either diocesan authority or pontifical law.

IGNATIUS AND WOMEN

Ignatius relied not only on the donations of wealthy benefactresses but also on their social patronage in securing the good graces of powerful local interests when establishing his colleges. This friendship was sometimes bought at a high price. His reluctance to involve himself with female aspirants to the Jesuit life stemmed in particular from two episodes involving Isabel Roser and the Spanish Infanta Juana of Austria.

Isabel, a widowed early benefactress from Barcelona, resolved to move to Rome with two companions in 1542 in order to place herself under obedience to Ignatius. When Ignatius resisted her pleas she petitioned the pope to allow her to make profession in the Society of Jesus and to oblige Ignatius to accept her vows. The petition was granted and in 1545 she and her companions made their solemn profession as Jesuits into Ignatius' hands. Difficulties arose almost immediately, for Isabel was as rash as she was determined. The affair culminated in Isabel and her nephews, who stood to inherit her fortune, accusing Ignatius of misappropriation of goods.[8] A court hearing resolved the matter in favour of Ignatius, who successfully appealed first to have the sisters' vows commuted to vows of obedience to the diocesan bishop and then to free the Jesuits in perpetuity from the spiritual direction of women living together in community and wishing to place themselves under obedience to his Society.[9] This was not the last attempt by women to enter the Society but Ignatius, forewarned by this experience and similar troubles he observed among the Dominicans and Franciscans, remained adamant.[10]

It proved less easy to resist the determination of Juana of Austria, daughter to Charles V and sister to Philip II, to live as a Jesuit. A deeply religious woman of high intelligence and considerable political acumen, she is the only female in history to have become a member of the Society of Jesus under permanent vows.[11] In 1554 the emperor appointed her regent of Spain during Philip's marriage to Mary Tudor. Under the spiritual guidance of Francis Borgia the young widow lived in the palace of Valladolid as in a monastery and rapidly fell under the Jesuit spell. Her petition to enter the Society had to be taken seriously, and Ignatius appointed a commission to consider it. In strictest secrecy and with certain stipulations the Infanta, under the code name of Mateo Sánchez, was admitted as a Jesuit until her death in 1573, but this remains a unique case.[12]

MARY WARD, 1585–1645

Mary Ward's attempt to found a Jesuit-style congregation for women in the early seventeenth century fell foul both of post-Tridentine rulings on the enclosure of religious women and of Ignatius' strictures against a female branch of the Society of Jesus. Born into an English recusant family, Mary was one year old when the York butcher's wife, Margaret Clitherow, was pressed to death for harboring priests. Margaret belonged, as did Mary and her family, to an extended network of Catholic women who were inspired by the example of the English martyrs and the zeal of visiting underground priests to live a life of passionate commitment to their faith.[13] Despite there being no religious houses left in Britain, many of these recusant families lived according to an almost monastic regime within their homes, and became familiar with the Ignatian Spiritual Exercises through the ministry of itinerant Jesuits. These women experienced community life and assumed positions of religious leadership within the prisons where recusants followed, as best they could, a life of common prayer and religious instruction. Outside the prisons it was often less risky for Jesuits and other priests to seek the collaboration of women than of men, and a generation of women emerged such as Dorothy Vavasour, Anne Vaux, and Luisa de Carvajal who, at great risk to themselves, lived at the service of the Church while not being professed religious.[14]

Intent upon embracing a way of life now lost to Catholic Englishwomen, Mary fled to St-Omer, then in the Spanish Netherlands, in order to enter the strictest monastery she could find. Convinced that "women did not know how to do good except to themselves," she entered a monastery of Poor Clares at the instigation of her Jesuit confessor, first as an extern sister and later as the founder of a monastery for Englishwomen in Gravelines.[15]

Unfolding insights

This much-desired solitude and withdrawal from the world was to prove a false dream. In a letter of 1620 Mary Ward outlines her journey from a monastic to an apostolic vocation:

> it seemed to me most perfect to take the most austere Order, that a soul might give herself to God not in part but altogether, since I saw not how a religious woman could do good to more than herself alone. To teach children seemed then too much distraction . . . nor was of that perfection and importance as therefore to hinder

that quiet and continual communication with God which strict enclosure afforded.

To her dismay she came to understand that God was calling her to "some other thing," as yet unimagined, and, after a period of discernment under the guidance of her Jesuit confessor Roger Lee, she left the monastery.[16] In contrast with the story of Ignatius' early devotees, she expresses no initial attraction towards Ignatius himself nor to the Jesuit way of life. She was only aware that this "other thing" was not any other form of religious life currently on offer. In 1606 she returned to London, having made a vow of chastity, and did what apostolic work she could within the Catholic underground networks. A powerful mystical insight, known as the "Glory Vision," convinced her that she was not to be a Carmelite, as urged by her confessor, but that the "assured good thing," to which God was drawing her, would be greatly to God's glory. The Ignatian resonances of this experience are not lost on present-day commentators, but they shed no great light for Mary. With a group of companions, most of whom were related to members of the recent Gunpowder Plot, she set sail again for St-Omer in 1609, where they determined to live as religious. Their inability to clarify what sort of religious life they were to embark upon led to acute difficulty.

> Great instance was made by divers spiritual and learned men that we would take upon us some Rule already confirmed, several Rules were procured by our friends ... and earnestly urged to make choice of some of them. But they seemed not that which God would have done, and the refusal of them all caused much persecution, and the more because I denied all and could not say in what particular I desired or found myself called unto.

Clarity was not long in coming. In 1611 Mary received an intellectual understanding that she and her companions were to "'Take the same of the Society,' so understood as that we were to take the same both in matter and in manner, that only excepted which God, by diversity of sex, hath prohibited."[17]

Mary and her companions felt considerable relief to have discovered God's will at last. Their Jesuit neighbors and other advisors reacted with predictable horror, some at the thought of unenclosed female religious on the loose, others because they interpreted this as an attempt to live under Jesuit jurisdiction in the manner forbidden by Jesuit Constitution 588 after the Isabel Roser affair.[18]

Deciding to use the name Society of Jesus, as female Carmelites or Benedictines used the name of their male counterparts, gave rise to further objections.

> My confessor resisted, all the Society opposed, various plans were drawn up by several persons . . . These were . . . pressed upon us; there was no remedy but to refuse them. This caused infinite troubles. Then they would needs that at least we should take the name of some Order confirmed, or some new one, or any we could think of, but not that of Jesus. This the fathers of the Society urged exceedingly, and still do so every day, telling us that though they recognise that we will not be satisfied unless we take their Constitutions at least in substance, nevertheless they are unwilling that we use the same name or the same written form for our Rule.[19]

An initial attempt was made by Roger Lee to draw up a rule, but, while exhibiting certain Ignatian features, this proved too cautious and monastic for Mary.[20] In 1615 she received further spiritual confirmation, through the "Just Soul Vision," of the "singular freedom . . . entire application and apt disposition to all good works" in which she and her sisters were being called to live out this new apostolic vocation.[21]

The confidence afforded by this vision emboldened Mary to draw up a second plan, the *Ratio Instituti*, to be presented for papal approval to Paul V in 1616. By this time her companions had multiplied, and her understanding of a call to the apostolic life had made Mary insist on freedom from enclosure and from monastic practices and dress. The apostolic aims had spread from the education of girls to "the salvation of our neighbour . . . by any other means that are congruous to the times." The plan stresses two major innovations in governance: freedom from episcopal authority and the corresponding role of the General Superior.

Reactions

The Jesuits themselves showed a marked ambivalence towards Mary Ward's "English Ladies," referred to by many as "Jesuitesses." They received support from the likes of Roger Lee and from John Gerard, who had experience of women's apostolic potential from the English mission.[22] From others there was implacable opposition.[23] Jesuit ambivalence is illustrated by the fact that two illustrious Jesuit canonists were consulted on the legality of Mary Ward's venture. Lessius judged that it was legitimate, Suarez that it was not.[24] The Superior General, Claudio Aquaviva, denied that the English Ladies were sisters and forbade his men to direct the community. His successor, Muzio Vitelleschi, often showed personal kindness and support for Mary and her companions' work as long as it remained that of a pious association. Any mention of an order of Jesuitesses drew his unswerving opposition.[25] This was not only because of Constitution 588 but also because the English Ladies became weapons in the campaign waged against the Jesuits by secular clergy and Benedictines on the English mission. The secular clergy's instinctive mistrust of Jesuit innovations was only exacerbated by the unprecedented freedoms claimed by these "Galloping Girls," whom some did not hesitate to accuse of immorality, financial irregularity, and usurping priestly functions.[26] Mary Ward was undeterred and proceeded to open houses in other cities, including London, where her companions worked on the English mission and drew from George Abbot, Archbishop of Canterbury, the criticism that she "did more hurt than six or seven Jesuits." The comment provoked her into visiting Lambeth Palace and, on finding His Grace absent, leaving her signature carved with a diamond on a window pane.[27]

Catholic bishops were as divided as the Jesuits. Some welcomed Mary Ward's foundations in their dioceses, others objected either on canonical or juridical grounds when secular rulers supported the Jesuitesses on their territory.[28] Her years of apostolic experience convinced Mary not only of the aptness of women for the Jesuit way of life, but of the fundamental equality of women and men before God, a theological insight not universally shared at the time. Ascribing one Jesuit's conviction that women were not able to comprehend God as men are to his lack of experience, she urged her companions to be fearless in believing that women could "do great matters."[29] There is little mention of Ignatius in Mary Ward's writings.[30] While she and her sisters sought Jesuit confessors they were fully aware of the Society's ambivalence towards them and at no point sought to vow obedience to it.[31] It was the spirit of the *Exercises* and the *Constitutions*, especially their introductory *Formula*, outlining the innovatory freedoms in this way of life, by which they felt inspired and to which they felt called directly by God.

While members of differing nationalities increased and communities opened and flourished across Europe Mary realized the urgent need to have her Institute confirmed.[32] Deciding to plead her cause in person, she set out in 1621 with a few companions on foot across the Alps, braving the outbreak of war and plague and treacherous conditions in order to present her plan to the pope. While there were initial signs of approval for the companions' work among girls and women, including the reflection that if it continued so successfully it would put the brothels of Rome out of business, it became clear that canonical approval for an order of female Jesuits would not easily be forthcoming.[33]

In 1622 Mary wrote a two-page memorandum entitled *Reasons Why We May Not Change*, outlining her conviction that the Jesuit way of life, approved by the Church, was suitable for women and had been successfully tested over time by the virtuous lives and effective apostolates of her sisters. Appealing to social changes and their own experience she argued the need for a new form of religious life for women.[34] The appeals and arguments fell on deaf ears.

Suppression

Convinced that this enterprise was of God and could not be withstood, and deceived by Urban VIII's practised diplomatic shifts, Mary continued to hope that papal approval would come. While encouraging her to her face, the pope was preparing the suppression of Mary Ward's Jesuitesses and he set about ordering the closure of the houses and dispersal of the sisters.

Mary could not believe that this was being done by papal order and on 6 April 1630 wrote a letter to the houses in Trier, Cologne, and Liège urging the sisters to resist any attempt by enemies to bypass the pope and suppress their communities.[35] This and the visit to Liège by her loyal but impulsive Vicar, Winefrid Wigmore, to prevent the closure of the community, were to prove her undoing.[36] Both appeared to be urging disloyalty to the Church and to be placing Mary's authority as Superior General above that of the pope and his representatives. Some sisters submitted to the order of suppression; others, including senior figures, had abandoned the Jesuitesses when the storm broke. Winefrid and those remaining were interrogated in a manner that could not fail to confuse women uneducated in the refinements of theology and canon law.[37] Mary Ward made one final attempt to explain the Jesuitess vocation to Urban VIII and to appeal for justice, but, when she received no answer, wrote ordering all sisters, in the event of suppression, to obey without question.[38] This did not save her from being arrested and imprisoned in Munich on a charge of heresy, schism, and rebellion against the Church.[39]

The catastrophe of Mary Ward's imprisonment and the suppression of her congregation reverberated far beyond their immediate group. Sisters of various nationalities were rendered homeless and left without dowries to enable them to return home and marry or enter other orders.[40] The church authorities were unable to distinguish between Mary Ward's Jesuitesses, Ursulines, and members of other small groups and pious institutes who were living in legitimate communities and teaching girls. All were caught in the backlash of the storm that broke over the English Ladies.[41]

The bull of suppression, *Pastoralis Romani Pontificis*, destroyed any hope of establishing an order of unenclosed women religious in imitation of the Jesuits. The extreme violence of its language exhibits a deep-seated hostility to any attempt by women to transcend social and theological boundaries imposed on them.[42] A chilling reference to the question of a quiet judicial execution shows that Mary considered it a real possibility.[43] Once released from prison, her life was severely restricted by the surveillance of the Inquisition. Her homeless and destitute remaining sisters, whose status as unenclosed religious was thought so dangerous to their chastity, were forbidden to seek safety in residing together. In time they gathered into houses in Munich, Liège, Rome, and York, where Mary died during the English Civil War in 1645, the dream of a female branch of the Jesuits apparently destroyed forever.[44]

Aftermath

The "poisonous growths in the church of God" had been torn up by the roots, as the bull demanded, but their extinction "lest they spread themselves further" was not achieved. The handful of survivors in time became a network of apostolic women inspired by the Jesuit charism, dedicated to female education and devoted to the disgraced foundress.[45]

Subsequent attempts at canonical approval always foundered on the rock of *Pastoralis Romani Pontificis*. While attitudes to women and structures in the Church and society had changed, no pope felt able to rescind Urban VIII's ban on Mary Ward's English Ladies. Communities spread across Europe and eventually beyond, but recognition came slowly. In 1703 Clement XI's brief *Inscrutabili* ruled "Let women be governed by women" and approved eighty-one rules of Jesuit inspiration, while in 1749 Benedict XIV's Apostolic Constitution *Quamvis Justo* confirmed the office of Superior General not only for the surviving Institute but for all similar women's congregations of the future.[46] The price for this concession was to deny Mary Ward the name of foundress. It was as if she were disgraced all over again. Precious documents were destroyed, the *Painted Life*, a series of paintings depicting Mary's spiritual odyssey, was hidden away, but her memory and founding dream remained strong.

It even gave rise to the foundation in Ireland of a second branch of the order, known as Loreto Sisters, which, like the original remnant, spread across continents and into a third, North American, branch.[47] Given the enmity shown Mary Ward by the secular clergy, Jesuits and Benedictines, it is satisfying to note that her final rehabilitation by the Church and the confirmation of what was by then known as the Institute of the Blessed Virgin Mary was brought about in 1909 by a coalition of support from all three constituencies in collaboration with sisters of both branches.[48]

In 1979 and 1983 respectively, the oldest two branches of the IBVM were permitted to adopt edited forms of the Jesuit Constitutions.[49] Changes in canon law encouraged the first branch to adopt the fullest possible text, including the Jesuit fourth vow of universal mission, in 2003.[50] With this came a change of name. Its precarious formal status meant that Mary Ward's Institute had no stable name until the late nineteenth century. She herself had styled her group "Mothers of the Society of Jesus," and had always believed that God wished the name of Jesus to be included in their title.[51] In a compromise which honored both this wish and the autonomy of the Jesuits, the name of the first branch changed to Congregation of Jesus. Nearly four hundred years after the first foundation in St-Omer, Mary's dream was achieved in full.

JEAN-PIERRE MÉDAILLE: AN ATTEMPT FROM WITHIN

Even in Mary's lifetime, the situation in France was markedly more open to active apostolates for women. The 1516 Concordat, signed between Pope Leo X and Francis I, made the king effective head of the Church in France. The resulting assertion of Gallican privileges over Roman authority meant the delay in promulgating the decrees of the Council of Trent (1545–63) in France until 1615. The strong position of bishops within their own dioceses also had a profound effect on the development of new forms of religious life for women.[52] The early and mid seventeenth century saw the rapid spread of missions to the de-Christianized countryside by religious orders such as the Lazarists and the Jesuits, bent on regaining France for Catholicism. In an era marred by civil war, famine, and widespread disorder, reforming bishops like Francis de Sales and missionary religious like Francis Régis and Vincent de Paul realized the essential role that women could play in the nurturing of faith and the pastoral care of rural and urban poor alike. It became an era of unprecedented collaboration between clergy and women.

The Tridentine insistence on enclosure was an obstacle that must be overcome. The chief focus of Francis de Sales and Jane Frances de Chantal's new order of the Visitation became the holiness of its members. Their original desire for sisters to engage in apostolic activity fell victim to prevailing restrictions. The essence of Vincent de Paul and Louise de Marillac's Daughters of Charity was the sisters' mission to the poor. They were prepared to trade religious status for apostolic freedom, and won it by ensuring that the sisters took private vows, renewable annually, thus keeping them outside the canonical status of religious that necessitated enclosure. A number of bishops and priests were to take similar steps with women in their dioceses who felt drawn to an apostolic form of consecrated life.[53] One of the most remarkable instances of this was the collaboration between a Jesuit missioner, Jean-Pierre Médaille, and Henry de Maupas, bishop of Le Puy, as spiritual and juridical founders of a group of women who were to become the Petite Congrégation des Filles de Saint-Joseph.[54]

The *grand siècle* of Louis XIV was preceded by years of religious and civil wars. The sick and poor, urban and peasant, suffered horrifically and few institutions existed to bring them relief. Towns and cities established hospitals, while the spiritual elites of the Jesuit sodalities and the secretive Compagnie du Saint-Sacrement included in their ranks influential citizens determined to improve the lot of the destitute.[55] One of the most effective weapons in the Jesuits' assault on unfaith was the Marian Congregations, which gathered dukes and merchants, servants and artisans in whole-hearted commitment to faith and charity. Women also aspired to pray and work in the Congregations and the origins of the Sisters of Saint Joseph lie in service in the town hospital of the *Hôtel-Dieu* of Le Puy and the Ignatian inspiration of the Congregations.[56]

Médaille and Maupas never intended to found a religious order and were at pains to protect the members from enclosure by stressing their lay status.[57] With a mixed affiliation, including *agrégées*, women living self-sufficient lives in small rural communities, they wore the dress of widows, not nuns, and their chief purpose was to live devout lives in the service of the sick and destitute. Jesuit spirituality had already inspired Anne de Xaintonge, who concealed her desire to found an order on the Jesuit model by adopting the approved Ursuline rule.[58] There was no question of the Sisters of Saint Joseph wanting or attempting to be "Jesuitesses," although many communities sprang up in places where the Jesuits had settled.[59] Begun in 1649, within a generation they had spread widely through central France, and in 1651 royal Letters Patent guaranteed their rule and name but stressed the private nature of their consecration.[60] Médaille did not escape the censure of his contemporaries and the concern of the Jesuit Superior General for his involvement with this group of women, but the writings of the man described by his contemporaries as a "born missionary" show the high value he placed on women as socially committed evangelizers and his conscious attempt to transpose the Jesuit *Constitutions* for the female condition.[61]

The rule he provided for the sisters was a simplified summary, lacking their canonical status and thus less dangerous to adopt, yet inspired by *Constitutions* part VII, which by implication opened all apostolates to women save the priesthood itself.[62] The rule stressed that, for the Sisters of Saint Joseph, apostolic action was the true expression of the mystical life for this "*corps sans corps ... congrégation sans congrégation ... religion* (i.e., religious order) *sans religion*."[63] Apostolic endeavor was the founding principle and the driving force that mostly saved the congregation from later impulses towards monastic assimilation.[64] Their model of community was that of Jesuits dispersed on mission, and in the *sœurs agrégées*, whose vow of stability expressed their attachment to the congregation and its apostolate, we find the Jesuit figure of the spiritual coadjutor making the preferential choice to follow Christ.[65]

The Ignatian spirit endured to the extent of an eighteenth-century sister becoming a famed proponent of the Spiritual Exercises.[66] Considered by Médaille to be religious without a cloister, as with Mary Ward's foundation, subsequent generations would introduce a more monastic spirit and structures, and as their Ignatian roots grew more distant, so did the sisters also lose the poor as the predominant *locus* of their life.[67] The location of their apostolates, whether boarding schools, homes for the mentally ill, or prisons for Magdalenes, came to be centered within the sisters' homes, and it took the Revolution to return them to the establishment of small community groups, defined by their social goal and Ignatian origin, spread today in a worldwide federation.

CONCLUSION

The fate of Mary Ward's attempt to found an order of "women Jesuits" has been seen as the tragic outcome of an untimely prophetic vision or the mistake of a woman who could not accept the Church of her time as it was. Her French contemporaries had more room for maneuver in allowing women to live and work like Jesuits and Jesuits to collaborate with women. Future generations would struggle and compromise for survival, waiting four centuries for the institutional Church to catch up with the charism. The existence today of so many Ignatian women's congregations owes an unparalleled debt to the determined vision of some remarkable pioneering spirits both within the Society of Jesus and beyond it.

Abbreviations

Chron. Juan Alfonso de Polanco, *Vita Ignatii Loiolae et Rerum Societatis Iesu Historica [Chronicon]*, 6 vols. (Madrid: Typographorum Societas, 1894–98).

MI Font. Doc. *Monumenta Ignatiana. Fontes Documentales de S. Ignatio de Loyola* (Rome: Institutum Historicum Societatis Iesu, 1977)

Notes

1 *Saint Ignatius Loyola: Letters to Women*, ed. Hugo Rahner, trans. Kathleen Pond and S. A. H. Weetman (Edinburgh and London, Nelson, 1960), 253–54.

2 Ibid., 173–247; Cándido de Dalmases, *Ignatius of Loyola, Founder of the Jesuits: His Life and Work*, trans. Jerome Aixalá (St. Louis: Institute of Jesuit Sources, 1985), 88.

3 *Chron.*, ii:21, ii: 683–84.

4 *Saint Ignatius Loyola: Letters to Women*, 251, 260.

5 *MI Font. Doc.*, 696–711.

6 This was the case for the Daughters of Charity and the Ursulines, whose rule was the first in the Western Church written by a woman for women living outside monastic enclosure, although they accepted enclosure in the early seventeenth century in order to be recognized as nuns.

7 Mary Wright, *Mary Ward's Institute: The Struggle for Identity* (Sydney: Crossing, 1997), 70–77.

8 See William W. Meissner, *Ignatius of Loyola: The Psychology of a Saint* (New Haven: Yale University Press, 1992), 260–70.

9 *MI Font. Doc.*, 696–711; *Saint Ignatius Loyola: Letters to Women*, 262–95. Rahner's references to the "imprudent zeal of women," their "nervous hysteria" or "masculine intelligence" betray his own mind-set, but all sources agree that the disastrous Roser episode did lasting damage to the cause of female Jesuits.

10 *Saint Ignatius Loyola: Letters to Women*, 304–10, 315–24; Dalmases, *Ignatius of Loyola*, 253–55.

11 *Saint Ignatius Loyola: Letters to Women*, 52.

12 Ibid., 52–67.

13 Margaret and Mary shared the same spiritual director, Father John Mush. See James Walsh, "Introduction," in Gillian Orchard, ed., *Till God Will: Mary Ward through Her Writings* (London: Darton, Longman & Todd, 1985), xi–xvii.

14 See Philip Caraman, ed., *The Other Face: Catholic Life Under Elizabeth I* (London: Longmans, 1960), 135, 198–203; Jennifer Cameron, *A Dangerous Innovator: Mary Ward (1585–1645)* (Strathfield, NSW: St. Paul's, 2000), 14–18, 75–76.

15 Orchard, *Till God Will*, 9, 11–21.

16 Ibid., 23–25. Lee was to suffer Jesuit censure for his support, see Cameron, *A Dangerous Innovator*, 88–89.

17 Orchard, *Till God Will*, 27–29, 60–61.

18 Immolata Wetter, *Mary Ward: Under the Shadow of the Inquisition*, trans. Bernadette Ganne and Patricia Harris (Oxford: Way Books, 2006), 20–22.

19 Orchard, *Till God Will*, 33.

20 Ibid., 33–39. See also Francis Edwards, ed., *The Elizabethan Jesuits: Historia Missionis Anglicanae Societatis Jesu (1660) of Henry More* (London: Phillimore, 1981), 337–38; Wetter, *Mary Ward*, 23.

21 Orchard, *Till God Will*, 39–40, 43–46.

22 Gerard lent Mary his copy of the Jesuit *Constitutions* from which she drew her final and most Ignatian plan. A loose cannon, his lack of prudence was to cause Mary Ward's sisters considerable trouble. Gerard's support did not survive the suppression of the Institute. See Philip Caraman, ed., *John Gerard: The Autobiography of an Elizabethan* (London: Longmans, 1951); Henriette Peters, *Mary Ward: A World in Contemplation*, trans. Helen Butterworth (Leominster: Gracewing, 1994), 218–21; and Wetter, *Mary Ward*, 23–25 and 35–36.

23 Orchard, *Till God Will*, 48–50, 69, and Peters, *Mary Ward*, 468, n. 2, 121–22.

24 Cameron, *A Dangerous Innovator*, 93–94; Peters, *Mary Ward*, 145–57.

25 Cameron, *A Dangerous Innovator*, 123–24; Peters, *Mary Ward*, 326, 408, 485, 522.

26 Orchard, *Till God Will*, 48–50, 69; Cameron, *A Dangerous Innovator*, 118–23. Mary Ward, described as *"vergine d'animo virile,"* was accused of behaving like a priest, driving round Europe in a carriage and pretending to be a duchess *incognita*. See Peters, *Mary Ward*, 468–69.

27 Peters roundly disputes this famous tale, in her *Mary Ward*, 162.

28 Ibid., 183, 449–50, 495–96; Cameron, *A Dangerous Innovator*, 139–140; Wetter, *Mary Ward*, 31.

29 Orchard, *Till God Will*, 55–60.

30 In Rome at the time of Ignatius' canonization, Mary makes no mention of it. See Cameron, *A Dangerous Innovator*, 115.

31 Peters, *Mary Ward*, 438–40.

32   Cameron, *A Dangerous Innovator*, 101–10, 125–36.

33   Orchard, *Till God Will*, 71–77.

34   Peters, *Mary Ward*, 332.

35   To women brought up in a country without bishops the finer points of hierarchical authority were not always clear. See Wetter, *Mary Ward*, 33–35.

36   Ibid., 39–41.

37   Ibid., 42–58.

38   Ibid., 68–72. Peters remarks that it was this submission to the pope that proved her a true Jesuitess. See Peters, *Mary Ward*, 565.

39   Peters, *Mary Ward*, 569; Wetter, *Mary Ward*, 74. Imprisoned near the same time as Mary, Galileo has received apologies from the Church so far lacking to the female innovator.

40   Peters, *Mary Ward*, 515.

41   Ibid., 474–80; Wetter, *Mary Ward*, 147–57.

42   Wetter, *Mary Ward*, 129–40, 213–18; Peters, *Mary Ward*, 566.

43   Orchard, *Till God Will*, 107.

44   Wetter, *Mary Ward*, 164–73; Orchard, *Till God Will*, 117–21.

45   Cameron, *A Dangerous Innovator*, 157–61.

46   Ibid., 203–5; Wright, *Mary Ward's Institute*, 53–86, 196–217. See also Wetter, *Mary Ward*, 196–98.

47   Wetter, *Mary Ward*, 199–203. The North American and Irish branches amalgamated in 2004 and are now known as the Institute of the Blessed Virgin Mary.

48   Ibid., 203–11.

49   Cameron, *A Dangerous Innovator*, 161–62.

50   A remarkable concession, given that not all Jesuits are permitted to take it.

51   See Cameron, *A Dangerous Innovator*, 99–100, and Peters, *Mary Ward*, 488. Cf. John W. Padberg, ed., *The Constitutions of the Society of Jesus and their Complementary Norms* (St. Louis: Institute of Jesuit Sources, 1996), 3 #1.

52   See Alain Tallon, *La France et le concile de Trente (1518–1563)* (Rome: Ecole française de Rome, 1997), 219–47.

53   Marguerite Vacher, *Des 'régulières' dans le siècle: les sœurs de Saint-Joseph du Père Médaille aux XVIIe et XVIIIe siècles* (Clermont-Ferrand: Adosa, 1991), 33–37.

54   Keen to emphasize its hiddenness and humility, in emulation of the secret Catholic confraternities of his day, Médaille called the enterprise his *"petit dessein."* See Vacher, *Des 'régulières' dans le siècle*, 366.

55   Both were much involved with the *dévot* party, combining pro-Catholic political aims with personal devotion and good works. See Alain Tallon, *La Compagnie du Saint-Sacrement, 1629–1667: Spiritualité et société* (Paris: Cerf, 1990); Raoul Allier, *La cabale des dévots, 1627–1666* (Paris: Colin, 1902); Louis Chatellier, *L'Europe des dévots* (Paris: Flammarion, 1987).

56   See Anne Hennessy, "In Search of a Founder: The Life and Spiritual Setting of Jean-Pierre Médaille SJ, Founder of the Sisters of St. Joseph"

(unpublished dissertation, Berkeley, 1988, 160–82), and Vacher, *Des 'régulières' dans le siècle*, 86–94.

57 Vacher, *Des 'régulières' dans le siècle*, 101–5.

58 Ibid., 36.

59 Ibid., 161–63.

60 Ibid., 107, 129–36; Hennessy, "In Search of a Founder," 178–83.

61 Vacher, *Des 'régulières' dans le siècle*, 65, 126, 135, 141, 367; Hennessy, "In Search of a Founder," 188–90.

62 Vacher, *Des 'régulières' dans le siècle*, 318.

63 Ibid., 110–18, 151, 202, 207–8.

64 Attempts were made to assimilate the congregation to the pattern of the Visitation order, but the apostolate prevailed as a ruling principle. See Vacher, *Des 'régulières' dans le siècle*, 307.

65 Ibid., 320, 359. Cf. the English Jesuitess "Sister Dorothea" living her consecration and apostolate in anonymity; Cameron, *A Dangerous Innovator*, 94–97. Jesuit spiritual coadjutors do not take the fourth vow, a vow of apostolic mobility.

66 Ibid., 260–61.

67 Ibid., 122, 190–201, 368–69. A new version of the sisters' Constitutions, printed in Vienne in 1694, was considerably more monastic in tone. The Vienne community would eventually seek enclosure. See 207–8, 247–51, 339, 352, 359, 370–72. This may also reflect a certain ambivalence towards the poor within the Compagnie du Saint-Sacrement itself, which aimed at the same time to embrace Christ in the poor and contain them as a potentially disruptive social element. See also Tallon, *La Compagnie du Saint-Sacrement*, 141–57.

8 Jesuits in Poland and eastern Europe

STANISŁAW OBIREK

INTRODUCTION

It is hard to believe that at the time when almost all European countries were facing violent religious conflicts Poland welcomed different dissidents in faith. This fact is well known in Polish historiography and is seen as a symbol for Polish tolerance. In fact Poland received Italian Antitrinitarians, German Lutherans, Dutch Mennonites, English Quakers, and Huguenots – all those who were denied religious freedom in their own countries.[1] We might have in mind today's America; nevertheless, it was, as a matter of fact, Catholic Poland, but of the sixteenth century! We have to add that it was a different Poland and a different Catholicism, closer to the England of Henry VIII than to Rome. A good illustration for that is the primate of Poland, Jakob Uchanski, who was not very concerned by the possibility of being put on trial by Pope Paul IV in 1559, and who was justly seen as "a potential head of the Polish national church."[2] It was also about that Poland that Erasmus of Rotterdam, having many friends there, said *Polonia mea est*, and his influence on the Polish Reformation and Counter-Reformation is well known.[3] Perhaps also the humanistic education,[4] which Jesuits were propagating, contributed to his popularity.[5] In any case, it was clear that when Cardinal Stanislaw Hosius, one of the most prominent representatives of Counter-Reformation tendencies in the Polish Church, and an active participant at the Council of Trent (1546–63), invited them in the year 1564, his dream was to use Jesuits for fighting against Reformation. At that time Hosius was considered to be one of the candidates for the papacy, mainly because of his rigid position towards the Reformation.

This date is important because the Society of Jesus was already different from the Jesuits as founded in 1540 by Ignatius Loyola: "The Society in 1565 was different in important respects from what it was in 1540 ... The Society conformed to the inevitable laws of sociology affecting any group that grows rapidly from an informal bonding among friends to a worldwide organization numbering its members in the thousands."[6] Hosius had had an occasion to meet representatives of this new and dynamic religious order at the Council of Trent, among them some (for example Diego Laínez) who were strongly supporting papal authority. This powerful organization was seen as a providential tool in the battle against Reformation.

The reasons for looking for help from the outside were many. There was the growing popularity of the new religious ideas among Polish and particularly Lithuanian Catholics, where the powerful Radziwill family gave full support to the Calvinist Church. Also, the first officially Lutheran country in Europe was founded in the year 1525 in the neighborhood of Poland: Prussia, with an important intellectual center in Königsberg. At that time the Polish episcopate was more interested in politics than in religious renovation of the Church. This fact is understandable if we remember that Polish Catholic bishops were, automatically, members of the parliament, and the primate of Poland had an important function during the period between the death of a king and the election of a new one as *interrex* – responsible for the legal aspect of the new king's election.

HISTORIOGRAPHY: BETWEEN PAMPHLETS AND APOLOGY

In 1963 Janusz Tazbir published an anthology, *Anti-Jesuit Literature in Poland 1578–1625*, which gave an interesting view of the negative image of the Jesuits in sixteenth- and seventeenth-century Poland.[7] This anthology was the main source of information about the Society of Jesus in Poland for years. Most likely, the beginning of a new approach toward the Catholic Church *per se* was possible only after the collapse of Communism in central Europe in 1989. It is worth mentioning some themes that were considered at the conference organized in 1991 in Cracow and afterwards published: The political aspect of the Polish Jesuit theater; The Renaissance and Jesuit humanism; Marcin Poczobut, S. J., and the Catholic Enlightenment; The role of the works by Father Piotr Skarga, S. J., in the heritage of St. Dymitr from Rostow and other Russian writers; Father Piotr Skarga's vision of the Church of the East; The vision of the state in the sermons by Father Piotr Skarga (it was not accidental that such vast attention was dedicated to Peter Skarga; later we will consider his impact on central and eastern European Catholicism); The role of the Polish Jesuits in educational work from 1565 to 1773; The role of the Jesuits in the musical culture of the seventeenth-century

Polish Republic.[8] In fact Janusz Tazbir, one of the leading Polish historians, wrote in his article on "Anti-Jesuit Literature in Poland" that there is need for a new perspective in dealing with the Jesuits' past: "For a long time there were those who looked on [Jesuits'] history through panegyrical glasses, others only through pamphlets. Today we try to take the middle road, remembering that only indifference kills. In fact, pamphlets are usually written only about movements and people that leave a permanent sign on the history of politics and culture."[9] If we take the number of pamphlets written against the Jesuits as a measure for their political and cultural importance we will be surprised. It is enough to think of the extraordinary popularity of *Monita Secreta*, written by the former Polish Jesuit Hieronim Zahorowski,[10] which became a world bestseller and a source for many slanderous stereotypes about the Jesuits.

A look into the pamphlets written against the Jesuits gives us a more precise idea of why the Jesuits were so controversial in the Polish Kingdom: they were seen as an alien element in Polish society and too close to the royal court. But of course these two reasons do not explain the whole phenomenon. An interesting book was published in the year 1872 by Stanisław Załęski[11] under the provocative title *Was Poland Destroyed by Jesuits?* Nevertheless, that book does not really help us to comprehend the history of the black legend of the Jesuits.

THE FIRST GENERATION

The establishment of the Jesuits in Poland in the sixteenth century was not easy. Although the first Jesuit, Alfonso Salmerón, arrived in Poland in the year 1555, he was made to feel unwanted, since his efforts to meet King Sigismund Augustus were unsuccessful. In a letter to Ignatius of Loyola he complained not only of the Polish beer, but also of the general lack of interest in inviting Jesuits into the Polish Commonwealth. His memorandum delayed the arrival of the Jesuits in Poland by nearly a decade.[12] A few years later, Peter Canisius was no more fortunate, despite his personal charm and the fact that he had made friends with a considerable number of humanists in Poland. Nevertheless, his memories of Poland and of the Polish people were always affectionate, and he dreamed of being able to return to that country: "If my superiors were to allow it I would be glad to stay in Poland for the rest of my life."[13] Given that Canisius was called the "second Apostle of Germany," his opinion is particularly interesting.[14]

When the Jesuits finally arrived in Poland, they rapidly became the most dynamic element in the confrontation with the Reformation movement,[15] in various ways from education to court preaching. The most decisive impact on this process was that of the first generation of Polish Jesuits. Many of them entered the Society of Jesus in Rome and were educated at the Roman College. Some of the most important were, first, Jakub Wujek (1541–97), an erudite biblical scholar; his Polish translation of the Bible shaped the style of Polish biblical language for centuries. Piotr Skarga (1536–1612) was the author of *Lives of Saints* [Żywoty Świętych], which influenced enormously the religious imagination not only of Poland but of all of the Slavic world. He was also the court preacher of Zygmunt III for nearly twenty-five years (1588–1611). Stanisław Warszewicki (1530–91), before joining the Jesuit Order, studied under Melanchthon in Wittenberg; as a Jesuit he was sent as the papal envoy to Stockholm in 1574, when King John III of Sweden showed interest in becoming a Catholic. Warszewicki was also involved in educating the king's son Zygmunt, the future king of Poland. Those individuals were very important for the creation of a positive image of Jesuits. We have to admit that the first and the most interesting generation of the Polish Jesuits was very different from the successive ones. Most of the former were mature when they joined the Order, and went through the same path that Hosius (who, as we saw, was a representative of the hard line against Reformation) took before them: from Erasmianism, or humanism, to confessionalism full of pathos and sometimes even aggressive, to disciplined and dynamic piety, and, due to human weakness, to rules and prescriptions adopted as the final aim instead of as mere tools.[16] To this first generation we have to add the first Polish Jesuit saint, Stanisław Kostka (1550–68), who directly after his death in Rome became the most popular Polish saint and the patron of Catholic youth.

The next generations of Jesuits made an important contribution to central and eastern European culture, but it was not as impressive as that of the previous one. Let us remember just three names: Mateusz Kazimierz Sarbiewski (1595–1640), who was described as the Horace of Poland, the author of *Lyricorum Libri Tres* [Three Books of Lyrics], and the court preacher of Władysław IV; Adam Adamandy Kochański (1631–1700), the court mathematician of Jan III Sobieski, who left extensive correspondence with Gottfried Wilhelm Leibniz; and Marcin Poczobut (1728–1810), also a mathematician and an astronomer, a member of the Royal Academy of Science (London), and of the French Royal Academy. The question of whether they were excellent scholars because they were Jesuits, or simply because of their personal talents, has remained open.

It is also relevant that the first superiors were foreigners, mostly Italians; this fact, on the one hand, helped them to keep their distance from local politics, but, on the other hand, it also created the impression that the Jesuits were not a part of Polish culture. This was probably the reason why this situation was changed as soon as the majority of the candidates to the Society were from Poland, and mainly from one social class, the gentry (*szlachta*).

SHADOWS AND LIGHTS OF JESUIT EDUCATION

It is well known what Roland Barthes said about the influence of Jesuit education in France[17] (they taught France how to write); this is even more true concerning education in central and eastern Europe. Let us remember what John O'Malley said about the Jesuits' schools:

> The schools brought about other important changes in the Society – in its relationship to culture, in a pattern of living off endowment rather than alms, and to some extent even in the classes of society to whom the Jesuits would minister. Although the Jesuits' most official documents never baldly stated it, the schools became a part of the Jesuits' self-definition. They symbolized and powerfully helped effect changes that set off from the first eight or twelve years of Jesuit history all that followed.[18]

This statement by O'Malley is very true regarding the presence of the Society of Jesus in central and eastern Europe.[19] It is appropriate to quote a laconic remark by Stanislaw Bystroń, a Polish anthropologist, as a kind of characteristic of some religious orders in Poland: "Thus, the *szlachta* would drink with the Franciscans of Strict Observance; learn the precepts of the ascetic life from the Carmelites; but send their children to the Jesuit schools, and seek counsels from the Jesuits in the most serious matters."[20] This statement is loaded with religious, social, and political consequences. It means, in fact, that Jesuits were extremely influential, and in a way responsible for the shape of Polish Catholicism.

The Jesuits to a great degree taught Polish *szlachta* how to read and how to write. The question is open if they also were masters of good style. But what O'Malley wrote on Jesuits as a "teaching order" is particularly accurate concerning the situation in the Polish–Lithuanian Commonwealth:

> The Jesuits were the first religious order in the Catholic Church to undertake formal education as a major ministry. They became a "teaching order." The boldness of the decision for its day is difficult

for us to recapture. Its importance for the culture of early modern Catholicism was incalculable. By the time the Society was suppressed by papal edict in 1773, it was operating more than eight hundred universities, seminaries, and especially secondary schools almost around the globe. The world had never seen before nor has it seen since such an immense network of educational institutions operating on an international basis.[21]

The fate of the Jesuits' universities and schools was similar to the fate of the Society of Jesus as such. In some places they were welcomed and in some violently rejected. In the huge Polish–Lithuanian Commonwealth they experienced differentiated reception, from enthusiasm (in Vilnius) to open hostility (in Cracow). Indeed, in Cracow the Jesuits spent a lot of energy trying to fight the monopoly of the old Academia Krakowska without any positive result, and in Vilnius they founded their own Academy, and created a cultural center, which radiated Western culture not only to Lithuania, but also to Ukraine, Belorussia, Latvia, and Russia. We are still far from a complete picture of the impact of Jesuit education on eastern and central European culture. But we can say, together with Eugenio Garin, that it was education with strongly ideological aspiration,[22] and probably it was also the reason why other confessions were so critical towards the partially successful attempt to have a monopoly in this field in the Polish–Lithuanian Commonwealth. Nonetheless, it is noteworthy that all Christian denominations were influenced by humanistic tradition, mainly by the heritage of Erasmus of Rotterdam.[23]

As Bystroń stated, Jesuit education was very popular and influential among the Polish *szlachta*. The number of colleges was around forty, at different educational levels. This number is not so impressive if compared to hundreds of colleges and many universities in western Europe, but the function of a bridge between West and East should be underlined.

What made the central and eastern European situation of the Society of Jesus unique was the suppression of the Order, in 1773. In that year, two hundred members who worked as Jesuits in the Polish Commonwealth found themselves, after the first partition of Poland, henceforth part of Russia, as citizens of Tsarina Catherine II the Great. Most of them worked in Połock College, which soon became an Academy.[24] The Tsarina, after visiting Połock and after a debate with her counselors, decided to preserve the Jesuits as teachers, and gave them extensive autonomy. Thanks to her decision, the Society of Jesus survived and after some years could be restored. In Prussia, the Jesuit educational system did not meet the expectations of Frederick the Great, who preferred to control all education systems, and after a few years he simply expelled the Jesuits from his territory. This explains why the fate of the Jesuits who became citizens of Frederick the Great in Prussia was different from the fate of the Jesuits in Russia. This differentiated attitude toward the Jesuit Order after its suppression could also be an interesting case study of the complex relationship between politics and religion. In the rest of Poland, under the Polish king Stanisław August, most of the former Jesuits (after the suppression of the Order all of the Jesuits were forced to look for new work) became active in the Commission of National Education, founded in 1773 by the king himself.[25] This fact can be seen as the Jesuits' contribution to the Polish Enlightenment. In fact, most of those who were prepared for teaching had made their studies in western Europe, mainly in Italy and France. A good example is Marcin Poczobut, who after the suppression of the Society of Jesus became the rector of Vilnius Academy and was involved actively in the Commission for National Education. We can say that he was prepared, on the one hand, to make use of new philosophical and theological insights in his scientific and educational activities, and, on the other hand, to remain faithful to tradition and Catholic doctrine. In other words, such a combination of theological and scientific interests would have brought Poland more fully into the Catholic Enlightenment, in prayer as well as in practice. That this did not come to pass constituted not only Poczobut's tragedy, but also that of the Jesuits. It was ultimately a significant loss for the Catholic Enlightenment as a pan-European phenomenon.[26]

TOO CLOSE TO THE ROYAL COURT

The presence of the Jesuits in the royal courts of Europe has been extensively studied by Robert Bireley,[27] but he did not pay much attention to the Polish Commonwealth. The decisive impact of the Jesuits on the religious situation began with their collaboration with the Polish king Stefan Batory (1574–84)[28] who, as a fervent Catholic monarch, was very much interested in ideological support of the Society of Jesus. Therefore, he gave them full support in founding new colleges, including the most important educational institution, the Academy of Vilnius that he founded in 1579. Also his successor, Zygmunt III (1588–1632), was educated by Jesuits, and was well known for his sympathy toward the Society. Piotr Skarga, for example, was not only the court preacher for almost twenty-five years but also a close friend of the royal family.[29] It is likely that this close association of the Jesuits with the royal court contributed to the opinion that they were more interested in politics than in religion.

The reason why kings were looking for Jesuits as advisors, preachers, and confessors was that the new religious order was strongly supporting the existing political system. For Skarga, the division between the state and the Church did not exist, because, in his opinion, both of them were supposed to serve the same purpose. One Church within one state – that was his idea. He was strongly influenced by biblical models, and he used the example of God as the model of kingship in the patristic tradition. God was said to recommend autocracy, or government under one head, who is above all others. Such a head is like God who alone rules heaven and earth. Being strongly criticized, Skarga tried to confute the criticism of such an idea by pointing out the differences between absolute dominion, based on God's law, and tyranny. Here he quoted the Old Testament tradition according to which Israel's kings ruled thanks to God's grace, and on the basis of His law.[30]

From pamphlets we know that their opponents saw the Jesuits as a group strongly involved in politics, and particularly supportive of the dynasty of the Habsburgs, which was not very popular in the Polish–Lithuanian Commonwealth. So it is not surprising that, in 1606, Mikołaj Zabrzydowski's army of mutineers (who considered themselves *rokoszanie* – a social group exercising their time-honored privilege of withdrawing their loyalty from a bad monarch) called for the expulsion of the Jesuits from the Polish–Lithuanian Commonwealth. One of the reasons on which they based their demand was the foreign provenance of the Society, and hence its connections with foreign powers (they meant the Habsburgs), and certain activities seen as counter to the interests of the Polish state (they meant the Jesuit support for the king's endeavors to increase his power). It became common to associate the Jesuits with Machiavelli's theory of political power, an association that was vividly disputed by the Jesuits and their supporters. This opinion was shared not only by Protestants, with whom Jesuits were fighting on the doctrinal level, but also by some Catholics.[31]

INCULTURATION: SARMATISM AND JESUITS

One of the most characteristic qualities of the Society of Jesus is its ability to inculturate the Christian message in different cultural and religious contexts. As a matter of fact, this "inculturation" practice became a kind of trade mark of the Jesuits' pastoral activity, was the cause of many conflicts with the Roman Curia, and was probably one of the reasons why the Order was suppressed in 1773. It is well known what Jesuits did in Asia and South America. The achievements of Matteo Ricci in China, or of the Guaraní Republic in South America, are examples of the ability to translate Christianity into Asian or American culture. But scholars have not paid much attention to the case of central and eastern Europe.

In the beginning, this pastoral practice was seen with suspicion by Rome, but today is accepted as positive, and in a way prophetic – adopted by the Catholic Church at the Second Vatican Council in the 1960s. The most important intuition of the Jesuits related to their practice of inculturation was the realization that the Western form of Christianity was only one of many possible ways to be a Christian. This understanding may be obvious today, but in the sixteenth century was viewed by many as heresy. In fact, there can be ambiguous results of a strategy of inculturation. The Polish or central and eastern European experience can be an interesting case study. And perhaps it might be more appropriate to name inculturation as a syncretic process.[32] It is also important to remember that the Society of Jesus was a part of the history of Christianity, which was characterized by confusion with European culture. This perspective (Christianity identified with Western culture) was largely overcome by Vatican II. What Karl Rahner said in this context is instructive:

> Theologically speaking, there are three great epochs in Church history, of which the third has only just begun and made itself observable officially at Vatican II. First, the short period of Jewish Christianity. Second, the period of the Church in a distinct cultural region, namely, that of Hellenism and of European culture and civilization. Third, the period in which the sphere of the Church's life is in fact the entire world of Christianity.[33]

Rahner's observation could imply that the Jesuits, as an institution, have at times been as much or more part of a European culture as they have been apostles of a purely religious message. They may have given priority to defending the existing, Western institution of the Catholic Church and her claim to be the embodiment of the only true explanation of the Christian message. This is also true concerning the Jesuit presence in the Polish–Lithuanian Commonwealth. When Jesuits arrived in Poland, they intended to change Polish society, but with time they actually became a part of that society. What I have in mind here is the phenomenon conventionally known as the Sarmatization of Polish Catholicism. The concept was first used by Janusz Tazbir to refer to the influence of pre-Christian customs and behavior on Christian society as a whole.[34] Tazbir was less interested in the Jesuits' influence on Polish society than in the "Sarmatization" of the Order's members, and the price that the Jesuits paid for this.[35] Tazbir's opinion is that the Jesuits succumbed to this process:

> The Jesuits did not withstand the process of the Sarmatization of Polish Catholicism, which reached its apogee at the turn of the seventeenth and eighteenth centuries. By this term I mean the adaptation of religious concepts, views of the past, and eschatological ideas to the political and constitutional structure of the Polish–Lithuanian Commonwealth, and their mixture with folklore and the local historical tradition.[36]

It seems that the Jesuits contributed to the construction of a theological justification for the concept of the state and its structure held by the majority of the *szlachta* (Polish gentry). It seems that with the passing years they felt more and more at home with this concept, and became an integral part of the state. In other words, in the Jesuits' balance of accounts for work accomplished in the seventeenth century it would be hard to overlook the fact that ultimately Sarmatism had the upper hand with the Society's cultural elite.

Is that fact really an adequate description of the Jesuit presence in Polish culture? This was one of the questions that the participants in an academic conference on the relations between Jesuits and Polish culture, held in 1991 in Cracow, tried to answer.[37] This conference provided an opportunity for formulating research postulates rather than answers. Some of these postulates were realized in a volume published ten years later on the contribution of the Polish Jesuits to the development of science and culture in the Polish–Lithuanian Commonwealth and under the Partitions.[38]

In any case, certain controversial elements in the character of the Polish *szlachta* did not spare the Jesuits either. As early as 1614, Father General Claudio Acquaviva was calling the attention of Father Visitor Giovanni Argentini to this: "Something of vanity has been observed in our people in Poland of gentle stock, and hence also of haughtiness, such as that at the slightest offence they bring to the fore their gentle birth, comparing themselves with others and regarding themselves as better."[39] It is not surprising that the special importance of the *szlachta* in public life provoked a tendency among the Jesuits to emulate the *szlachta*, e.g., by changing family names and embracing a hedonistic lifestyle that entailed the neglect of religious life.] This tendency was severely criticized by the superiors in Rome.

In 1634, Father Provincial Marcin Hincza admonished the rectors of the colleges that some of the masters who were not of noble birth had assumed gentlemen's surnames and were using "gentle" surnames for their students, too, which smacked of vanity and had to be stopped; they should be using their former names. The rectors themselves had earned a reprimand in 1648 from Father Provincial Szczytnicki for pursuing a lifestyle that was totally out of line with the community life expected by the Society. They left the house too frequently and without good reason, to make social calls or visit relatives; they spent considerable sums on four-horse carriages and hired bursary singers to accompany them; they were mindful of their own needs but insensitive to the needs of others. Such warnings and reprimands were an expression of the continual effort being made to counteract the bad side of Old Polish social conduct, to which the Jesuits, now more frequently recruited from among the gentry, were susceptible.

Nevertheless, the Jesuits became so deeply integrated in Polish society that we could speak of a syncretic process, which only in recent years gained recognition in Catholic theology.[40]

UNDER THE WINGS OF THE RUSSIAN TSARINA

There was a real paradox and an unusual coincidence: the Catholic religious order that was known for its fidelity to the papacy was suppressed by Pope Clement XIV in 1773, and was saved by non-Catholic monarchs. And more than that: the Catholic Polish–Lithuanian Commonwealth was divided between three neighbors – Orthodox Russia, Protestant Prussia, and Catholic Austria (1772), and Jesuits, working in Russia (from 1773 till 1820) and Prussia (for a few years), could continue their activity, while in Catholic Austria and the rest of the Polish Kingdom they were suppressed.[41] This paradox was expressed wittily by Frederick the Great of Prussia: despite the exertions of his Most Catholic Majesty of Spain, his Most Apostolic Majesty of Portugal, his Most Christian Majesty of France, and the Holy Roman Emperor, the Jesuits had been saved by his Most Heretical Majesty and her Most Schismatical Majesty. "Most Heretical Majesty" expelled them a few years later, but her "Most Schismatical Majesty" Catherine the Great, and her successors, preserved them till 1820, the year in which they were expelled from

Russia. However, by that time the Society of Jesus was restored (in 1814), and could absorb the Jesuits from Russia practically around the whole world.

This period in Russia from 1773 till 1820 presents a most exciting example of development that offers, again, a case study that deserves particular attention.[42] The influence of the Academy of Połock and of the Collegium Nobilium (1805–15) in St. Petersburg especially deserves more attention, as they were centers of the radiation of Western culture and Catholicism in Orthodox Russia. The restoration of the Society of Jesus in 1814 would hardly have been possible without the personal support of the Russian tsars, who allowed Jesuits to open many schools and missionary stations in the extensive Russian territory. An important role was played by Father Gabriel Gruber who was elected in 1802 to be the superior general of the Jesuits in Russia. Most likely, it is impossible to understand fully nineteenth-century Russian literature and political thought without this presence of Jesuits in the Russian Empire. We can also add that the Polish king was following the example of other Catholic Majesties when he suppressed the Society. He transferred its property to the Commission for National Education, founded in the same year. Nevertheless, at the same time, many former Jesuits were engaged in the activities of the Commission founded by the king.[43] It is one of the reasons why in the Polish historiography we find the concept of "Catholic Enlightenment," which indicates the involvement of clergy in the process of modernization and adaptation of the Catholic Church into the new cultural situations of the eighteenth century. "Suppressed" Jesuits continued to contribute to a process of inculturation.

Notes

1   Cf. J. Tazbir, *A State without Stakes: Polish Religious Toleration in the Sixteenth and Seventeenth Century*, trans. A. T. Jordan (New York: Kosciuszko Foundation, 1973).

2   "Some of the bishops even secretly sympathized with the new faith; the primate Uchanski himself was suspected of seeing himself as a potential head of a Polish national church, while his close friendship with Frycz Modrzewski could cast doubt on the orthodoxy of the titular leader of the church in Poland. Rome was not unaware of such doubt." Ibid., 119.

3   He sold his library to Polish reformer Jan Laski who influenced not only the Polish but also the European Reformation.

4   B. Natoński, "Humanizm jezuicki i teologia pozytywno-kontrowersyjna: szkola polska w XVI wieku" [Humanism of Jesuits

and Positive-controversial Theology], in *Dzieje teologii katolickiej w Polsce* [The History of Catholic Theology in Poland], vol. II (Lublin: Katolicki Uniwersytet Lubelski, 1972).

5 "Some recent studies on the relationship between Erasmus and St. Ignatius, beginning with Marcel Bataillon, have been instructive in this regard. While attempts to find a textual dependence of the *Spiritual Exercises* on the *Enchiridion* have been largely abandoned, though there are indeed some remarkable similarities in phrasing, we are today far removed from the earlier judgment that these two reformers are irreconciliably opposed." J. O'Malley, "Introduction," in *Collected Works of Erasmus: Spiritualia* (Toronto: University of Toronto Press, 1988), 30–31.

6 J. O'Malley, *The First Jesuits* (Cambridge, MA: Harvard University Press, 1993), 14.

7 J. Tazbir, *Literatura antyjezuicka w Polsce 1578–1625* [Anti-Jesuitical Literature in Poland 1578–1625] (Warsaw: Ludowa Spółdzielnia Wydawnicza, 1963).

8 Only in 1991 was a new perspective on the role played by the Order in central and eastern European history presented. It happened when historians of the Jesuit Order and its critics met in Cracow in order to discuss the presence of the Jesuits in Polish culture. The contributors to the conference showed how deeply this presence shaped the character of central and eastern European Christianity: from theater to music, from philosophy to architecture. One of the results of that conference was the awareness of how significant and controversial was the impact of the Order on other Christian confessions; however, the relations with other religions were not considered at that conference. L. Grzebień and S. Obirek, eds., *Jezuici i kultura polska* [The Jesuits and Polish Culture] (Cracow: Wydawnictwo WAM, 1993).

9 J. Tazbir, "Literatura antyjezuicka w Polsce" [Anti-Jesuit Literature in Poland], in *Jezuici a kultura polska* [Jesuits and Polish Culture] (Kraków: Wydawnictwo WAM, 1993), 333.

10 S. Pavone, *The Wily Jesuits and the Monita Secreta* (St. Louis: Institute of Jesuit Sources, 2005).

11 S. Załęski, *Czy jezuici zgubili Polskę?* [Was Poland Destroyed by Jesuits?] (Lwów: Przegląd Powszechny, 1872).

12 S. Obirek, "The Jesuits and Polish Sarmatism," in J. O'Malley et al., eds., *The Jesuits: Cultures, Sciences, and the Arts, 1540–1773* (Toronto: University of Toronto Press, 1999), 555–63.

13 Peter Canisius, *Epistulae et Acta*, ed. Otto Braunsberger, 8 vols. (Freiburg: Herder, 1896–1923), II: 358, 361.

14 Cf. J. Oswald and P. Rummel, eds., *Petrus Canisius – Reformer der Kirche. Festschrift zum 400. Todestag des zweiten Apostels Deutschlands* (Augsburg: Sankt Ulrich Verlag, 1996).

15 B. Natonski, "Początki Towarzystwa Jezusowego w Polsce" [The Beginning of the Society of Jesus in Poland], in J. Brodrick, ed., *The Origin of the Jesuits* (Polish translation) (Cracow: Wydawnictwo WAM, 1969).

16 Cf. J. Błonski, *Mikołaj Sęp Szarzyński a początki polskiego baroku* [Mikolaj Sep Sarzynski and the Beginning of Polish Baroque] (Kraków: Wydawnictwo Literackie, 1967), 31.

17 R. Barthes, *Sade, Fourier, Loyola* (Paris: Editions du Seuil, 1971).

18 O'Malley, *The First Jesuits*, 15.

19 S. Bednarski, *Upadek i odrodzenie szkół jezuickich w Polsce. Studium z dziejów kultury i szkolnictwa polskiego* [The Decline and Renaissance of Jesuits in Poland. Study on the Culture and School System in Poland] (Kraków: Wydawnictwo Księży Jezuitów, 1933).

20 S. Bystroń, *Dzieje obyczajów w dawnej Polsce: Wiek XVI–XVIII* [The History of Manners in Old Poland: The Sixteenth to Eighteenth Centuries] (Warsaw: Państwowy Instytut Wydawniczy, 1932), 347.

21 O'Malley, *The First Jesuits*, 15–16.

22 "L'educazione è liberale perchè è di liberi e rende liberi. La scuola gesuitica riconosce un solo tipo d'uomo, un compito specifico preciso; in essa non circola più quella preoccupazione continua di libertà; in essa domina un principio d'autorità. Non si tratta di aiutare l'uomo ad essere libero di scegliere da se; la scelta è fatta, si tratta di rendere il soldato della Chiesa ben armato ed addestrato." E. Garin, *L'educazione in Europa (1400–1600)* (Bari: Laterza, 1957), 214.

23 B. Bauer, *Jesuitische 'ars rhetorica' im Zeitalter der Glaubenskaempfe* (Frankfurt am Main: Peter Lang Verlag, 1986).

24 M. Inglot, *La Compagnia di Gesù nell'Impero Russo (1772–1820) e la sua parte nella restaurazione generale della Compagnia* (Roma: Pontificia Università Gregoriana, 1997).

25 J. Popłatek, *Komisja Edukacji Narodowej. Udzial byłych jezuitów w pracach KEN* [The Commission for National Education. The Participation of Former Jesuits in the Works of CNE] (Cracow: Wydawnictwo WAM, 1973).

26 Cf. M. O'Connor, "Oświecenie katolickie i Marcin Poczobut" [Marcin Poczobut, S.J., and the Catholic Enlightenment], in Grzebień and Obirek, *Jezuici a kultura polska*, 351–52.

27 R. Bireley, *Hofbeichtvaeter und Politik im 17. Jahrhundert* (Freiburg, 1970); *The Counter-Reformation Prince: Antimachiavellianism or Catholic Statecraft in Early Modern Europe* (Chapel Hill: University of North Carolina Press, 1990).

28 S. Obirek, *Jezuici na dworach Batorego i Wazów 1580–1668* [The Jesuits at the Courts of Stefan Batory and the Vasa Dynasty 1580–1668] (Kraków: Wydawnictwo WAM, 1995).

29 S. Obirek, *Wizja Kosciola i państwa w kazaniach ks. Piotra Skargi SJ* [The Vision of Church and State in the Sermons of Piotr Skarga, S.J.] (Kraków: Wydawnictwo WAM, 1994), 169–85.

30 S. Obirek, *Wizja państwa w nauczaniu jezuitów polskich w latach 1564–1668* [Vision of the State in the Teaching of the Polish Jesuits 1564–1668] (Kraków: Wydawnictwo WAM, 1995).

31 S. Obirek, "Antymakiawelizm jezuicki" [Jesuit Antimachiavellianism], in *Jezuicka ars educandi* (Kraków: Wydawnictwo WAM, 1995).

32   I'm using this term in the sense of Carl Starkloff, elucidated in his *A Theology of the In-Between: The Value of Syncretic Process* (Milwaukee: Marquette University Press, 2002).

33   K. Rahner, "Towards a Fundamental Theological Interpretation of Vatican II," *Theological Studies* 40 (1979), 721.

34   M. Bogudzka, *The Lost World of Sarmatism: Custom as the Regulator of Polish Social Life in Early Modern Times* (Warsaw: Polish Academy of Science, 1996).

35   Cf. J. Tazbir, "Jezuici między Rzeczpospolitą i Rzymem" [The Jesuits in the Polish–Lithuanian Commonwealth], in his *Szkice z dziejów papiestwa* [Sketches from the History of the Papacy] (Warsaw, 1989), 75.

36   Ibid., 96.

37   See L. Grzebień and S. Obirek, eds., *Jezuici i kultura polska* [The Jesuits and Polish Culture] (Kraków: Wydawnictwo WAM, 1993).

38   I. Stasiewicz-Jasiukowa, ed., *Wkład jezuitów do nauki i kultury w Rzeczpospolitej Obojga Narodów i pod zaborami* [The Contribution of the Polish Jesuits to the Development of Science and Culture in the Polish–Lithuanian Commonwealth and under the Partitions] (Kraków: Wydawnictwo WAM, 2004).

39   S. Załęski, *Jezuici w Polsce* [The Jesuits in Poland], 5 vols. (Lwow-Kraków: Przegląd Powszechny, 1900–6), II: 273.

40   See Carl Starkloff, in his book, *A Theology of the In-Between: The Value of Syncretic Process*, 140: "It is my hope that this book might contribute to the creation of a village that expresses the best in village life – hospitality and conversation, and not the worst, such as conflict and manipulation. I realise that this village seems destined to be pluralistic, and that all dialogue must accept the fact of historical pluralism, certainly of cultures ... and in the historical experience of religion."

41   Inglot, *La Compagnia di Gesù*.

42   Apart from the well-known monograph by M. Inglot, cited above, I use the results of research by I. Kadulska, *Akademia Połocka: Osrodek kultury na Kresach 1812–1820* [The Połock: Center of Culture in the Borderlands 1812–1820] (Gdańsk: Uniwersytet Gdański, 2004).

43   Popłatek, *Komisja Edukacji Narodowej*.

Part III

Geographic and Ethnic Frontiers

9 The Jesuit enterprise in sixteenth- and seventeenth-century Japan

M. ANTONI J. ÜÇERLER

PORTUGUESE INDIA AND THE BEGINNINGS OF THE JAPANESE MISSION

The story of the Jesuit mission in Japan cannot be told without reference to earlier events in India, which was an important center of Christian missionary activity from the beginning of the sixteenth century. The exploratory journeys of Vasco da Gama (1469–1524) along the Indian coast in 1498 culminated in the conquest of Goa in 1510 for the Portuguese crown by Affonso de Albuquerque (1453–1515). The fate of the Indian missionary enterprise is inextricably linked to that of Japan from the time of Francis Xavier (1506–52), who first arrived in India on 6 May 1542 as papal legate and nuncio. Xavier had been sent to India by Ignatius of Loyola (1491–1556) at the request of Pope Paul III (1468–1549) and undertook the long journey from Lisbon via Mozambique with King John III (1502–57) of Portugal as his patron. The Jesuits, however, were not the first religious order to set foot in India or in Goa under the Portuguese. They were preceded by the Franciscans, who arrived in India in 1500, and the Dominicans, who came in 1503. The Augustinians, on the other hand, began their missionary activities in India only in 1572.

Since the final decades of the fifteenth century, Spain and Portugal had become rivals in maritime exploration and conquest. As a result of various arguments over sovereignty, arbitration was left to the papacy. Pope Alexander VI (1431–1503) stepped in to mediate in 1481 and again in 1493. The papal bull *Inter Caetera* effectively "divided" the world into the East and West Indies by drawing an imaginary line in the Atlantic Ocean and granted the Portuguese and Spanish both civil and ecclesiastical administration over all lands "discovered and yet to be discovered" in a system that subsequently came to be known as the *padroado real* in Portugal and the *patronato* (or *patronazgo*) *real* in Spain.[1] The two nations formalized their agreement to the terms of such a division by signing the Treaty of Tordesillas on 7 June 1494.[2]

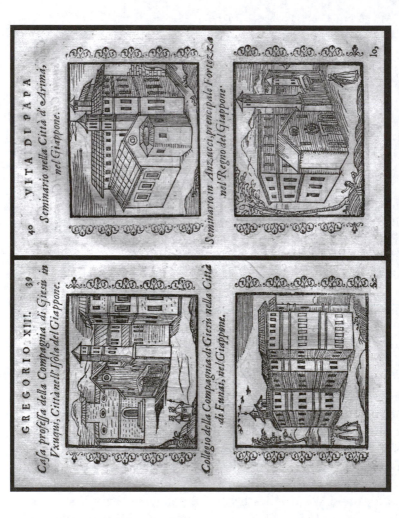

Figure 9.1. Engravings of the Jesuit novitiate, schools, and college established in Japan in 1580 by Alessandro Valignano (1539–1606), in Marc-Antonio Ciappi, *Compendio delle heroiche et gloriose attioni et santa vita di Papa Gregorio XIII* (Rome: Stamperia degli Accolti, 1596), 39–40. Archivum Romanum Societatis Iesu, Early Printed Books Collection.

As a result of this system of royal patronage, which had its own legal framework of rights, privileges, and obligations known as the *ius patronatus*, the Portuguese crown established in 1534 the episcopal See of Goa, which was destined to play an important role in the life of many churches in the East, including Japan and China.[3] In 1557 it became an independent archbishopric and primatial See of the East Indies. Its suffragan dioceses included Cochin in southern India (1557), Malacca (1557), Macau (1575), and Funai in Japan (1588). The first bishops both of Macau and Funai were Jesuits, Melchior Carneiro (1516–83) and Sebastião Morais (1534–89) respectively. The first bishop to actually set foot in Japan, however, was the Jesuit Pedro Martins (1542–98), who arrived in 1596. Luís Cerqueira (1551–1614), who governed the Japanese Church for many years and established the first seminary for native clergy, succeeded him in 1598.

Back in Goa, the governor asked Xavier for more Jesuits to be sent from Europe in order to work at the College of St. Paul or "of the Holy Faith," which had been founded by secular clergy in 1541 and was supported by lay benefactors.[4] It was first called the "Seminary of the Holy Faith" and its primary mission was the religious education of Indian and East African children and youths.[5] The Jesuits were asked to take over its administration in 1548, and three years later King John III of Portugal donated both the seminary and the college in perpetuity to the Society of Jesus.[6] António Gomes (c. 1520–54), its first Jesuit rector, reports in 1548 how the Jesuits are striving to follow the teaching methods and curriculum of the University of Paris and spiritual discipline of the Jesuit College of Coimbra.[7] One cannot exaggerate the importance this institution played in the lives and formation of generations of Jesuit missionaries – some of whom subsequently embarked on the Society's missionary endeavors throughout India while others studied there before being assigned to mission posts further east in Malacca, Macau, or Japan. It was also at the College of Goa in 1556 that the Jesuits set up the first moveable-type hand press for the printing of books in Portuguese, Latin, and Tamil, and it was there that the first Indians received their formation before being ordained to the secular priesthood.[8] For all practical purposes, the College of Goa was the Jesuit intellectual gateway to the East and it performed the same function in Asia as the Roman College or the College of Coimbra did in Europe.

It was also in India that, after a number of years of preaching and working with the poor both in Goa and further south along the Malabar and Pearl Fishery Coasts, Xavier planned further exploits, including his trip to Japan. During an earlier sojourn in the strategic Portuguese fort of Malacca (Melaka) in 1547, he had met Yajirō, a Japanese samurai from Kagoshima who convinced Xavier that he should preach the Christian faith in Japan. At the end of that year, Yajirō and two other Japanese accompanied Xavier back to India, where they were instructed in the faith and baptized at the College of St. Paul. Xavier then chose two Jesuit companions, Cosme de Torres (1510–70) and Juan Fernández (1526–67), to make the journey with him to Japan.[9] Having departed from Goa in mid-April, after a brief stay in Malacca the party reached Kagoshima, in the feudal realm of Satsuma, on 15 August 1549. The missionaries soon realized that no work could be undertaken without the consent of the local lord. They also discovered that the country was divided into sixty-six realms or kingdoms and that Japan was a country in the midst of a turbulent civil war. The initial arrival of the Portuguese in Japan in 1542 (or 1543) – the first Europeans to set foot in Marco Polo's "Zipangu" – preceded that of Xavier by only six or seven years. But this time inclement weather had actually brought the Portuguese to the coast of Japan, just off Tanegashima Island, unlike the earlier voyage of Christopher Columbus, who erroneously believed he had reached the fabled kingdom described by Polo after exploring the coast of Cuba in 1492.

Xavier was so impressed by his first encounter with the Japanese that in an early missive to Rome he enthusiastically describes the people as the "best that have as yet been discovered."[10] This oft-quoted assessment was to have a long-term impact on the missionary approach that generations of his successors would adopt and justify as the correct way of proceeding in Japan (and later China). Although Xavier spent no more than two years in Japan, he succeeded in gaining footholds in a number of cities throughout the country. Besides the domain of Satsuma, where he was received by Shimazu Takahisa (1514–71), he established a small mission in Hirado, controlled by Matsuura Takanobu (1529–99), and in Yamaguchi, with the permission of the local daimyo, Ōuchi Yoshitaka (1507–51). He also conferred with Ōtomo Yoshishige (1530–87), the influential daimyo of Bungo, who would become a Christian in 1578 and have a major impact on the way the Jesuits defined their missionary methods thereafter.

As Xavier and his companions were foreigners who had come from India, a number of Japanese thought that they represented a new sect of Buddhism. This misunderstanding was compounded by their lack of sufficient knowledge of the Japanese language, the limited grasp of Christian doctrine by Yajirō, whom Xavier had no choice but to rely on for translations, and the major mistake he committed when he adopted a common term employed by the Shingon sect to describe Buddha, *dainichi nyōrai*, to express the Christian concept of a trans-cendent, omnipotent, and triune God. Once they became aware of the problem, the Jesuits were very careful not to make further use of Buddhist or Shinto terminology to convey Christian concepts; instead they resorted to using transliterations of Latin words.[11]

EXPANSION OF THE ENTERPRISE AND ALESSANDRO VALIGNANO

In the years that followed under the guidance of Xavier's companion and successor, Cosme de Torres (1510–70), the mission rapidly expanded, although the Jesuits had to leave Yamaguchi in 1557 when their patron, Ōuchi Yoshinaga (1540–57), was defeated by Mōri Motonari (1497–1571). Gaspar Vilela (1525–72), who had come to Japan the previous year, succeeded in obtaining permission from the shogun, Ashikaga Yoshiteru (1546–65), to establish a Jesuit presence in Kyoto in 1560, though he faced continuous opposition from Buddhist bonzes. In spite of these difficulties and other hardships, he succeeded three years later in converting a number of prominent samurai and scholars including Takayama Zusho or Dom Dário (1531–96) and his son, Takayama Ukon or Dom Justo (1552?–1615), lords of Settsu, one of the five home provinces (*Gokinai*) surrounding the capital. Vilela was greatly aided in his work by an elderly half-blind Japanese brother, Lourenço Ryōsai (1525–92), who was a great preacher, debater, and interpreter. Vilela was succeeded by Luís Fróis (1532–97), a keen observer and student of Japanese culture as well as a prolific writer, to whom we still owe today much of our knowledge about the early history of the Jesuit mission. He was, in fact, an eyewitness to many of the events he wrote about. He was in Kyoto when Oda Nobunaga (1534–82) took over the capital in 1568 and met with him on numerous occasions before Nobunaga's untimely death in 1582.[12] Fróis was joined in Kyoto in 1570 by the Italian Organtino Gnecchi-Soldo (1530–1609), who would for years minister to Christians in the capital. In 1576 the latter built the first church in the capital, which came to be known as the "Temple of the Southern Barbarians" (*Namban-dera*) and attracted much attention.[13]

During the same period in Kyushu, another Portuguese Jesuit, Luís d'Almeida (1525–83), set up a hospital in 1557 in Funai (Bungo), in the domain of Ōtomo Yoshishige. D'Almeida thus became the first European physician to introduce Western medical knowledge to

Japan. Another important breakthrough came when Ōmura Sumitada (1533–87) was baptized in 1563 by Cosme de Torres. The Jesuits had promised him that the Portuguese *nau* would come to his harbor of Yokoseura if he looked favorably upon the Christian religion. Dom Bartolomé, as the Jesuits would refer to him in their correspondence, thus became one of the Jesuits' chief patrons. In 1571 the Portuguese "black ship" (*kurofune*) entered the natural harbor of Nagasaki in his domain for the first time. For half a century thereafter, Portuguese trade with Japan would take place almost exclusively through this port. Sumitada's conversion and its aftermath highlights the uneasy balance in Kyushu between the economic interests of the local warlords and their Portuguese trading partners on the one hand, and the missionary ambitions of the Jesuits on the other. This situation was in marked contrast with Jesuit efforts in the Kansai region, where economic considerations played no part in the choice to embrace the new faith among either the nobles or the general population.

When Cosme de Torres died in 1570, Francisco Cabral (1533–1609) took over the leadership of the mission with only eleven Jesuits under him. During his tenure, the Church grew rapidly and the number of Jesuits increased to fifty-five by 1579, including seven Japanese Jesuits and over a hundred *dōjuku* or lay catechists who assisted the missionaries and lived together with them but were not formally members of the Order.[14] That year the Japanese Church began another important chapter in her history. Alessandro Valignano (1539–1606), an Italian nobleman, arrived in Kuchinotsu, a port in the domain of Arima Harunobu (1567–1612). He had been appointed Visitor (*Visitador*) to all Jesuit missions east of the Cape of Good Hope by the Superior General, Everard Mercurian (1514–80), in September 1573.[15] He was granted a sweeping range of administrative powers and reported directly to the General in Rome. He had read much about the successes of the Jesuits in Japan before his arrival but was dismayed to find that the mission was beset by serious problems.[16] After carrying out an extended visitation of Jesuit mission posts, he blamed Cabral for not having fostered a correct understanding among the Jesuits of the Constitutions of the Order and its way of proceeding. Moreover, he faulted the mission superior for the lack of harmony he found between the European and Japanese Jesuits on account of Cabral's contempt for the Japanese and their customs as well as his harsh treatment of them. This detrimental attitude, Valignano believed, was at the root of all the mission's problems. He was confirmed in this view by Ōtomo Yoshishige, whom he quotes as having told him that "it was a sign of diminished intelligence for a motley handful of foreigners to try to induce Japanese lords to renounce their customs and the etiquette of their own land and adapt themselves to the foreigners ... and to their barbaric and vulgar ways."[17] Valignano's reaction to this rebuke as well as to his own misgivings was to hold a series of consultations in 1580 and 1581 at Usuki, Azuchi, and Nagasaki. By the time he ended his first visitation of the country in 1582 and left for Macau, he had reorganized the mission and relieved Cabral of his post as mission superior. The new method of evangelization he proposed would be that of accommodation to Japanese culture. This would require, however, special training for the foreign missionaries. Moreover, it would mean admitting more native candidates to the Society. Thus, he decided to establish in 1580 a novitiate in Usuki and a college of higher studies in Funai, where both European *and* Japanese humanities, as well as philosophy and theology, were taught. The purpose of the program was to instill the students with the proper etiquette, customs, and ceremonies of Japan and to engage them in the pursuit of virtue, piety, and sound doctrine. Besides these two institutions that were located in the domain of Ōtomo Yoshishige, he also founded two preparatory schools for noble youths aged twelve to eighteen in Arima, on land given to him by Harunobu, and at Azuchi, the castle-town built by Oda Nobunaga. It was from among these young noblemen that he chose in 1582 four boys for a highly successful Japanese Christian "embassy" to Europe.[18] These and other initiatives by Valignano must be seen against the background of his assessment of the Japanese missionary enterprise as "the most important and profitable in the whole of the Orient" and the people of Japan as "of great civility, prudence, understanding and subject to reason."[19]

Despite Valignano's enthusiasm for Japan, he was unable to avoid the harsh realities of the *sengoku* or "warring states" and the political compromises they entailed. One decision in particular was to have a long-term effect on the fate of the Jesuits. Ōmura Sumitada, compelled by his enemy Ryūzōji Takanobu (1530–84) to become his vassal or perish, was determined not to lose the advantages afforded to him by the Portuguese ship that regularly docked in his harbor. After talks with the Visitor, he took the extraordinary step on 9 June 1580 of "donating" the ports of Nagasaki and Mogi to the Society of Jesus.[20] For seven years the Jesuits were the *de facto* rulers and responsible for both its civil and ecclesiastical administration. Moreover, they benefited from the harbor dues paid by the Portuguese, which Sumitada gave to the missionaries. The Jesuit General, Everard Mercurian, reluctantly agreed to this highly irregular situation under canon law, in view of the dramatic circumstances in which Sumitada had been placed. This donation proved to be a mixed blessing to say the least. When in June 1587 Hideyoshi defeated Shimazu Yoshihisa (1533–1611), the last obstacle to his complete domination of Kyushu, the *kampaku* was not amused to observe that the Jesuits were occupying a key harbor that was partly fortified. While still at Osaka Castle, in May 1586 he received Gaspar Coelho (1529–90), the mission superior who had taken over from Cabral. At the audience he assured Coelho of his good will and listened to the ill-advised vice-provincial as he made promises to seek the support of both the Portuguese and the Christian lords in Kyushu for Hideyoshi's future campaigns. Coelho imprudently repeated this line of reasoning when he met with Hideyoshi near Hakata in late July 1587 aboard the ultralight armed vessel that the vice-provincial had acquired to repel pirate (*wakō*) attacks. Hideyoshi had heard and seen enough. On 24 July he issued a decree expelling the missionaries from Japan. As the Jesuits made remonstrations that their immediate departure was not possible for lack of vessels, he subsequently eased his order and allowed them to remain provided that they never again preach in public, for "Japan [was] the land of the gods."[21] It is interesting to note that while there were 111 Jesuits in Japan at the time, the number grew in 1591 to 142 – the highest number ever. This was also made possible by another important circumstance. Pope Gregory XIII had confirmed in 1575 and again in 1577 that Japan lay in the Portuguese sphere of influence and in 1585, shortly before his death, he made the Japanese mission the exclusive domain of the Society of Jesus.[22]

In view of Hideyoshi's decree, when Valignano sailed for Japan in 1590 with the four youths who were returning from their embassy to Europe, he was able to enter the country only wearing his official hat as ambassador of the Viceroy of India. This second visitation of Japan lasted until 1592. During that time, the Jesuits began using one of their most important new tools. The Visitor had returned with a Gutenberg hand press, acquired by Diogo de Mesquita (1553–1614) while the embassy was in Lisbon. Between 1590 and 1614 it was used to print a wide range of devotional works for Japanese Christians, as well as dictionaries and study aids for the missionaries, both in Romanized script and in Japanese characters. It also marked the first time moveable type was used in Japan.[23] In the decade after Hideyoshi's expulsion order, the Jesuits had to stay out of sight and often moved both the press and the college from one remote location to the next at a moment's notice.

This precarious arrangement quickly evolved into a major crisis when the *San Felipe*, a Spanish galleon bound for Acapulco and laden with rich cargo, ran aground off the coast of Tosa on 19 October 1596. While Hideyoshi was considering what to do, he was given information about the Spanish that changed the fortunes of Christianity in Japan forever. The pilot of the ship, Francisco de Olandía, was reported to have told the Japanese authorities that Spain would not tolerate her ships being taken illegally in such a fashion. Moreover, he allegedly claimed that it was a common strategy for Spain first to send ahead missionaries to distant lands in order to render the natives docile, and then to arrive with soldiers to conquer them.[24] Enraged by these reports, Hideyoshi initially planned to round up and execute all Christians in Osaka and Kyoto. However, in the end only twenty-six Christians were arrested. The number included six Franciscan friars who had arrived in 1593 from the Philippines, three Japanese Jesuits in training, and seventeen lay Christians, among whom there were three children aged twelve to fourteen. These men, women, and children began their month-long trek by foot to Nagasaki, where they were crucified in Japanese fashion at Nishizaka, a hill overlooking the harbor, on 5 February 1597. The mission was nonetheless afforded respite when the following year Hideyoshi died. The power struggle that ensued culminated in the famous battle of Sekigahara in October 1600, from which Tokugawa Ieyasu (1543–1616) and his supporters emerged victorious. Despite the fact that a number of prominent Christian daimyos, including Konishi Yukinaga (1555–1600), had allied themselves with the faction of his main enemy, Ishida Mitsunari (1560–1600), for a time Ieyasu continued to tolerate Christianity. In fact, the future shogun had not abandoned hope of still reaping the benefits of trade with the Portuguese and the Spanish and exhibited no fear that the Iberians might pose a military threat to his own recently secured hegemony over Japan.

PERSECUTION DURING THE TOKUGAWA PERIOD AND THE END OF THE MISSION

The mission suffered a major setback in 1612, when the Christian daimyo, Arima Harunobu (Dom Protásio), was accused of having attempted to bribe the new administration for personal financial gain. He was found guilty and in June of that year executed. Shortly thereafter, Ieyasu issued his first anti-Christian edict in areas under the direct control of the shogunate. This prohibition was extended to the whole country in February 1614, which marks the beginning of a more systematic persecution of Christianity throughout the country. Eight months later, on 28 October, the governor of Nagasaki, Hasegawa Fujihiro Sahyōe (1567–1618), ordered all Christian clergy to leave the city and make their way to the port of Fukuda in preparation for immediate deportation. Of the 115 Jesuits still in the country at the time, 65 left for Macau on three small ships and another 23 boarded a vessel bound for Manila. They were accompanied by 53 *dōjuku*. Takayama Ukon, Naitō Tokuan (d. 1626), and several hundred other Christians followed them into exile and embarked for the Philippines. The remaining 27 Jesuits did not leave the country and went into hiding.[25] In 1611, just before these events, the Japanese mission had been elevated to the status of an independent province, of which China would be a vice-province. The first provincial superior was Valentim Carvalho (1559–1631).

As the persecution intensified over the next decade, a number of public executions took place both in Nagasaki (10–12 September 1622) and in Edo (4 and 24 December 1623).[26] The latter came in the wake of the abdication of Tokugawa Hidetada (1579–1632) in favor of his second son, Iemitsu (1604–51), who was determined to stamp out the Christian religion at any cost. A curious interlude took place in 1632, when the Portuguese Jesuit Sebastião Vieira (1574–1634) was taken to Edo, where he had the unexpected opportunity to read a compendium of the Catholic faith in the presence of Iemitsu himself. Reason of state prevailed over any religious argumentation and the shogunate decided to continue the nationwide extirpation of Christianity.[27] To further this goal, in 1633 they issued the first of five *sakoku-rei* or decrees of "national seclusion." In October of that year Christóvão Ferreira (1580–c. 1654), the Jesuit vice-provincial, apostatized after six hours of *ana-tsurushi* or the torture of the pit. More than just a setback, his fall sent shockwaves throughout the Society of Jesus, both in Asia and in Europe. Thereafter, Jesuit attempts to enter the country were intended first and foremost as moral rescue missions. While capture, torture, and death were certain, the purpose of these missions was to persuade Ferreira, who had been given the new name Sawano Chūan, to recant his apostasy and to make amends for his lapse.[28]

Though they had never heard of Tertullian, the Japanese authorities implicitly acknowledged the truth of his famous dictum that "the blood of Christians is the seed" of the Church.[29] Their tactics changed accordingly and their primary purpose shifted from eliminating Christians to coercing them – and missionaries in particular – to apostatize rather than allowing them to die as martyrs. They hoped to demoralize the Christian community by destroying their faith from within. No one proved to be more adept at this ominous task than Inoue Chikugo no kami Masashige (1585?–1661), who acted as the Japanese anti-Christian Inquisitor or head of the "office-for-religious-reconversion" (*shūmon aratame-yaku*) from 1640 to 1658. The *kirishi-tan yashiki*, a center for detention, interrogation, and torture of Christians who had been discovered, was established in Edo in 1646 and continued to operate till the end of the eighteenth century.

The final political blow to the Christian mission came in 1637 with the outbreak of the Shimabara Rebellion. Its immediate cause, however, was not religious. The local lord, Matsukura Katsuie (1597–1638), had imposed heavy taxes that amounted to extortion and resulted in famine among the populace. Cruel punishments were meted out to those who tried to evade the taxes or were otherwise unable to pay up. The fact that the majority of the rebels were Christians confirmed the authorities in their suspicions that not only foreign missionaries but indeed Christianity itself was a pernicious and subversive force in Japan in direct opposition to Tokugawa hegemony. A hundred thousand men were dispatched to quell the rebellion. With the aid of Dutch artillery, Hara Castle, the center of the uprising, finally fell on 12 April 1638. In the ensuing slaughter that spared neither women nor children, 37,000 people within the precinct lost their lives. The issue of the final of the five "closed country" decrees followed in 1639, which precluded any further contact with the Portuguese.

The last two Jesuit expeditions to succeed in entering the country in the seventeenth century, albeit in secret, were led by the Italian Antonio Rubino (1578–1643). The first group of four Jesuits and five laymen arrived in August 1642, while the second group reached the shores of Hirado in June 1643. All were eventually apprehended and tortured; and the majority – but not Rubino – apostatized. Among these Pedro Marques (1576–1657), the provincial superior, and Giuseppe Chiara (?–1685) later retracted their apostasies and died in Edo in 1657 and 1685 respectively; the Japanese brother, Andrés Vieira, died at the *kirishitan yashiki* in 1678 and therefore had presumably also retracted his apostasy.[30]

The last foreign (secular) priest to enter Japan was Giovanni Battista Sidotti (1668–1714), who spent seven years under house arrest after his capture in 1708. He became famous for having engaged in scholarly debate Arai Hakuseki (1657–1725), the Japanese Confucian scholar and influential advisor on policy to Tokugawa Ienobu

(1662–1712). Hakuseki recorded his extended conversations with Sidotti as well as the knowledge he acquired from him about the West, its geography, and Roman Catholicism in his *Seiyō kibun* or *Tidings of the West*, a three-volume work he composed in 1715.[31] Sidotti was subsequently left to die of starvation in a hole in 1714, after the authorities discovered he had baptized an elderly couple who had served as his caretakers during his captivity.

The disappearance of the Jesuits and other missionaries did not spell the end, however, of Christianity in Japan. In a truly remarkable show of perseverance, pockets of Japanese Christians, in particular on Ikitsuki Island off Hirado and on the Gotō Islands, survived by going underground and reorganizing themselves with lay elders chosen to head each community. In the end, without any clergy to assist or instruct them, the "hidden Christians" or *kakure kirishitan* ended up mixing folk culture together with elements of Shinto and Buddhist rituals into their Christian religious expressions. As "imperfect" as this highly eclectic form of Christianity may have been, it bore witness to the tenacity with which they held on to the faith and traditions of their ancestors insofar as they were able to remember, understand, and transmit them in secret from one generation to the next.

This selective account of over two centuries of the Jesuit enterprise in Japan might leave the reader perplexed as to how to assess this unique mission, caught up in the turbulence of civil war, national unification, and the relentless persecution that literally and physically extinguished the Jesuit presence by the mid-seventeenth century. One historian has described this story as "a vision betrayed" while another calls it "a mission interrupted."[32] In view of the harrowing persecution that Christians were subjected to, it is legitimate to ask whether the enterprise was not in the end indeed a failure. Certainly the statistics in question are noteworthy. When Xavier left Japan in 1551 there were between 700 and 1,000 Christians. This number grew to 30,000 in 1570, 100,000 in 1579, when Valignano first arrived, and approximately 150,000 by 1585. By the end of the century there were at least 350,000 Christians, although there may have been as many as 600,000 baptisms by 1614, when Christianity was proscribed, reaching an overall total of approximately 800,000 (including infant baptisms) by 1626, after which the data become uncertain.[33] The estimated population of Japan in 1600 was twelve million. In view of the Tokugawa regime's systematic obliteration of any outward trace of Christian culture or faith in Japan, some scholars have come to the conclusion that the long-term impact of what Charles Boxer called the "Christian

Century" was minimal if not nil.[34] While it is true that the mission was abruptly interrupted, that many had been forcibly converted by over-zealous Christian warlords, and that others had apostatized under duress or otherwise, the relative "success" before the onslaught of the persecution as well as the determination of the "hidden Christians" to maintain their faith would suggest that Christianity had in fact taken root in Japanese soil. The legacy of the Jesuit enterprise and of those who embraced the Christian faith in Japan thus continues to elude a definitive assessment and invites historians to explore further.

Notes

1   For a general introduction on royal patronage in Portuguese Africa and Asia see Charles R. Boxer, *The Portuguese Seaborne Empire, 1415–1825* (Manchester: Carcanet Press, 1969; repr. 1997), 228–48. For the texts of the papal bulls see Levy Maria Jordão, ed., *Bullarium patronatus Portugalliæ regum in ecclesiis Africæ, Asiæ atque Oceaniæ ...*, 3 vols. (Lisbon: Ex Typographia Nationali, 1868–70).

2   See Emma Falque, "Bulas alejandrinas de 1493. Texto y Traducción," in Juan Gil and José Maria Maestre, eds., *Humanismo latino y descubrimiento* (Cadiz: Universidad de Cádiz; Seville: Universidad de Sevilla, 1992), 11–35; Francisco Mateos, "Bulas portugesas y españolas sobre descubrimientos geográficas," *Missionalia Hispanica* 19 (1962), 5–34, 129–68.

3   The terms of the *ius patronatus* of Portugal and the privileges of the king vis-à-vis the pope were more clearly defined in 1514.

4   See Georg Schurhammer, *Francis Xavier: His Life, His Times*, trans. M. Joseph Costelloe, 4 vols. (Rome: Jesuit Historical Institute, 1973–82), II: 235–43, 273–75. For Xavier's description of the college in his letter to Ignatius of Loyola (Goa, 20 September 1542), see Georg Schurhammer and Josef Wicki, eds., *Epistolae S. Francisci Xaverii aliaque eius scripta*, 2 vols. (Rome: Monumenta Historica Societatis Iesu, 1944–45; repr. 1996), I: 132–37.

5   See Charles R. Boxer, "The Problem of the Native Clergy in the Portuguese and Spanish Empires from the Sixteenth to the Eighteenth Centuries," in G. J. Cuming, ed., *The Mission of the Church and the Propagation of the Faith*, Studies in Church History, 6 (Cambridge: Cambridge University Press, 1970), 85–105.

6   See John III's letter of donation (Almeirim, 20 February 1551) in *Documenta Indica*, ed. Josef Wicki, Monumenta Missionum, Monumenta Historica Societatis Iesu, 18 vols. (Rome: Institutum Historicum Societatis Iesu, 1948–88), II: 189–93.

7   See António Gomes to Simão Rodrigues (Goa, 20 December 1548) in *Documenta Indica*, I: 411–12.

8   Georg Schurhammer and G. William Cottrell, Jr., "The First Printing in Indic Characters," *Harvard Library Bulletin* 6/2 (1952), 147–60; Anant

K. Priolkar, *The Printing Press in India: Its Beginnings and Early Development* (Mumbai: Marathi Samshodhana Mandala, 1958), 1–27.

9   For short biographies of these and other Jesuits, see Charles O'Neill and Joaquín M. Domínguez, eds., *Diccionario histórico de la Compañía de Jesús*, 4 vols. (Rome: Institutum Historicum Societatis Iesu; Madrid: Universidad Pontificia Comillas, 2001).

10 For the original letter of Xavier to his companions in Goa (Kagoshima, 5 November 1549) see Juan Ruiz-de-Medina, ed., *Documentos del Japón*, 2 vols. (Rome: Institutum Historicum Societatis Iesu, 1990–95), 1: 142. For an English translation see *The Letters and Instructions of Francis Xavier*, ed. and trans. M. Joseph Costelloe, S. J. (St. Louis: Institute of Jesuit Sources, 1992), 297.

11 On Balthasar Gago's reform of Christian terminology, see his letters to Jesuits in India and Portugal (Hirado, 23 December 1555) in Ruiz-de-Medina, *Documentos del Japón*, 1: 569–70. For a more detailed discussion see Georg Schurhammer, *Das kirchliche Sprachproblem in der japanischen Jesuitenmission des 16. und 17. Jahrhunderts* (Tokyo: Deutsche Gesellschaft für Natur- u. Völkerkunde Ostasiens, 1928).

12 For a short discussion on the Jesuits and Nobunaga, see Jeroen Lamers, *Japonius Tyrannus: The Japanese Warlord Oda Nobunaga Reconsidered* (Leiden: Hōtei Publishing, 2000), 171–87.

13 See Luís Fróis' letter to the Society of Jesus in Portugal (Usuki, 9 September 1577) in Roman Archives of the Society of Jesus (ARSI), *Iap.–Sin.*, 8/ii, fols. 154r–159v, reproduced in Josef Franz Schütte, *Introductio ad Historiam Societatis Jesu in Japonia* (Rome: Institutum Historicum Societatis Iesu, 1968), 610–11.

14 The Society of Jesus was to rely heavily on two other categories of such assistants, *kambō*, i.e., laymen who were in charge of churches and helped with baptisms and funerals especially in rural areas where priests could rarely visit, and *komono*, i.e., domestic servants who worked in the residences, churches, and schools. Between 1582 and 1609 there were altogether between 500 and 900 such assistants in all three categories, including the *dōjuku*. See Schütte, *Introductio*, 376–80.

15 For a more detailed account see my "The Jesuit Enterprise in Japan (1573–1580)," in Thomas M. McCoog, ed., *The Mercurian Project: Forming Jesuit Culture, 1573–1580* (Rome: Institum Historicum Societatis Iesu; St. Louis: Institute of Jesuit Sources, 2004), 831–75. For more on Valignano and his career see Josef Franz Schütte, *Valignano's Mission Principles for Japan*, trans. John J. Coyne, 2 vols. (St. Louis: Institute of Jesuit Sources, 1980–85); Joseph F. Moran, *The Japanese and the Jesuits: Alessandro Valignano in Sixteenth-Century Japan* (London: Routledge, 1993); and my "Alessandro Valignano: Man, Missionary, and Writer," in Daniel Carey, ed., *Asian Travel in the Renaissance* (Oxford: Blackwell, 2004), 12–41.

16 See Valignano to Mercurian (Kuchinotsu, 5 December 1579), in ARSI, *Iap.–Sin.*, 8/i, fol. 242r.

17 See Valignano to Mercurian (Usuki: 27 October 1580), in ARSI, *Iap.–Sin.*, 8/i, fols. 298r–300r, translated and discussed in Schütte,

Valignano's Mission Principles, 1/1: 252–55. For his criticisms of Cabral and an account of his interview with Ōtomo Yoshishige, see his letter to Claudio Acquaviva (Goa, 23 November 1595) in *Documenta Indica*, XVII: 259–88 (esp. 267–68).

18   See Michael Cooper, *The Japanese Mission to Europe, 1582–1590: The Journey of Four Samurai Boys through Portugal, Spain and Italy* (Folkestone: Global Oriental, 2005).

19   Alessandro Valignano, *Sumario de las cosas del Japón (1583)* ..., ed. José Álvarez-Taladriz, Monumenta Nipponica Monographs, 9 (Tokyo: Sophia University Press, 1954), 131–32.

20   For the original document see ARSI, *Iap.–Sin.*, 23, fols. 9r–10v. For Valignano's justification of his actions, see his letter to Mercurian (Nagasaki, 15 August 1580) in ARSI, *Iap.–Sin.*, 8/1, fols. 277r–279r and his *Sumario (1583)*, 77–80. See also Schütte, *Valignano's Mission Principles*, 1/1: 327–34.

21   See George Elison, *Deus Destroyed: The Image of Christianity in Early Modern Japan* (Cambridge, MA: Harvard University Press, 1988), 115–18; and his "Christianity and the Daimyo," in John Whitney Hall, ed., *The Cambridge History of Japan*, vol. IV, *Early Modern Japan* (Cambridge: Cambridge University Press, 1991), 347–53; 359–65.

22   For the apostolic constitutions *Super Specula* (23 January 1575) and *Ex Pastorali Officio* (28 January 1585) and his *viva voce* declaration, *Summi Sacerdocii Curam* (13 December 1577), see Leo Magnino, *Pontificia Nipponica. Le relazioni tra la Santa Sede e il Giappone attraverso i documenti pontifici*, 2 vols. (Rome: Officium Libri Catholici, 1947–48), I: 16–22.

23   See Diego Pacheco, "Diego de Mesquita, S.J. and the Jesuit Mission Press," *Monumenta Nipponica* 26 (1971), 431–43.

24   The Franciscans denied the pilot had ever made any such statement and countered by claiming that it had been the Jesuits and the Portuguese who had accused the Spanish of employing such methods. See Charles R. Boxer, *The Christian Century in Japan, 1549–1650* (Berkeley: University of California Press, 1951), 163–67, 415–24; Elison, *Deus Destroyed*, 136–41, 425–28.

25   See Schütte, *Introductio*, 200, 344–45, 746 and his *Monumenta Historica Japoniae I. Textus Catalogorum Japoniae* ... (Rome: Monumenta Historica Societatis Iesu, 1975), 559, 576–77.

26   See Juan Ruiz-de-Medina, *El Martirologio del Japón (1558–1873)* (Rome: Institum Historicum Societatis Iesu, 1999), 217–23.

27   See ibid., 249–50.

28   For a detailed account of Ferreira see Elison, *Deus Destroyed*, 185–211.

29   See Tertullian, *Apologeticus adversus gentes pro christianis*, 50.

30   See Ruiz-de-Medina, *Martirologio*, 256–58; Schütte, *Introductio*, 373–75.

31   See Ruiz-de-Medina, *Martirologio*, 257; Elison, *Deus Destroyed*, 237–42. For the text of the *Seiyō kibun*, see *Arai Hakuseki zenshū*, ed. Ichijima Kenkichi, 6 vols. (Tokyo: Kokusho Kankō-kai, 1905–7), IV: 741–97.

32 See Andrew C. Ross, *A Vision Betrayed: The Jesuits in Japan and China, 1542–1742* (New York: Orbis, 1994); Michael Cooper, "A Mission Interrupted: Japan," in Ronnie Po-Chia Hsia, ed., *A Companion to the Reformation World* (Oxford: Blackwell, 2004), 393–407.
33 For an analysis of these statistics, see Schütte, *Introductio*, 408–34.
34 This is the assessment of George Elison in *Deus Destroyed*, 248–49.

10 Jesuits in China

NICOLAS STANDAERT

HISTORICAL OVERVIEW

In the last letter that is preserved from Francis Xavier, written from the island of Shangchuan off the shore of China two weeks before his death on 3 December 1552, he expressed his hope of going to China despite the many difficulties involved. It was, however, thirty years before Matteo Ricci (1552–1610) obtained permission for a permanent residence on the mainland (in 1583). The Jesuit presence during the next two hundred years can roughly be divided into five periods, each covering approximately thirty to forty years.[1]

The first period, from 1583 to 1616, was the time of the pioneers.[2] It was characterized by Matteo Ricci's activities.[3] Not only did he gradually develop a missionary strategy under the encouragement of the Visitor of Asia, Alessandro Valignano (1539–1606); Ricci was also responsible for an "ascent to Beijing," a movement from the south to the north and from the periphery to the center. In 1610, at the moment of the death of Matteo Ricci, there were merely sixteen Jesuits in China, eight Chinese and eight foreigners, with around 2,500 Christians. A few years later, in 1616–17, an anti-Christian movement forced the Jesuits to withdraw to the center of the country.

Around 1620, when the situation calmed down, a new group of missionaries initiated a second period. These included several Jesuits versed in mathematics or Aristotelian philosophy, among them Johann Adam Schall von Bell (1592–1666). Due to their efforts, Jesuits were involved in large-scale translation activities, of both religious and scientific writings. There was also a territorial expansion: first in the central Jiangnan region, next in the provinces of Fujian and Shaanxi–Shanxi. In the 1630s, in addition to the arrival of the mendicant orders, there was also a change in the Jesuit missionary policy. Jesuits made a double shift: in Beijing they mainly sought imperial protection and contacts with court officials who became more important than the *literati*, while at the local level they moved their attention to the lower levels of the *literati* and to commoners.

The year 1644, when the Ming court fell and was superseded by the Manchu leaders of the Qing, is more the symbolic than the effective date of a new period. By that time most of the early missionaries and their Chinese elite acquaintances had died, but Johann Adam Schall von Bell provided the transition and was almost immediately appointed to the post of Director of the Astronomical Bureau. From that time onward until the 1770s Jesuits assumed leading positions in the Bureau. In the early years of the Qing dynasty, despite the numerous internal disturbances in China, Christian communities expanded due to the organization of confraternities. A conflict about the calendar in the years 1664–65 resulted in the expulsion of all Jesuits, except four, to Canton. This period of exile was important because the Jesuits discussed with other religious orders the policy concerning the Chinese rites. In 1671 they were allowed to return to their former mission areas. In the subsequent years, Jesuits consolidated with vigor and publicity the efforts they had undertaken before the exile. While Ferdinand Verbiest (1623–88) was actively involved at the court, where he taught mathematics to the Kangxi emperor (reigned 1662–1722), many others dynamically promoted the expansion of Christian communities in the provinces.

In 1688, the year in which Verbiest died, the first three Chinese Jesuits to become priests were ordained on the mainland. The year 1688 was also characterized by the arrival of the French Jesuits who represented a new type of European Jesuit. Known as "Mathématiciens du Roy," they did not fall under the Portuguese *patroado*, but were supplied with pensions from the French king, Louis XIV, while being corresponding members of the newly founded Académie royale des sciences. The increasing number of French Jesuits who worked directly at the court resulted in a conflict between them and the Portuguese Jesuits working at the Astronomical Bureau. As a result, the French mission was separated from the Portuguese vice-province in November 1700. Though a considerable part of their efforts was dedicated to the Rites Controversy, the French Jesuits became known for their preoccupation with scientific matters, such as the major project of mapping the whole of China. Their writings about China also influenced European Enlightenment thinkers.

During the reign of the relatively tolerant Kangxi emperor, the Jesuits succeeded in preventing several times the expulsion of the missionaries. After his death, however, Christianity was proscribed. In 1724, many missionaries in the provinces were deported to Canton, and were expelled to Macao in 1732, including eighteen Jesuits. While the division between "Portuguese" and French Jesuits continued to exist and to be important, this final period brought about a more articulated division between those Jesuits legally in the service of the emperor at the capital, and those who now illegally and secretly did pastoral work in the provinces outside Beijing. In order to sustain the local communities, the Society of Jesus accepted more Chinese into its ranks. Some of them spent part of their formation in Europe. In 1773, the Society of Jesus was dissolved, a dissolution which was promulgated in China in 1775. The former Jesuits remained in China working there as secular priests, subject to bishops or apostolic vicars.

STATISTICS

While in total over 400 Jesuits were active in China during this whole period of 1583–1775, in terms of statistics the number of Jesuits who served at any one time was small. During the whole period, their number never reached one hundred. The general statistical trend shows a pyramidal structure reaching its zenith around 1700, with a progressive increase in the number of Jesuits in China until 1700, and a progressive decline thereafter. In fact, from 1583 till 1688 there were fewer than forty Jesuits working at the same time in China. In the 1690s there was a sharp increase due to the more favorable situation for Christianity. Exceptional years were 1701–3 when more than ninety Jesuits operated in China. After these golden years, the missionary presence began to decline, because of the Rites Controversy and imperial proscription of Christianity. Due to the Canton exile of 1724 and the subsequent expulsion of 1732, their number was reduced. But since new court Jesuits were allowed to enter the country and Chinese Jesuits were ordained, until the dissolution, there were for most of the time between fifty and seventy Jesuits in the country. Knowing that China's total population increased from about 150 million in the early seventeenth century to more than 250 million in the middle of the eighteenth century, numerically speaking the Jesuits had a very limited impact.

The statistical data can also be broken down according to the most important nationality groupings. The number of Portuguese Jesuits followed quite closely the evolution of the total Jesuit contingent. The French Jesuits arrived en force in 1688–98 and were to play an important role throughout the eighteenth century. In the early seventeenth century there was a small number of Chinese Jesuits, but after a complete decline in the middle of the century their number increased.

In the eighteenth century they played a major role. Between 1732 and 1743 the number of Chinese Jesuits increased significantly, from six to twenty-two. In 1748, they constituted one third of the Jesuits in China and thus became the largest nationality group among the Jesuits, a situation that continued for about twenty years.

JESUIT CORPORATE CULTURE

The Jesuits of the early period laid the foundations of a strategy that would characterize their missionary policy during the following two centuries. It had been conceived by Alessandro Valignano and creatively put into practice by Matteo Ricci and his successors. It can be described by four major characteristics:[5]

1 A policy of accommodation or adaptation to Chinese culture. Valignano, who had been disappointed by the limited degree of the adaptation of the Jesuits in Japan to Japanese culture, insisted in the first place on knowledge of the Chinese language. Probably inspired by the Japanese situation, the first Jesuits dressed like Buddhist monks. In 1595, after nearly fifteen years of experience, they changed their policy and adapted themselves to the lifestyle and etiquette of the Confucian elite of *literati* and officials. Ricci was responsible for this change. This new policy would remain unchanged throughout the seventeenth and eighteenth centuries and for most Jesuit missionaries Ricci became the reference point with regard to the accommodation policy.

2 Propagation and evangelization "from the top down." Jesuits addressed themselves to the literate elite. The underlying idea was that if this elite, preferably the emperor and his court, were converted, the whole country would be won for Christianity. The elite consisted mainly of *literati* who had spent many years of their life preparing for the examinations so as to enter officialdom. In order to enter into contact with this elite, M. Ricci studied the Confucian classics and, with his remarkable gift of memory, became a welcome guest at the philosophical discussion groups that were organized by this elite. In the early period, several of them converted to Christianity: Paul Xu Guangqi (1562–1633), Leo Li Zhizao (1565–1630), Michael Yang Tingyun (1562–1627) and Philip Wang Zheng (1571–1644).[6] From the 1630s, however, the contacts with the *literati* elite weakened, and became mainly focused on the court and court officials in Beijing.

3 Indirect propagation by using European science and technology in order to attract the attention of the educated Chinese and convince them of the high level of European civilization. Jesuits offered a European clock to the emperor, they introduced paintings that surprised the Chinese by their use of geometric perspective, translated mathematical writings of Euclid, translated books on the calendar, agriculture, and technology, and printed an enormous global map which integrated the results of the latest world explorations. From the middle of the seventeenth century, well-trained Jesuit scientists occupied positions at the Astronomical Bureau and became gradually involved in court activities. In the hope of strengthening the position of Christianity, they were teaching mathematics, involved in cannon building, participating in diplomatic negotiations with Moscow, mapping China, and preoccupied with artistic activities such as painting, architecture, and construction of artifacts (clocks, glass, and enamelware). The most well-known Jesuit in this regard is Giuseppe Castiglione (1688–1766). Often there was a subtle interplay between the missionaries and the emperor, in which both sides took advantage of the other for their own purposes. The missionaries tried to please the emperor as much as possible, while the emperor, from his side, amply availed himself of their services and led them even to make ambivalent choices.

4 Openness to and tolerance of Chinese values. In China, Jesuits encountered a society with high moral values for which they expressed their admiration. They were of the opinion that the excellent social doctrine should be complemented with the metaphysical ideas of Christianity. However, Jesuits rejected Buddhism and Neo-Confucianism, which, in their eyes, was corrupted by Buddhism. They pleaded for a return to original Confucianism which they considered to be a philosophy based on natural law. In their opinion it contained the idea of God and therefore they also used traditional Chinese names for God.[7] Finally, they adopted a tolerant attitude towards certain Confucian rites, like the ancestral worship and the veneration of Confucius, which they declared to be "civil rites." These aspects would result in the "Rites Controversy" and in their condemnation in the early eighteenth century.[8]

The Jesuit corporate culture in China, however, is not only the result of a conscious and well-defined policy conceived by Jesuits themselves. It is also to a large extent the result of their reaction to what China was and who the Chinese were. In other words, their corporate identity was shaped by the Chinese other as well. If the Jesuits in China became who they became, it was also because the "other" encouraged them actively or passively to become like that. There are many examples of how Jesuits' activities were shaped by the Chinese, including by those who opposed their ideas and actions.[9] Many of them can be summarized under the label "cultural imperative," a characteristic belonging to the structure of Chinese religious life in late imperial China.[10] No marginal religion penetrating from the outside could expect to take root in China (at least at a high social level) unless it conformed itself to a pattern that in late imperial times was more clearly defined than ever. Confucianism represented what is *zheng* ("orthodox" or "orthoprax") in a religious, ritual, social, and political sense. In order not to be branded as *xie* ("heterodox" or "heteroprax") and to be treated as a subversive sect, a marginal religion had to prove that it was on the side of *zheng*. In other words, the adaptation was not only a choice, but was also to a large extent constantly imposed on the Jesuits. In this process, it was the Chinese who occupied the dominant position, since they effectively hosted the foreigners on their own territory, obliging them to adapt to the native culture. The clearest example of this was the predominance of the Chinese or Manchu language throughout the exchange. With the exception of a very small number of Chinese educated for the priesthood, no Chinese involved in the interaction learned a foreign language.

Another example is the field of sciences and technology. If Chinese scholars of the early seventeenth century were attracted by the science brought by the Jesuits, it was because prior to their arrival Chinese *literati* were already interested in practical learning. The search for "solid learning" or "concrete studies" was a reaction against some intuitionist movements originating from a Neo-Confucian school in the late sixteenth century. In the early seventeenth century, an influential intellectual and political movement re-established the importance of "things in the world." It was this preceding quest that led to the unique interaction between them and the Jesuits. Also, at the end of the seventeenth century, missionaries with a specific scientific training were sent to China in order to respond to the quest of the court and, especially in the eighteenth century, their artistic and technical activities were largely determined by the court. Finally, one may also point out that Chinese society imposed some limits on the activities of the Jesuits. It is indeed remarkable that Jesuits apparently were not able to accommodate themselves to certain aspects of Chinese culture because they were too difficult to master or were too different from the European background. This concerns aspects of Jesuit corporate culture in Europe and many parts of the world, but which were not put into practice in China. The clearest example is that of schools and education. Despite their hope to replace the contents of the Chinese exams with Aristotelian philosophy, Jesuits were never able to adopt the well-established Chinese education system.

BUILDING COMMUNITIES OF EFFECTIVE RITUALS

The image of the Jesuit mission in China in contemporary and modern sources is predominantly one of an elite mission. This image is evoked by several factors: the general policy of the Jesuits to propagate "from the top down"; the actual conversion of some high officials in the late Ming period who are referred to in many Chinese and Western books as examples of the success of this policy; the publication of many books, including scientific texts, by both missionaries and converts indicating a notable activity among a literary elite; the presence of Jesuits who worked in the imperial service; and, finally, a general knowledge of Christianity predominantly based on published sources that inevitably draw attention to literate groups.

The image of the Jesuit mission as primarily elite is cast in a different light if one looks at the statistics of the Christian population.[11] A rather rare and very specific statistic of 1636 shows that the elite represented only 1.33 percent of the total Catholic population, while the number of literate persons probably did not exceed 10 percent of the total Catholic population. In other words, by far the largest group of Christians were illiterate commoners. Jesuits often complained about the fact that most Christians were *pauperes* (people with little property). But they also saw it as proof that it was more difficult for the rich to enter the Kingdom of God since they were too attached to the world, to their wealth, and to their concubines. Primary sources on these commoners, however, are much scarcer in comparison to sources about the elite. Still, the strongest and most durable incorporation of the Jesuit missions did take place among the popular levels of society where it took the form of communities of effective rituals.

At the level of these communities, Christianity was shaped by Chinese religious culture. The clearest example of this is the organization of the Church. Chinese Christians were not organized in parishes, i.e., geographical units around a church building, but in *hui* (assemblies or associations), which in Chinese society were one of the most important ways of lay participation in the life of the Buddhist or Taoist clergy.[12] These associations were often constituted according to age, sex, and social background, with laypeople as leaders. The activities of the groups differed, from activities stressing personal cultivation to devotion to works of charity. They were established on the initiative of Chinese Christians or Jesuit missionaries. As a result, they represented a fusion of traditional Chinese and Christian elements. Jesuits, who were well acquainted with societal life such as the Sodality of Mary in Europe, encouraged the establishment of such associations in China. Important, however, is that Jesuits merely reinforced a traditional pattern within the Chinese context, and that their converts probably needed little encouragement to set up such bodies by themselves. In the late Ming period Chinese Christians, such as Yang Tingyun and Wang Zheng, patterned their communities on Confucian or Buddhist models, some of them with an explicitly charitable purpose. In the early Qing, associations were a mixture of a Chinese type of social organization and European-inspired congregations, actively promoted by Francesco Brancati (1623–71). Around 1665, there were around 140 congregations in Shanghai while there were more than 400 Christian congregations in the whole of China.

These communities of Christians (*christianitas*) were present in both cities and villages. The incorporation of Christianity at this local level took place in the form of what can be described as "communities of effective rituals": groups of Christians whose life was organized around certain rituals (mass, feasts, confession, etc.). These rituals were related to faith and doctrine, and were organized by a liturgical calendar. They were "effective" both in the sense that they built a group and that they were considered by the members of the group as bringing meaning and salvation. On these lower levels, adaptation to the Confucian imperative was less important, and accommodative strategies explaining the Christian message in Confucian terms less necessary. Jesuits working at this level were not necessarily engaged in the translation of mathematical writings or the study of Confucian classics. They announced the Christian Gospel in a very explicit way (without underexposing aspects that were difficult to accept), and referred to Bible stories and stories of European saints and sages. They gave the Spiritual Exercises to individuals and organized retreats for groups. Jesuits practiced rituals (mass, confession), performed exorcism, conducted a pastoral strategy of fear and hope (with the idea of heaven and hell), and spread tales of the supernatural that were not different from Taoist or Buddhist popular traditions. Chinese primary sources show how in small communities of Chinese converts in remote provinces Jesuits had to compete, not with learned Buddhist monks and anti-Christian scholars, but rather with local Taoist masters, sorcerers, and faith healers. There also Jesuits engaged in practices that, at least in the eyes of Chinese authorities, fully belonged to the sphere of potentially subversive cults. The Christian communities gradually came to function on their own. An itinerant priest (in the early period a foreigner, but in the eighteenth century predominantly Chinese) would visit them once or twice a year; in certain cases, the communities themselves moved to the city for one day of liturgical activity. Most Jesuits were most of the time involved in fostering these communities through pastoral care. These aspects also form part of Jesuit corporate culture, although they have often been considered as marginal by historiography.

APOSTOLATE THROUGH BOOKS

In addition to pastoral activities, Jesuits were involved in many other activities that found their reflection in the publication of books. They in fact actively promoted an "apostolate through books" (*Apostolat der Presse*).[13] Herein they were helped by the flourishing of the publishing and printing industry in late Ming and early Qing China that played an important role not only in the intellectual changes of that time but also in the spread of Christianity. Indeed, by making dissenting opinions widely available, publishers and writers helped to create an intellectual environment that was conducive to the spread and reception of other streams of thought. In contradistinction to other countries where printing was often introduced by missionaries, in China Jesuits took full advantage of the well-developed printing industry that was already present. The simplicity of block printing made it possible for books to be published not only by official and commercial publishers, but also by private *literati*, families, or other small institutions (e.g., churches), which made reproduction in large or small quantities very easy. Moreover, the low prices made it possible to produce simple prayer books, catechisms, and leaflets for the widest possible readership. The absence of an effective institutional structure in either Ming or Qing China for systematic prepublication censorship of texts explains why missionaries and Christians were free to print and distribute their teachings.

As a result, the apostolate through books became one of the major means of spreading Christianity among the elite. Moreover, in addition to the numerous writings that made Christian doctrine and Western sciences known to a large public, writings directed at an inner-Church public increased as the number of Christians grew. The number of texts produced in Chinese by missionaries and Chinese Christians is quite impressive. For the seventeenth century, in addition to some 120 texts dealing with the West and its sciences, some 470 texts can be identified that are mainly related to religious and moral issues, of which some 330 were written by missionaries, most of them Jesuits.

It was again the Chinese scholars who entered into contact with the first Jesuits who to a large extent initiated the apostolate through books. The Chinese interest in the world map hanging in Ricci's room led to the relatively rapid transmission of the latest Renaissance knowledge about cartography, astronomy, and mathematics. Ricci published at least four versions of a world map in Chinese. In addition, he translated mathematical and astronomical writings with the help of Chinese scholars, especially Xu Guangqi and Li Zhizao. All these translations were based on works by Christophorus Clavius (1538–1612), astronomer and author of the Gregorian calendar reform, with whom Ricci had studied at the Roman College. Ricci's publication activities were not limited to scientific works. Besides catechetical writings, he published several humanistic writings which proclaimed wisdom from the West and which were explicitly written for a general, non-Christian readership. Since Ricci discerned Stoicism in ancient Confucianism, collections of edifying Stoic aphorisms became building blocks both for entering into dialogue with Confucianism and for introducing Christianity.

Ricci in many ways laid the foundation of the Jesuits' publication activities in the seventeenth and eighteenth centuries. After his death, Niccolò Longobardo (1565–1655) transformed Ricci's spontaneous and almost individual transmission into a "project" in terms of both planning and personnel. Longobardo sent Nicolas Trigault (1577–1628) to Europe to collect books and personnel. Trigault came back with a large library and several qualified Jesuit scientists. These would be the major source of the transmission of Renaissance culture that took place until the 1680s and can be divided into scientific and religious writings. The arrival of the French Jesuits initiated a new period, especially in the field of sciences. In the eighteenth century the transmission of Chinese culture to Europe became significantly more important.

Scientific writings

A first initiative stimulating the translation of scientific works into Chinese was the calendar reform project of the 1630s.[14] The main characteristic of this project is that it was largely initiated and led by the Chinese converts Xu Guangqi and Li Zhizao. After a proposal by Xu Guangqi to put the Jesuits to work on calendar reform was accepted in 1629, several Jesuits began compiling an astronomical compendium, with the help of some twenty Chinese specialists. The result of this work, *Calendar Compendium of the Chongzhen Era* (1631–35), comprised twenty-two works in 137 volumes and included texts that were based on European documents of a very recent date. The result of the work done at the Calendar Office mainly benefited the newly established Qing dynasty (beginning in 1644), to which Schall offered his service. In the seventeenth century, all Chinese preoccupied with astronomy or mathematics were aware of the works that had been translated in this project.

A rather ambitious project, but a less successful one, was the effort of the Jesuits to introduce Aristotelian philosophy in China. In this case, the initiative was mainly taken by Jesuits themselves, who, by emphasizing Aristotelianism, attempted to reproduce what was the basis of their own education. They were convinced that a good knowledge of this philosophy, including its stress on logic and dialectics, was required for understanding Western thought and sciences. There were two major translators: Francisco Furtado (1589–1653) collaborated with Li Zhizao and took the well-known Coimbra commentaries (*Commentarii Collegii Conimbricensis SJ*, 1592–1606) on Aristotelian philosophy as his primary source. Alfonso Vagnone (1568/69–1640) worked in collaboration with several Chinese converts of the Shaanxi–Shanxi region, on Chinese adaptations of *Ethica Nicomachea*, *De Coelo et Mundo*, and *Meteorologica*.

The most ambitious project in the field of sciences and (natural) philosophy was undertaken by Ferdinand Verbiest. In 1683 he presented to the Kangxi emperor a collection of 60 volumes entitled *Qiongli xue* [Study of Fathoming Principles] to be printed by the court, as he expected. It included most of the aforementioned Aristotelian works, but also writings belonging to the philosophy of nature or *Physica* (such as mechanics, ballistics, and medicine). Verbiest not only wanted to expose the foundation of Western astronomy and faith, but also hoped that this philosophy would be adopted as part of the curriculum for the Chinese state examination system. To his disappointment, the emperor returned the collection with the remark of his advisors that the style and content did not correspond to Chinese wisdom.

After his death, the arrival of French Jesuits brought a new impulse to scientific investigations, although their proposals also led to some conflict with their Portuguese confreres. Characteristic of their publications is that they were often published with imperial patronage. Due to their contacts with Europe, new astronomical information was transmitted to China. For instance, in the eighteenth century, Jesuits produced several Chinese star maps and catalogues, which were based on the recent observations of French astronomers at the Paris Observatory. While teaching the Kangxi emperor mathematics the French Jesuits prepared several manuscript textbooks based on Ignace-Gaston Pardies's (1636–73) *Elémens de Géométrie* (Paris, 1671). These were first written in Manchu and then translated into Chinese. Due to the incorporation of Jesuits' mathematical manuscripts into a collection commissioned by the emperor in 1623, Western mathematics was integrated into a broader corpus, which constituted the discipline as reconstructed under imperial patronage. One of the greatest projects that the French Jesuits undertook was overseeing the imperial survey of the Chinese empire in 1708–17. By the first decade of the eighteenth century the need for an accurate geographical representation of China was quite apparent to the Kangxi emperor because of the rapidly expanding Manchu–Qing empire and because of earlier rebellions. Support from the emperor, combined with a sufficient number of Jesuits trained in cartographic technique and enough background information on the areas to be covered, allowed the Jesuits to contemplate the production of a complete, scientifically produced atlas based on a survey of the Chinese empire. Within a decade, 1708–17, this immense work was finished.

Religious-devotional writings

The catechetical, theological, and religious writings of the Jesuits are numerous and represent the main currents of their time in Europe.[15] The Jesuits carried with them the distinction between supernatural and natural theology that was common in Europe. Where supernatural theology was founded on revelation, natural theology was the knowledge that humans can have of the existence and nature of God by means of reason. The distinction between supernatural and natural theology influenced the division between two major genres of catechetical writings: the *Dottrina Christiana*, based on revelation, and the *Catechismus*, based on natural theology (not to be confused with the modern "catechism").

Jesuits produced several versions of the *Dottrina Christiana*, a rather small booklet, usually called *Tianzhu jiaoyao*. These works included the Chinese version of the most important prayers, the Ten Commandments, the creed, a list of the seven sacraments, the fourteen works of mercy, the eight beatitudes, the seven capital sins and the seven opposing virtues, and usually other short items, which vary from edition to edition. They were destined for literate catechumens, those who prepared themselves for baptism. Besides explanations of the *Dottrina* in its entirety, books with detailed commentaries on certain parts of it were published as well (e.g., explanations of the Lord's Prayer or the creed). Apart from some exceptions, these were not meant for outsiders.

The second genre was meant for people who were hardly acquainted with Christian teachings. A *Catechismus* tried to explain these fundamental notions through argumentation and to convince people of their truth according to the principles of natural reason. Often such a catechism had an apologetic nature and was written in the form of a dialogue. It was more substantive than prescriptive and also more intellectual and philosophical in approach. The most important *Catechismus* is Matteo Ricci's *Tianzhu shiyi* [The True Meaning of the Lord of Heaven] (1603).[16] It became the foundation for introducing the basic Christian teachings and this far beyond the seventeenth century. Several works appeared that treated some of the aspects included in *Tianzhu shiyi* in greater detail: creation, the soul, the angels, original sin and the retribution of good and evil. These writings were primarily based on the works of Thomistic theology as the missionaries had been taught these in their formation. It was not until 1645 that Lodovico Buglio started to partially translate Thomas Aquinas' *Summa Theologiae* (mainly *Pars Prima*), published in thirty volumes during the years 1654–78.

Dottrina Christiana virtually always contained a list of the seven sacraments, sometimes followed by short explanations. There were, however, not many separate treatises on the sacraments. Most treatises deal with confession and eucharist: for example, two books by Giulio Aleni (1582–1649), who was very active in the Fujian mission. This shows that, besides baptism, these two sacraments were not only often administered, but also needed a continuous explanation in the Christian community. As for the eucharist, an important concern was to teach converts how they should 'attend' mass (and not, as nowadays, participate in it). In his treatise on the mass Aleni had developed (supposedly based on European models) an allegorical explanation of the successive parts of the mass, which symbolically represented the mysteries of Jesus' life from his Incarnation to the Last Judgment. For liturgy, Lodovico Buglio also translated substantial parts of the liturgical manuals, in view of the formation of a Chinese clergy and in the expectation that Rome would grant new permission for an administration of the sacraments in Chinese by Chinese. In 1685, Philippe Couplet (1622–93) donated a copy of the Chinese Missal to the pope, but permission to celebrate the liturgy in Chinese did not follow.

In addition to these catechetical writings, Jesuits also engaged in other types of religious publication. Although during his stay in Rome Trigault had obtained permission for a translation of the Bible into Chinese in 1616, the Jesuits did not engage in such an enterprise, occupied as they were with the other projects, especially the reform of the calendar. Still, biblical narratives are present in other writings. A chronological *Life of Christ* by Giulio Aleni was based on *Vita Christi*, a popular work by Ludolphus de Saxonia (c. 1300–78). An illustrated companion volume contained Chinese adaptations of the copper engravings of Jerónimo Nadal's (1507–80) *Evangelicae Historiae Imagines* (Antwerp, 1593). Exegetical writings are rather rare. Among the prayer books, *Shengjiao rike* [Daily Exercises of the Holy Religion] (1665) represents a unique case in the history of prayer books since it has been in use for more than three hundred years. The translations were taken partly from the *Memorial de la Vida Christiana* of the Spanish mystic Luís de Granada, O. P. (1504–88). There was a also Chinese translation of Thomas à Kempis' *Imitatio Christi* (*Contemptus Mundi* in the "Granada" version). It was published posthumously, not by missionaries but by Chinese converts (c. 1680).

Contrary to the former category, which was meant for a broad public but eventually had a limited circulation, the writings of this category were intended for a confined, mainly inner-Church audience where they had a relatively wide readership. Several were translated by authors who were also known for their translations of scientific works. This confirms how the "religious" and "scientific" sides of their activities formed an integrated whole. Moreover, many Chinese scholars collaborated in their production, and can therefore rightly be called co-authors.

Books for Europe

Jesuits transmitted not only European knowledge to China, but also Chinese knowledge to Europe.[17] Writings such as Matteo Ricci's and Nicolas Trigault's *De Christiana Expeditione apud Sinas* (Augsburg, 1615), Álvaro de Semedo's (1585–1640) *Imperio de la China* (Madrid, 1642), and Martino Martini's (1614–61) *Novus Atlas Sinensis* (Amsterdam, 1654), all translated into several European languages, reached a wide readership. They treated both the different aspects of Chinese culture and the progress of Christian missions. Some writings were more apologetic in nature: Ferdinand Verbiest's *Astronomia Europaea* (Dillingen, 1687) and Louis Le Comte's *Nouveaux mémoires sur l'état présent de la Chine* (Paris, 1696) defended the Jesuit mission policy. The first translation of Chinese classics that aroused considerable attention was *Confucius Sinarum Philosophus* (1687), edited by Philippe Couplet (1622–93). The book contains an extensive introduction as well as the translations of three of the major Confucian books. In the eighteenth century a major source of information was the Jesuit letters, *Lettres édifiantes et curieuses*, published in different editions from 1702. Two other important comprehensive collections were: Jean-Baptiste Du Halde's *Description géographique, historique, chronologique, politique et physique de l'Empire de la Chine et de la Tartarie chinoise* (4 vols., Paris, 1735) and *Mémoires concernant l'histoire, les sciences, les arts, les moeurs, les usages des Chinois* (16 vols., Paris, 1776–1814) with as main authors Antoine Gaubil (1689–1759), Jean-Joseph-Marie Amiot (1718–93), and Pierre-Martial Cibot (1727–80). They discuss subjects as diverse as Chinese history, music, philosophy, literature, sciences, etc., in most cases based on Chinese primary sources.

These writings provoked different reactions in Europe. Aside from the inner-Church discussions about the Rites Controversy, Gottfried Wilhelm Leibniz's (1646–1716) broad interest in Chinese culture may duly be called unique among philosophers in early modern times. Leibniz gained a significant part of his knowledge about China through correspondence with Jesuits, among them the Figurist Joachim Bouvet (1656–1730) whose approach was partly adopted by Leibniz. While the Jesuits used their traditional concepts to deal with China, their very description of China influenced Enlightenment thinkers such as Charles de Montesquieu (1689–1755), François-Marie Voltaire (1694–1778), and Jean-Jacques Rousseau (1712–72). They used the missionaries' portrait of China as a test for their own theories. It appears that Jesuit writings about China, and more importantly the debates and the various interpretations that they provoked in the French intellectual context, contributed to several break-ups in the encompassing notion of "religion" in Europe: the split between the true Christian religion and a religion that was true but not Christian; the break between religion and morality; the breach between religion and history. In the end, these different changes resulted in a split between "religious" and "non-religious" spheres. It is only because of the birth of something like "non-religion" that "religion" as such became the subject of scientific study in the nineteenth century, as a separate domain of human life, to be distinguished from morality, philosophy, and science.

The history of the Jesuits in China was not simply a successful transmission of knowledge by a "generation of giants." The interaction and communication that took place between them and their Chinese partners was such that very often they were not the originators of a dialogue, but joined a dialogue that was already in progress. This dialogue is still going on today, both in the discussions on their achievements, and in the life of the Christian communities that trace their origin to Jesuit missionary activity.

Notes

1   There are not many general surveys of the history of the Jesuits in China; for a short survey and bibliography, see Claudia von Collani, "Jesuits," in N. Standaert, ed., *Handbook of Christianity in China, vol. 1: 635–1800* (Leiden: Brill, 2000), 309–21; the most comprehensive histories are Liam Matthew Brockey, *Journey to the East: The Jesuit Mission to China, 1579–1724* (Cambridge, MA: Harvard University Press, 2007) and Jean-Pierre Duteil, *Le mandat du ciel: Le rôle des Jésuites en Chine* (Paris: Éditions Arguments, 1994); for collective writings with selected topics, see, e.g., Catherine Jami and Hubert Delahaye, eds., *L'Europe en Chine: Interactions scientifiques, religieuses et culturelles aux XVIIe et XVIII siècles*, Mémoires de l'Institut des Hautes Études Chinoises, 34 (Paris: Collège de France, 1993); Federico Masini, ed., *Western Humanistic Culture Presented to China by Jesuit Missionaries (XVII–XVIII Centuries): Proceedings of the Conference Held in Rome, October 25–27, 1993*, Bibliotheca Instituti Historici Societatis Iesu, 49 (Rome: Institutum Historicum Societatis Iesu, 1996); Charles Ronan and Bonnie Oh, eds., *East Meets West: The Jesuits in China, 1582–1773* (Chicago: Loyola University Press, 1988).
2   On this period, see George H. Dunne, *Generation of Giants: The Story of the Jesuits in China in the Last Decades of the Ming Dynasty* (Notre Dame: University of Notre Dame Press, 1962).
3   There are many studies on M. Ricci; the most comprehensive is Johannes Bettray, *Die Akkommodationsmethode des P. Matteo Ricci S. J. in China* (Rome: Pontificia Università Gregoriana, 1955); in English see, e.g., the book by Jonathan D. Spence, *The Memory Palace of Matteo Ricci* (New York: Viking, 1984); for the edition of his *Journal*, see Pasquale M. d'Elia, ed., *Fonti Ricciane*, 3 vols. (Rome: La Libreria dello stato, 1942–49); the Latin version was translated into English: see *China in the Sixteenth Century: The Journals of Matthew Ricci, 1583–1610*, trans. Louis J. Gallagher (New York: Random House, 1953).
4   See Nicolas Standaert, "The Jesuit Presence in China (1580–1773): A Statistical Approach," *Sino-Western Cultural Relations Journal* 13 (1991), 4–17. For biographical data about the Jesuits who went to China, see Joseph Dehergne, *Répertoire des jésuites de Chine de 1552 à 1800* (Rome: Institutum Historicum Societatis Iesu, 1973); for a short biography and bibliography, see Louis Pfister, *Notices biographiques et bibliographiques sur les jésuites de l'ancienne mission de Chine (1552–1773)* (Shanghai, 1932).

5 See Nicolas Standaert, "Jesuit Corporate Culture as Shaped by the Chinese," in J. W. O'Malley, G. A. Bailey, S. Harris, and T. F. Kennedy, eds., *The Jesuits: Cultures, Sciences, and the Arts, 1540–1773* (Toronto: University of Toronto Press, 1999), 352–63.

6 See Nicolas Standaert, "The Four Principal Converts," in Standaert, *Handbook of Christianity in China*, 404–20.

7 For the Jesuits' attitude towards Confucianism, see Paul Rule, *K'ung-tzu or Confucius? The Jesuit Interpretation of Confucianism* (Sydney: Allen & Unwin, 1986).

8 On the Rites Controversy, see David E. Mungello, ed., *The Chinese Rites Controversy: Its History and Meaning*, Monumenta Serica Monograph Series, 33 (Nettetal: Steyler Verlag, 1994); see also Nicolas Standaert, "Rites Controversy," in Standaert, *Handbook of Christianity in China*, 680–88.

9 On the Chinese reaction, see especially Jacques Gernet, *Chine et christianisme: Action et réaction* (Paris: Gallimard, 1982; 1990); *China and the Christian Impact*, trans. J. Lloyd (Cambridge: Cambridge University Press, 1985).

10 On this topic, see Erik Zürcher, "Jesuit Accommodation and the Chinese Cultural Imperative," in Mungello, *The Chinese Rites Controversy*, 31–64.

11 See Nicolas Standaert, "Number of Chinese Christians," in Standaert, *Handbook of Christianity in China*, 380–93.

12 See Nicolas Standaert, "Associations for Lay-People", in Standaert, *Handbook of Christianity in China*, 456–61.

13 Bettray, *Akkommodationsmethode*, 181ff.; A. Dudink and N. Standaert, "Apostolate through Books," in Standaert, *Handbook of Christianity in China*, 600–31.

14 See Catherine Jami, "Science and Technology: General Reception," in Standaert, *Handbook of Christianity in China*, 689–710.

15 Dudink and Standaert, "Apostolate through Books," 608ff.

16 For an English translation, see Matteo Ricci, *The True Meaning of the Lord of Heaven (T'ien-chu shih-i)*, trans. Douglas Lancashire and Peter Hu Kuo-chen, ed. E. Malatesta (St. Louis: Institute of Jesuit Sources; Taibei: Ricci Institute, 1985).

17 See Dominic Sachsenmaier, "Cultural Transmission to Europe," in Standaert, *Handbook of Christianity in China*, 879–906; David E. Mungello, *Curious Land: Jesuit Accommodation and the Origins of Sinology*, Studia Leibnitiana Supplementa, 25 (Wiesbaden: Steiner Verlag, 1985).

11 The Jesuits in New France

JACQUES MONET

Seventy-five years after the approval of the Society of Jesus by Pope Paul III in 1540 and fifty-five years after the death of its founder, Ignatius Loyola, the French Jesuit priests Pierre Biard (1567–1622) and Ennemond Massé (1575–1646) set foot in New France at Port Royal, 22 May 1601. "It is according to our divine calling," Ignatius Loyola had written, "to travel to various places and to live in any part of the world where there is hope of God's greater service and the help of souls";[1] and in New France these "Blackrobes," as they were soon affectionately called, immediately began to reach out to the aboriginal peoples of the vast new land.

They went first to a band of Mi'kmaq living nearby whose chief Membertou had been baptized thirteen months earlier by Jessé Fléché, a diocesan priest accompanying a small expedition sponsored by the governor of Acadia. Membertou and his family were the first aboriginal people to receive solemn baptism in New France. Two years later the two Jesuit priests, having been taken prisoner by the English, were returned to France. In the long run, this first Jesuit mission, despite its short duration, would, in its frequent recounting, inspire many vocations among the students of the Jesuit colleges in France.

Jesuits returned to New France in 1625, this time to the settlement founded in 1608 by Samuel de Champlain at Quebec, whose population numbered only around seventy. Three priests, Ennemond Massé again, Charles Lalemant (1587–1674), and Jean de Brébeuf (1593–1649), as well as two Jesuit brothers, François Charton (1593–1657) and Gilbert Burel (1585–1661), landed there on 15 June 1625. They would be followed by new arrivals almost every year until by 1760 some 330 had come and seven Canadian-born young men had joined the Order.

The first task of the early pioneers was to make themselves familiar with the various places, people, and aboriginal languages. The second was to convince Cardinal Richelieu to found a company of wealthy Catholic courtiers, merchants, and officers of state whose donations and commercial interests could support the colony. This would be the Compagnie des Cent Associés, established in 1628. "Notre Dame des Anges" (Our Lady of the Angels) was the name they gave their residence, which included a school room, in which in 1632 they began teaching two boys, one of seven and the other of ten years of age.

A third task was to reach out to the Native people. They followed the wanderers, the Montagnais at first, and then the Algonquins. They made their way into the forests, along the waterways, across the portages and through the woods. "The history of their labours," George Bancroft wrote two centuries later with only a little exaggeration, "is connected with the origin of every celebrated town in the annals of French America. Not a cape was turned, nor a river entered, but a Jesuit led the way."[2] By 1745, Gabriel Drouillettes (1610–81) had brought the Gospel to the nations along the Atlantic coast, Charles Albanel (1616–96) to those on James Bay, while Claude Allouez (1622–80), Jean-Pierre Aulneau (1705–36), and Godefroy Coquart (1706–65), scouring three thousand miles along the Great Lakes and on to the prairies as far as Lake Winnipeg, had made contact with some twenty-three peoples of differing languages and customs. Most famously, Jacques Marquette (1637–75) had discovered the great waterway that would bring Christianity into the lives of thousands more in the heart of the continent.

The most illustrious of the early Jesuit missions is the tragic failure of Saint Jean de Brébeuf and his companions in Wendake. They had hoped to establish there a church that would be at once fully Catholic and fully Wendat. The Wendat, allied with the French since the founding of Quebec as fur-trading and military partners, formed a more compact sedentary nation of efficient farmers numbering in 1615 close to 30,000 people spread out in some twenty villages. By the late 1630s, they were served by seven churches, most of them begun by Brébeuf, whose style was to live among the Wendat in their villages.

In 1639 Jérôme Lalemant (1593–1673), who succeeded Brébeuf as superior in 1638, decided to build Sainte-Marie, as a central fortified residence for the missionaries and for the Christian Wendat, "a house of prayer and a home of peace."[3] He saw it as the center of a larger community in which aboriginal and white people would dwell together in harmony, where the rites and the traditions of the Wendat and the Europeans could be strengthened and enriched by the values of the Gospel. At its busiest, in 1648, it housed twenty-three Jesuits and twenty-three *donnés* (young French laymen who volunteered to serve the missionaries for a time), four boys, seven domestics and eight soldiers. In addition to a "European compound" that included a Jesuit residence and a chapel, it held a church, a farm large and varied enough to make the mission relatively self-sufficient, a hospital, a school, and a large compound of longhouses for some 200 Christian Wendat and others who, at any given time during the year, might number as many as 500. It was there that Joseph Chihwatenha, the first Wendat leader to be baptized (16 August 1637), made the Spiritual Exercises of Saint Ignatius in January 1640, a few months before he was murdered, probably because he had become a Christian.

Conversions of adults were rare at first, and the Blackrobes suspect. People felt perplexed at their preaching, buffeted about between heaven, purgatory, and hell, in constant danger of eternal destruction ... like a birch-bark canoe caught in the rapids. In addition they realized the presence of the French among them was bringing disease and death, Blackrobes apparently spreading the illness.[4] The epidemic of smallpox and dysentery in 1634, the contagion of malignant influenza in 1636, and a second plague of smallpox in 1639 reduced the Wendat population to 12,000, one fifth of the estimate Brébeuf and Champlain had made some twenty years earlier.

Gradually, however, through the example of the Jesuits' courage and energetic ability, and the attractiveness of Brébeuf's commonsense personality and supernatural wisdom, the faith began to make progress. There were 120 baptisms between June 1643 and March 1644. In the public and social life of Wendake, new converts soon exercised a considerable ascendency, thus drawing more of their people to Christianity. By the end of the 1640s, the faith had taken solid root in Wendake.

The mission, however, was doomed! The Wendat and the Iroquois, deep in tribal warfare for generations, had become embroiled in the intrigues of the Dutch, English, and French rivalries, in the politics of the fur and brandy trades. A first wave of Iroquois attacks hit Wendake in 1648. Within eighteen months, one village after another was destroyed, and about one thousand Wendat Christians taken prisoner. By the spring of 1650, six of the Blackrobes had been put to an atrocious death and Sainte-Marie had been burned to the ground lest its supplies fall into the hands of the enemy. Surviving Blackrobes and Wendat went off to distant shores: some to Lake Superior and posts to the west where, with Claude Allouez, they organized the Mission of Chekouamegon in 1665. About 300 others went eastwards, eventually to Loretteville, near Quebec, where, encouraged by Joseph-Marie Chaumonot (1611–93), they practiced their faith with such holiness and charity that the site of their church became a place of pilgrimage for the French.[5]

Eight of the heroes of the Wendat mission were canonized by Pope Pius XI on 29 June 1930 and declared to be the secondary patrons of Canada (after Saint Joseph) by Pope Pius XII on 16 October 1940. They are Jean de Brébeuf; Gabriel Lalemant (1610–49) nephew of Charles and Jérôme, who had just come to Wendake when he was captured with Brébeuf and put to death with him; Isaac Jogues (1607–46), who was Master of the Works in the construction of Sainte-Marie and was twice captured by the Iroquois: in 1642 on a return trip to Quebec for provisions, when his companion, René Goupil (1608–42), was slain for making the sign of the cross over a native child; then a second time, in 1646, when on a peace mission to the Iroquois he was killed along with the *donné* Jean de La Lande (1629–46); Antoine Daniel (1601–49), who fell riddled through with arrows and bullets at the door of the church in his mission at Teanaostaiaë as he sought to help his parishioners escape; Charles Garnier (1605–49), a gentle fearless man who was killed while he was helping the wounded during the Iroquois attack on his mission of Etharita; and Noël Chabanel (1613–49), a gifted linguist who suffered acutely in Wendake for not being able to learn Wendat, and bound himself by a vow to remain in New France until death. They and dozens of others, such as Joseph Chihwatenha and his wife Marie Aonetta, have since continued to inspire people down to the present.

Fervent Christians, the thousand or so Wendat victims of the invasion were reduced to slavery in the Iroquois country; they were rediscovered by the Jesuits five years later. Simon Le Moyne (1604–65), commissioned by the Governor of New France, began making contact with the Iroquois as an ambassador of peace. In 1666 the Iroquois actually asked for French Blackrobes and Jean Pierron (1631–1700) headed a small group of Jesuits who answered the call. (It may be at that time that his colleague Philippe Pierson (1642–88) composed the *De Religione*, a summary of religious doctrine to help the Christians in their new circumstances and, to this day, celebrated as the longest text ever written in the Wendat language.[6]) They met the young Kateri Tekakwitha. In 1675 she was baptized, a conversion that brought her continuing threats of death, until she succeeded in fleeing to Kanawake, the Iroquois Christian village near Montreal. There she became known for her life of austerity and saintliness.[7] Her biography, written by her spiritual director, Claude Chauchetière (1645–1709), and published shortly after her death, inspired many to visit her tomb, where miracles have continued to be reported ever since.

Is the inspiration the spirit of the devout? The Jesuits of New France were indeed of that "mystical" era, the French Counter-Reformation, when pious religious and lay men and women led intense lives of prayer, seeking union with God through contemplation, bodily mortification, and self-surrender – lives often rewarded with visions and deep spiritual insights.[8] Brébeuf was one of these. So were Isaac Jogues, Simon Le Moyne, and Claude Allouez, the latter held by some to be, after Brébeuf, the greatest missionary in the annals of New France. They considered it a grace and a privilege to suffer for their faith, in fact to be called to die for it. On hearing, for instance, of the martyrdoms of Brébeuf and Lalemant, Francesco-Giuseppe Bressani (1612–72), who had himself suffered cruelly at the hands of the Iroquois, wrote to his superior:

> Do not imagine that the rage of the Iroquois and the loss of many Christians, and of many catechumens can bring to naught the mystery of the cross of Christ and the efficacy of his blood. We shall die, we shall be captured, burned, butchered. Be it so. Those who die in their beds do not always die the best deaths. I see none of our company cast down.[9]

As Jesuits they sought the *magis*, that is, to do ever more and more for Jesus Christ. As in the "Third Week" of the Spiritual Exercises, their suffering and death could but bring them into greater conformity with Him.

Probably in reaction to the Lutheran emphasis on *sola fides*, the high-born and high-minded men and women of the French Counter-Reformation were also convinced that austerity and prayer were not enough without good works. To an extent Quebec, rather than the mission territories, was the main beneficiary of that spirituality. Paul Le Jeune (1591–1664), the superior of the whole mission, laid there the solid foundations of institutions that have since well stood the test of time. An active, enterprising, optimistic organizer as well as a refined intellectual, he established Notre-Dame-de-Recouvrance, the first public church in Quebec, which would become, in 1664, the first cathedral parish in the first diocese established north of Mexico; he also saw to building two chapels that were eventually transformed into permanent parishes: one in 1634 in the settlement Champlain was creating in Trois-Rivières, the gathering ground of Algonquin, Montagnais, and Wendat traders; the other, in 1635, in Tadoussac, at the mouth of the Saguenay, another meeting place where hundreds of Native people came every year to greet the trading vessels arriving from France.

In 1632 Le Jeune wrote to his superior in Paris, Barthélémy Jacquinot (1569–1648), a letter that became the first of the famed Jesuit *Relations*, or, to give them their full title, *Relations de ce qui s'est passé de plus remarquable aux missions des Pères de la Compagnie de Jésus en la Nouvelle-France*. Indeed, for the next forty years (1633–73) these yearly accounts of settlement life and missionary activity in New France, disseminated through the network of the Jesuit colleges, inspired many Jesuits to volunteer for work in North America and, avidly read by the French public, drew enthusiastic support both for the missions and for the progress of the colony. To the ethnographers and historians of the future they would also provide a well-spring of minute details on the reactions of the early white settlers and their adaptation to the new world. They are also invaluable accounts of the culture and life of the aboriginal people.[10]

By 1634, the school room in Notre-Dame des Anges was proving inadequate. Le Jeune added more space to open a college in 1635. It was the first such in North America, and it eventually evolved without interruption into Laval University. In 1648, a new half-quadrilateral stone building three stories high was built for it by Brother Jean Liégeois (1600–55). Liégeois was the designer as well as the foreman (of three brothers and three *donnés*). He had been apprenticed with the noted Jesuit architect Brother Etienne Martellange (1569–1641), who is credited with introducing Baroque architecture into France. Liégeois traveled back to Paris for advice and supplies at least three times during the building of the college. His building was added to in 1725 when the quadrilateral was completed according to some of his plans. It is of this latter building that the Swedish scientist and traveler Pieter Kalm wrote in 1749:

> The Jesuit college is much more striking than the governor's palace because of the nobility of its architecture. It would suit very well as a residence for a prince, if it were better located. It's about four times the size of the Governor General's residence, and the most beautiful building of the city.[11]

The student body grew slowly but steadily. There were five boys in 1635, sixteen in 1655, and 120 in 1669, being taught in the eight-year program by five professors in 1669 and sixteen in 1676. At the outset catechism, elementary Latin and native languages were the only subjects taught; later on grammar, classical poetry and literature were added as well as rhetoric with, later still, science, geography, mathematics, the principles of navigation and, after 1658, two years of

Thomistic philosophy. Astronomy was introduced in the 1640s by Giuseppe Bressani, the only Italian (and non-francophone) Jesuit to serve in New France. Then in 1671 at the personal request of Louis XIV, who sent the necessary devices and tools, the *donné* Jean de Saint-Martin began to teach hydrography. The king paid him 300 *livres* a year, as he did Saint-Martin's successor after 1674, Louis Jolliet, the co-discoverer of the Mississippi.

The college followed strictly the *Ratio studiorum* of the Jesuit colleges in Europe which focused on integrating intellectual, physical, and spiritual formation. Hence ballet, drama, and rhetoric: a Latin oration in October 1657, for example, to welcome a new Governor – Jean de Lauzon – *latina oratione et versibus gallicis*, or a grand playing of Corneille's *Le Cid* in 1652, or again on 28 July 1658 a spectacular outdoor pageant prepared by Paul Ragueneau (1608–80) and spoken in French, Latin, Wendat, and Algonquin.

As the years passed, Le Jeune's college also became the colony's main language school and center of learning, its precious library constituting the colony's main cultural institution. The library grew steadily from 1635 onwards until in the 1760s it held close to 1,000 volumes. These included a volume of Latin proverbs published in 1583; the 1531 edition of the works of Erasmus; the mathematical works of Christopher Clavius (1538–1612); the missionary writings of Alexandre de Rhodes (1583–1618); and what is considered to be the first book written in North America, the *Affectus Amantis Christum Jesum* composed at Sainte-Marie by Pierre Chastellain (1606–84) and published in Paris in 1647.[12]

As Le Jeune's efforts to attract native youngsters to a classical education at the college proved a failure his foundation came to serve almost exclusively the sons of French settlers. The same could not be said, however, for the school he inspired for the education of young girls. In his *Relation* of 1635 he called out what became his very famous cry: "Is there nowhere in France a woman who has heart enough to found for us here a convent school for girls which could be put under the direction of a brave and courageous widow?"[13] His appeal was heard, and doubly so: first by Marie-Madeleine de la Peltrie, a very rich young widow who persuaded the Ursuline mystic Marie de l'Incarnation and two companions from the monastery at Tours to come with her to found a convent in Quebec; second by Marie, Duchess of Aiguillon, another very rich young widow and a niece of Richelieu. She approached the Augustinian hospital sisters of Dieppe, who easily agreed on sending three of their number to open an *Hôtel-Dieu* near the Jesuit College in Quebec.

Were these six nuns the first women religious ever to leave Christian lands for the "foreign missions"? In any event their foundations, serving both French and Native people, have both survived very successfully into the twenty-first century.[14]

When Le Jeune left office as superior of the Jesuits at the end of 1639 he had truly established solid foundations. Among the French the faith was sound, strong, and robust; lived with pride. Among the Native peoples, it was held courageously but still terribly fragile. In fact, for all his energy and zeal, Le Jeune, like so many of his contemporaries, had not appreciated the Native culture. He was convinced that before becoming good Christians the Native people had to be "civilized" into the French way of life.

One who did appreciate and respect the aboriginal people was Brébeuf. "If I were asked to advise anyone who was beginning to work among the Native people," he wrote typically and after a quarter-century of experience, a short time before his death, in the *Relation of 1649*,

> I would tell them frankly what I think they will themselves learn by experience, that is, that they must be very careful not to condemn outright a thousand things which are part of Indian customs. It is easy to treat as "irreligious" what is merely clumsy, and to see the devil's intervention in what is merely human. People often think they must forbid as impious what is done in all innocence, or at most, because of some silly, but not criminal, custom. These customs can be gradually abolished, gently and efficaciously, by inducing the natives themselves to find out their irrelevance; to laugh at them, and to abandon them through their own judgement and knowledge. Remember that it is difficult to see all in one day, and time is the most reliable teacher that one can consult.[15]

Like Brébeuf, most of the more successful Jesuits realized they had much to learn from the Native peoples and their environment. There were some essentials: how to follow a true course through strange forests; how to sleep through freezing nights without freezing to death; how to make slitted wooden goggles against snow blindness; how to fish through the ice with nets; how to get accustomed to mosquitoes. There was a way of life, the choice of food, the use of medicinal herbs, the times for eloquence and oratory, the times for silence, for listening to the sounds of the wind blowing through the trees. Within two generations, they had learned to appreciate much of the "nobility" in native culture.[16]

They were men of the dawning age of reason, schooled in the leading colleges in France. They wrote dictionaries and commentaries on the native languages, and, with a keen sense of precision and scientific accuracy, they prepared miscellanies and reports on their discoveries. At the beginning of one such, Brébeuf insists: "I assure you that I shall state nothing that I have not seen myself or have not learned from persons very worthy of belief."[17] Their *Relations* abound in minute descriptions of animals, fish, and insects; of wild fruit, maple syrup, earthquakes, the climate, comets. Chapter X of the *Relation* of 1664–65, for instance, is obviously intended for the astronomers and scientists at the University of Paris. It describes thirteen observations of comets that all read more or less like this one:

> On the following day, December 22, at a quarter past four in the morning, the Comet's altitude was 15 degrees, 15 minutes; that of Spica, 21 degrees, 54 minutes; and the Azimuth between the Comet and Spica, 38 degrees, 22 minutes. The Star was East of the Comet; and consequently the latter's southern declination was 27 degrees, 31 minutes, and its right ascension, 162 degrees, 51 minutes.[18]

Another paragraph goes like this:

> We purposely omit the observation taken on the second, seventh, eleventh, thirteenth, fourteenth, and fifteenth of the same month of January, the high wind and excessive cold having disturbed our instruments, which we were unable to readjust with all the exactness necessary on such occasions.[19]

In addition to the *Relations* and the dictionaries of the native languages, the two most celebrated works of the Jesuits of New France are the *Moeurs des Sauvages amériquains, comparées aux moeurs des premiers temps* by Joseph-François Lafiteau (1681–1746), published in 1724, and the *Histoire et description générale de la Nouvelle-France, avec le Journal historique d'un voyage fait par ordre du roi dans l'Amérique septentrionale* by Pierre François-Xavier de Charlevoix (1682–1761), published in 1744. Like the *Relations* both of these have ever since been invaluable sources to scholars. Lafiteau's *Moeurs* has become a classic especially among anthropologists and ethnologists.[20] Charlevoix's *Histoire*, which was preceded in 1724 by a *Vie de la Mère Marie de l'Incarnation*, was eventually translated into several languages. The *Histoire*'s glowing description of the natural resources of New France is in fact credited with convincing the English to attack and conquer Canada.

Were the Jesuits in all this acting as agents of the French crown intent on strengthening and expanding its commercial and territorial empire? Would they even have understood the question, convinced as they were that their preaching of the Catholic faith coincided perfectly with the interests of the Most Christian King? It was the king who saw it as his duty to impose Pierre Biard and Ennemond Massé on the traders sailing to Port Royal in 1611. It was Marie de' Médici, the Queen Regent, who gave Paul Le Jeune a commission in 1632 to act as Governor over the colony in case of emergency. In the 1650s he and Charles Lalemant were her first two choices to be the first bishop of Quebec. (They refused, and instead Le Jeune in 1658 successfully secured from the Roman authorities the appointment of François de Laval in opposition to a Sulpician who would have been more respectful of the "liberties of the Gallican Church.")

Isaac Jogues and Simon Le Moyne were undoubtedly acting in the king's name as ambassadors to the Iroquois in 1646 and in the peace missions of the 1650s. So, less obviously, was Claude Allouez when, on 4 June 1671, as chaplain and principal orator, he accompanied François de Saint-Lusson to the Jesuit mission near Sault-Ste. Marie to proclaim the taking possession, in the king's name and in the presence of native chiefs from fourteen nations, of all the western territories "from the seas of the North and west to that of the south." By then New France had been made a royal province in 1663, mainly on the urging and strong advice of Paul Le Jeune, whose first letter to the young Louis XIV clearly made no distinction between Church and State. "Behold your colony of New France at the feet of Your Majesty," it began:

> .... As you will see by this account, a small band of Indians has reduced it. Listen, if it please Your Majesty, to her languishing voice, nay, to her dying words: "Save me, she cries, I am going to be bereft of the Catholic faith; they are tearing from my hands the fleur-de-lys. I shall be no longer French. They are taking from me the beautiful name I have so long carried."[21]

The power and glory of the *Roi Soleil* promoted the spread of the Gospel. Conversely, aboriginal nations who became Catholic also proved to be the most faithful and reliable allies. The Jesuits, who came to master the native languages – Allouez, for instance, was comfortable in over two dozen dialects, Marquette could preach fluently in six – were the diplomatic go-betweens. They reported, however, to their provincial superior in Paris, who himself reported to the Superior General in Rome. And it was one of the two latter, not the king, who decided on every assignment of each Jesuit missioned to New France.

The day did come, however, when the interests of the Jesuits, of the king, and of the pope did clash. That was in 1764, when the Society of Jesus was suppressed in France, an event that proved to be the harbinger of its suppression in the whole Church in the brief *Dominus ac Redemptor*, by Pope Clement XIV in 1773. New France, renamed the Province of Quebec, had, however, passed into the British Empire in 1760. Although forbidden to recruit, the dozen or so Jesuits in the colony at the time continued their work, as they did after 1773, the laws of the Empire not allowing the publication of the papal brief. They disappeared gradually. Pierre Potier (1708–81), an indefatigable philologist and the most prolific writer of his day on the languages both of the French Canadians and of the Native people, founded the mission of Notre Dame-de l'Assomption, on the south side of the Detroit River, in 1767 and served there until his death.[22] The last to pass away was Jean-Joseph Casot (1728–1800), who had come to Quebec as a brother during the Seven Years' War in 1757 and, because of the shortage of priests, had been ordained in 1766. Until his death at the beginning of the new century, he lived in a wing of the old college in Quebec, the remainder of the building occupied as a barracks for British troops.

Was this the way the Jesuits' world ended? With a whimper?

No. Restored by Pope Pius VII in 1814, nine French Jesuits returned to Canada in 1842. That, however, is another story.

Notes

1   *Rules of the Society* (Woodstock, MD: Woodstock College Press, 1956), 95. See also Augustus Coemans, *Commentary on the Rules of the Society of Jesus* (El Paso, TX: Revista Católica Press, 1942), 78.

2   George Bancroft, *History of the United States* (London: George Routledge and Co., n.d.), III: 783.

3   *The Jesuit Relations and Allied Documents, 1611–1800*, ed. Reuben Thwaites (Cleveland: Burrow Brothers, 1896–1901) (hereafter JR, Thwaites).

4   Thomas Worcester, S.J., "A Defensive Discourse: Jesuits on Disease in Seventeenth–Century New France," *French Colonial History* 6 (2005), 8.

5   The Jesuit story of Wendake is detailed in Lucien Campeau's *La Mission des Jésuites chez les Hurons, 1634–1650* (Montreal: Editions Bellarmin, 1987). It is volume 46 of the Bibiliotheca Instituti Historici Societatis Jesu published by the Institutum Historicum Societatis Jesu, Rome. In 2001 it came out in a translation by William Lonc and George Topp as *The Jesuit Mission to the Hurons, 1634–1650*, which is volume 3 in the series Early Jesuit Missions in Canada, published by William Lonc, produced and distributed by Steve Catlin, Martyrs'

Shrine, Midland, Ontario. Campeau's analysis and conclusions have been challenged and defended variously, most notably by James Axtell, *The Invasion Within: The Contest of Cultures in Colonial North America* (New York: Oxford University Press, 1985); Denys Delage, *Le pays renversé: Amérindiens et européens en Amérique du nord-est, 1600–1664* (Montreal: Boréal Express, 1985); Marc Jetten, *Enclaves amérindiennes: Les "réductions" du Canada, 1637–1701* (Sillery: Septentrion, 1994); Guy Laflèche, *Les saints martyrs canadiens* (Laval: Les Editions du Singulier Ltée, 1988); and Bruce Trigger, *Natives and Newcomers: Canada's "Heroic Age" Reconsidered* (Montreal and Kingston: McGill-Queens University Press, 1985). See also Robert Toupin, *Arpents de neige et Robes Noires* (Montreal: Editions Bellarmin, 1991), esp. 18, 81–97.

6 See John L. Steckley *De Religione: Telling the Seventeenth-Century Jesuit Story in Huron to the Iroquois* (Norman: University of Oklahoma Press, 2004).

7 See Allan Greer, *Mohawk Saint: Catherine Tekakwitha and the Jesuits* (Oxford: Oxford University Press, 2005).

8 See Louis Châtellier, *The Europe of the Devout* (Cambridge: Cambridge University Press, 1980); Elizabeth Rapley, *The Dévotes: Women and Church in Seventeenth-Century France* (Montreal and Kingston: McGill-Queens University Press, 1990).

9 Bressani to Vincenzo Carafa, quoted in T. J. Campbell, *Pioneer Priests of North America, 1642–1710* (New York: America Press, 1910), II: 42.

10 The *Relations* (1632–72) were first gathered together in the 1850s by teams of researchers supervised by the *abbé* Charles-Honoré Laverdière, professor at Laval University, and published (1858) in three volumes thanks to a grant from the Government of Canada marking the 250th anniversary of the founding of Quebec. Between 1896 and 1901 the American historian Reuben Gold Thwaites edited in seventy-three volumes *The Jesuit Relations and Allied Documents, 1611–1800* (Cleveland: Burrow Brothers, 1896–1901), which were reprinted in 1959 by Pageant Books Inc., New York. In the "Thwaites edition" an English translation faces every French, Italian, or Latin text and the thousands of accompanying notes are in English only. A third edition, by Lucien Campeau, S.J., began appearing in 1967 in the *Monumenta Novae Franciae* (Rome: Institutum Historicum Societatis Jesu; Montreal: Editions Bellarmin). When Fr. Campeau died in March 2003 he had reached vol. IX (1657–61). This *Monumenta* edition contains hundreds of documents that were unknown to Thwaites. Each one is carefully and critically edited as well as amply annotated in French; each is published only in its original French, Italian, or Latin. See Luca Codignola, "The Battle Is Over: Campeau's *Monumenta* vs. Thwaites' *Jesuit Relations, 1602–1650*," *European Review of Native American Studies* 10 (1996), 3–10.

11 Quoted in Camille de Rochemonteix, S.J., *Les Jésuites et la Nouvelle France* (Paris: Letouzey et Ané, 1895), I: 221ff.

12 There are apparently only two copies of this book still extant, one in the Bibiliothèque Nationale in Paris and the other in the Bibliothèque du Collège de l'Immaculée Conception, now housed at Collège Brébeuf in Montreal. The bulk of the library of the old college went to what is now Laval University at the time of the death of Jean-Joseph Casot (1728–1800), the last Jesuit of the *ancien régime*. Many of the books were given or sold by Casot to benefactors and friends in the 1790s and have made their way into various private or public libraries.

13 JR, 1635, Thwaites, VII: 261. In most quotations from Thwaites I have refined the translation.

14 The long and remarkable story of the Ursuline and Augustinian sisters can best be found in Dom Guy-Marie Oury, O. S. B., *Les Ursulines de Québec, 1639–1953* (Sillery: Septentrion, 1999); and in François Rousseau, *La croix et le scalpel: Histoire des Augustines de l'Hôtel-Dieu de Québec*, 2 vols. (Sillery: Septentrion, 1989–94).

15 JR, 1649, Thwaites, XXXIII: 144.

16 See Olive P. Dickason, *The Myth of the Savage* (Edmonton: University of Alberta Press, 1984).

17 JR, 1636, Thwaites, X: 8.

18 JR, 1664–65, Thwaites, L: 73. On the observations and reports of the early Jesuits, see also Léon Pouliot, S. J., *Etude sur les Relations des Jésuites* (Paris: Desclée de Brouwer, 1940).

19 JR 1664–65, Thwaites, L: 75.

20 See Carl Starkloff, S. J., *Common Testimony* (St. Louis: Institute of Jesuit Sources, 2002), for a discussion of its important relevance to modern missiology.

21 Paul Le Jeune to Louis XIV, 1661. JR 1660–61, Thwaites, XLVI: 197.

22 See Robert Toupin, S. J., *Les Ecrits de Pierre Potier* (Ottawa: Les Presses de l'Université d'Ottawa, 1996).

12 Racial and ethnic minorities in the Society of Jesus

THOMAS M. COHEN

The first Jesuits were committed in theory to admitting all qualified men, regardless of lineage. In practice, however, Jesuit unanimity concerning admissions was fragile.

The principle of ignoring lineage in admitting new members to the Society was enshrined in the Constitutions and upheld – with a handful of exceptions – throughout Ignatius' life. Jesuits were among the most vocal and effective opponents of statutes of "purity of blood" (*limpieza de sangre*), which required that candidates for a wide range of civil and ecclesiastical positions throughout the Iberian world prove that they were from Old Christian families. Opposition to *limpieza* among the first Jesuits was rooted in Ignatius' insistence on inclusiveness and on unity within the Society. It was strengthened by the Jesuits' pastoral ideals and above all by their concern that their mission work in Europe and throughout the Iberian empires proceed free of challenges to the validity of conversion.

After the death of Ignatius, however, Jesuit unity was threatened from many quarters. The most sustained threat came from Spain and Portugal in the form of opposition to the admission of Christians of Jewish descent – known as New Christians – to the Society. Throughout the sixteenth century, however, Jesuits debated the admission of a wide range of other minorities.

Ignatius had no contact with Jews or New Christians as a youth. Indeed, the Basque country in which he grew up was fiercely proud of its Old Christian heritage and passed an ordinance prohibiting New Christians from settling in the region. Although Ignatius affirmed the Old Christian heritage of his family and his province when he was questioned by the Inquisition about his lineage and about his ties to the Spanish mystics known as *alumbrados*, he strongly opposed *limpieza* in theory and practice.[1]

The Spanish Jesuit Pedro de Ribadeneira (1526–1611), one of Ignatius' most trusted companions, recounted three occasions on which Ignatius expressed his desire to be bound by blood to the Jewish people. "One day when we were eating together in front of many people," Ribadeneira recalled,

> at one point, speaking of himself, [Ignatius] said that he would hold it to be a special grace of Our Lord to come from the lineage of the Jews. And he pursued the point, saying: "What, for a man to be able to be of the family of Christ Our Lord and of Our Lady the glorious Virgin Mary!" He spoke these words with such an expression and with so much feeling, that tears came forth, and it was something that was widely noted.[2]

When the Spanish nobleman Pedro de Zárate objected, "saying, 'Jew?,' and spitting at this name," Ignatius responded by giving him "so many reasons for this [point of view], that [Ignatius] truly persuaded him to wish to be of the lineage of the Jews."[3] These and other statements and actions (including Ignatius' active ministry to the Jews of Rome from the time he began living there in 1538) demonstrate that, well before founding the Society, Ignatius had renounced the antipathy towards Jews that was common in the Basque country of his youth.[4]

Ignatius' first sustained contact with a New Christian occurred when he moved to Paris, where he studied with Diego Laínez. Laínez, a descendant of Spanish Jews, would become one of the most trusted companions of Ignatius, and would serve as the second General of the Society. Ignatius' friendship with Laínez strengthened his commitment to admitting New Christians to the Society. The Constitutions and the writings of Ignatius' companions demonstrate, however, that Ignatius' ideas about New Christians were rooted in a deeper commitment to equality within the Society and to Ignatius' repeated affirmations of the Jewish heritage of all Christians.

Although Ignatius decided to include a question about lineage in the final version of the General Examen – the questionnaire given to prospective members of the Society – he affirmed in his words and in his actions that lineage was not to be a basis for exclusion.[5] The secular clergy and most religious orders barred, by law or custom, the admission of New Christians.[6] In contrast, the Jesuits under Ignatius, Laínez, and Francis Borja became known throughout Europe as a haven for New Christians, including some of the most prominent members of the Society during the sixteenth century. This reputation was disturbing to many within and outside the Society.

During the Society's first five years, Ignatius appears to have discussed the New Christian question only with Laínez and other

confidants who supported his policy of inclusion. The first member of
the Society to directly confront Ignatius concerning this policy was
Antonio Araoz, a distant cousin of Ignatius who was a leader in the
dissident faction of Jesuits that emerged after Ignatius' death. The logic
of Araoz's many appeals to Ignatius – underscoring the need to take into
account anti-New Christian sentiment in Spain when making decisions
on admissions – was already apparent in a 1545 letter that addressed this
subject. "Father," Araoz wrote, "until the Society is better known and
better established in Castile, it seems wise to reconsider the policy of
admitting New Christians, because for many people this [policy] alone is
already a poison."[7] The following year Araoz wrote to Ignatius:

> Regarding the admission of New Christians, it is no doubt a holy
> thing not to discriminate among persons, nor does the Lord
> permit us to do so ... nevertheless, for the common good, and in
> conformity with the temperament of the regions in which we
> find ourselves, it is well to consider this question, at least in order
> to examine [applicants] with more vigilance and rigor.[8]

During Araoz's service as Provincial in Spain, he sought not simply to
prompt a reconsideration of the New Christian question but to persuade
Ignatius to exclude New Christians from the Society, taking the side of
the archbishop of Toledo, Juan Martínez de Siliceo, in Siliceo's protracted
struggle with Ignatius and the Society during the early 1550s. Siliceo,
who in 1547 had introduced in Toledo some of the most rigorous purity
of blood statutes in Spain, objected to the Society's policy of admitting
New Christians and threatened to prohibit the Jesuits from administer-
ing the sacraments in his diocese. Ignatius' response was firm. In the
instructions concerning the dispute that he sent to Francisco de
Villanueva, rector of the new Jesuit college at Alcalá and a defender of
the New Christians in the Society, Ignatius concluded simply:

> The continuation of our ministries of preaching and confessing is
> the first thing to be sought, in order that the divine service not be
> interrupted. There is no need to think about coming to an agree-
> ment with the archbishop or about accepting his designs and
> making our constitutions conform with his. Let him apply himself
> to understanding his own affairs.[9]

Throughout the remaining three years of his life, Ignatius provided a
similarly firm response – a response that was rooted in the concrete
ministries of the Society – to other efforts from within and outside the
Society to amend the Constitutions and exclude New Christians. The

Society ultimately compromised with Siliceo, agreeing to suspend the admission of New Christians in Spain and to submit to Siliceo's authority. The Society viewed these concessions, however, as temporary measures taken to restore peace with Siliceo, and had no intention of implementing the suspension. Moreover, Ignatius never contemplated amending the Constitutions, and he discouraged any discussion of the subject among his companions. The election of Laínez to succeed Ignatius as General ensured that New Christians would continue to be welcomed into the Society.

After the death of Ignatius in 1556, differences within the Society concerning the admission of New Christians hinged, like many other issues, on individual interpretations of Ignatius' intentions. A small group of Jesuits, led by Araoz, continued to call attention – quietly, for the time being – to the harm to the Society's ministries and reputation that was allegedly caused by the prominence of New Christians in the Society. Laínez's response to this argument was as firm as Ignatius' had been. In an undated letter to Araoz written after Ignatius' death, Laínez invoked the memory of Ignatius in explaining his own position on the New Christian question.

> In my view (and I believe it is the view shared throughout the Society), we cannot apply this remedy – that is, not admitting men of this kind into the Society – and even if we could, it would not be wise ... for if you remember, Your Reverence wrote about this matter to Our Father [Ignatius], and at that time Our Father, having considered it and commended it to Our Lord, resolved against [your advice], and accordingly he placed this decision in the Constitutions that were approved in the last General Congregation [in 1556, after the death of Ignatius] ....[10]

The inviolability of the Constitutions' provisions concerning lineage was maintained throughout the generalates of Laínez (1556–65) and Borja (1565–72). Moreover, Jesuits during these two generalates avoided making public their concerns about the admission of New Christians. This policy of discretion would change, however, upon the death of Borja.

The logical successor to Borja was Juan de Polanco, a Spanish New Christian who was one of Ignatius' early companions. The expected election of a second General of Jewish descent provoked strong opposition among a small but vocal minority within the Society. This group, which was dominated by Portuguese Jesuits who were frequently at odds with their Spanish colleagues, opposed not only the election of Polanco but also the acceptance of New Christians on an equal footing in the Society. Polanco's opponents did not explicitly state that they rejected his candidacy because he was of Jewish descent. They did state, however, that after three Spanish generals it was time for a change. Although national rivalries were a factor in the opposition to Polanco and were an important source of division in the development of the Society as a whole during the sixteenth century, the true motives of Polanco's opponents were never in doubt, either within or outside the Society. The opposing faction convinced Pope Gregory XIII (reigned 1572–85) to decree that Borja's successor not be a Spaniard. Although the decree was subsequently withdrawn and the election was a nominally free one, the Society chose Everard Mercurian (1514–80), a Belgian, as its fourth General.

Antagonism towards New Christians was rooted both in the Iberian preoccupation with *limpieza* and in the contention that certain unalterable characteristics of the New Christians placed them in permanent conflict with the Society and with the Church as a whole. In 1573 such views were not yet being disseminated in Jesuit memorials, even memorials that were privately circulated. But the unprecedented intervention of the pope in the election of Mercurian and the absence of strong leadership emboldened the opponents of the New Christians within the Society. It was to combat the increasingly bitter divisions that threatened the Society that Antonio Possevino (1533–1611) wrote a long memorial to Mercurian in 1576.[11]

Possevino, who served as secretary to Mercurian from 1573 to 1576, was almost certainly of Jewish descent.[12] The stated purpose of his memorial was to urge Mercurian to write a "letter of unity" that would call attention to the growing divisions within the Society and demand that those who fomented these divisions desist from doing so. Possevino contended that in the absence of such a letter the Society, which was one of the few religious orders that had only one observance, risked being divided by an "irremediable schism."[13] Possevino's memorial was the most important effort during the generation after Ignatius' death to call attention to the need to rid the Society of lineage-based discrimination. Possevino anticipated the vitriolic character of the attacks on the New Christians that would be launched in the course of the debate leading up to the 1593 vote by the fifth General Congregation on whether to exclude New Christians from the Society. In a memorial written on the eve of the vote, the Portuguese Jesuit Manuel Rodrigues argued:

> Although we may know all these men to be Christians and to be constant in the faith, surely the Society should hold them at a

distance because of their character, for they stand opposed to the purity of true religion. They are ... enemies of the cross of Christ, restless, scheming, men who humble others that they themselves might be exalted. They seek the highest offices and wish to be called "rabbi."[14]

Acknowledging Mercurian's fear of addressing the divisions within the Society, Possevino underscored the need to eliminate distinctions based on lineage. He affirmed that whether one looked to the Constitutions, or to "the example of past Father Generals," or finally to

the disposition of Divine Providence manifested in Sacred Scripture, one cannot see how this fear [of addressing internal divisions] can be borne within a Society whose Institute should be distinguished by the blood that is found in its freedom, and in the fact that it permits no preference for lineage, or for human concerns – which are vestiges of paganism – or for its own honor, such as not allowing oneself to be touched by others or to greet them, as is the custom of some infidels about whom Father Alessandro Valignano [Visitor of the Jesuit missions in Asia] has recently written to Your Paternity.[15]

This passage constitutes one of the most powerful critiques of the concept of purity of blood to be found in the vast literature – contemporary and modern – on the subject. For Possevino, debates about nation and lineage were inextricably linked to debates about the Jesuit missionary enterprise. Illustrious lineage depended on Jesuit ideals, not on blood. During the years since the death of Ignatius, Jesuit opposition to the concept of purity of blood had focused on Ignatius' own legacy and on Scripture. Possevino added to these an appeal to the ongoing development of Jesuit pastoral ideals and finally to the common humanity and intelligence of his contemporaries in the Society.

Mercurian declined to write the letter that Possevino requested, and the fifth General Congregation decreed that "in no case is anyone ... of Hebrew or Saracen stock, henceforth to be admitted to the Society. And if by error any such will have been admitted, he should be dismissed as soon as this impediment has been shown to exist."[16] Possevino was not present at the congregation, and among the more than fifty electors only two, including the great writer and missionary José de Acosta, cast dissenting votes. The decree was revised at the sixth General

Congregation in 1608, limiting investigations of individual lineages to five generations and making these investigations less intrusive.[17] The debate leading up to the decree and the decree itself, however, played a decisive role in Jesuit debates concerning a series of other lineage-based exclusions in the mission fields that remained a source of division within the Society until the Suppression.

The missionary experience was central to Possevino's argument for unity. In addressing the New Christian question, Possevino sought as well to address the larger problem of equality within the Society as it moved into new mission fields in Asia, Africa, and America. Drawing on the personal experience of his fellow Jesuits in the missions, Possevino insisted that conflicts over lineage and nationality constituted a pagan survival that needed to be expunged from the Society. If Jesuits were to continue to question the suitability of fellow Europeans for admission to the Society, how would they respond to requests to join from non-European converts and their descendants? Only a policy of inclusion could prevent the pernicious effects that the countenancing of discrimination would have on the missionary enterprise.

Like the debate about the admission of New Christians to the Society, the debate about the admission of Asians, Africans, and Amerindians gave rise to a sustained conflict between theory and practice. The two debates were different, however, in at least three important respects. First, the papacy, beginning in the early sixteenth century, officially supported the ordination of non-European clergy. Second, the Portuguese crown, which had campaigned against the admission of New Christians to the Society, sought – with varying degrees of insistence – to promote the development of the native clergy. Third, the Spanish monarchs did not share the commitment of their Portuguese counterparts to the ordination of native clergy. This commitment was stronger in theory than in practice, but it was an important factor in the fitful development of the native clergy, especially in Asia, before the nineteenth century.[18]

In *Exponi Nobis*, the bull sent to King Manuel I of Portugal in 1518, Pope Leo X directed that Ethiopians, Indians, and Africans be admitted to the clergy.[19] Although the Society would open two seminaries in Africa (in Angola and Kongo), it ordained only a handful of Africans before the Suppression.[20] Similarly, as noted below, although the Society's college in Goa educated African students, these men were not admitted to the Society.

In America, the Jesuits never considered the question of ordaining indigenous people, despite the affirmation of Paul III, in *Sublimis Deus*

(1537), of the spiritual capacities of the Indians. In Spanish America, Brazil, and New France, Jesuits spoke indigenous languages with most of their native converts. Few of these converts learned Spanish, Portuguese, or French. None studied Latin with the Jesuits, though Indians (especially Indian children) on Jesuit missions throughout America memorized Latin for singing mass.[21] In Brazil, where the Society was the first religious order to establish a mission, the Jesuits struggled to find an adequate indigenous vocabulary with which to teach basic Christian beliefs and practices to the nomadic Indians. In contrast, the Jesuits were relative latecomers to Spanish America, arriving in 1568 in Peru and in 1572 in Mexico. By this time the church hierarchy in both viceroyalties had prohibited the ordination of Indians, blacks, and mestizos.[22]

In Asia the Society, like the rest of the regular clergy, was more resistant than the secular clergy to native vocations. Jesuits throughout Asia as well as in Rome conducted a wide-ranging and frequently acrimonious debate about the desirability and feasibility of ordaining native clergy in Asia. Especially in the case of India, this debate was often inserted into a larger debate about miscegenation, which was famously encouraged by D. Affonso de Albuquerque, the first viceroy. Both Francis Xavier (1506–52) and Alessandro Valignano (1539–1606) linked their opposition to the admission of Indians to the Society to their opposition to race mixture and their conviction that Indians were inferior to Europeans. The church that the first Jesuits sought to introduce in India was to be a replica of the European church. Xavier and his colleagues did not consider in India the strategy of accommodation that their successors would pursue in China.[23] Writing to Ignatius in 1549, Xavier stated his reservations concerning the admission of Indian clergy. In response, Ignatius outlined five measures to strengthen Jesuit education in India, emphasizing the need to open more colleges. Six years later, after the death of Xavier, Ignatius observed that, although students in India needed to be more rigorously tested than Europeans because they were new to the faith, the more talented among them should be encouraged to enter the Society.[24]

Despite the misgivings about Indians in general and Indian students in particular that were expressed by Xavier in his 1549 letters to Ignatius, the Society that year was placed in charge of the Seminary of Santa Fé in Goa, which had been established in 1541 for the purpose of educating Indian clergy.[25] The seminary's constitutions stipulated that, in addition to admitting ten boys from Goa, the seminary was to admit eight boys from Abyssinia, six from Malabar, the Moluccas,

China, Pegu, and Gujarat, six to eight from Sofala, Mozambique, and Madagascar, "and up to six from other nations in this region where there is a need and where [the students] might bring forth fruit."[26] The seminary was thus a genuinely international enterprise. No Europeans, mestiços (men of mixed European and Asian descent), or castiços (Europeans born in Asia), however, were to be admitted.

Among the Jesuits charged with educating the boys was Nicolò Lancilotto, whose conflicted views about the ordination of native clergy in India reflected the larger divisions within the Society concerning this issue. Lancilotto's early writings – some dating to before the seminary was formally entrusted to the Society – reflect his confidence in the talents of his students. In a 1545 letter he noted that among the sixty boys in the seminary "there are eight who compose in Latin ... but they have no teacher who instructs them well, and who pushes them to speak Latin and memorize some texts." Nonetheless, Lancilotto continued, the Jesuits "are beginning to ask the boys to speak only in Latin."[27] Writing to Ignatius the following year, Lancilotto, sounding what was to become a common theme in letters of missionaries throughout the Iberian world, lamented the lack of Jesuits to teach in India. The seminary students were reading Terence, Virgil, Ovid, Cato, Jerome, and Erasmus, and Lancilotto professed that "they have great talent."[28]

In 1548 Lancilotto was transferred to Quilon and succeeded by António Gomes, the Portuguese rector who continued to lead the seminary when it was entrusted to the Society. According to a 1551 letter from Lancilotto to Ignatius, some of the boys jumped over the walls and ran away from the seminary, and the rest, in a move that Lancilotto opposed, were dismissed by Gomes, who admitted several Portuguese boys to replace them.[29] When Xavier returned to Goa in 1552, he banished Gomes to Diu and ultimately dismissed him from the Society. Xavier had no intention of allowing Asians and Africans to enter the Society as priests. Nonetheless, he insisted that the Society follow to the letter the seminary's charter to educate non-European boys.[30]

In the meantime Lancilotto's hopes for the training of native priests in India had faded, notwithstanding his opposition to the dismissal of the Asian and African boys from the seminary. Writing to Ignatius from Quilon in 1550, Lancilotto voiced his despair about the character of the Indians and about the poor quality of the conversions that had been performed in India, including many that had been performed by Lancilotto himself during his first years in the mission.[31] In a similarly despairing letter to Ignatius the following year about the seminary students whom he had praised in 1546, and from whom he had been separated for three years, Lancilotto wrote: "Among them there were many who were not only uncivilized but wild and incapable of all learning and virtue ... and [they] could in no way be trained unto virtue and good manners, because they did not know our language and spoke only like parrots."[32]

The Jesuits' growing concerns about the intellectual and spiritual abilities of their students combined with the Society's separation of itself from both the Indian and Portuguese communities in Goa to create an unofficial ban on the admission of native clergy. In comparison with other religious orders working in Portuguese India, the Society's refusal to admit native clergy was striking. Between Xavier's arrival in 1542 and the suppression of the Society in India in 1773, only one Indian – Pero Luís Bramane – rose to the priesthood in the Society. Pero Luís, who was ordained in 1560, was an effective pastor who pleaded with his superiors to admit more Indians to the Society, but his requests were not heeded, and Pero Luís himself was never permitted to take his fourth vow.[33]

It was not until the generalate of Mercurian – during which, as we have seen, the Society was increasingly divided about the admission of New Christians – that the Society formally banned the admission not only of Indians but also of mestiços. Moreover, the Society placed a series of new restrictions on the admission of castiços.[34] The Society's policy caused widespread resentment among Indians, most notoriously in the case of the brahmin Mateus de Castro, bishop of Chrysopolis and vicar-apostolic of Bijapur. Though he had studied at the Collegio Urbano and won praise from the Propaganda Fide in Rome, Castro was scorned as "a bare-bottomed Nigger" by the Jesuit patriarch of Ethiopia, Dom Afonso Mendes.[35]

It was in China – the mission field on which Xavier increasingly placed his hopes during his last years – that the Society conducted its most sustained and successful effort to ordain native clergy. Among the central points that the Jesuits in China addressed in connection with native clergy were questions about the advisability of compromising the identification of Christianity with European missionaries; divisions along generational and national lines; divisions between Jesuits at the court in Beijing and those in the mission field; and differences concerning the potential of Chinese priests to master Latin, honor vows of celibacy, and accept other key elements of the priestly vocation.[36]

The Italian Jesuit Matteo Ricci (1552–1610) was preoccupied with the problem of native clergy well before he arrived in China in 1582. Writing from Goa, where he spent almost four years en route to the China mission, Ricci strongly criticized his Portuguese colleagues in the Society for their refusal to ordain Indian priests and for the humiliation to which Europeans had subjected the Indians, both Christian and non-Christian.

> No one has shown [the Indians] as much understanding as have our Fathers. It is for this reason that they have a special love for us. If now they are to be made to feel that even our Fathers are against them and do not want to enable them to hold their heads high and to make it possible for them to aspire to any office or benefice on a basis of equality with Europeans, as education enables them to do, I am very much afraid that they will come to hate us.[37]

Ricci, like Ignatius and Possevino before him, insisted that intellectual and spiritual gifts be the principal criteria for admission to the Society, and that considerations of lineage be excluded. During the early years of the China mission, a small number of Chinese Christians – four or five in any given year – served the Society as lay brothers.[38] Ricci laid the foundation for Jesuit missionary strategy in China, which featured the accommodation of Chinese culture by the Society, the focusing of mission work on the Chinese elite, and the use of Western science as a means of stimulating interest in Christianity.[39] It was not until after Ricci's death, however, that the Jesuits began the long process that would lead to the ordination of Chinese priests.

Like previous Jesuit efforts to admit ethnic and racial minorities, the first efforts to establish a native clergy in China were both helped and hindered by the Jesuit hierarchy in Rome. Also like previous efforts, the effort to ordain Chinese clergy was shaped in large part by national differences within the Society.

In 1613 Niccolò Longobardo (1565–1655), who succeeded Ricci as superior of the China mission, sent Nicolas Trigault (1577–1628) to Rome. Trigault's main goal – in addition to stimulating interest in and obtaining material support for the China mission in Europe – was to persuade the general, Claudio Acquaviva (general 1580–1615), to establish a new province. In this way Trigault sought to remove the China mission from the jurisdiction of Portuguese Jesuits who opposed the Italians' efforts to train native clergy, and who were reluctant to divert resources to China from the more successful missions in Japan.[40]

Acquaviva, citing the newness of the China mission, had ordered in 1606 that no Chinese priests be ordained, but he appears to have changed his mind during the intervening years, for he granted Trigault's request to establish a new province and did not hinder Trigault's pursuit of the other goals of the mission. Upon arriving in Rome, Trigault quickly enlisted the help of the Jesuit cardinal Robert Bellarmine in obtaining the permission of the Holy Office to ordain Chinese priests and to introduce a Chinese liturgy.[41] Trigault also obtained a dispensation from Pope Alexander VII which provided for the ordination of men who were not proficient in Latin. This dispensation was one of the key elements of the Jesuits' proposal to ordain mature members of the *literati* class in China.

These promising concessions did not, however, produce the concrete results for which Trigault and the China Jesuits hoped. Acquaviva died in 1615 before the new China province had been formally established, and the Chinese liturgy was never introduced, although the decree that approved it was promulgated in China.[42] By the time Trigault returned to China, Christians were being persecuted, the survival of the mission was in doubt, and the Jesuits' collaboration with Chinese within the Society remained limited to work with laymen.

A small number of Chinese overcame the obstacles to ordination by studying in Europe. The first of these, Zheng Weixin (1633–73), known as Manuel de Siqueira, entered the Society in 1651 and was ordained in Coimbra in 1664, returning to China in 1668.[43] Several other Chinese Jesuits were trained in Rome and Paris during the seventeenth and eighteenth centuries.[44] Most of the Chinese Jesuits, however, were *literati* who were ordained in China according to the 1615 language dispensation.[45] Supported by Superior General Giovanni Paolo Oliva (general 1664–81) and by King Pedro II of Portugal, the Italian Jesuit Prospero Intorcetta (1625–96) began an effort in the 1670s to train "literati of ripe age and virtue."[46] By this time the need to train native clergy, especially in areas that were not subject to Spanish or Portuguese rule, was also of vital concern to the papacy, as may be seen in the instruction given to Msgr. François Pallu by Pope Innocent XI before Pallu's departure for Asia: "We would rather learn that you have ordained one native priest than that you have baptized 50,000 pagans. The Jesuits have baptized many such, but subsequently their work has vanished in smoke because they did not ordain native priests."[47] These instructions reflect the impatience of the papacy with the failure of the religious orders in general and the

Iberian Jesuits in particular to train significant numbers of native clergy.[48] As the China Jesuits continued to be divided on this subject, the elevation of Intorcetta to the post of vice-provincial in 1687 – along with the ordination of the first Chinese bishop, Luo Wenzao of Nanjing, in 1685 – enabled Intorcetta to begin to implement his plans. After receiving training in Macau, three Chinese priests entered the Society in 1688.[49] Although the erratic behavior of one of these priests and a new wave of persecution of Chinese Christians limited the development of the native clergy in subsequent years, more than twenty Chinese priests entered the Society between 1688 and 1755, when the Society was suppressed in China. These men made up about one third of the fifty to seventy Jesuits working in China in 1755.[50]

Only after the Suppression (1773–1814) did the national origins of members of the Society come to reflect the international character of the Society's pastoral ideals and practices. The Society has made a concerted effort, especially since 1945, to recruit men from a wide range of national, racial, and ethnic backgrounds. This effort is consistent with the effort of the Catholic Church after Vatican II to promote the indigenous character of the Church throughout the world. Cardinal J. Paracattil underscored this effort – to which the changing composition of the clergy is contributing – in his address to the 1970 Synod in New Delhi: "The Catholic Church is neither Latin nor Greek nor Slav, but universal. Unless the Church can show herself Indian in India and Chinese in China and Japanese in Japan, she will never reveal her authentically Catholic character."[51] At the beginning of the twenty-first century, for the first time in the Society's history, its largest assistancy – the South Asia Assistancy – is to be found outside the United States and Europe.[52]

Notes

1 New Christians were prominent among the *alumbrados*, whose orthodoxy was suspect.
2 Ignatius of Loyola, *Monumenta Ignatiana. Scripta de Sancto Ignatio de Loyola*, 2 vols. (Madrid, 1904–18), I: 398f.
3 Ibid., 399.
4 The only book-length study of Ignatius' ideas about Jews and New Christians (as well as about Muslims) is James W. Reites, *St. Ignatius and the People of the Book: An Historical-Theological Study of St. Ignatius of Loyola's Spiritual Motivation in His Dealings with the Jews and Muslims* (Rome: Pontificia Universitas Gregoriana, 1977).

5 The wording of the question – "Has [the applicant] come from a family long Christian (*christianos antiguos*) or one recently converted (*modernos*)" – departed from the standard terminology of the day, which distinguished between Old Christians (*cristianos viejos*) and New Christians (*cristianos nuevos*). See *The Constitutions of the Society of Jesus*, trans. George E. Ganss (St. Louis: Institute of Jesuit Sources, 1970), General Examen, 3.36 (p. 88).

6 See Reites, *St. Ignatius and the People of the Book*, 163–68.

7 *Epistolae mixtae ex variis Europae locis ab anno 1537 ad 1556 scriptae*, 5 vols. (Madrid, 1898–1901), I: 241.

8 Ibid., V: 643f.

9 Ignatius of Loyola, *Monumenta Ignatiana. Sancti Ignatii de Loyola Societatis Iesu fundatoris epistolae et instructions*, 12 vols. (Madrid, 1903–11), IV: 64.

10 Laínez to Araoz, quoted in Pedro de Ribadeneira, *Patris Petri de Ribadeneira Societatis Iesu Sacerdotis Confessiones, Epistolae Aliaque Scripta Inedita*, 2 vols. (Madrid, 1920–23), II: 250f.

11 Archivum Romanum Societatis Iesu, Congregationes 20/B, fols. 206–12. For a detailed analysis of the memorial, see Thomas M. Cohen, "Nation, Lineage and Jesuit Unity in Antonio Possevino's Memorial to Everard Mercurian (1576)," in *A Companhia de Jesus na península ibérica nos séculos XVI e XVII: Espiritualidade e cultura* (Porto: Universidade do Porto, 2004), 543–61.

12 For an analysis of Possevino's family background and of some of his principal writings on Jews and New Christians, see John Patrick Donnelly, "Antonio Possevino and Jesuits of Jewish Ancestry," *Archivum Historicum Societatis Iesu* 55 (1986), 3–31.

13 Archivum Romanum Societatis Iesu, Congregationes 20/B, fol. 206r.

14 "De Baptizatis ex Progenie Judaeorum" (1593), in Archivum Romanum Societatis Iesu, Institutum 186e, fol. 337v, quoted in Francisco de Borja Medina, "Ignacio de Loyola y la 'limpieza de sangre,'" in Juan Plazaolo, ed., *Ignacio de Loyola y su tiempo* (Bilbao: Mensajero, 1992), 586.

15 Archivum Romanum Societatis Iesu, Congregationes 20/B, fol. 207r.

16 See *For Matters of Greater Moment: The First Thirty Jesuit General Congregations* (St. Louis: Institute of Jesuit Sources, 1994), ed. and trans. John W. Padberg, S.J., Martin D. O'Keefe, S.J., and John L. McCarthy, S.J., Congregation 5, decree 52.

17 The decree was not formally rescinded by the Society until the twenty-ninth General Congregation in 1946. Ibid., Congregation 6, decree 28.

18 It was the crown that ultimately enforced the laws prohibiting discrimination against native clergy that most members of the church hierarchy in Portugal and throughout the empire had long resisted.

19 *Corpo Diplomatico Portuguez*, 16 vols. (Lisbon: Academia Real das Sciencias, 1862–1959), II: 15.

20 Charles R. Boxer, *The Church Militant and Iberian Expansion, 1440–1770* (Baltimore: Johns Hopkins University Press, 1978), 9ff.

21 The most important attempt to instruct Native Americans in Latin during the colonial period was undertaken by the Franciscans at the Colegio de Santa Cruz de Tlatelolco in Mexico. See David A. Lupher, *Romans in a New World: Classical Models in Sixteenth-Century Spanish America* (Ann Arbor: University of Michigan Press, 2003), 229–34.

22 See ibid., 232; and Boxer, *Church Militant*, 15f.

23 See Francis Xavier, *Epistolae S. Francisci Xaverii*, ed. George Schurhammer and Joseph Wicki, 2 vols. (Rome: Monumenta Historica Societatis Iesu, 1944 [repr. 1996]), ii: 22. For an excellent analysis of the racial thought of Xavier and his successors, see Ines G. Zupanov, *Missionary Tropics: The Catholic Frontier in India (16th–17th Centuries)* (Ann Arbor: University of Michigan Press, 2005). On Jesuit policies concerning the native clergy, see Carlos Mercês de Melo, *The Recruitment and Formation of the Native Clergy in India (16th–19th Century): An Historico-Canonical Study* (Lisbon: Agência Geral do Ultramar, 1955).

24 See Polanco, writing on behalf of Ignatius, in Josef Wicki, ed., *Documenta Indica*, 18 vols. (Rome: Institutum Historicum Societatis Iesu, 1948–88), iii: 308, quoted in John Correia-Afonso, "Ignatius and Indian Jesuit Vocations," in Teotónio R. de Souza and Charles Borges, eds., *Jesuits in India: In Historical Perspective* (Macau: Instituto Cultural de Macau/Xavier Centre of Historical Research, 1992), 78.

25 The seminary under the Jesuits came to be known as the College of Saint Paul, and the Jesuits throughout Asia were known as *paulistas*.

26 *Documenta Indica*, i: 120.

27 Ibid., i: 41.

28 Ibid., i: 145.

29 Melo, *Recruitment and Formation*, 79f.

30 Ibid., 81.

31 See Charles R. Boxer, *Race Relations in the Portuguese Colonial Empire, 1415–1825* (Oxford: Oxford University Press, 1963), 59–63.

32 *Documenta Indica*, ii (1550–53): 169, quoted in Melo, *Recruitment and Formation*, 79.

33 See Zupanov, *Missionary Tropics*, Epilogue.

34 For the text of Mercurian's letter, which was sent in 1579 to Ruy Vicente, Provincial in Goa, see Melo, *Recruitment and Formation*, 166.

35 Theodore Ghesquière, *Mathieu de Castro, premier vicaire apostolique aux Indes* (Leuven, 1937) 32, quoted in Charles R. Boxer, "The Problem of the Native Clergy in the Portuguese and Spanish Empires from the Sixteenth to the Eighteenth Centuries," in Geoffrey J. Cuming, ed., *The Mission of the Church and the Propagation of the Faith*, Studies in Church History, 6 (Cambridge: Cambridge University Press, 1970); rpt. in J.S. Cummins, ed., *Christianity and Missions, 1450–1800* (Aldershot: Ashgate, 1997), 99; see also Melo, *Recruitment and Formation*, 154 and *passim*.

36 On these and other factors that contributed to the long delay in ordaining Chinese priests, see Nicolas Standaert's chapter in the present

volume; also Nicolas Standaert, ed., *Handbook of Christianity in China*, vol. *1: 635–1800* (Leiden: Brill, 2001); Liam Matthew Brockey, *Journey to the East: The Jesuit Mission to China, 1579–1724* (Cambridge, MA: Harvard University Press, 2007), 142–51; Dauril Alden, *The Making of an Enterprise: The Society of Jesus in Portugal, Its Empire, and Beyond, 1540–1750* (Stanford: Stanford University Press, 1996), 262–66; and Boxer, "The Problem of the Native Clergy."

37   Matteo Ricci, *Opere storiche*, ed. Pietro Tacchi-Venturi, 2 vols. (Macerata: Girgetti, 1911–13), II: 20f., quoted in George H. Dunne, *Generation of Giants: The Story of the Jesuits in China in the Last Decades of the Ming Dynasty* (Notre Dame: University of Notre Dame Press, 1962), 25.

38   Nicolas Standaert, "Number of Missionaries," in Standaert, ed., *Handbook*, 301.

39   Claudia von Collani, "Jesuits," in ibid., 310.

40   Dunne, *Generation of Giants*, 171; on national and generational rivalries in the China mission, see Brockey, *Journey to the East*, 147–50.

41   Dunne, *Generation of Giants*, 164; von Collani, "Jesuits," 310.

42   Dunne, *Generation of Giants*, 165.

43   See Francis A. Rouleau, "The First Chinese Priest of the Society of Jesus: Emmanuel de Siqueira, 1633–1673 (Cheng Ma-no, Wei-hsin)," in *Archivum Historicum Societatis Iesu*, 28 (1959), 3–50. Chinese priests who entered other religious orders and the secular clergy studied in several cities in Europe – including the Collegio dei Cinesi in Naples – as well as in Manila and Siam.

44   Standaert, "Chinese Christians Going Abroad," in Standaert, ed., *Handbook*, 449.

45   Standaert and John Witek, "Chinese Clergy," in ibid., 462f.

46   Intorcetta memorial (1674) to Fr. João Cardoso, Provincial of Japan, quoted in Brockey, *Journey to the East*, 149.

47   Pope Innocent XI to Msgr. François Pallu (1680) in R. Steele, trans., *An Account of the State of the Roman Catholic Religion Throughout the World, Written for Pope Innocent XI by Monsignor Cerri* (London, 1715), 113f., quoted in Boxer, "The Problem of the Native Clergy," 101.

48   Ibid.

49   Brockey, *Journey to the East*, 150f.; Standaert and Witek, "Chinese Clergy," 463.

50   Brockey, *Journey to the East*, 151; Standaert and Witek, "Chinese Clergy," 463.

51   Quoted in Enrique Dussell, "Theologies of the 'Periphery' and the 'Centre': Encounter or Confrontation?," in V. Elizondo, C. Geffré, and G. Gutierrez, eds., *Different Theologies, Common Responsibility: Babel or Pentecost?* (Edinburgh: Clark, 1987), 88.

52   In 2004 there were 3,683 Jesuits in India and 3,309 in the United States. The size of the difference is expected to continue to increase during the coming years. See *Supplementum Catalogorum Societatis Iesu 2005* (Rome: Apud Curiam Praepositi Generalis, 2004). By 2008 there were fewer than 3,000 U.S. Jesuits.

Part IV
Arts and Sciences

13 Jesuit architecture in colonial Latin America

GAUVIN ALEXANDER BAILEY

Few architectural traditions were as deeply affected by the Society of Jesus as those of colonial Latin America, particularly South America between the late sixteenth and late eighteenth centuries.[1] Whereas the Jesuits made a profound impact on the architecture of other parts of the world – notably Baroque Italy, central Europe, and Flanders – Jesuit monuments played a paradigmatic role in certain regions of Latin America, frequently inspiring trends that would prevail for decades thanks to structural, stylistic, and decorative innovations. Such were the *cuzqueño* Baroque, a bold and unique variant of Baroque architecture that arose phoenix-like from the rubble of the 1650 Cuzco earthquake, and the so-called "Mestizo Style," an extraordinarily creative movement in architectural sculpture that spread rapidly through the southern Andes between the 1660s and the 1820s. In other regions, such as modern-day Paraguay, parts of Argentina, and lowland Bolivia, the Jesuits so dominated the built environment that Jesuit architecture and regional architecture were one and the same. Despite this profound architectural legacy in colonial Latin America, the Jesuits did not promote any single style. In fact, the buildings they constructed from Baja California to Chilean Patagonia were noteworthy for their lack of stylistic unity, the result both of their policy of adaptation to regional and indigenous forms and the unusually international background of Jesuit architects and designers.

The Jesuits arrived relatively late in many parts of Latin America, and consequently their influence on the visual arts took longer to develop in those areas. They reached New Spain (Mexico) in 1572, more than fifty years after the conquest and long after the Franciscans, Dominicans, and Augustinians had established major urban foundations and carved out prime mission territory in the former Aztec state.[2] The mendicant orders had already determined the architectural styles of the nascent colony and the Franciscans and Augustinians pioneered arts training among Amerindians, beginning

217

with Pedro de Gante's famed school of San José de los Naturales (1529) in Mexico City and soon also including rural mission art academies in places like Michoacán and the Yucatán.[3] Nevertheless, Jesuit foundations spread rapidly in New Spain following the 1573 foundation of the Colegio de San Pedro y Pablo in Mexico City – by 1581 they had already established bases in Puebla, Oaxaca, Veracruz, Valladolid (Morelia), and Pátzcuaro – and the churches and residences they built there would play an important although not defining role in the development of regional variants of the Baroque in the later seventeenth and eighteenth centuries. The Society also soon initiated missionary work in the unclaimed and distant lands of the north (Sinaloa, Coahuila, and Sonora, among other places) where their buildings enjoyed an influence comparable to that of their reductions in the southern cone of South America in the decades before their expulsion from Spanish territories in 1767.

The Society of Jesus also reached Spanish South America late enough (in 1567) that the earliest schools of architecture had already been established there by the mendicants. The severe Herreran and Serlian Renaissance churches and monasteries of the Peruvian Altiplano and their more fanciful Flemish Mannerist-inspired counterparts in Quito set the tone for early colonial architecture in the region.[4] As in New Spain, the mendicants had already begun training Native American artists, particularly in Quito where the Franciscans Jodoco Ricke and Francisco de Morales founded the flourishing arts school later known as the Colegio de San Andrés in 1551.[5] Nevertheless, with the arrival of Jesuit painter Bernardo Bitti (1548–1610) in 1574 and the foundation of the first Jesuit reduction in Spanish South America at Juli in 1576, the Jesuits quickly assumed a dominant position in the visual arts of the central and southern Andes, and the tragic but architecturally fortuitous earthquakes in Cuzco and Arequipa in the seventeenth century gave the Society a clean slate upon which to impose its stylistic imprint.[6] As in New Spain the Jesuits enjoyed almost untrammeled influence in the more remote mission regions, in this case primarily in the far north, south, and east of the continent.

Portuguese Brazil was the only place in the Americas where the Jesuits were the first to arrive.[7] The Jesuits reached Salvador (Bahia) in 1549 on the same ship as Tomé de Souza (1503–79), the colony's first Governor General. Although their mission was to convert the indigenous Tupi-Guaraní people they also soon made their mark on the main cities of the new colony, from Belém (Pará) in the Amazonian north to

São Paulo – a city founded as a Jesuit mission – to the south. The Jesuit missionary Manoel da Nóbrega (1517–70) built the boys' school in Salvador that went on to become the Colegio Máximo and was the oldest of the three colleges the Jesuits founded in Brazil, together with those of Olinda and Rio de Janeiro. The Society built some of the largest churches in the colony, and their buildings were usually located in commanding positions on hills and fronted by spacious patios. Although the Benedictines, Franciscans, and Carmelites soon joined in the building game, the Jesuits played a dominant role in the architectural and sculptural life of Brazil until their expulsion from Portuguese territories in 1758.

In this chapter I will survey six Jesuit foundations ranging from Peru to Paraguay. Owing to space constraints I have focused on the foundations I believe had the profoundest impact on the history of colonial architecture. I have limited myself to South America as Jesuit buildings enjoyed a much greater influence there than in New Spain. I will begin with the Church and College of the Transfiguration (better known as the Compañía) in Cuzco, because it is the prime example of the way the Jesuits were able to turn a disaster – in this case an earthquake – into an opportunity. As the 1650 temblor leveled nearly all of the churches in the central part of the city, the Jesuits were no longer at a disadvantage compared to the firmly established Franciscans, Dominicans, Mercedarians, and other orders that preceded them in the city.[8] Employing architects from within and outside the Society, they created the template for a vigorous new style characterized by a complex interrelation and layering of columns and entablatures (the horizontal part of the classical order) that would be copied throughout the bishopric of Cuzco through the end of the century. Strictly speaking the Compañía was not the first building in this new style – the cathedral façade (1649–c. 1654) was earlier – but because the new Jesuit church (1651–68) possessed much greater unity, this more visually satisfying structure was destined to become the prototype for the *cuzqueño* Baroque.

The original church of the Compañía was begun around 1578 directly on the site of the former palace of Huayna Cápac in the most important square in the former Inca capital, the Haukaypata, now the Plaza de Armas.[9] This audacious placement on the same square as the cathedral placed the church in direct competition with the latter, and caused considerable bickering from rival orders. The patron was Teresa Ordóñez, wife of the conquistador Captain Diego da Silva, and the building used blocks taken from the massive Inca fortress of

Sacsayhuamán, located on a nearby hilltop.[10] Thus, through placement, patronage, and building materials the Jesuit foundation became
a powerful symbol of Christian triumph over paganism. In building
this early church the Jesuits hired insiders, as with most of their early
foundations in the Americas. The Jesuit master carpenter Juan Ruiz
supervised the project and was likely its principal designer, and Brother
José Mosquera was in charge of the wooden roof (1584–85). The portal
was completed in 1587 along with the bell tower and the church was
consecrated in 1593. The lavish interior ornamentation – possibly the
greatest collaboration of Bitti and fellow Jesuit Pedro de Vargas
(1553–c. 1590) – included gilded retables, sculptures, and paintings
and took until 1605 to be completed. All that is left of this extraordinary interior, meant as a model for all of Peru, are a few reliefs and
paintings now in museums in Cuzco and Lima.[11]

The Compañía church that rose from the rubble in 1651 (Fig. 13.2)
may have been designed by the Flemish Jesuit Jean-Baptiste Gilles
(Juan Bautista Egidiano) – so say the Jesuit chroniclers – or the retable-
maker Martínez de Oviedo, who was also responsible for the façade,
and it included a main church, the Indian (Loreto) Chapel and
Penitentiary Chapel, and a spacious college arranged around a court-
yard.[12] Martínez first appears in the documents in 1664, when he
contracted to build "the portal of the said college and the towers of it,
until with perfection they are completed in conformance with the
drawings of them."[13]

The Compañía has one of the most unified interiors in Peruvian
colonial architecture (Fig. 13.1). Based on a Latin-cross plan, it has a
spacious nave and six side chapels separated by paired Corinthian
pilasters. The vaults are Gothic, a conservative element meant to
echo those in the adjacent cathedral. As in most of the grander Jesuit
structures in Peru, a lofty dome in the crossing dominates the space,
supported by four arches resting on giant Corinthian columns. The
interior positively glitters with gilded retables, particularly those of
the crossing with their twisting solomonic columns, rich ornamentation and sculptures – an assemblage that more than adequately com-
pensates for the lost program of Bitti and Vargas. The interior and
exterior of the church are integrated through structural similarities
between the façade and high altar retable that greet the visitor upon
entering the church.

The façade of the Cuzco Compañía was equally concerned with
seizing the viewer's attention, both through its liberal use of ornamentation and its harmony of form. By having the wall and columns step

Figure 13.1. Church of the Transfiguration, or Compañía, Cuzco. Façade.
Photo by Gauvin Alexander Bailey.

Figure 13.2. Church of the Transfiguration, or Compañía, Cuzco. Constructed 1651–68. Interior. Photo by Gauvin Alexander Bailey.

forward from the sides toward the center it directs our gaze inward
much like a stage backdrop – the effect is not coincidental as musical
performances, processions, and other events took place in front of this
very façade. There is also a typically Baroque emphasis on verticality,
with tall towers, a relatively narrow façade, and a central bay (that
of the door) that rises well above those on the sides. Equally Baroque is
the multiplication of elements, such as the paired niches/windows on
the sides of the second story and the dollhouse-like finial towers that
echo the real ones. The Compañía façade is richly layered and textured,
with freestanding Corinthian columns, bold entablatures, elaborately
carved friezes and panels, blind niches, and multi-colored stone, and it
contrasts sharply with the plain walls of the tower bases framing it on
either side. Entablatures serve as the primary unifying element.
Parallel entablatures on the first and top stories of the façade bind the
towers to the façade, the upper one forming a soaring trilobe curve as it
follows the contour of the niche below. Even the thinner entablatures
of the window frames on the towers connect with the choir windows
on the second story of the façade, and the window frames themselves
mimic the form of the façade as a whole. The assimilation of elements
found in the Compañía façade recalls the integrated role Jesuit foundations played in Cuzco and other Peruvian cities, with their network of
colleges, schools, clinics, pharmacies, and *tambos*, or guesthouses.

The so-called "Mestizo" (literally, "hybrid") style of architectural
sculpture dominated the southern Peruvian highlands between the
1660s and the dawn of Independence in the 1820s.[14] It is characterized
by visual richness, flattened but deep relief carving, a mosaic-like
distribution of decorative elements derived from Andean textiles, and
a plethora of indigenous motifs including references to Inca and pre-
Inca cosmology, the Inca crown or *mascaypacha*, representations of
Native Americans, and a panoply of local flora and fauna, from the
ubiquitous tube-shaped *cantuta* and Inca Lily to cactus flowers, cacao,
pumas, parrots, hummingbirds, monkeys, and a long-eared rodent
called a *vizcacha*.[15] Interestingly enough, the flora and fauna, while
native to Peru, frequently come from the distant jungle lowlands,
suggesting that they represent an idealized view of nature as a paradise
garden.

The scholarly debate over the Mestizo Style – basically hinging
upon whether it was a genuine fusion of European and indigenous
Andean motifs or merely a variant of European folk style – was one of
the most dominant and vituperative in the field of colonial Latin
American art, particularly in the decades immediately following the

Second World War.[16] The debate ended long ago and scholars have come out in favor of acknowledging the profound influence of indigenous motifs, pattern structures, and interpretations in this flourishing school. However, until I began my current monograph on the subject none of us realized the extent to which the Jesuits pioneered and nurtured the style, beginning with the church of Santiago, or the Compañía, in Arequipa (begun 1621) (Fig. 13.3). Through new documentary research I have determined that the Mestizo Style first appeared in 1663 with the Compañía side portal tympanum and not the 1678 choir vault at the nearby Dominican church as previously believed.[17] Not only does the Compañía have the earliest and most comprehensive collection of Mestizo Style carving in existence, but its splendid main façade (1698–99) became a model for countless churches in Arequipa, the Colca Valley, Collao (Lake Titicaca region), and Alto Peru (present-day highland Bolivia). A similar paradigmatic role was played by the four Jesuit churches in Juli, rebuilt in the seventeenth and early eighteenth centuries and the first to showcase the style in that region.[18]

The Jesuit college and church in Arequipa had two founders, the conquistador Diego Hernández Hidalgo and Antonio de Llanos, another feudatory resident of the city and a former mayor and chief justice.[19] The first two churches on the site toppled in earthquakes and the third (1605–10) was demolished because it was too modest to accommodate the city's growing congregation. The spacious fourth church began to take form in 1621, causing an enthusiastic Annual Letter to report that it "will be a magnificent thing indeed."[20] This fourth church, not completed until the early eighteenth century, is the structure standing today – one of the few churches to survive almost intact through the litany of earthquakes that ravaged the region between 1687 and 2001.[21] Like the Cuzco Compañía it was built on the same square as the cathedral (although here its property merely abutted it on one corner) and rivaled the latter in height and splendor.

The Arequipa Compañía follows a similar plan to that of Cuzco, based on a Latin cross with six nave side chapels and a dome at the crossing, although the nave and apse feature a more up-to-date barrel vault. On the interior, the surfaces of the nave walls are articulated with elegant Ionic engaged columns and a plain entablature with a projecting cornice supporting a wooden balustrade, and the dome is separated from the crossing by a prominent entablature of its own. The domed sacristy is covered entirely with brightly colored mural paintings, including illusionist architecture, jungle vegetation, angels, and

Figure 13.3. Church of Santiago, or Compañía, Arequipa (Peru). Begun 1621. Façade. Photo by Gauvin Alexander Bailey.

birds; however, only the dome, spandrels, and a few other details are original. Remnants of earlier decorative programs by Bitti and the Flemish Jesuit Diego de la Puente (1586–after 1656) survive, including Bitti's magnificent high altar painting of the *Virgin and Child* (c. 1603). The entire structure is built in fine *sillar* masonry (volcanic stone), which brings lightness to the interior even in the evening, and the language of its architecture is solemn and Classical, more Renaissance than Baroque.

The relative austerity of the interior does nothing to prepare us for the splendor of the main façade (1698–99), supervised by Diego de Adrián but – like nearly all Mestizo Style monuments – carved by Native American sculptors and masons.[22] The lavishly decorated portal is divided horizontally into two stories and a large tympanum-like pediment that is almost a story in its own right, and vertically into three bays with the widest one at the center. This basic grid plan stands out against a tapestry of flat, deep carving, much of it distributed like a mosaic of square or rectangular blocks of ornament. Few churches since have provided such a full repertoire of Mestizo Style motifs. The lower story is flanked by giant carved borders composed of serpentine monsters with massive maws which disgorge pomegranates, tobacco-like leaves, dahlias or cactus flowers, *cantuta* blossoms, scrolls, and mustachioed monster masks. Equally sumptuous panels appear between the columns, the areas surrounding the date inscriptions, the frieze over the lower story, and the borders and mosaic-like panel surrounding the window in the second story, including winged cherubs wearing *cantuta* earrings (as Andean women in Bolivia and Peru still do today), other human figures and masks (including one wearing the *mascaypacha*), tropical leaves and flowers, parrots and songbirds. There is no let-up in the decoration in the upper part of the façade – its frieze, tympanum-like pediment, and finials – which is also brimming with figures, plants, and other motifs. As in Cuzco, earthquakes provided a clean slate for other churches to copy the Arequipa Compañía. In this case, however, they took place after the church was already under construction. The 1687, 1715, and 1784 temblors destroyed almost every church in Arequipa (the cathedral was one of the worst hit) and architects and sculptors turned to the sole survivor – the Compañía – as the inspiration for their new portals, façades, domes, and towers. Echoes of the Jesuit church were still appearing as late as the early nineteenth century.

In Brazil the Jesuits built some of the most grandiose churches in all Latin America. The greatest of all is the Igreja de Jesus in Salvador

(Fig. 13.4), the fourth church on the site since 1590, and like so many Jesuit churches in the Americas it enjoyed a prominent position on the main square of the city, directly confronting the Franciscan church of São Francisco and overlooking the bluff and the lower harbor and sea.[23] Based on a design by the Jesuit architect Belquior Pires, the present structure was begun in 1657, reusing parts of the old building. The church was finished in 1672, and the sacristy ceiling was painted two decades later, in 1694. The Jesuit church at Salvador set the tone for future Jesuit buildings in Brazil through its restrained exterior, which was based on Italian and Portuguese late Renaissance models and adorned with Classical pilasters and pediments carved in low relief. Like a number of Jesuit foundations in Brazil, the Salvador church forms the focal point of a symmetrical arrangement of courtyards as in the great abbey churches of Germany and the royal Portuguese convent of Mafra (begun 1717).

The façade is based generically on the Jesuits' mother church of the Gesù in Rome (begun 1568); however, Pires has paid lip service to Portuguese tradition by adding small flanking towers.[24] The façade makes references to several Portuguese churches. It has the tight, grid-like compartmentalization of Coimbra Cathedral (also a Jesuit building, finished 1698), the pediment, pinnacles, and volutes recall the Arco dos Flamengos in Lisbon (1609), and the double order of colossal piers and alternating round and angular pediments are found on the Portuguese seat of the Society of Jesus, São Roque in Lisbon (begun 1567). The façade focuses on three monumental portals surmounted by niches containing statues of Ignatius of Loyola, Francis Xavier, and Francis Borja, works in marble dating from around 1746. The portals themselves look to other late Renaissance models, such as Michelangelo's Porta Pia in Rome (1561), which was known through engravings. The exterior uses solemn grey ashlar stone imported from Lisbon instead of the whitewash-and-stone combination so frequently used on Brazilian churches. The Salvador façade itself became the model for many churches in Brazil and even Portugal, where the Jesuit collegiate church at Santarém (1676) shows its influence.

The same Portuguese stone is used on the interior of the church, giving the impression that the east and west walls of the nave – both of which use the same pilasters and volutes – are inverted façades. In every other respect the interior provides a startling contrast with the outside (Fig. 13.5). Dominated by the glittering gold and rich Baroque carving of its main and side chapel retables and especially by the bold coffered ceiling with its angels, plant motifs and Jesuit monogram, the

Figure 13.4. Igreja de Jesus, Salvador, Bahia (Brazil). Constructed 1657–72.
Exterior. Photo by Gauvin Alexander Bailey.

Figure 13.5. Igreja de Jesus, Salvador, Bahia (Brazil). Interior. Photo by Gauvin Alexander Bailey.

interior evokes a world of pageantry and spectacle that is barely hinted at on the outside. The side chapels house no fewer than thirteen retables from different periods, including some by Jesuit sculptors João Correia, Luis Manuel, and Domingo Trigueros, and they also incorporate paintings by Jesuit artists such as Domingo Rodrigues and Eusebio de Matos – a testament to the high concentration of artistic skill among the Jesuit brothers of the early Society in Brazil.[25] The multi-story high altar, built between 1665 and 1670, dominates the main apse chapel (*capela-mor*) with its pairs of richly carved columns and background patterns formed of arabesques, cornucopias, sirens, and polychrome human heads. The two main Rococo side retables (1755) are among the last to be built and they represent the Jesuits' attempt to bring the iconography of their church up to date with European currents.

The sacristy (completed 1694) is one of the wonders of colonial art in Brazil, with its floor of inlaid marble and stone and its high tile dado on the walls, adorned with floral motifs in blue, green, and white. Recent work suggests that its complex iconographical program derives from the writings of the Brazilian Jesuit poet José de Anchieta (1534–97) and was also inspired by Rubens' painting cycle in the Jesuit church of Saint Ignatius (now Charles Borromeo) in Antwerp.[26] Above the dado is a series of biblical paintings on wood panel, one of them depicting the *Sacrifice of Isaac*. The sacristy is dominated by a paneled ceiling with twenty-one portraits of Jesuit heroes surrounded by animal and plant motifs and grotesque figures in bright colors. These men include Jesuit saints, such as Ignatius of Loyola and Francis Xavier, and beatified Jesuits, but the ceiling also incorporates several Jesuit martyrs, many of them only recently deceased, who had not yet achieved the dignity of sainthood.[27] The college library is also striking, with its monumental illusionistic ceiling painting attributed to Antônio Simões Ribeiro. Popular with Jesuits in particular and in Brazil in general, such illusionistic ceilings were based on a printed manual on perspective published between 1693 and 1700 by the Italian Jesuit painter and architect Andrea Pozzo (1642–1709). In the center of the library ceiling, which is painted to look like a view of the sky, is an allegorical figure of Wisdom, who is lifted into the upper world by allegories of Time and an angelic messenger with wings on her feet like Mercury. One of the symbols on the ceiling shows the helm of a ship, an allusion to maritime conquest, and perhaps also to the tragic martyrdoms of forty Jesuits who were attacked and sunk at sea while trying to reach Brazil in 1570.

Nowhere did Jesuit architecture make a greater impact than in the Cono Sur (southern cone) of South America, particularly present-day Argentina, Chile, and Paraguay.[28] The buildings the Jesuits constructed there were also among the most stylistically cosmopolitan in Latin America, with strong influences from Greater Germany, Switzerland, Bohemia, and Italy as well as contributions from a wide range of indigenous cultures. Although a handful of Jesuits were already operating in the region as early as 1585, their activities there began in earnest only after the creation of the Paraguay province in 1607. The Jesuits founded colleges and churches in a string of Argentine towns between 1611 and 1620, and it was during those years that they established their church and college of San Ignacio in Buenos Aires, at the time a small outpost on the edge of nowhere, with an unhealthy climate and at constant risk from pirates by sea and hostile Amerindians by land. The Jesuits first settled on the main plaza of the city, now the Plaza de Mayo, but in 1661 they moved two blocks south to their present location, now known as the Manzana de las Luces. There they built a college, residence, and a new church, also dedicated to Saint Ignatius. Nothing is known about the buildings the Society erected in these early years, but they were almost certainly nothing more than simple adobe structures with wooden roofs and little to dignify them with the title of "architecture."

The present church of San Ignacio is a creation of another era, the more prosperous early eighteenth century when the city's population exceeded 10,000 thanks largely to contraband trade (Fig. 13.6).[29] Jesuit enterprises in the Cono Sur had expanded as well, most notably in the Paraguay Reductions, and most of the Paraguay missionaries first passed through the port of Buenos Aires and stayed at the Jesuit residence. The oldest church still standing in Buenos Aires, San Ignacio was the grandest structure in the city at the time, and its elaborate façade and lofty tower (only the south one is original) must have made a deep impression on its citizens. San Ignacio was designed by central Europeans and Italians, who – like most of the non-Spanish Jesuit architects in the Cono Sur – came to the New World after the Spanish imperial government relaxed their restrictions on the number of foreign missionaries, particularly in two voyages in 1693 and 1716.

San Ignacio is a hybrid church. Begun in 1712, it was designed by the Bohemian architect Johann Kraus, S. J. (1660–1714) from Pilsen (Plzen), and most scholars credit him with the plan and basic profile of the church. Nevertheless, Kraus died only two years into the project, when the construction was taken over by a series of capable German

Figure 13.6. Church of San Ignacio, Buenos Aires. Constructed 1712–33.
Photo by Gauvin Alexander Bailey.

and Italian Jesuit builders and architects, including the master carpenter Johannes Wolff (b. 1691), the Italian architects Andrea Bianchi (1677–1740) and Giovanni Battista Primoli (1673–1747), and the master ironworker Peter Weger (1693–1733). Although it is tempting to assign the more Germanic parts of the church to the central Europeans and the more Italianate ones to the Italians, we know few details about the specific contributions of these Jesuit brother architects. Under Bianchi's direction the transepts were roofed and the south tower was finished, and he also widened some of the windows to give the interior more light. His successor Primoli, the celebrated architect of the Paraguay Reductions who was in Buenos Aires in 1728–30, probably finished the vaults of the roof. The final decorative details, including probably the garlands, finials, and urns of the façade, were added by Weger. In fact, Weger was still working on these finishing touches when he fell to his death from the scaffolding in 1733.

The façade has the most recognizably Germanic accent, particularly in the three open arches on the ground floor with their high inverted corbels, the prominent urn finials, and the delicate garlands dressing the windows and niches on the second story. The arched vestibule recalls the Benedictine abbey at Weingarten in Bavaria (1715–24) or the Jesuit Kollegienkirche in Salzburg by Johann Bernhard Fischer von Erlach (1696–1707), even though the Austrian church has a convex façade. The tall, multi-story towers flanking the façade are like those of the Benedictine church at Ottobeuren (1737–66) without the onion domes. The dome, partly enclosed in a high square drum and almost invisible from the street, is similar to the one later executed in the cathedral at Montevideo (designed 1784), and both churches also have a clerestory gallery over the side aisles, unusual in Spanish American architecture. The corbels, volutes, and other Germanic features of this Jesuit church reverberated throughout colonial Argentina, from the grand Jesuit *estancia* (ranch) churches surrounding Córdoba (some of them also designed by central Europeans) to Salta in the northwest.[30]

The Jesuits built some of their most original and influential foundations on the missions, beginning with their first reduction in Juli (founded 1576) on the shores of Lake Titicaca. However, far more famous are the Jesuit reductions in Paraguay.[31] Established in 1609 and firmly settled after 1641, the Jesuits built a network of thirty mission towns along the Uruguay and Paraná rivers in present-day Argentina, Paraguay, and Brazil boasting gargantuan churches and prolific workshops of talented Guaraní artists. The first churches the

Jesuits built on the Reductions were simple, three-aisled structures of wood and adobe, or occasionally sandstone, similar in design to the churches in the Chiquitos region of Bolivia (see below). The giant stone ruins which most people associate with the Reductions were the product of a later era in Reduction history, in the decades leading up to the Jesuit expulsion in 1767 when an ever increasing number of Jesuit artists and architects came from Europe, especially central Europe and Italy.

Two of the most impressive ruins, Trinidad (Paraguay) and São Miguel (now in Brazil), were designed by Primoli, who focused mainly on the Paraguay Reductions after his arrival in 1717. Primoli's reduction churches were three-aisled structures with prominent stone towers, and at Trinidad, owing to the presence of local lime deposits, the church was also vaulted in stone and had a stone dome which scholars now believe was inspired by that of San Ignacio in Buenos Aires.[32] Unfortunately, all of Primoli's buildings in Paraguay now lie in ruins. Although the Trinidad Reduction was founded in 1706, Primoli's church was begun around 1744, and after the architect's death in 1747 it was taken over by the Spanish Jesuit architect José Grimau (b. 1718) (Fig. 13.7). The church remained unfinished at the time of the Jesuit expulsion in 1767, and much of its nave never reached the height of the ceiling. The Latin cross structure is 58 meters long and would have been 11 meters high, and like the rest of the Reduction churches it has a flat apse flanked by a sacristy and countersacristy. As with all the churches in the region it was constructed by Guaraní masons, this time using fine dressed ashlar sandstone from Itaquí. Although the Trinidad church has a very conservative plan, its decorative details (such as the cartouches that adorn the porch) are unmistakably Baroque. The interior is carved with flattened tropical vegetation reminiscent of the Mestizo Style ornamentation of Peru and it features a frieze in the crossing in which thirty angels play musical instruments – a reflection of the importance of music in the life of the Reductions. The church contains many other testaments to the skill of the Guaraní stone carver, including dour figures of Saints Peter and Paul and a splendid altarpiece, carved into the wall, which depicts souls burning in purgatory. This latter image was adapted from an engraving of a painting by Peter Paul Rubens (1577–1640).

Of all the surviving Reductions, Trinidad gives the visitor the best idea of the original urban setting of the missions, a scheme that blended a Baroque love of spectacle with indigenous traditions of urbanism. The mission complex, which extended over eight hectares

Figure 13.7. Church of the Reduction of Trinidad (Paraguay). Constructed 1744–67. Interior. Photo by Gauvin Alexander Bailey.

and was centered on a large formal plaza, included the main church, the Jesuit residence and workshops, ten apartment blocks for the Guaraní, a secondary, single-aisled church, and a massive stone bell tower. Reduction planners adopted features from indigenous towns, designing Amerindian residential quarters to accommodate to Guaraní social and kinship groups. The long, one-story apartment blocks were arranged along the side of a main plaza opposite the church, with individual cubicles for each family, and they were surrounded by a verandah on stone columns that allowed people to spend most of their time outside as they were accustomed, suspending their hammocks between the columns. The large formal plaza was the center of religious spectacle, but here it was designed in a more theatrical way than was standard in Spanish grid-plan towns. A main avenue led directly to the church, opening up a dramatic vista, and the church, college, and cemetery took up one entire side of the square. Dance, music, and speeches were important features of pre-contact Guaraní religion, and the Jesuits did their best to incorporate these features into the life of the mission. Missionaries like the Italian Domenico Zipoli (1688–1726) wrote and staged full-length operas in Guaraní and Chiquitos, complete with indigenous costume and instruments.

Music had an even greater influence on the architecture of the Jesuit reductions in Chiquitos, in lowland Bolivia, one of the few regions in South America that preserves the three-aisled wooden basilica churches originally constructed by most religious orders throughout Latin America before they replaced them with grander buildings of stone (Fig. 13.8).[33] Although the Jesuits had tried to missionize the Chiquitos Indians as early as 1587, when fathers Martínez and Samaniego worked with them out of Santa Cruz, they had little sustained contact with the tribes until José Francisco de Arce led an expedition in 1691 into the vast region east of Santa Cruz between the Paraguay and Guapay rivers and sandwiched between the Gran Chaco and Brazil.[34] The sixteenth-century explorer Ñuflo de Chávez referred to the thirty-one tribes in the region as "Chiquitos" ("little ones") in reference to the narrow doors of their homes. Although Arce's expedition was a failure (he was killed in 1715), the Chiquitos reductions soon flourished beyond anyone's expectations. Before the expulsion in 1767 the Chiquitos region boasted seven Jesuit houses and twenty-nine reductions, manned by 152 Jesuits. The seven towns that have restored missions today comprise San Javier, Concepción, San Ignacio, San Miguel, Santa Ana, San Rafael, and San José.

Figure 13.8. Church of San Rafael de Chiquitos (Bolivia). Constructed 1747–49. Exterior. Photo by Gauvin Alexander Bailey.

Except for San José, which is built of stone, all of these missions were constructed entirely of adobe and wood by indigenous artisans and decorated with richly carved retables, statues, confessionals, and other furnishings made with a local hardwood called *ajunau*. As in Paraguay, the indigenous carpenters and sculptors demonstrated an exceptional ability to adopt European styles and a natural skill with wood. Several of these structures survived the expulsion of the Jesuits, the collapse of the Spanish Empire, and wars with Brazil and Paraguay. Enough were left for the Swiss Jesuit Felix Plattner and the Swiss architect Hans Roth to restore them to their original appearance beginning in the 1970s, a process that continues today at San José.

Many of these churches were the brainchild of a much earlier Swiss visionary, Father Martin Schmid (1694–1774). Born in Zug in Catholic central Switzerland, Schmid reached South America in 1729, leaving behind him an accomplished career as a musician. Beginning in 1730 and continuing into the late 1750s, the indomitable Schmid worked at the Chiquitos reductions of San Javier, San Rafael, and Concepción, and possibly also San Ignacio and San Miguel. He founded choirs, manufactured musical instruments from harps to flutes, wrote and copied masses, operas, and motets, and designed churches and helped carve some of their statues and retables. A brilliant mathematician, Schmid related the proportions of their construction to musical harmonies so that each mission church was built in a series of different musical "keys," allowing the architecture to resonate metaphorically with the musical life of the missions.[35] The churches are low, wide, barn-like structures with ample eaves and separate bell towers. All of them have three aisles, in homage to the basilicas of the Early Church, and their adobe façades are painted with Baroque scrolls, shells, and balustrades. The roofs are supported by massive wooden columns carved from single trees. The best-preserved façade is at Santa Ana, a simple stucco front painted with short twisted columns, resembling candlesticks, which end before they reach the roof level. The churches are especially impressive on the inside, not only because of their sheer size (especially at the reconstructed church of San Ignacio, now a cathedral, and at Concepción), but also because of the richness of their carved and gilded wooden retables, pulpits, and confessionals, some of them decorated with glittering pieces of mica as they were in colonial times.

As in Europe and Asia, the Jesuits were architectural innovators in colonial Latin America and their churches, residences, and colleges served as models for later foundations both within and outside the Society. However, this innovativeness was always responsive to the regional idiosyncrasies of their location and the men who designed, built, and decorated them, resulting in a legacy as diverse as their enterprise was extensive.

Notes

1   For two recent surveys of Jesuit architecture in Latin America, see Ramón Gutiérrez and Graciela María Viñuales, "The Artistic and Architectural Legacy of the Jesuits in Spanish America," in John W. O'Malley and Gauvin Alexander Bailey, eds., *The Jesuits and the Arts: 1540–1773* (Philadelphia: St. Joseph's University Press, 2005), 269–310; Luisa Elena Alcalá, *Fundaciones jesuíticas en Iberoamérica* (Madrid: Viso Ediciones, 2002). For recent surveys of colonial Latin American art and architecture in general see Gauvin Alexander Bailey, *Art of Colonial Latin America* (London: Phaidon, 2005) and Ramón Gutiérrez, *Arquitectura y urbanismo en iberoamérica*, 4th edn (Madrid: Cátedra, 2002).
2   J. Gutiérrez Casillas, "Mexico," in Charles E. O'Neill and Joaquín María Domínguez, eds., *Diccionario histórico de la Compañía de Jesús*, 4 vols. (Rome and Madrid: Institutum Historicum Societatis Iesu, 2001), III: 2465. The classic work on Jesuit architecture in Mexico is Marco Díaz, *La arquitectura de los jesuitas en la Nueva España* (Mexico City: Universidad Nacional Autónoma de México, 1982). Recently there has been a surge of interest in Jesuit architectural and arts patronage in New Spain, among which the work of Clara Bargellini is particularly valuable. See Clara Bargellini, "Jesuit Devotions and Retablos in New Spain," in John W. O'Malley, Gauvin Bailey, Steven J. Harris, and T. Frank Kennedy, eds., *The Jesuits: Cultures, Sciences, and the Arts, 1540–1773* (Toronto: University of Toronto Press, 1999), 680–98; Clara Bargellini, "Iglesia de la Casa Professa, Ciudad de México, México," in Alcalá, *Fundaciones jesuíticas*, 293–99. The journal *Artes de México* is currently publishing several monographs devoted to Jesuit visual arts in New Spain, including: *Colegios jesuitas* (Mexico City: Artes de México, 2001); *Jesuitas: Misiones* (Mexico City: Artes de México, 2003); *Jesuitas: Arte y espiritualidad* (Mexico City: Artes de México, 2004); and *Jesuitas: Arte y espiritualidad II* (Mexico City: Artes de México, 2005).
3   See Bailey, *Art of Colonial Latin America*, 213–17.
4   On the influence of Sebastiano Serlio and other late Renaissance models on early mendicant architecture in Spanish South America, see Antonio San Cristóbal, *Puno: Esplendor de la arquitectura virreinal* (Lima: Peisa, 2004), 61–80; Gauvin Alexander Bailey, "'Just Like the Gesù': Sebastiano Serlio, Giacomo Vignola, and Jesuit Architecture in South America," in *Archivum Historicum Societatis Iesu* 70/140 (July–December 2001), 233–64; Valerie Fraser, *The Architecture of Conquest: Building in the Viceroyalty of Peru, 1535–1635* (Cambridge: Cambridge University Press, 1990), 108–53.

5　On the Colegio de San Andrés see Bailey, *Art of Colonial Latin America*, 217. Andrea Lepage, Ph.D. candidate in the Department of the History of Art and Architecture at Brown University, is completing an important new study of this school.

6　On Bitti see José de Mesa and Teresa Gisbert, *El manierismo en los Andes: Memoria del III encuentro internacional sobre barroco* (La Paz, Unión Latina, 2005), 49–86; José de Mesa and Teresa Gisbert, *Bitti un pintor manierista en sudamérica* (La Paz: Universidad Mayor de San Andrés, 1974).

7　L. Palacín, "Brasil," in O'Neill and Domínguez, *Diccionario histórico*, 524–30. The classic work on the Jesuits in Brazil is Lucio Costa, "A arquitetura jesuítica no Brasil," *Revista do Serviço do Patrimonio Historico y Artistico Nacional* 5 (Rio de Janeiro, 1941), 9–104. For a brilliant new book on Brazilian Rococo architecture that includes discussion of Jesuit monuments and has an extensive bibliography, see Myriam Andrade Ribeiro de Oliveira, *O rococó religioso no Brasil e seus antecedentes europeus* (São Paulo: Cosac & Naify, 2003).

8　For a recent survey of Cuzco Baroque, see Roberto Samanez Argumedo, "Las portadas retablo en el barroco cusqueño," in Ramón Mujica Pinilla *et al.*, eds., *El Barroco Peruano* (Lima, 2002), 145–99. On the Compañía, see Luis Eduardo Wuffarden, "Iglesia y Colegio de la Transfiguración, Cuzco, Perú," in Alcalá, *Fundaciones jesuíticas*, 116–29; Rubén Vargas Ugarte, *Los jesuitas del Perú y el arte* (Lima: Talleres Iberia, 1963), 66–73; Harold E. Wethey, *Colonial Architecture and Sculpture in Peru* (Cambridge, MA: Harvard University Press, 1949), 56–60.

9　Wuffarden, "Iglesia y Colegio," 117.

10　Vargas, *Jesuitas del Perú*, 66–68; Wethey, *Colonial Architecture*, 57.

11　Some of these reliefs have recently been published in color in Mesa and Gisbert, *Manierismo*, 57–65.

12　Wuffarden, "Iglesia y Colegio," 120–22; Vargas, *Jesuitas del Perú*, 68–70; Wethey, *Colonial Architecture*, 57–60.

13　Wuffarden, "Iglesia y Colegio," 122.

14　See in particular the work of Teresa Gisbert: *Iconografía y mitos indígenas en el arte* (La Paz: Gisbert & Cia., 2004); *El paraíso de los pájaros parlantes: La imagen del otro en la cultura andina*, 2nd edn (La Paz: Plural Editores, 2001).

15　On the *mascaypacha* and its significance, see Tom Cummins, "Silver Threads and Silver Needles: The Inca, the Spanish, and the Sacred World of Humanity," in Elena Phipps *et al.*, *The Colonial Andes: Tapestries and Silverwork, 1530–1830* (New York: Metropolitan Museum of Art, 2004), 11.

16　For a survey of the literature see ch. 1 of my forthcoming book *The Andean Hybrid Baroque: Convergent Cultures in the Churches of Colonial Peru*. See also Antonio San Cristóbal, *Arquitectura planiforme y textilografica virreinal de Arequipa* (Arequipa: Universidad Nacional de San Agustín, 1997).

17　Bailey, *Andean Hybrid Baroque*, ch. 2.

18 Ibid., ch. 5.
19 Ricardo Mariátegui Oliva, *La Compañía* (Lima: Biblioteca Arte de Arequipa, 1952), 8; Emilio Harth-Terré, "La portada de la iglesia de la Compañía de Jesús en Arequipa," *El arquitecto peruano* (January–March 1958), 15; Vargas, *Jesuitas del Perú*, 61; Luís Eduardo Wuffarden, "Iglesia y Colegio de Santiago, Arequipa, Perú," in Alcalá, *Fundaciones jesuíticas*, 149.
20 Vargas, *Jesuitas del Perú*, 61.Vargas gives no source for this quotation.
21 Wethey, *Colonial Architecture*, 141; Mario J. Buschiazzo, *Arquitectura colonial* (Buenos Aires: Guillermo Kraft, 1944), 115. Only the tower, rebuilt repeatedly (the present tower dates from 1919), did not escape destruction.
22 My revised dating and attribution of the façade derive from new archival discoveries to be published in my monograph *The Andean Hybrid Baroque*.
23 On the Igreja de Jesus in Salvador, see Costa, "A arquitetura jesuítica," 33–35; Germain Bazin, *L'architecture religieuse baroque au Brésil*, 2 vols. (Paris: Librairie Plon, 1956), I: 56–85. For excellent pictures in color, see Percival Tirapeli and Wolfgang Pfeiffer, *As mais belas igrejas do Brasil* (São Paulo: Metalivros, 2001), 38–41.
24 Bazin, *L'architecture*, 58–66.
25 Costa, "A arquitetura jesuítica," 33–35.
26 On the sacristy see Luís de Moura Sobral, "Ut Pictura Poesis: José de Anchieta e as Pinturas de Sacristia da Catedral de Salvador," *Barroco* 18 (1997/2000), 209–46; Luís de Moura Sobral, "Pintura, santos y propaganda: La sacristía del antiguo colegio de los jesuitas de Salvador, Bahía," in Ana María Aranda *et al.*, eds., *Barroco iberoamericano: territorio, arte, espacio y sociedad* (Seville: Ediciones Giralda, 2001), 393–403. For a recent study of the Antwerp cycle, see Anna C. Knaap, "Seeing in Sequence: Peter Paul Rubens' Ceiling Cycle at the Jesuit Church in Antwerp," *Nederlands Kunsthistorisch Jaarboek* 55 (2004), 155–95.
27 It is extremely unusual for Jesuit iconography to contain so many images of uncanonized Jesuits, but there is a very important model for this ceiling in the Jesuits' main novitiate in Rome, S. Andrea al Quirinale. In a fresco cycle in the recreation room and residence of the Roman novitiate, painted sometime between the 1590s and 1611, the visitor was presented with a plethora of images of Jesuit martyrs, including many who had not been canonized, in one case lined up like trophies in a trophy-case. See Gauvin Alexander Bailey, *Between Renaissance and Baroque: Jesuit Art in Rome, 1565–1610* (Toronto: University of Toronto Press, 2003), 61–68.
28 On the cosmopolitan makeup of Jesuit artists and architects in the Cono Sur see my articles: "Cultural Convergence at the Ends of the Earth: The Unique Art and Architecture of the Jesuit Missions to the Chiloé Archipelago (1608–1767)," in O'Malley *et al.*, eds., *The Jesuits II: Cultures, Sciences, and the Arts, 1540–1773* (Toronto: University of Toronto Press, 2006), 211–39; "The Calera de Tango of

Chile (1741–67): The Last Great Mission Art Studio of the Society of Jesus," *Archivum Historicum Societatis Iesu* 74/147 (January–June 2005), 175–206; "The Jesuits and the Non-Spanish Contribution to South American Colonial Architecture," in Hilmar M. Pabel and Kathleen M. Comerford, eds., *Early Modern Catholicism: Essays in Honour of John O'Malley* (Toronto: University of Toronto Press, 2001), 211–40.

29   On the church of San Ignacio, see Alberto de Paula, *Colegio de San Ignacio* (Buenos Aires: Manrique Zago, 1997); *Historia general del arte en la Argentina*, 2 vols. (Buenos Aires: Academia Nacional de Bellas Artes, 1982), 1: 190–94; José León Pagano, *El Templo de San Ignacio* (Buenos Aires: Academia Nacional de Bellas Artes, 1947); Stella Genovese-Oeyen, *Buenos Aires Colonial: Arquitectura Jesuitica del Siglo XVIII: La iglesia de San Ignacio* (Buenos Aires: Academia Nacional de Bellas Artes, 1946).

30   On the Jesuit estancia churches in the Sierras de Córdoba, see Carlos Page, *La estancia jesuítica de Alta Gracia* (Córdoba: Universidad Católica de Córdoba, 2004); Carlos Page, *El camino de las estancias* (Córdoba: Comisión del Proyecto, 2002); Antonio Lascano González, *Monumentos religiosos de Córdoba colonial* (Buenos Aires: S. Amorrortu y hijos, 1941); Mario Buschiazzo, *La estancia de Santa Catalina* (Buenos Aires: Academia Nacional de Bellas Artes, 1940); Mario Buschiazzo, *La estancia jesuítica de Jesús María* (Buenos Aires: Academia Nacional de Bellas Artes, 1940).

31   On the arts of the Jesuit Reductions in Paraguay, see Gianni Baldotto and Antonio Paolillo, *El barroco en las reducciones de Guaraníes* (Treviso: Soraimar, 2004); Gauvin Alexander Bailey, *Art on the Jesuit Missions in Asia and Latin America, 1540–1773* (Toronto: University of Toronto Press, 1999), 144–82; Bozidar D. Sustersic, *Templos Jesuítico-Guaraníes* (Buenos Aires: Universidad de Buenos Aires, 1999); Manrique Zago, ed., *Las misiones jesuíticas del Guayrá* (Buenos Aires: Manrique Zago, 1995); Paul Frings and Josef Übelmesser, *Paracuaria* (Mainz: Grünewald, 1982).

32   Sustersic, *Templos Jesuítico-Guaraníes*, 311–14.

33   On the Chiquitos missions, see Pedro Querejazu, *Las misiones jesuíticas de Chiquitos* (La Paz: Fundación BHN, 1995); Eckart Kühne, ed., *Martin Schmid, 1694–1772* (Lucerne: Historisches Museum, 1994).

34   A. Menacho and J. Baptista, "Bolivia," in O'Neill and Domínguez, *Diccionario histórico*, 1: 480–81.

35   Stefan Fellner, "'Weillen ich die musik verstehe': Musikalische Entwurfsprinzipien in der Architektur Martin Schmids," in Kühne, *Martin Schmid*, 75–88.

14 The Jesuits and the quiet side of the scientific revolution

LOUIS CARUANA

There is little doubt that European intellectual development, in various fields, has been marked by the contribution of Jesuits. The emergence of the natural sciences is no exception. Just three years before the first publication of Nicolaus Copernicus' *De Revolutionibus*, the Society of Jesus was officially founded in 1540. Eleven years later, we see the beginnings of what eventually became the Roman College, a center of learning whose influence regarding theology and natural philosophy extended over all Europe and beyond. The Jesuits' apostolic style took shape therefore during the turbulent years of the birth and development of natural science. The scientific revolution has been studied in various ways. Some early accounts favor a so-called Whig interpretation whereby the sequence of events is seen as a steady, victorious march from the age of darkness towards the light. Other, more responsible accounts reconstruct the narrative in terms of paradigm-shifts. In many of these accounts, the Jesuit project in the sixteenth and seventeenth centuries is often portrayed as ending in a tragic failure. Jesuits are depicted as being at first favorable to the new science. There is then the decree from higher authorities that blocks their open attitude; and henceforth they become the major resistance to scientific progress. The result of their opposing efforts in this area is then portrayed as a total failure.[1] Fortunately, more recent accounts of how science develops are more sophisticated and responsible. Imre Lakatos proposed that our main focus should be on research programs. This idea was certainly a step in the right direction. It invites historians to concentrate first on the core of such projects in terms of theories that are considered indisputable by a specific group of researchers. This core is seen as surrounded by a protective belt of auxiliary hypotheses that explain why the core theories should not be rejected when contradictory evidence arises. The task of researchers is therefore to formulate the simplest, and thus most acceptable, auxiliary hypothesis that saves the core. On this account, perseverance with the core project is of the essence of scientific practice.[2]

My aim in this paper is to work within the framework of this sophisticated version of scientific change so as to gain a deeper understanding of the Jesuits' role in the scientific revolution. Their received research program was Aristotelian cosmology. Their efforts to construct one protective belt after another to shield the core principles involved in this cosmology were fueled not only by the basic instinct to persevere, as Lakatos describes. It was propelled as well by the impact of official prohibitions from the side of church authorities that tended to avoid change. The clash between Copernicanism and the Church is marked primarily by three dates. The first condemnation occurred in 1616. This was directed primarily against Copernicanism as a theory. The second, more drastic, condemnation occurred in 1633: Copernicanism was declared heretical and Galileo was placed under house arrest. The third significant year was 1757 when the Congregation removed the 1616 decree from the new edition of the Index of forbidden books. This meant that the previous condemnations were effectively, although not officially, withdrawn. The Galileo case cannot, however, be associated exclusively with these three dates. It has had repercussions along the centuries up to our own times. To situate this essay within reasonable limits, I will concentrate on a period of about a hundred years, starting from the first condemnation of 1616 and ending in the early eighteenth century. My basic assumption will be that the church restrictions, represented primarily by the two condemnations, were not as paralyzing for Jesuit intellectuals as has often been thought. They left considerable space for maneuvering. Valuable contributions to the debates that were forging the very heart of the emerging new paradigm were still possible. Within this space, Jesuits were not engaged in spectacular new discoveries. Nevertheless, they exerted an important influence. They were essentially engaged in the indispensable task of exhausting all the potential of Aristotelian cosmology. In this essay, I will show how they did this primarily by trying to build intellectual bridges to ensure coherence between three regions of the cosmological imagination of the time. They struggled first to safeguard coherence between the received Aristotelian view, the new empirical data, and everyday experience. The obvious way to save the idea of a stationary earth was to support the proposal of Tycho Brahe, in which planets revolve around the Sun while the Sun itself revolves around a stationary earth. Aware of the mounting evidence against the earth's privileged position, however, they realized that this option was being steadily undermined. Various strategies were therefore adopted. To identify these strategies, I will determine first the exact nature of the restrictions imposed on Jesuit scholars by church authorities. After this first section, I will identify three prominent strategies evident in Jesuit writings. In the concluding section, these strategies will be briefly evaluated and discussed in the light of the intellectual output of Jesuits in later centuries leading up to our own times. The overall result throws light on how scientific development depends on the space left available by social and political restrictions.

THE SPACE AVAILABLE AFTER THE PROHIBITIONS

A prohibition is a kind of boundary. It does not in itself determine what should be said or taught. It only indicates what should not. The sanctions that proscribed the Jesuits from endorsing Copernicanism did not block their activity completely. Let me first distinguish the situation before the early 1600s from the situation afterwards.

Before the early 1600s, Jesuits were used to three main constraints. These were all included in official documents produced by the Society itself. They were norms about their apostolic style.[3] The first is found in their own Constitutions, officially approved in 1558. In Part IV we find Aristotle being given uncontested prominence in the kind of formation the Jesuits were meant to have: "In logic, natural and moral philosophy, and metaphysics, the doctrine of Aristotle should be followed, as also the other liberal arts."[4] This shows something of the founder's confidence in the approved doctrine of the time. In various points in the Constitutions, Ignatius had included concessions for different times and places. Many commentators have seen in these concessions his particular wisdom in government. As regards doctrine, however, he had never contemplated the possibility of a new cosmology. For him, Aristotle apparently was to be the only point of reference for the entire Society for ever. The second constraint was an important nuance added to the Constitutions by the Third General Congregation in 1573. Commenting on the part of the Constitutions just quoted, this Congregation specified that, in philosophy, Aristotle had to be taught not for his own sake but as a support for theology. In this way the ultimate aim of philosophical studies, which included the study of physics, was made clear. Theologians were given the final word.

The third constraint was more substantial: the 1599 *Ratio Studiorum*. This document charted the educational policy of the rapidly growing Jesuit colleges across Europe. It took some years to compile because it was the result of deliberation by the fifth General Congregation concluded in 1593. It is worthwhile highlighting this

Congregation's groundwork before referring directly to the *Ratio* itself. In Decree 56 of the Congregation, we find the following significant directives:

(1) By all means, Ours should consider St. Thomas as their special teacher, and they should be obliged to follow him in scholastic theology, first, because our Constitutions commend this to us in §1 of chapter 14 of part 4 and the supreme pontiff, Clement VIII, has indicated that he desires it; and second, because letter K of chapter 1 of part 8 of the Constitutions admonishes us to select the doctrine of one writer, and at this time there can hardly be a doctrine more solid and safe. St. Thomas is deservedly regarded by all as the prince of theologians.

(2) Nonetheless, Ours are not to be understood as being so bound to St. Thomas that they may not deviate from him in any respect. For those very ones who most strongly profess themselves to be Thomists differ from him at times. And it is not fitting that Ours be more tightly bound to St. Thomas than are the Thomists themselves.

(3) In questions that are purely philosophical and also in those pertaining to Scripture and the canons, it will also be permissible to follow others who have professedly been engaged in those areas.[5]

Following these directives, those responsible for the final version of the *Ratio* summarized the issue in the following clear mandate:

Teachers of philosophy should not depart from Aristotle in matters of any moment unless there happens to be something foreign to the teaching that academics everywhere approve or, even more so, if there is question of a teaching that is contrary to the orthodox faith. If there are any arguments of this or another philosopher against the faith, they should strongly endeavor to refute them, in accord with the Lateran Council.[6]

The Jesuits were aware of the possibility of finding elements in the Aristotelian corpus that go against the faith. Moreover, they saw themselves not as innovators, called to explore new intellectual territory, but as followers of the general trend of responsible scholars. For a deviation from Aristotle to be acceptable, the basic criterion was to wait for the debate to subside. Jesuit scholars were then expected to adopt the opinion of the majority. Although this looks very much like a conservative strategy, one needs to recall that, at that time, the *Ratio* was overall a courageous, innovative document.[7] It allowed even for disagreement with Aquinas: "one is never to talk of St. Thomas without honoring him, following him willingly whenever possible; one is to depart from him with reverence and reluctance."[8]

These three factors determined the Jesuit frame of mind as the new cosmology was on the verge of sweeping across Europe. The second phase of prohibitions can be seen as starting after the early 1600s. As Rome went through the Galileo crisis, the Vatican condemned Copernicanism in 1616 and then, in 1633, declared it heretical, placing Galileo under house arrest. Another prohibition arose from the Jesuit authorities themselves, who wanted to update their position after the Vatican decision. Their official statement was the *Ordinatio pro Studiis Superioribus* of 1651, one of the fruits of the Ninth General Congregation. This was practically a list of philosophical and theological opinions declared forbidden in Jesuit teaching. The main idea was that Aristotle and Aquinas had to be given preeminence, and that the most common opinion should be adhered to. In spite of this conservative attitude, we find yet again that some doors were left open. Some points that had seemed certain about thirty-five years earlier were not included. For instance, the fluidity of the heavens had been considered an unacceptable opinion. The *Ordinatio* never included this in its list. It implied thereby that, even though fluidity contradicts Aristotle's theory of solid spheres, it could be taught if ever it became the more common opinion.

These prohibitions had various effects on Jesuits.[9] In general, the pronouncements of the Roman Inquisition, set up in 1542, had high authority even though they lacked the status of infallible teaching. The Jesuit Giovanni Battista Riccioli, in his *Almagestum Novum* (1651), described the moral obligation imposed on Catholics by the 1633 condemnation:

> As there has been no definition on this matter by the Sovereign Pontiff or by a General Council directed and approved by him, it is in no way of faith that the sun moves and the earth is motionless; ... Still, all Catholics are obliged ... at least not to firmly teach the opposite of what the decree lays down (*& saltem ad non docendum absolute oppositum*).[10]

Strictly speaking, the Roman Inquisition had the authority to exercise its powers in all Catholic countries except Spain, which had its own Inquisition. In practice, however, it had no power outside Italy. Sovereigns of France and of Germanic lands, even though Catholic, would not tolerate interference from Rome. There was always the possibility that the Roman authorities would impose spiritual sanctions such as excommunication on offenders beyond the Italian peninsula, but they never in fact did so in the case of Copernicanism.[11]

In brief, then, the constraints on the Jesuit intellectual output in the latter half of the seventeenth century were of various kinds. Whatever the reasons behind them, they did leave some space for maneuvering. They obliged the Jesuits to trace a risky path across slippery intellectual territory. Jesuits were obliged to refute Copernicanism. They felt obliged also, for the sake of intellectual integrity, to accept genuine evidence when they saw it. They wanted to avoid both useless speculation and uncritical revisionism. How did they manage all this?

PROBABILITY ARGUMENTS

The first Jesuit strategy worth highlighting involves the question of certainty. Endorsing or defending Copernicanism was not an option. This ban, however, did not forbid anyone from discussing and evaluating the probability of the claims of heliocentrism. Taking this opportunity, Jesuits started to slide away from an attitude of clear-cut distinctions between truth and falsity, as was fashionable in high scholasticism. They embarked on a more subtle discussion of the merits of the different, contesting hypotheses.

History shows that changes of ideas are never abrupt. New explanations that gain credibility do so gradually: from being regarded as certainly false to being regarded as somewhat possible, then to being regarded as perhaps probable, and finally to being regarded as warranted or true. The main ingredient here is hypothetical reasoning. For medieval schoolmen, such reasoning was an exercise in entertaining ideas that did not fit the accepted system. An absurdity for Aristotelian and Ptolemaic science could nevertheless be entertained. Some explanations started thus to be mentioned and discussed only, as it were, for the sake of the argument. Spelling out the forbidden claim, however, is already a slight concession. It allows a peep at its consequences; and this makes all the difference. The schoolmen were encouraged in this procedure by the theologians' admonition that God's omnipotence cannot be restricted by the limitations of the Aristotelian or Ptolemaic paradigm. The impossibilities of natural philosophy thus became possibilities *de potentia Dei absoluta*. This is just one illustration of how, if the climate of opinion changes, or if new evidence becomes available, what had been considered anathema may become an acceptable possibility. In his discussion on this point, the historian Amos Funkenstein writes:

> Even where schoolmen in the Middle Ages traded Aristotle's "impossibilities" for possibilities *de potentia Dei absoluta*, they regarded them only as incompossible with our universe. With the usage of ideal experiments in the seventeenth century many such incompossibles became limiting cases of our universe; even if they do not describe our universe, they are necessary to explain it.[12]

This offers a good sketch of what the Jesuits did in the aftermath of the Galilean controversy. Constrained to work within the boundaries of the various prohibitions, the Jesuits started by ignoring Copernicanism. They then started including it in textbooks as a false hypothesis. This inclusion allowed it to be described and even sometimes discussed at length. The Jesuits were thus instrumental in making Copernicanism shift from being seen as false because impossible, to being considered possible but improbable, and finally to being considered possible and probable – which is just a step away from being considered true. This technique was effective especially after the *Ordinatio* of 1651. As indicated above, this document obliged Jesuits to stick to Aristotle and Aquinas, but did so in a way that explained how departures from these authors could be made. As a consequence, the *imprimatur* was also available to those who made a judicious use of "probable" and "hypothesis." Jesuit scholars were thus allowed to publish commentaries on various aspects of the new cosmology even though the official position of the Vatican was against them. This strategy is evident in various works of the time, especially in those published in the German-speaking provinces. On this, Marcus Hellyer writes: "Provided Aristotle or St. Thomas' opinion was granted a degree of probability, other opinions could be openly discussed."[13]

There are two crucial consequences of the Jesuit use of probability: one concerns biblical interpretation, and the other the role of superiors. The point about biblical interpretation refers to the principle of accommodation. Put simply, this principle stipulates that Scripture speaks a human language appropriate, or accommodated, to the mentality of the time. Aquinas spells it out: "Scripture speaks according to the opinion of the people."[14] This is to be distinguished from a related but different idea, often referred to by the term "concordism." This idea concerns a specific way of interpreting the Bible. It stipulates that, whenever well-established empirical evidence stands opposed to some biblical claim

about physical nature, the Bible should be given an appropriate rein-
terpretation so that its descriptions regain coherence with empirical
data. For instance, the six days of creation in Genesis need to be
reinterpreted as six very long periods of time so as to be in line with
current views on the age of the universe. Concordism corresponds to a
maximalist version of the principle of accommodation as opposed to a
minimalist version.[15] Concordism is maximalist in the sense that the
Bible is assumed to contain all science and metaphysics. This content,
heavily clothed in metaphors, remains inaccessible to the uneducated
masses of the various periods in the course of history. The minimalist
version is the exact opposite. The Bible is here assumed neutral as
regards physics and metaphysics. It is assumed lacking in significant
descriptive content regarding the nature of things. Hence, on the
minimalist view, the Bible neither contradicts science nor contains it
in a hidden way.

These various trends were all very important during the Galileo
controversy. In his letter to the Duchess Christina, Galileo insisted
that, if time were to stand still in the Ptolemaic universe, it is not
enough that "the sun in Gibeon stand still," as written in Joshua 10:12.
The sphere of the fixed stars must cease to move, as well. Hence,
Galileo argued, whether we accept Ptolemy or Copernicus, there is
no way of interpreting the biblical text as descriptively responsible.
There is no science being clothed by ordinary language here. Whether
we follow Ptolemy or Copernicus, the text has to be considered meta-
phorical. It is clear, therefore, that Galileo was a champion of the
minimalist version of the principle of accommodation. His opponents,
on the contrary, were crude maximalists, insisting on the supreme
relevance of the descriptive content of the biblical text, even when
such content was marginal as regards the main point of the text.

With the Jesuits' use of probability arguments, the case for such
crude maximalist ideas was considerably weakened. Once they started
to include in textbooks Copernicanism as a hypothesis worthy of discussion, the arguments of those who used the Bible against heliocentrism were progressively undermined. Copernicanism underwent the
stages mentioned above. From being seen as false because impossible,
it started being considered possible but improbable, and finally was
considered possible and probable. Geocentrism underwent the opposite development; and so did the maximalist understanding of
Scripture. The idea that the Bible contains hidden but true descriptions
of the deep nature of the material world used to be accepted as true.
Due to the Jesuits' probability-tinted reasoning, its status started to

shift. It gradually came to be considered possible but improbable, until it finally ended up being considered impossible. This is not to say that the descriptive content of Scripture was sloughed off completely. Details of a historical nature, ranging from simple facts, like the fact that Jacob had twelve sons, to specific dates for battles and political changes, were always retained as genuine descriptions. These are central to the message of the text.[16] Other details, however, found their way into the text only as decorative extras. Cosmological ideas are among these latter. The Jesuits' way of engaging in intellectual work after the Galileo case was instrumental in uncovering the true features of the principle of accommodation, namely as stipulating that God, in His infinite wisdom, had accommodated His message to the various mentalities in the course of history not by adjusting, simplifying, and packaging the truths of cosmology, but by adjusting and simplifying those of theology.

Apart from these issues regarding biblical interpretation, there is a second significant consequence of the Jesuit recourse to probability arguments. This second consequence concerns the role of superiors. As the new cosmology found its way into textbooks, the evidence in its favor started becoming stronger. Some aspects of the ancient cosmology, like celestial immutability and the reality of qualities, soon became untenable. This made Copernicanism gain credibility. Jesuit natural philosophers started adopting a more positive attitude towards the new cosmology. Since they were constrained to avoid admitting its truth, however, they had to think of a way of presenting the stark incompatibility of the two systems in the very same book. They often did this by shifting the responsibility on to superiors. They practically started putting the blame gently on superiors for not allowing them to draw the obvious conclusions regarding the superiority of the new cosmology. The Jesuit Claude Miliet Dechales, who taught mathematics in Jesuit colleges in Marseilles and Lyons in the 1670s, was typical. In spite of his sympathies towards Copernicanism, he still felt obliged to reject it. He applied therefore the last available argument: loyalty to Scripture and the Church. He admits that Copernicus gives the simplest explanation. In the same breath, however, he adds that the Church has to be obeyed. If it were not for the authority of Scripture, he himself would be a Copernican.[17] Something similar is found in the writings of the Jesuit Melchior Cornaeus (1598–1665), theology professor at Würzburg University. At one point in his 1657 philosophy textbook, he draws a clear contrast between what he thinks is correct and what his superiors want. The specific question wasn't about the motion of the heavens, but about the reality of the distinct qualities of heaviness and lightness, as prescribed by Aristotelians. Cornaeus writes:

> What I have just taught about heaviness and lightness according to the opinion of learned men, I myself have openly taught and held for many years. Now because the authority of my superiors commands something else, I say that it is probable that heaviness and lightness are two positive qualities ... And because authority commands that we subscribe to this opinion, I subscribe and I approve of it.[18]

The responsibility is clearly shifted on to church authorities. The initial discussion on the merits of the various competing hypotheses has resulted in one of the hypotheses becoming much more probable than the other. When the only justification for the old cosmology became superior authority rather than demonstration, the case for the new cosmology became much stronger. As a strategy in managing the cultural tensions of the scientific revolution, this is basically a way of exhausting slowly but steadily the heuristic potential of the received research program.

ANACHRONISTIC SPECULATION REGARDING ANCIENT AUTHORS

Another Jesuit strategy involved addressing questions of this kind: What would the major philosophers of antiquity have said had they been with us today? The form of this question is particularly valuable. It acknowledges the respect due to ancient authorities. It acknowledges moreover the irrefutable value of the new evidence. A very clear example of this strategy can be seen in some arguments presented by Cornaeus. In his textbook mentioned above, he tackles the issue of celestial incorruptibility. Aristotle had repeatedly claimed that the heavens and the stars are immutable and incorruptible. They were made up of the fifth element, the ether. This belief started to be challenged from the late sixteenth century onwards because of various new astronomical observations: comets, sunspots, and hitherto unknown stars or planets. The argument advanced by Cornaeus involved imagining what Aristotle would have said had he been aware of these observations:

> If Aristotle had lived today, and had seen how we observe changes and conflagrations in the Sun, without any doubt he would have changed his mind and would have agreed with us. The same reasoning applies

to the planets, of which the Philosopher never knew more than seven. We nowadays, however, by the use of the telescope (access to which he never had) know for certain that there are more.[19]

What kind of reasoning is involved here? No doubt, Cornaeus presupposes a good knowledge of Aristotle. It is precisely this good knowledge of Aristotle that enables him to go beyond the usual Aristotelian picture. In other words, Cornaeus felt justified in affirming the counterfactual conditional statement: if Aristotle were alive today, he would have agreed that there are changes in the heavens. This is the first step towards a kind of slippery slope. If the statement is true, then it leads to the idea that, if Aristotle had agreed to celestial mutability, he would have seen the need to adjust his entire cosmology. This in turn leads to the more radical claim that, if Aristotle had seen the need to adjust his entire cosmology, he would have become a Copernican. Political correctness demanded that only the first claim be explicitly stated.[20]

The Jesuits were here essentially following the example set by Galileo himself, who at times argued in a similar fashion. In his *Dialogue Concerning the Two Chief World Systems*, we find him highlighting the importance of sense experience in scientific reasoning. He explicitly states that "we do have in our age new events and observations such that if Aristotle were now alive, I have no doubt he would change his opinion. This is inferred from his own manner of philosophizing." Aristotle's conversion would have resulted, according to Galileo, from the crucial principle of giving priority to sense experience over natural reason.[21]

From these remarks, it is clear that what I am calling the strategy of anachronistic speculation was a powerful weapon in the hands of those who, like the Jesuits, were open to innovation and yet sought to respect tradition. This strategy was essentially associated with the idea of rediscovering the real Aristotle. Peripatetic doctrine had to be cleaned up from errors that had become encrusted upon it since scholastic times. As bits of this peripatetic doctrine were replaced by new ideas and concepts, a variety of systems was tried out.[22] Such piecemeal replacement and adjustment continued all through the century I am considering in this essay and even beyond.

ACCUMULATION OF DATA

The third and final strategy I want to highlight involves the avoidance of speculation. With evidence in favor of the new cosmology gaining strength, and with the prohibition against Copernicanism still in force, some Jesuit scholars dedicated themselves to sporadic and patchy accumulation of knowledge without any theoretical synthesis. They acknowledged the existence and usefulness of novel ideas and observations, but did not worry much about the need to ensure a coherent system. This strategy has both negative and positive aspects.

The negative aspects include the fact that, as a research strategy, it tended to engender eclecticism. The clearest example here is Athanasius Kircher (1602–80), Jesuit professor of mathematics at the Roman College and founder of a renowned museum there. In his *Mundus Subterraneus*, he simply fills pages and pages with descriptions of a bewildering variety of novelties without any coherent synthetic explanation. The novelties he includes strike the modern reader for their sheer variety, ranging from useful geological or biological descriptions to useless folklore. It is difficult not to agree with William B. Ashworth, Jr., who admits that the Jesuits "do indeed seem to merit the praise they have frequently received. And yet when all this is said and acknowledged, there still remains the unavoidable feeling that Jesuit science was somehow seriously deficient." The main reason for his judgment is Kircher, who "sandwiches descriptions of fossil fish between accounts of gems bearing the images of cities and stones in the shape of John the Baptist, and he can sustain such a mélange for hundreds of pages. There is no suggestion that some authorities might be more reliable than others; every fact or observation seems to be given equal weight."[23] Traces of eclecticism can be seen even in Riccioli's *Almagestum*, especially where he discusses new stars. He lists fourteen possible explanations for their appearance, together with the advantages and disadvantages of each.[24] He does not, however, make any attempt to choose one of these explanations. He gives the impression that trying to arrive at the correct one was not really important. In his judgment, the time was apparently not ripe for taking the risk of suggesting a philosophical superstructure for all the facts available. He, like Kircher and others who adopted this strategy, limited himself to gathering information. He postponed the task of establishing explanatory coherence to future generations.

This negative aspect is counterbalanced by at least one significant positive aspect: the beneficial shift of attention from theory to observation. The very meaning of the term "observation" was changing during the scientific revolution. In scholastic natural philosophy, "experience" had taken the form of universal statements. This was because statements of singular events were not evident and indubitable, but relied on fallible historical reports. Peter Dear explains:

In a sense, the Aristotelian model of a science adopted by the Jesuits implied that scientific knowledge must be *public* – the conclusions of scientific demonstration would in principle be truths perfectly graspable by all, because they were derived from necessary, logical connections between terms formulated in premises commanding universal assent. Singular experiences were not public, but known only to a privileged few; consequently, they were not suitable elements of scientific discussion.[25]

In the early seventeenth century, Jesuit scholars started to include singular experience. Their work enhanced the status of discrete events, which thus started to have a role as properly accredited knowledge about the world. The Jesuits worked essentially to establish two crucial elements in the chain of justification. Private, singular, actual experience was related to public, potential experience; and this public, potential experience was related to universal, self-evident truths. Thus, habitual private experience, which roughly corresponds to the modern understanding of "experiment," started to gain its importance in scientific demonstrations. The hunt for more and more evidence became the central issue. One can see, therefore, how the pressure of the Roman Inquisition did not stifle the development of science in Catholic countries but redirected its attention. It made scientists shift from theory construction to collection of data. Jesuit astronomers, for instance, shifted from theoretical to observational astronomy. Some of them were quite successful in this area: Riccioli and Grimaldi, because of this new shift, managed to map the surface of the moon with remarkable accuracy.[26]

CONCLUSION

My original aim was to show how, all through the century following Galileo's first condemnation, Jesuit scholars were, in spite of everything, engaged in genuine science. The prohibitions originating from the Vatican and from their own Jesuit curia did leave some valuable space for maneuvering. Exhausting all the potential of the received research program was still possible. Of the various strategies in this endeavor, I highlighted three: the introduction of probable judgments in natural philosophy; anachronistic speculation of what ancient authorities would have done had they been faced with the new evidence; and the simple accumulation of data. The fact that Jesuits' research program turned out to be regressive does not show that their efforts were unscientific. Once the idea of a crucial experiment, as a gestalt switch between paradigms, is rejected as completely unrealistic, we must acknowledge the importance of perseverance within a given research program. It is a vital constituent of genuine scientific method. Seen in this light, the common assumption that seventeenth-century Jesuits were blinkered, reactionary Aristotelians, keen on blocking at all costs the advance of natural science, loses all its plausibility.

Can these strategies help us understand the intellectual output of Jesuits in later centuries? If we start with the major Jesuit figure dominating the period just after the one covered in this essay, Ruder Bošković (1711–87), we find similar efforts being made even though Aristotelian cosmology was by then quite evidently a regressive research program. Bošković started as a defender of Tycho Brahe's system but soon became convinced that Newtonianism should be substituted for peripatetic natural philosophy. His main concern was centered on saving the everyday experience of an immobile earth. So he devised his impressive theory of the two kinds of space: a relative space in which the earth is in motion as described by Newton and an absolute space in which the earth stands still. By his time, the balance of probabilities in cosmology had tilted definitely towards heliocentrism. Anachronistic reasoning involving ancient authors had become largely irrelevant. In spite of this, Bošković can be seen as engaged in work that was still in line with the broad Jesuit effort of exhausting all the potential of a received research program before discarding it. He was effectively still stretching out to its limits the idea of the immobility of the earth as suggested by daily experience.[27]

A similar stance can be seen in Jesuit scientific work through much of the eighteenth, nineteenth, and twentieth centuries. Two of the major highlights in this later period were the rise of evolutionary biology and the advances in astronomy. The way Jesuits have been involved in these two areas shows a similar concern to explore all the possibilities before moving on, and a concern to accumulate data.[28] Innovation and revolutionary thinking is never valued in and for itself. On the contrary, the main concern seems to be safeguarding the coherence of a unified system of thought ranging from science to philosophy and theology. It is not surprising that the need to resist the fragmentation and eventual disintegration of knowledge has been expressly recalled by recent Jesuit Generals.[29]

This style of work situates its protagonists inevitably on the quiet side of scientific revolutions. For historians, the tendency is to keep the harbingers of new successful research programs in the limelight. Less attention is given to those who do the spadework to ensure that a genuine revolution is called for. Both roles, however, are indispensable for scientific practice. Jesuit scientists have tended to take the latter.[30]

Notes

1   For an example of such simplistic historiography, see Andrew D. White, *A History of the Warfare of Science with Theology in Christendom* (New York: Appleton, 1896; republished Prometheus Books, 1993).

2   Imre Lakatos, "Falsification and Methodology of Scientific Research Programmes," in I. Lakatos and A. Musgrave, eds., *Criticism and Growth of Knowledge* (Cambridge: Cambridge University Press, 1970), 95–195.

3   I draw here from Marcus Hellyer, *Catholic Physics: Jesuit Natural Philosophy in Early Modern Germany* (Notre Dame: University of Notre Dame Press, 2005).

4   Ignatius of Loyola, *The Constitutions of the Society of Jesus and Their Complementary Norms*, trans. G. E. Ganss, S. J. (St. Louis: Institute of Jesuit Sources, 1996), Part IV, ch. 14, §3.

5   J. W. Padberg, S. J., M. D. O'Keefe, S. J., and J. L. McCarthy, S. J., *For Matters of Greater Moment: The First Thirty Jesuit General Congregations* (St. Louis: Institute of Jesuit Sources, 1994), 207. Surprisingly, point 1 of this official text of the Congregation misquotes the Constitutions. The point indicated by the letter K does not in fact deal with following a single *author* but a single *doctrine*. Moreover, although point 2 shows an opening towards some diversity, it is still centered on Thomistic interpretation. The scientific revolution did not fit into this model. The stationary earth had been defended by Aristotle in *De caelo* 2.13.293b.16–32 and 2.14.296a.24–26; and by Aquinas in his commentary on *De caelo*.

6   Cf. Padberg *et al.*, *For Matters of Greater Moment*, 199. The Fifth Lateran Council (1512–17) had decreed that, in the search for truth, faith should be given priority over the exercise of reason.

7   Critics of the Jesuits submitted the *Ratio* to the Inquisition twice. See J. Consentino, "Le matematiche nelle 'Ratio Studiorum' della Compagnia di Gesù," *Miscellanea Storica Ligure* 11/2 (1970), 171–213.

8   *Ratio Studiorum*, para. 6 [212]. Note that Jesuit Thomism is not equivalent to Dominican Thomism. See Rivka Feldhay, "Knowledge and Salvation in Jesuit Culture," *Science in Context* 1 (1987), 195–213; in her judgment (201), "Jesuit Thomism, in comparison with Dominicans', was mainly distinguished by its particular openness, stemming from the Jesuits' quest to educate the entire Catholic secular elite on the one hand, and from the independent intellectual interest developed by the second generation of scholars, on the other hand." See also Francis Winterton, "Philosophy Among the Jesuits," *Mind* 12

(1887), 254–74; Steven J., Harris, "Transposing the Merton Thesis: Apostolic Spirituality and the Establishment of the Jesuit Scientific Tradition," *Science in Context* 3 (1989), 29–65.

9   I have not exhausted all the prohibitions. For more cases of censorship, see Richard J. Blackwell, *Galileo, Bellarmine and the Bible* (Notre Dame: University of Notre Dame Press, 1991), 149; M.-P. Lerner, "L'entrée de Tycho Brahe chez les jésuites, ou le chant du cygne de Clavius," in Luce Giard, ed., *Les jésuites à la Renaissance: Système éducatif et production du savoir* (Paris: Presses Universitaires de France, 1995), 145–86.

10   Giovanni Battista Riccioli, *Almagestum Novum* (Bologna: Ex typographia hæredis Victorij Benatij, 1651), Tome i, Liber ii, Caput iii, Scholia, 52.

11   The attitudes of Jesuits depended also on their country: for Germany and Italy see Hellyer, *Catholic Physics*; for the situation in France, see John I. Russell, S. J., "Catholic Astronomers and the Copernican System after the Condemnation of Galileo," *Annals of Science* 46 (1989), 365–86. In France, the effects of the 1633 condemnation were not uniform. For instance, on the one hand, we find Descartes abandoning the publication of his nearly complete manuscript *Le Monde*. On the other hand, we find an edition of Galileo's condemned *Dialogues* published at Lyons in 1641, in defiance of the Index; it even had a formal *imprimatur* from the diocesan authorities.

12   Amos Funkenstein, *Theology and the Scientific Imagination from the Middle Ages to the Seventeenth Century* (Princeton: Princeton University Press, 1986), 17.

13   Hellyer, *Catholic Physics*, 46.

14   *Summa Theologiae* 1–2, Q 98 a3. The principle goes back to at least Augustine, who argued that God "knows much better than man what pertains by accommodation to each period of time (*qui multo magis quam homo novit, quid cuique tempori accommodate adhibeatur*)," Aurelius Augustinus, *Epistulae*, ed. Al. Goldbacher, Pars iii (Vienna: F. Trempsky; Leipzig: G. Freytag, 1904), Epistula 138. 1.5, p. 130.

15   I draw this distinction from Funkenstein, *Theology and the Scientific Imagination*, 213–19.

16   See Robert Bellarmine's letter to Foscarini (12 April 1615) in Blackwell, *Galileo, Bellarmine and the Bible*, 265–68.

17   See Russell, "Catholic Astronomers."

18   Melchior Cornaeus in his *Curriculum Philosophiae Peripateticae, ut Hoc Tempore in Scholis Decurri Solet* (Würzburg, 1657), ii: 107, quoted in Hellyer, *Catholic Physics*, 51.

19   Cornaeus, *Curriculum*, 503. This attitude shows a marked shift from the decades preceding the Galileo controversy, when Jesuits used to defend Aristotelian celestial incorruptibility by proposing that comets and novae are special divine signs. Cf. William Wallace, *Galileo and His Sources: The Heritage of the Collegio Romano in Galileo's Science* (Princeton: Princeton University Press, 1984), 141.

20 The idea of celestial incorruptibility was the Achilles' heel of the old cosmology. Even those who, decades after Galileo's time, still rejected Copernicanism conceded defeat on the question of the heavens' incorruptibility. One can detect the development in textbooks. For instance, the Jesuit Leonardus Cinnamo is still discussing in 1715 the question of the incorruptibility of the heavens as a sub-question of whether the heavens are nobler than the earth (see L. Cinnamo, S.J., *Microscopium Aristotelicum* (Palermo: G. Bayona, 1715), Sec. II, 8). By 1739, the situation changes. In chapter II of a 1739 textbook by Antonio Mayr, S.J., entitled *Philosophia Peripatetica Antiquorum Principiis, et Recentiorum Experimentis Conformata*, vol. III: *Physicae Particularis Pars I* (Ingolstadt), the heavens are taken as indeed corruptible. Mayr even includes biblical evidence for this (§847).

21 See Galileo Galilei, *Dialogue Concerning the Two Chief World Systems, Ptolemaic & Copernican*, trans. S. Drake (Berkeley: University of California Press, 1953), 50. See also Wallace, *Galileo and His Sources*, 301. The origins of this mature attitude towards Aristotle can be traced back to Albertus Magnus: "Whoever believes that Aristotle was a god, must also believe that he never erred. But if one believes that Aristotle was a man, then doubtless he was liable to error just as we are" (*Physica*, lib. VIII, tr. I, xiv).

22 This claim is amply justified in E. Grant, *Planets, Stars, and Orbs: The Medieval Cosmos, 1200–1687* (Cambridge: Cambridge University Press, 1994); by the late seventeenth century, "bits and pieces of Aristotelian cosmology were replaced by bits and pieces of the new cosmology. Strange cosmological mosaics developed, none of which could win much support" (679).

23 William B. Ashworth, Jr., "Catholicism in Early Modern Science," in D. C. Lindberg and R. L. Numbers, eds., *God and Nature: Historical Essays on the Encounter between Christianity and Science* (Berkeley: University of California Press, 1986), 136–66; quotations from 155. On Kircher's style, see Paula Findlen, "Scientific Spectacle in Baroque Rome: Athanasius Kircher and the Roman College Museum," in Mordechai Feingold, ed., *Jesuit Science and the Republic of Letters* (Cambridge, MA: MIT Press, 2003), 225–84.

24 Riccioli, *Almagestum*, Tome II, Liber VIII, Sectio II, Caput XVII, 174–77.

25 Peter Dear, "Jesuit Mathematical Science and the Reconstitution of Experience in the Early Seventeenth Century," *Studies in the History and Philosophy of Science* 18 (1987), 133–75 (the quotation is from 143).

26 Cf. Russell, "Catholic Astronomers." By 1773, of the world's 130 astronomy observatories, thirty were operated by Jesuits. There are now thirty-five lunar craters named in honor of Jesuit scientists.

27 See Žarko Dadic, "Boškovic and the Question of the Earth's Motion," in I. Macan and V. Pozaic, eds., *The Philosophy of Science of Ruder Boškovic* (Zagreb: Institute of Philosophy and Theology, 1987).

28 See B. Brundell, "Catholic Church Politics and Evolution Theory, 1894–1902," *British Journal of the History of Science* 34 (2001),

81–95; S. Maffeo, *The Vatican Observatory: In the Service of Nine Popes*, trans. G. V. Coyne (Notre Dame: University of Notre Dame Press, 2001).

29 On the fragmentation of knowledge, see P. Arrupe, "Theological Reflection and Interdisciplinary Debate," in Pedro Arrupe, S. J., *Jesuit Apostolates Today*, ed. J. Aixalá, S. J. (St. Louis: Institute of Jesuit Sources, 1981), 33–42; "The Intellectual Apostolate in the Society's Mission," ibid., 111–26. See also Peter-Hans Kolvenbach, "The Jesuit University in the Light of the Ignatian Charism," Address to the International Meeting of Jesuit Higher Education, Rome, 27 May 2001 (available on the Internet at http://users.online.be/~sj.eur.news/doc/univ2001e.htm).

30 Acknowledgments: Pontifical Gregorian University Library, Rome, for professional help in the Rare Books Section; Dr. Michael Hoskin for useful comments.

Part V
Jesuits in the Modern World

15 The Suppression and Restoration

JONATHAN WRIGHT

A satisfactory modern history of the Jesuits' suppression remains to be written. The paucity of detailed evidence from many provinces is frustrating, although recent studies have shown how accurately local variants of the Suppression and its aftermath can be reconstructed.[1] There is also a major conceptual issue obstructing any account of the destruction of the most dynamic religious order in the Roman Catholic world. How could it possibly have come to pass? A series of national suppressions in Portugal, France, and Spain (their colonies and satellite states included) culminated in the 1773 papal brief *Dominus ac Redemptor* which blotted out the Jesuits' corporate existence across almost the entire globe. It was, as John Henry Newman later put it, "one of the most mysterious matters in the history of the Church."[2]

Crucially, we must abandon the notion of a simple, over-arching explanation of the Suppression. In earlier historiography, this was harder to achieve than one might suspect, not least because the Suppression occurred at a moment when grand historical movements were seemingly in full flow. It has always been tempting to assume that one of these movements was responsible for the Society's demise. The Enlightenment is just one case in point. A religious order that was portrayed (often with scant justification) as stubbornly obscurantist seemed an obvious target for the self-styled syndics of reason and progress. Nor were the French *philosophes* bashful about claiming credit for the Jesuits' destruction.

At face value, this was an attractive suggestion. Men like Diderot and (with rather more nuance) Voltaire hardly shied away from criticizing the Society, and French Jesuits, notably Guillaume-François Berthier, editor of the *Journal de Trévoux*, launched scathing attacks on the Enlightenment's most sacred project, the *Encyclopaedia*.[3] Perhaps an even wider perspective is available: perhaps the destruction of the Jesuits was part of process of secularization that culminated in the French Revolution. This was certainly a notion peddled by Jesuits and ex-Jesuits both during and after the revolutionary era.[4]

Unfortunately, positing the Jesuits as the natural adversaries of the Enlightenment (assuming we can even talk about a unified Enlightenment "movement") is untenable. For one thing, the Jesuits and the Enlightenment had much in common: an unapologetically positive view of human nature; a fascination with the world's diverse cultures; an unshakeable belief in the power of education; and an unquenchable passion for science.[5] The Jesuit order had its die-hard Aristotelians, but it also made astonishing contributions to countless scientific disciplines. The Society was not simply a refuge for outmoded thinkers, and the leaders of the French Enlightenment knew as much. As Jean Le Rond d'Alembert admitted in 1765, the recently deceased French branch of the Society had actually been rather skilled "in the matter of sciences and lights."[6]

For another thing, even if they *wanted* to crush the Jesuits, the high priests of Enlightenment simply lacked the wherewithal to carry through their vision. Even in France, that task largely fell to the Jansenist elements within the Paris Parlement. And what of Spain, Portugal, and the rest of the world, where many anticlerical Enlightenment nostrums were markedly less popular?

This all serves to make the point that striving for some over-riding explanation of the Jesuits' destruction is a mistake. No single explanation fits the facts of the various national suppressions. As another example, it is correct to see the Spanish suppression as a symptom of Charles III's regalist vision of the Church, to which the Jesuits were a conspicuous challenge, but such motivation does not hold good in France, where Louis XV was reluctant to remove the Society. Similarly, efforts to extrapolate from the French experience towards the role of a "Jansenist International" in the Suppression are instructive but only partially convincing.[7]

Of course, the Jesuits' enemies all had access to the familiar charge sheet of the Society's supposed misdemeanors. There was the lax moral theology allegedly preached by Jesuit casuists, the fact that Jesuit missionaries in China and India had seemingly made too many syncretic concessions to local cultures, the fact that Jesuits were members of a supranational organization in a Europe made up of national Churches that had grown weary of Roman interference. At the level of myth and fantasy, there was a shared repertoire of supposed Jesuit abuse, ranging from regicide, to sexual perversion, to avaricious profiteering. This shared anti-Jesuit culture undoubtedly facilitated the suppressions, and in certain countries aspects of it played a key role. Ultimately, though, each of the national suppressions has to be explained as a discrete *political* event, governed by particular grudges and aspirations.

Certainly, the national suppressions gained encouragement from one another and in their wake, as an act of justification, a coherent logic of worldwide destruction rapidly emerged. But in reaching that point local political circumstances had been the engine of suppression. That, and the fact that in three kingdoms, as we are about to see, the Jesuits had suffered extraordinarily bad luck: opportunities had arisen that allowed the Society's enemies to pounce. What follows is a synoptic account of these three bizarre processes. By recounting the facts we get most of the way towards an explanation.

PORTUGAL

On the morning of All Saints' Day 1755 an earthquake struck Lisbon, killing as many as 30,000 people. In its aftermath, Jesuit priests were rumored to have suggested that it had been God's way of chastising Portugal for its sins. Such mutterings infuriated Sebastião José de Carvalho e Mello, better known to history as the Marquis of Pombal. He was perhaps the most influential politician in Portugal and it fell to him to engineer the destruction of the Jesuits within the realm of King Joseph I. He hated the Jesuits with a *political* passion.[8]

His animus against the Society had been fueled in the aftermath of the 1750 Treaty of Madrid. The Jesuits had long been tending the spiritual needs of the Guaraní people of Paraguay, gathering them together into well-organized settlements, or reductions. With the 1750 treaty, Portugal and Spain had exchanged territories, and seven of the Jesuits' reductions were transferred to Portuguese rule. This was wildly unpopular among many of the affected Guaraní, not least because they were expected to decamp many miles across the Uruguay River. Resistance and violence ensued, European troops were obliged to put down the rebellion and, back in Portugal, the Jesuits were accused (unfairly) of fomenting the entire escapade. Pombal was convinced that the Jesuit reductions represented something of a state-within-a-state and he also shared the popular delusion that the reductions were a source of fantastical Jesuit wealth.[9]

Pombal was still more irritated by the Jesuits' power at home. He had a specific, modernizing vision for Portugal, and alongside streamlining the economy and increasing revenues, he also sought to snuff out all challenges to royal authority. He had two main bugbears: the stubbornly independent aristocracy and the Society of Jesus: an organization with, by Pombal's reckoning, far too much influence through its role in education and its traditional role as confessor to the great and the good. Throughout the late 1750s Pombal chipped away at the Society's position: banishing various confessors from court, spreading endless anti-Jesuit propaganda and, most satisfyingly of all, convincing Rome to appoint Cardinal Saldanha to investigate the Jesuits' supposedly immoral commercial activities.

His greatest opportunity arose on 3 September 1758, when someone tried to assassinate the king. Joseph I was only wounded in the right shoulder and arm, but Pombal seized his moment. At one stroke, by ascribing responsibility to the right people, he could attack both the aristocracy and the Jesuits. In the second week of December, the arrests began. Various nobles and a handful of Jesuits were taken into custody. Accusing Jesuits of would-be king-killing, as Pombal well knew, was an astute tactic: the Society had been dogged by such charges throughout its history, most recently in France back in 1757 when Roger Damiens had tried to assassinate Louis XV.

Subsequently, the path towards casting the Society out of Portugal on the grounds that they were, essentially, enemies of state was remarkably uncluttered. In January 1759 it was formally announced that Jesuits had played a principal role in the assassination attempt and death-sentences were passed down. In the coming months, the Portuguese Jesuits were restricted to their houses, officially suppressed in April and, in September, the vast majority of Portugal's Jesuits were transported to ports from which they embarked upon their sea-journeys to the Papal States. In the coming years, as news of the banishment slowly traveled around the world, Jesuits in many of the Portuguese colonies were also obliged to return to Europe.[10] A number of priests remained in Pombal's jails for many years and, in a final act of revenge, the Jesuit Gabriel Malagrida was executed on 2 September 1761 for his supposed role in the assassination attempt against Joseph I. The banishment of the Jesuits was undoubtedly part of a larger political program – a counterpart to Pombal's severing of relations with Rome and his efforts to gain control of the local Inquisition. But it would be a mistake to cast these as anti-religious measures. They were about power, and the banishment of the Jesuits had been a localized and, objectively speaking, efficient exercise in political legerdemain. Nonetheless, it had consequences that rippled out far beyond the borders of Portugal.

FRANCE

The French branch of the Society of Jesus had always endured a turbulent history. When the idea of Jesuits arriving in France had first been mooted during the sixteenth century, many voices (uneasy secular clergy, rival religious orders and Sorbonnistes notable among them) had been raised in protest, and the Society had initially only been granted permission to serve as teachers at its various colleges, *not* to establish a legal, corporate presence in the realm. The reign of Henry IV had (at least within lands overseen by the Paris Parlement) brought a period of banishment in the wake of Jean Chatel's regicidal assassination attempt, and the seventeenth century saw the growth of two determined anti-Jesuit factions: those of Gallican sympathies – people who insisted on the independence of the French Church and resented the interference of Rome – and, even more crucially, the Jansenists.

There is no space here to look closely at the theological wrangling between Jesuits and Jansenists.[11] Suffice to say, the two camps espoused radically different views on the operation of grace and how mankind might be saved from eternal perdition. To the Jansenists, inheritors of an Augustinian theological sensibility, mankind was wretched, adrift, and utterly dependent on the mercy of God to achieve salvation. The Jesuits, on the whole, adopted a far more optimistic position, stressing the role of free will and human effort in the salvific economy. There was exaggeration and calumny on all sides of the debate. The Jansenists, most famously in the *Provincial Letters* of Blaise Pascal, claimed that the Jesuits' sanguine attitudes caused them to dispense laxist, easy-going moral advice. The Jesuits suggested that the Jansenists were little more than predestinarian Calvinists in disguise.

On the face of things, it was an argument that, between the 1650s and the second decade of the eighteenth century, the Jesuits won. The principal text of the Jansenists, the *Augustinius* of the Flemish theologian Cornelius Jansen, was condemned, in spite of the best efforts of French Jansenists such as Antoine Arnauld, and French clergymen were compelled to sign anti-Jansenist formularies. Latterly, the Jansenists' symbolic stronghold, the convent of Port Royal, was disbanded and, in 1713, the papal bull *Unigenitus Dei Filius*, which condemned 101 propositions propounded by Pasquier Quesnel, seemed to toll the death knell of French Jansenism.

In fact, Jansenism proved to be more robust, especially as it transmuted from a largely theological movement into a well-organized political pressure group. By the early 1760s there was no doubting the Jesuits' influence in France. They had long cornered the market as influential confessors and, as of 1762, their 3,330 representatives controlled nine novitiates, 25 residences, 21 seminaries, and 111 colleges.[12] But they also had enemies. Earlier humiliations had not been forgotten and the practice of refusing sacraments to dying, unrepentant Jansenists – a trend that had escalated during the 1750s – only added new venom to the Jansenist cause.[13] Within the pages of their influential journal, the *Nouvelles Ecclésiastiques*, the Jansenists sniped away at every aspect of the Society of Jesus' activities. Within the Paris Parlement, a recognizable Jansenist party – many, though not all, of whom were still partly motivated by the old theological arguments – awaited its chance of revenge.

In 1756, ships carrying produce from the West Indies to France were seized by the British. This spelled disaster for the Jesuit Antoine Lavalette, who had built up an impressive business in Martinique and Dominica producing cash crops and acting as an agent for Martinique residents wanting to transfer monies to France. Unfortunately, in the process, he had amassed considerable debts with various French financial houses. When his ships were captured in 1756, the fragile bubble burst and a number of Lavalette's creditors sought restitution. The spectacle of a Jesuit priest engaged in commerce was damaging enough – wholly contrary to the tenets of canon law, at first blush – but the key moment arrived when the aggrieved parties began to claim that the Society of Jesus as a whole was responsible for the errant priest's debts.[14]

A series of legal battles ensued and in 1760 the consular court in Marseilles ruled that the entire Society was indeed liable. The enormous amounts of money involved made it necessary for the Society to appeal the decision. Fatefully, they took their case to the Parlement of Paris: as we have seen, a body that was home to a determinedly anti-Jesuit party. In May 1761, the Parlement duly upheld the decision of the lower court regarding the Society's financial responsibilities, but by this point the Jansenist party within the Parlement had begun to seize an opportunity to launch a far broader attack on the Jesuits. With the compliance of sympathetic allies, they did so with consummate political skill (they only numbered fifteen to twenty out of the 150 members able to vote), recruiting any anti-Jesuit constituencies that were available to them. Those of a Gallican stripe were informed that the Jesuits, with their special vow of obedience to the pope, were a potential fifth column within the French Church. The historically minded were presented with evidence that the Jesuits had never even been granted the right to corporate existence in France. Perhaps most effectively of all, much was made of the suggestion that the Society's organization was utterly despotic and, as such, an insidious threat to French political life.

Over the next two years a chaotic political drama unfolded.[15] The Society's Institute was examined and denounced and, on 6 August 1761, Parlement ruled that the Jesuits were to abandon their schools and to desist from taking on new recruits. There were attempts at compromise and delay, not least because the king and most of the French episcopate did not relish the idea of the Society's total suppression. The notion of a distinct French branch of the Society, independent of the leadership in Rome, was mooted, although this was always a dead letter since the Jesuit hierarchy, not least the Superior General Lorenzo Ricci, could never countenance the idea.[16] Gradually, the prospect of outright suppression loomed ever larger, especially as other regional parlements followed Paris's lead by condemning the Society's activities. Finally, in November 1764, the Society was dissolved in France and its colonies by a reluctant Louis XV.

SPAIN

In the business of suppression, outside of the chronological sense of the word, France did not "follow" Portugal, and Spain assuredly did not "follow" France. Spain was home to a little under 3,000 Jesuits during the 1760s, many of whom were scattered around 117 Jesuit-run colleges, including such influential institutions as the Colegio Imperial and the Seminario de Nobles in Madrid.[17] Most of the nostrums of the francophone Enlightenment received a decidedly lukewarm reception in the kingdom though Spain *was* enjoying something of a *Catholic* Enlightenment of its own. Nor could the devotional credentials of Charles III, monarch since 1759, be called into question. The problem for the Jesuits was that Charles III had a very distinctive vision of how the Spanish Church should be. He was a passionate believer in an ecclesiastical system in which the king's authority ought to be uncontested and, so far as possible, undiluted. The influential, supranational Jesuits did not fit into his plans.

Into the bargain, Charles had a profound personal dislike of the Society of Jesus, cultivated during his time as ruler of Naples by Bernardo Tanucci. Charles also frowned at the Jesuits' dogged opposition to one of his most cherished projects: the canonization of the seventeenth-century Mexican bishop Juan Palafox y Mendoza – a famous adversary of the Society.

It took more than a king to uproot the Spanish Jesuits, of course, and, once again, a confluence of various strains of anti-Jesuit feeling conveniently came together. During the early 1760s a number of reformist and regalist-minded politicians – including Pedro de Campomanes and José Moñino – gained influence at court. There was also an upsurge of opposition to Jesuit moral teaching and impassioned talk of potential educational reform to which the Jesuits were perceived as an obstacle. Nor was the Society's cause helped by the perennial animosity of other religious orders and the secular clergy. Recent scholarship has reminded us of just how diverse both regalism and anti-Jesuit sentiment were during the 1760s, but they undoubtedly represented the dominant political mood.[18] All that was lacking, once again, was an excuse to attack the Society. It arrived in the spring of 1766.[19]

On 20 March the unpopular finance minister, the Marquis of Esquilache, enacted legislation that forbad the wearing of broad-brimmed hats and capes: they provided, so it was averred, too good a disguise for criminals. This assault on traditional costume was the final straw for the people of Madrid who were already smarting under the consequences of bad harvests, high prices, and rising taxes. They turned their fire on Esquilache and days of violent riots ensued during which the king was forced to flee the capital. Peace was soon restored but the government was dumbfounded by what had happened: indeed, the crisis of 1766 represented a huge blow to Charles III's reformist agenda. There was a need to allot blame. All eyes turned to the Jesuits.

Committees of the Extraordinary Council of Castile were set up to gather evidence and, in a memorandum drawn up by Campomanes, the riots were blamed on Jesuit agitation. And not just that: a savage attack was launched against the entire Jesuit enterprise. It was accused of encouraging rebellion, of being a mire of avarice, of possessing an inherent revulsion for rulers and authority and, of course, of having no role to play in the future of Spain.[20] Charles signed off on this condemnation at the end of February 1767 and, after the decree of banishment had been kept a closely guarded secret for several weeks, Jesuit houses and communities were surrounded by troops and emptied out in late March and early April. After being stripped of most of their possessions, the residents were transported to the coast to begin their journey into exile.

When news came of a fresh consignment of banished Jesuits heading towards the Papal States, the pope was obliged to turn them away on the grounds that he lacked the resources to support them. After sojourning in Corsica, many of the exiled priests and brothers finally settled in northern Italian cities such as Bologna and Ferrara. In the coming years their ranks would be swelled by some of the thousands of

Jesuits banished from Spain's colonies in Asia and the Americas, and by exiles from Spain's satellite states in Europe – Naples, Parma, and Sicily.[21]

The Spanish expulsion would have many unlooked-for consequences. In South America, for instance, it would be remembered as a conspicuous example of arbitrary Bourbon rule and would find a place in the cultural memory that eventually bred that continent's independence movements.[22] In the shorter term, however, the events of 1767 provoked one unavoidable question: having been cast out of Portugal, Spain, and France, was the total destruction of the Society of Jesus simply a matter of time?

SUPPRESSION

During the next six years, there were clearly still signs of life and, as late as 1769, the Jesuits of Freiburg embarked on a major renovation of their *Gymnasium*.[23] It was abundantly clear, however, that the courts of Spain, France, and Portugal were determined to destroy the entire Jesuit Order and applied enormous pressure on Rome: it was also a huge advantage that none of these powers was at war with one another and so they could present a united front. In 1768, the Duke of Parma enacted legislation that brought ecclesiastical appointments firmly under his control and forbad the promulgation of papal bulls in the duchy without the duke's express permission. The pope immediately declared the new laws null and void. Such blatant papal interference in Parma's affairs granted the Bourbon powers a perfect opportunity to remind the pope of his vulnerable position. In retaliation, France occupied Avignon and Venaissin while Naples seized the papal towns of Benevento and Pontecorvo.[24]

Here was a none-too-subtle threat, but so long as Clement XIII remained as pope the Jesuits were fairly secure. All of this was to change with the arrival of a papal election in May 1769.[25] The conclave was dominated by the issue of the Jesuits, with ambassadors lobbying hard for a candidate who was willing to carry through the suppression. In the event, Cardinal Lorenzo Ganganelli won the day, securing 46 out of 47 votes. There has always been speculation as to whether, and in what form, Ganganelli explicitly promised the representatives of the Catholic powers that he would snuff out the Jesuits. Whatever happened, there was clearly a sense at the time that his election boded very badly for the Society of Jesus. Writing from Rome, the English Jesuit John Thorpe reported that "the unanimous election of Cardinal

Ganganelli was no sooner divulged about the city than everyone looked upon the Jesuits ... to be inevitably ruined."[26]

As matters turned out, the new pope Clement XIV failed to do the great powers' bidding quite as quickly as they might have liked. He skilfully dallied and demurred, launching small-scale attacks on the Society – removing their control of the Irish College in Rome, failing to lend them papal musicians on ceremonial occasions, etc. – but refusing to destroy them outright. The position of Catholic Austria also gave some hope to the Jesuits. If Maria Theresa could be induced to protect the Society in her kingdoms then the chances of total suppression would be greatly reduced. Ultimately, however, Maria Theresa simply side-stepped the issue. While maintaining great respect for the Society's intellectual pedigree she had, during the 1750s and 1760s, made efforts to reduce its influence – destroying its near-monopoly in higher education and its stranglehold on the role of royal confessors – and to question its moral teaching. She was also, not least because of the lure of marriage alliances with France, reluctant to alienate the Bourbon powers. Disastrously for the Jesuits, she announced that if the Society's total suppression came to pass, she would acquiesce in it.[27]

The game was now up. With the arrival of a new Spanish ambassador, José Moñino, in Rome in March 1772, a final assault was launched on the pope's procrastination. With considerable assistance from Moñino, a papal brief of suppression was drawn up, signed on 21 July 1773, and promulgated on 16 August. It seemed to Clement XIV as if "I have cut off my right hand."[28]

SURVIVAL AND RESTORATION

On 27 January 1815, a correspondent of *The Times* in London complained that "the revival of the order of the Jesuits by the present pope, after they had been totally abolished by a predecessor of his ... appears to be an event of no ordinary importance, and I cannot but feel considerable surprise at the apathy and indifference which are manifested in the subject by the states of Europe in general and by this country in particular."[29] He made a good point. In comparison with the dramatic events of the Suppression, the official worldwide papal restoration of Loyola's Society in July 1814 was a surprisingly uncontroversial event. Perhaps part of the reason was the fact that the Society of Jesus had never really disappeared.

There is no doubting the wide-ranging, often cataclysmic, consequences of the Suppression. Jesuit properties were placed in new hands, the Jesuits' educational duties were passed on to other religious orders, numerous missionary vineyards were all but deserted. Some priests suffered terribly, not least the Society's Superior General Lorenzo Ricci who ended his days languishing incarcerated in Rome's Castel Sant'Angelo. But the future was not nearly so bleak for many ex-Jesuits.

Many took up new careers in the secular clergy or, notably in Austria, continued their lofty academic progress unchecked. In isolated pockets, it even proved possible to retain a vibrant corporate existence. In Prussia (temporarily) and Russia (throughout the suppression years), the papal brief of suppression was never operative and Jesuit communities endured – gaining official papal recognition in Russia in 1804. England also offered something of a refuge. The educational enterprise begun at St.-Omer, France, in 1593, which had been obliged to decamp to Bruges after the French suppression, then to Liège in 1773, finally found a new, permanent home at Stonyhurst in Lancashire in 1794.[30] Elsewhere – in Canada, for instance – Jesuit communities, while not permitted to take on new novices, were at least allowed to dwindle gently away rather than having to face immediate destruction. And even where a Jesuit corporate existence was deemed illegal, ex-Jesuits determined to establish new religious orders that maintained the Loyolan spiritual vision (and, in some cases, even their properties). The Select Body of the Clergy and the Corporation of the Roman Catholic Clergy in the United States, Pierre-Joseph de Clorivière's Society of the Fathers of the Heart of Jesus in France, and the colorful Fathers of the Faith of Niccolò Paccanari were notable instances of this trend.[31] Gradually, in England, Parma, the United States, and the Kingdom of the Two Sicilies, for instance, *bona fide* Jesuit communities began to re-emerge.

This was a story of extraordinary resilience and individual determination, perhaps best encapsulated by the dogged efforts of Joseph Pignatelli to keep the Jesuit identity alive in straitened circumstances.[32] But just as the Jesuits' suppression was largely the result of unhelpful political circumstances, so its return can best be explained by a major shift in Europe's political orientation: while the Jesuit Order had been slumbering, the French Revolution had happened. The nations that had cast the Jesuits out now confronted the legacy and (as they perceived it) the continued menace of anticlericalism, secularism, and republicanism. By the second decade of the nineteenth century, the Catholic world was desperate to find ways to stem this ominous tide, to erect bulwarks of throne and altar. In this work, the

Church found its eloquent theorists, but it also required its symbols and its champions. The Society of Jesus, which could easily, if inaccurately, be portrayed as the most conspicuous victim of unhealthy new trends in European political life, stepped into the breach.

The words of the papal restoration of the order said it all. "Amidst these dangers of the Christian Republic ... we should deem ourselves guilty of a great crime towards God if ... we neglected the aids which the special providence of God has put at our disposal." The bark of Peter was "tossed and assaulted" by endless storms, so why not turn to the Jesuits, the "vigorous and experienced rowers who volunteer their services"?[33] There was more bluster than substance in such words. As of 1814, the newly revived Society of Jesus was feeble, diminished, and it would never regain its former influence in European political and intellectual life. As John Carroll, ex-Jesuit, first bishop of Baltimore, and a prime example of how the suppression years could be put to advantage, admitted: "many years will be necessary to reproduce such men as formerly adorned the Society by their virtues and talents."[34] Ultimately, though, bluster was what counted in 1814. If it is inordinately difficult to explain the Jesuits' suppression, it is surprisingly easy to account for their re-establishment. They had never abandoned hope and, in the summer of 1814, much of Catholic Europe craved their return. It is precisely that simple, and it is sobering to reflect on what a difference forty-one turbulent years could make in European politics.

Notes

1 Many older accounts of the Suppression remain indispensable, including the relevant volumes of L. Von Pastor, *The History of the Popes from the Close of the Middle Ages*, 40 vols. (London: Routledge and Kegan Paul, 1923–53) and A. Astrain, *Historia de la Compañía de Jesús en la asistencia de España*, 7 vols. (Madrid: Sucesores de Rivadeneyra, 1902–25). J. A. M. Crétineau-Joly, *Clément XIV et les Jésuites* (Paris: Mellier, 1847) is also still useful. Recent localized studies of the Suppression and its aftermath include P. Shore, "The Suppression of the Society of Jesus in Bohemia," *Archivum Historicum Societatis Iesu* 65 (1996), 138–56; D. G. Thompson, *A Modern Persecution: Breton Jesuits under the Suppression of 1762–1814*, Studies on Voltaire and the Eighteenth Century 378 (Oxford: Voltaire Foundation: 1999), 5–182; D. Alden, "The Suppression of the Society of Jesus in the Portuguese Ascendancy in Asia: The Fate of the Survivors, 1760–77," in A. Disney and E. Booth, eds., *Vasco da Gama and the Linking of Europe and Asia* (Oxford: Oxford University Press,

2001), 361–86; J. Flaga, "Le sort des Jésuites polonaises après la suppression de l'ordre en 1773," *Revue d'Histoire Ecclésiastique* 97 (2002), 892–908; T. McCoog, ed., *Promising Hope: Essays on the Suppression and Restoration of the English Province of the Society of Jesus* (Rome: Institutum Historicum Societatis Iesu, 2003).

2 C. S. Dessain, ed., *The Letters and Diaries of John Henry Newman*, vol. xii (London: T. Nelson, 1961), 117.

3 A. Cazes, "Un adversaire de Diderot et des philosophes," in *Mélanges offerts par ses amis et ses élèves à M. Gustave Lanson* (Paris: Hachette, 1922), 235–49; J. E. Barker, *Diderot's Treatment of the Christian Religion in the Encyclopédie* (New York: King's Crown Press, 1941); J. McManners, "Voltaire and the Monks," in W. J. Sheils, ed., *Monks, Hermits and the Ascetic Tradition*, Studies in Church History 22 (Oxford: Blackwell, 1985), 319–42.

4 See B. N. Schilling, *Conservative England and the Case Against Voltaire* (New York: Columbia University Press, 1950), ch. 13.

5 On Jesuit scientific culture see L. Caruana's essay in this volume, and the relevant contributions in J. O'Malley, G. Bailey, S. J. Harris, and T. F. Kennedy, eds., *The Jesuits: Cultures, Sciences, and the Arts, 1540–1773* (Toronto: Toronto University Press, 1999) and M. Feingold, ed., *Jesuit Science and the Republic of Letters* (Cambridge, MA: Harvard University Press, 2002).

6 J. Le Rond d'Alembert, *Sur la destruction des Jésuites en France* (Paris, 1765), 42. See C. M. Northeast, *The Parisian Jesuits and the Enlightenment*, Studies on Voltaire and the Eighteenth Century 288 (Oxford: Voltaire Foundation, 1991), 176–215; D. Van Kley, *The Jansenists and the Expulsion of the Jesuits from France, 1757–1765* (New Haven: Yale University Press, 1975), 208–28; R. Porter and M. Teich, eds., *The Enlightenment in National Context* (Cambridge: Cambridge University Press, 1981).

7 D. Van Kley, "Catholic Conciliar Reform in an Age of Anti-Catholic Revolution," in J. E. Bradley and D. Van Kley, eds., *Religion and Politics in Enlightenment Europe* (Notre Dame: University of Notre Dame Press, 2001), 46–118.

8 K. Maxwell, *Pombal, Paradox of the Enlightenment* (Cambridge: Cambridge University Press, 1995); K. Maxwell, "Pombal: The Paradox of Enlightenment and Despotism," in H. Scott, ed., *Enlightened Absolutism: Reform and Reformers in Later Eighteenth-Century Europe* (Ann Arbor: University of Michigan Press, 1990), 75–118; S. J. Miller, *Portugal and Rome, c. 1748–1830: An Aspect of the Catholic Enlightenment* (Rome: Pontificia Università Gregoriana, 1978).

9 B. Ganson, *The Guaraní under Spanish Rule* (Stanford: Stanford University Press, 2003) and P. Caraman, *The Lost Paradise: An Account of the Jesuits in Paraguay* (London: Sidgwick and Jackson, 1976); C. R. Boxer, *The Portuguese Seaborne Empire, 1415–1825* (New York: Knopf, 1969), 186.

10 A. Weld, *The Suppression of the Society of Jesus in the Portuguese Dominions* (London: Burns and Oates, 1877) is still valuable. Dauril

Alden is currently working on *The Suppression of an Enterprise: The Destruction of the Society of Jesus in Portugal, Its Empire and Beyond, 1750–1777.*

11 See W. Doyle, *Jansenism: Catholic Resistance to Authority from the Reformation to the French Revolution* (New York: St. Martin's Press, 2001); J. McManners, *Church and Society in Eighteenth Century France*, 2 vols. (Oxford: Oxford University Press, 1998), II: 345–455; B. R. Kreiser, *Miracles, Convulsions and Ecclesiastical Politics in Eighteenth-Century France* (Princeton: Princeton University Press, 1978).

12 McManners, *Church and Society*, 509.

13 J. Rogister, *Louis XV and the Parlement of Paris, 1737–1755* (Cambridge: Cambridge University Press, 1995).

14 Van Kley, *The Jansenists and the Expulsion*, 90–107; D. G. Thompson, "The Lavalette Affair and the Jesuit Superiors," *French History* 10 (1996), 206–39; D. G. Thompson, "French Jesuit Wealth on the Eve of the Suppression," in W. J. Sheils and D. Wood, eds., *The Church and Wealth*, Studies in Church History 24 (Oxford: Blackwell, 1987), 307–19.

15 Van Kley, *Jansenists and the Expulsion*; McManners, *Church and Society*, II: 530–61; D. Van Kley, *The Religious Origins of the French Revolution: From Calvin to the Civil Constitution* (New Haven: Yale University Press, 1996); M. Fumaroli, "Between the Rigorist Hammer and the Deist Anvil: The Fate of the Jesuits in Eighteenth-Century France," in J. O'Malley, G. Bailey, S. J. Harris, and T. F. Kennedy, eds., *The Jesuits II: Cultures, Sciences, and the Arts, 1540–1773* (Toronto: Toronto University Press, 2006), 682–90. J. Swann, *Politics in the Parlement of Paris under Louis XV, 1754–1774* (Cambridge: Cambridge University Press, 1995) emphasizes the role of the Duke of Choiseul.

16 D. G. Thompson, "General Ricci and the Suppression of the Jesuit Order in France," *Journal of Ecclesiastical History* 37 (1986), 426–31.

17 W. J. Callahan, *Church, Politics and Society in Spain, 1750–1874* (Cambridge, MA: Harvard University Press, 1984), 28.

18 S. J. Stein and B. H. Stein, *Apogee of Empire: Spain and New Spain in the Age of Charles III, 1759–1789* (Baltimore: Johns Hopkins University Press, 2003).

19 A. Hull, *Charles III and the Revival of Spain* (Washington, DC: University Press of America, 1981), ch. 7; J. Lynch, *Bourbon Spain, 1700–1808* (Oxford: Oxford University Press, 1989), 280–90; C. C. Noel, "Clerics and Crown in Bourbon Spain, 1700–1808: Jesuits, Jansenists and Enlightened Reformers," in Bradley and Van Kley, *Religion and Politics*, 119–53; J. Andrés-Gallego, *El Motín de Esquilache, América y Europa* (Madrid: Consejo Superior de Investigaciones Científicas, 2003).

20 D. Beales, *Prosperity and Plunder: European Catholic Monasteries in the Age of Revolution, 1650–1815* (Cambridge: Cambridge University Press, 2003), 160.

21 M. Mörner, ed., *The Expulsion of the Jesuits from Latin America* (New York: Knopf, 1965).

22 M. Picón-Salas, *A Cultural History of Spanish America from Conquest to Independence* (Berkeley: University of California Press, 1962), 137–38.

23 M. R. Foster, *Catholic Revival in the Age of the Baroque: Religious Identity in Southwest Germany, 1550–1750* (Cambridge: Cambridge University Press, 2001), 223.

24 O. Chadwick, *The Popes and European Revolution* (Oxford: Oxford University Press, 1981), 364–68.

25 L. Szilas, "Konklave und Papstwahl Clemens XIV," *Zeitschrift für Katholische Theologie* 96 (1974), 287–99.

26 J. Thorpe, "Notes on Passing Events at Rome, etc, before, at the period of, and after the Dissolution of the Society," Jesuit English Province Archives, MS M24, fol. 3.

27 D. Beales, "Joseph II and the Monasteries of Austria and Hungary," in N. Aston, ed., *Religious Change in Europe, 1650–1914* (Oxford: Oxford University Press, 1997), 161–84; D. Beales, *Joseph II* (Cambridge: Cambridge University Press, 1987), 455–64.

28 N. Atkin and F. Tallett, *Priests, Prelates and People: A History of European Catholicism since 1750* (Oxford: Oxford University Press, 2003), 35.

29 *The Times*, 27 January 1815, p. 3, col. 5.

30 Von Pastor, *History of the Popes*, XXXIX: 177–329; D. L. Shlafly, Jr., "The Post-Suppression Society of Jesus in the United States and Russia: Two Unlikely Settings," in O'Malley *et al.*, *The Jesuits II*, 772–85. Maurice Whitehead is currently pursuing a research project on the educational work of the English Jesuits during this period. Visit www.swansea.ac.uk/history/research/spencer_project/.

31 T. Clemens, " 'Les Pères de la Foi' in France: 1800–1814," *Archivum Historicum Societatis Iesu* 57 (1989), 233–65; *Recherches autour de Pierre de Clorivière: Actes du colloque public des 18 et 19 octobre 1991* (Paris: SIPS, 1993).

32 J. N. Tylenda, *Jesuit Saints and Martyrs*, 2nd edn (Chicago: Loyola Press, 1998), 385–87.

33 *The Bulls of Popes Clement XIV and Pius VII for the Suppression and Re-Establishment of the Order of Jesuits* (London, 1815), 8.

34 T. O'Brien Hanley, ed., *The John Carroll Papers*, 3 vols. (Notre Dame: University of Notre Dame Press, 1976), III: 351.

16 Jesuit schools in the USA, 1814–c. 1970

GERALD McKEVITT

In 1855, James Oliver Van de Velde, Jesuit bishop of Natchez, Mississippi, described the educational ministry of the restored Society in America. "Wherever our Fathers have commenced colleges," he told an English friend, "they have succeeded beyond their expectations." They thrived even though "in most cases they were foreigners, Belgians and French, scarcely acquainted with the language of the country."[1] The bishop's boast underscored a defining feature of early Jesuit schooling: its domination by Europeans. Although American- and English-born Jesuits directed Georgetown College (founded 1789) following the Society's reconstitution in 1814, succeeding institutions were forged by émigré clerics. St. Louis University was run by Belgians; French expatriates launched institutions in Alabama, Kentucky, and New York; and Woodstock College, the Order's national seminary in Maryland, was the creation of exiled Neapolitans. German Jesuits, deported by Bismarck's *Kulturkampf*, founded five schools across the northeast from New York to the Mississippi River. In the Far West, Italians and other immigrant priests operated colleges in Santa Clara, San Francisco, Denver, Spokane, and Seattle.

The schools' foreign provenance had far-reaching implications. As the historian Philip Gleason has observed, Catholic institutions, including those run by Jesuits, stood apart socially, organizationally, and ideologically from native academies. They were socially distinct because the majority of teachers and students were newcomers. Organized along European lines by refugee clerics subject to European oversight, they were also administered differently than mainstream colleges. And they stood apart ideologically because their convictions about curricula and student discipline were imported from abroad. However, in order to satisfy the wants of clientele and to cope with competitive pressures, the Jesuits sought to make their colleges culturally appealing. The resulting push and pull between

278

Figure 16.1. Church of Saint Ignatius, University of San Francisco, California, 2004. Photo by Thomas Worcester.

their desire to retain a distinctive identity and their need to serve the society for which they existed has been (and remains) an ongoing tension within Jesuit institutions.[2] Over the years, their uniqueness manifested itself in a host of features – from a belief in the superiority of a classical education to a disparagement of vocational training; from an insistence on integrating high school and collegiate education to an insistence on moral formation after other American schools had long since abandoned it.

The transplanted educators championed training in Latin and Greek in the New World just as they had in the Old. That the ancient languages offered superior schooling was a conviction shared by most early American educators – although they would abandon that position later in the century. Jesuits of the sixteenth century had insisted on classicism for utilitarian reasons (Latin had been the language of the educated classes and the essential tool for understanding and influencing culture), but nineteenth-century academics, living in vastly different times, embraced a new rationale for mastering Virgil and Homer: intellectual formation. Ancient literature and languages not only imparted abiding and universal values, Jesuits argued, they also provided "the most efficient instrument of mental discipline."[3] With their complicated syntax and grammar, the highly inflected classical idioms were ideal tools for the maturation of intelligence and for laying bare the laws of thought and logic. In addition to literary studies, their curriculum included the natural sciences, mathematics, philosophy, and, to a lesser degree, theology.

Jesuit pedagogy, embodying the ideals of the late Renaissance, addressed the whole of human experience by promoting both intellectual and moral formation. "The acquisition of knowledge, though it necessarily accompanies any right system of education, is a secondary result of education," Boston College declared in 1894. "Learning is an instrument of education, not its end. The end is culture, mental and moral development." "We must never forget that education differs essentially from instruction," officials at St. Louis University added, "and its office is less to fill the memory with facts or the understanding with knowledge, than to develop the faculties of the mind and to prepare them for the work of life."[4]

The apex point of all studies was rhetoric. Mastery of *eloquentia perfecta*, or articulate wisdom, meant not merely the ability to communicate with ease and elegance, but "the capacity to reason, to feel, to express oneself and to act, harmonizing virtue with learning."[5] To this end, students analyzed ancient masters of elocution such as Cicero and Demosthenes. They participated in dramatic productions that inculcated lessons of virtue, enhanced memory, and perfected oratorical expertise. In American eyes, "only gold is idolized more than an eloquent speaker," a Georgetown priest recounted.[6] "Good speechmaking means more to them than rhetoric and philosophy."[7]

The schools were explicitly Christian in purpose, not merely value-oriented, to use a contemporary term. Although "education consists chiefly in informing the mind and in training the powers of intellect and will," wrote Robert Fulton of Boston College, "the chief result of education is the religious formation and religious training." Formal theological instruction did not occupy a large place in the early curriculum, but the schools promoted spiritual values and moral training through an all-inclusive network of devotional symbols suffusing every aspect of campus life. Religious holidays abounded while Marian sodalities promoted piety and good example. All students attended obligatory church services and Catholics went to confession at least once a month. In sum, the regimen of the school, the personal relationship of student and teacher, and weekly catechetical instruction – all aimed at inculcating the principles and practices of Christian faith.[8]

As in Europe, the Jesuit *collegium* comprised two integrated departments, the first of which was roughly equivalent to the modern high school and the second to collegiate studies. The typical student entered around the age of twelve and graduated with a Bachelor of Arts degree seven or eight years later. "There is no use," a California Jesuit cautioned, "in sending boys to a well-conducted and disciplined Seminary of learning at seventeen, eighteen, or nineteen" when they "know no other rule of living but that of wild and unrestrained self-will." Youths with such dispositions would regard the college as a house of correction or state prison. In their insistence on an early start, the Jesuit institutions were not unlike other American colleges, including mid-nineteenth-century Harvard whose average aspirant was sixteen years old.[9] By the twentieth century, however, the Society's union of preparatory school and college set their establishments uncomfortably apart from the mainstream.

Students came from all economic classes. St. Xavier College, a New York commuter school, drew the sons of working-class families because its location at the center of Manhattan's developing mass transit system made it economically and geographically accessible.[10] Founders intended Boston College to be "a low-tuition college for day scholars." "No student, however poor, is refused admission because he is unable to pay tuition," officials reported in 1899, "and of the four hundred young men registered in the college, scarcely more than half do so."[11] Although the Jesuits preferred to run day schools necessitating fewer personnel and lower costs, they opened boarding colleges at Georgetown, Fordham, Denver, Spokane, and Santa Clara. Because they required additional fees, those establishments inevitably enrolled a more restricted clientele. By 1880, the Order's twenty institutions in the United States were evenly split between residential and commuter colleges.[12]

By enrolling students of diverse nationalities, races, and economic backgrounds, the typical Jesuit college fostered shared cultural values. The sons of newly arrived European immigrants filled classrooms from Boston to San Francisco. Native American youths attended industrial boarding schools in six western states and Alaska. Academies in New Mexico and California came into existence to educate Spanish-speakers brought into the United States by the Mexican War. "Whether native or Eastern, Mexican or South American, English, French, or Italians, Catholic or Protestant, Jew or Gentile, they were Santa Clara boys," a student recalled.[13] The colleges aimed at strengthening the faith of immigrant children in a culture often unfriendly to Catholicism while preparing them to participate in American society. In the process, students encountered faculty mentors who themselves wrestled with the challenge of acculturation. Most of the schools attracted significant non-Catholic populations, although few were as ecumenical as Santa Clara College, half of whose enrollees in 1868 were Protestant.

The majority of students at Jesuit colleges, like those at other US institutions, did not remain long enough to earn a diploma. Americans were not interested in prolonged years of study, lamented a priest in Cleveland. "They first intend to make money as soon and as quickly as possible."[14] Of the nearly six thousand students attending Jesuit colleges in 1884, less than 2 percent graduated with the classical Bachelor of Arts degree. The Bachelor of Science diploma was far more in demand.[15]

Overseas superiors expected the American schools to follow European precedents. "I desire that in all things the Society assume the same form and proceed in the same manner as in Europe," wrote Superior General Roothaan in 1834. "As far as circumstances will permit, let nothing new be introduced." But the realities of American life demanded compromise. "Hardly anyone seeks a liberal arts training curriculum like ours," sighed an official of St. John's College in New York. "Those whose interest is business, and that's the largest part of the nation," disdained Latin and Greek. Students destined for careers in "law, medicine, and other professions don't give any more attention to literary studies than illiterates do."[16] Classicism was an even harder sell in the West. "Oh what a waste of time are Latin and Greek," a San Francisco teacher noted ruefully in 1866, "for so many students that I now see working for a living – as grocer, butcher, and who knows what else!" As late as 1890, only five of the twenty-seven American Jesuit institutions, most of them in the East, offered an exclusively classical course.[17]

While superiors abroad urged adherence to tradition, missionary educators argued for adaptation. No college should be "a bed of Procrustes," insisted the American-born Walter P. Hill of St. Louis University, "into which every mind is forced and compressed, and there fashioned and shaped into one dead uniformity." The aim of education was a constant, namely "the training of truly Christian generations," he said, but we must "take the world as it is, and apply the system of education to it in every way in which it is willing to receive it."[18] An upwardly mobile clientele demanded a flexible curriculum. Therefore, in addition to the classics, most schools offered an English program leading to a Bachelor of Science diploma. Emigré schoolmasters in the West adjusted their curricula to regional interests by offering instruction in the sciences, including mineralogy and assaying.

Mercantile training constituted another compromise, although most Jesuits privately disdained vocational education. In 1894, teachers at St. John's College dismissed the commercial course as "the Refuge of Idlers," even though it attracted 38 percent of the student body. Such instruction might be "greatly suited to the temperament and training of Americans, who from their very cradle are engaged in the accumulation of money," a Californian scoffed, but it is "very foreign to our customs, by which boys are educated in the study of the humanities and natural sciences."[19] Georgetown College barred mercantile training for decades, but it was highly popular elsewhere. By 1890, eighteen Jesuit institutions in the United States offered the course.[20]

Although the schools of the Society attempted to preserve the iconic status of the classics, the traditional curriculum gradually waned in popularity elsewhere. In response to rapid industrial growth and westward expansion, a more diversified course of studies emerged in the United States that prized professional development and research. In that new world, Cicero and Demosthenes seemed irrelevant. As a consequence, by the end of the nineteenth century, the Society's institutions drifted into an academic backwater and enrollments dropped. Major American universities began rejecting alumni of Jesuit high schools and colleges who applied for admission. In 1899, the Harvard president Charles Eliot delivered a stunning public critique of the Society's schools. Writing in the *Atlantic Monthly*, America's leading promoter of electivism condemned the "uniform prescribed education" favored by the Jesuits as "impossible and absurd."[21] The foreign character of their institutions alienated still others, including fellow Catholics. Bishop Richard Gilmour of Cleveland, Ohio, resisted the founding of John Carroll College because he feared it would be unsuited for America. "The Jesuits of this diocese are German and not ready for Cleveland," he charged in 1883. "The highest interest of the Church and State demand that we Americanize our people." Similar complaints were heard in the West. "The Italian Fathers no longer enjoy the support and following of the people that they once had," a California Jesuit reported in 1896.[22]

Smarting from such criticisms, Jesuits began to reappraise their policies. Although officials continued to assure superiors in Europe that the courses of studies were just as they were done "in an established college in the old world," in fact, changes were afoot.[23] With more native-born men entering the Order, Jesuits debated how they might embrace change. The lifting of European supervision of many of the Society's operations in America after the turn of the century and the elevation of former missionary jurisdictions to independent provinces facilitated that process. As Jesuits in the United States assumed more leverage over their affairs, their schools began slowly to inch toward the educational mainstream. Colleges in the Northeast adhered to the liberal arts curriculum, but conformity to more practical secular goals became a requisite for survival in the Midwest where land grant colleges and state universities held sway. William Banks Rogers of St. Louis University typified a new generation of reform-minded presidents. "Boys do not care for the rigid course" in the classics, he warned in 1904. "Whether a course that keeps so many boys away from us is the best in the present time is a subject for serious consideration." When Harvard Law School rejected a St. Louis graduate because his studies had been insufficiently comprehensive, Rogers implemented improvements assuring that degrees from his institution would be recognized "at the principal national and state universities."[24]

When public universities began requiring four years of secondary schooling for admission, the integrated seven-year Jesuit program fell to pieces. Acknowledging that union was "utterly at variance with the general educational practices of the country," Jesuits separated their high school and collegiate departments.[25] Thus, in 1900, Boston College, while retaining its adherence to classics, expanded its preparatory program from a three- to a four-year course, thereby providing more time for the study of modern languages, mathematics, and history. By the end of World War I, all of the twenty-five Jesuit colleges in the United States had administratively severed collegiate from high school programs.

Redefinition of the secondary curriculum had a domino effect, forcing a reappraisal of collegiate studies. At the same time, the ascendancy of schools of professional education obliged both high schools and colleges to offer a greater variety of subjects. Although a prescribed curriculum centered on literary studies still prevailed, undergraduate courses in law, engineering, journalism, and pre-medicine began to appear in college catalogs.[26] The Bachelor of Science degree, which had been discontinued at many institutions, was reintroduced. Academic modernization was accompanied by a relaxation of European codes of strict student discipline and supervision. "Character-training and the inculcation of Christian principles" was still "the principal aim of their work," authorities insisted, but "instead of repressing the generous promptings of youth, let us rather strive to develop in them a spirit of initiative."[27]

Among the forces reshaping the educational landscape, none was more powerful than the regional accrediting association. Although contrarians decried standardization "as a means of destroying the small college," most Jesuit educators foresaw that no institution could afford to disregard rankings.[28] "The day is not far distant when our college diplomas and high school certificates will be of little value to the owners unless our institutions have the standing recognized by the state," warned the Society's Missouri province in 1915. "As we cannot set the standard, we shall have to follow."[29] Determined to chart a new course, a group of Jesuit academics, led by President Edward P. Tivnan of Fordham University, in 1921 formed the Inter-Province Committee to push for modernization. "There should be on the part of all a full realization of standardization," it decreed. "All our colleges and high schools should strive to meet the requirements" of their regional associations by upgrading curricula, improving libraries, and supporting doctoral training for Jesuit faculty.[30]

East Coast colleges, influenced by the more traditional Ivy League, were less subject to standardization. But institutions in the Midwest swiftly accommodated to norms imposed by the authoritative North Central Association and by state universities dedicated to business, scientific, and technological education. Accordingly, Greek was no longer required for the A.B. degree in the Society's schools in the Central States. Catalogs and programs were revised to conform to other American colleges; classrooms and libraries were improved; admission standards became more formal and more rigorous; the quality of the faculty was upgraded; and athletic programs and financial management became subject to closer scrutiny.

With the gradual fading of Latin and Greek, other subjects filled the vacuum. The main beneficiaries of waning classicism were religion and philosophy, which were viewed not merely as instruments for imparting a humanistic education, but also as antidotes to the materialism and skepticism of the day. The shift that occurred at Loyola College in Baltimore was typical. Religious instruction, which had constituted 2 percent of the undergraduate curriculum hours in 1895, had by 1928 expanded to 10 percent. The formative role once ascribed to classical literature also shifted to philosophy, which at Loyola grew from 12 percent to 23 percent.[31] Philosophy had always occupied a central place in the Jesuit core curriculum but, because few Americans remained in college long enough to earn a degree, a mere handful completed the philosophy requirement. Between 1816 and 1912, only 3.4 percent of all the students who attended the twenty-eight American Jesuit colleges and universities actually finished the entire course. Formerly concentrated as a capstone in the senior year, philosophy was now distributed over three undergraduate years as the distinguishing feature of Jesuit education.[32] Even students enrolled in professional studies took the full sequence. Philosophy "knits together all the various threads of learning," declared the Georgetown president Joseph Havens Richards, "and makes of them one consistent and harmonious fabric. Thus it becomes the great principle of unity in education."[33]

Theology, once imparted by religious discipline and devotional practices, also advanced to a more prominent academic place. Enemies of the Church "are constantly forging new weapons" against religious belief, Jesuits of the Midwest declared in 1918. "The whole world, Catholic and non-Catholic, is in ferment over biblical questions, and educated laymen must have sufficient knowledge to meet the difficulties and objections." Since Catholics were insufficiently versed in Scripture and church history, "more vitality ... is needed in our teaching of religion." Handbooks that were chiefly pastoral were replaced by texts that addressed "the principal modern difficulties urged against the Faith."[34] Wilhelm Wilmer's *Handbook of the Christian Religion*, a scholarly and substantial tome ("just the sort of book our graduates should take out into the world with them," one Jesuit wrote) was adopted across the country.[35]

Jesuits pointed to their distinctive curriculum as a contribution to society. While succumbing to greater specialization, the Society had retained the holistic and formative feature that had always been central to its pedagogical system. "We can safely say that we are not only not out of touch with the times," boasted Thomas J. Campbell, president of Fordham College, "but better equipped than most men" to offer a superior collegiate education. "Our teaching in law, medical, dental and other professional schools is necessary for the welfare of the individual, family, church and state," added Herbert C. Noonan, former president of Marquette University, in 1925. It is superior because it emphasizes philosophy and is "in accord with human wisdom."[36]

Few innovations were as dramatic as the Society's pursuit of university standing for its colleges. "We were losing caste as educators" by 1900, a priest in St. Louis explained, and "being looked upon as high school teachers and little more."[37] The fact that increasing numbers of Catholics sought professional careers provided an additional stimulus to expansion. Rather than lose students to secular universities "where doctrines contrary to the Faith and teaching of the Church are disseminated," Catholic educators began to found graduate and professional schools of their own.[38] In 1902, Omaha's Creighton University started a trend by acquiring a medical school. Within a few years other colleges, notably in the Midwest and West, became universities by incorporating schools of law, medicine, dentistry, journalism, and engineering. Some Jesuit educators questioned the wisdom of rapid expansion. We have been seized by "a frenzy for multiplying and increasing enrollments beyond our capacity in men and money to take proper care of them," an official wrote around 1927. "Too many of us have become enamored of mere size."[39] Because the juggernaut of proliferation could not be slowed, however, many institutions consigned themselves to mediocrity.

The inauguration of graduate studies prompted schools to assume titles reflecting their new status. These name changes testified to a desire to integrate institutions into the American mainstream by associating them with a city instead of with a saint. Thus, St. John's College in New York was rechartered in 1907 as Fordham University. St. Ignatius College in Cleveland distanced itself from its German origin in 1923 by becoming John Carroll University, honoring a bishop whom a spokesman identified as "one hundred percent American."[40] Seven years later, California's St. Ignatius College became the University of San Francisco.

Intercollegiate athletics provided another means of winning recognition. "We are getting lots of publicity from the papers," exclaimed a Jesuit administrator in 1929, "since Ohio State succeeded in getting our best tackle from us. This has brought us into the limelight very much."[41] Educators emphasized the connection between American values and Catholic values. "Seeing that on all sides there is a cry for Americanization and much is made of education for citizenship," declared the Inter-Province Committee in 1921, "it should be made clear to all that the training given [in] our colleges illustrates the fundamental principles of real patriotism and is the best preparation for successful citizenry."[42]

The inauguration of graduate and professional education was accompanied by a diminution of clerical presence. "It is becoming increasingly evident that we shall not be able to man our high schools and colleges exclusively with Jesuit teachers," educators reported in 1924. "Lay teachers will be called upon to teach a number of our courses." By 1930, the percentage of Jesuit faculty nationwide had declined to between 40 and 60 percent, a shift that raised eyebrows in some quarters.[43] That a non-Catholic professor was teaching a course in biology, "a dangerous subject," provoked a small crisis in Cleveland. "Since he is a non-Catholic," an official advised, "he should be dropped as soon as possible as this can be done in justice."[44]

Curricular expansion meant that women entered the classrooms for the first time. In some cases this resulted from a university's having acquired a pre-existing professional school that already enrolled females. In 1909, a woman was awarded the B.S. degree by Marquette University, probably the first granted to a female in the history of the Order. Others were admitted at the insistence of bishops eager to spare Catholics from attending secular institutions where they "are forced to imbibe materialistic and infidel ideas." Still other women enrolled because so few Catholic institutions were open to them. By 1939, 26.6 percent of the 42,583 students enrolled in Jesuit universities in the United States were female.[45] The coming of women did not prompt significant institutional reorganization, however, until the introduction of undergraduate coeducation several decades later.

With the launching of professional training, fund-raising took on greater urgency. Enhanced revenues were needed not only to run larger institutions with more programs, but also because accreditation agencies required endowments. Colleges began to appeal for support not just to alumni and to Catholics, but to the public at large. Campaign slogans employed in fund drives in the 1920s typified the new approach. "Boston College serves the public" was the theme of a New England campaign while another in California depicted Santa Clara as "Your College – My College – Everybody's College."[46] The quest for broader patronage prompted a unprecedented emphasis on cultivating good public relations, a maneuver that sometimes resulted in downplaying a school's Catholic affiliation. In 1923, when President A. C. Fox of Marquette University – intending to explain to a non-Catholic public that Marquette was open to students of all faiths – described the school as "non-sectarian," he was criticized for secularizing the institution. Four years later, a Vatican official accused American Jesuit schools of being insufficiently "Catholic" because of their increasing reliance on non-Catholic professors and because their presidents exercised too little influence over faculty and the religious life of students.[47]

These criticisms were not without effect. Charges of secularism pushed the schools to define their religious character more narrowly, evidenced, for example, by greater emphasis on recruiting Catholic students and faculty. Dissatisfaction with their lackluster academic standing spurred painful reappraisals. Although there had been an upturn in the number of earned Ph.D.s among Jesuits in the 1920s, the ongoing paucity of professionally trained faculty remained a source of embarrassment.[48] That quality was indeed a problem showed in the difficulty with which universities struggled to win certification. In 1932, eight of the fourteen Jesuit law schools in the nation failed to meet the requirements of the American Bar Association. Two years later, when the American Association of University Professors issued its list of sixty-three graduate schools qualified to prepare candidates for the doctorate, no Jesuit institution was included. In 1937, the American Medical Association evaluated the Society's five medical schools in the United States, ranking St. Louis University as "among the twenty best schools in the country" while three others were judged "distinctly unsatisfactory."[49] Such failures undercut morale, a professor in the Midwest lamented. "Catholic schools must labor to improve themselves to overcome their own inferiority complex."[50] We "are on trial before the [American] hierarchy who say we have no outstanding men," a Jesuit educator wrote ominously to superiors in Rome. They claim "that we are mediocre as a class, that we are four flushers" or shams.[51]

Alarmed at these inadequacies, the Jesuit Superior General, Wlodimir Ledochowski, formerly an opponent of educational reform, now became an advocate of change. In 1931, he formed the U.S. Commission on Higher Studies to forcefully upgrade the American schools through greater national cooperation. Three years later, he created the Jesuit Educational Association headed by a powerful "commissarius," Daniel M. O'Connell, who was charged with giving "new direction and fresh impulse" to renovation. Under O'Connell's firm hand, fresh urgency was given to regional accreditation, academic professionalism, modernization of administration, and graduate studies for Jesuits so that "our standard may be equal to the best in the country."[52]

Pressed to amend, the schools achieved progress in the inter-war decades. In the 1930s, an increase in the number of college-age students and enhanced Catholic upward mobility resulted in increased enrollments. As Catholics began to feel more at home in America, schools of social work appeared on several campuses. The founding of labor schools plunged other Jesuit institutions into the thick of American industrial life in ways inconceivable even a generation earlier. The colleges and universities played a prominent role in an intellectual resurgence that transformed American higher education in the 1930s. Inspired by a revival of scholastic philosophy and theology, this so-called Catholic Renaissance challenged modernity's rejection of God, supernatural revelation, and the Church by proposing a holistic Catholic culture as a superior alternative.[53] There were many things that non-Catholic schools did better, a Jesuit report conceded in 1932, but for them "religion is taboo"; and they "fail to give their students any abiding and satisfactory philosophy of life. They are content to give them knowledge and not wisdom."[54]

Although Jesuit institutions continued to glory in their distinctiveness, changes that occurred in American higher education after World War II propelled them to greater conformity with other colleges and universities. With a majority of Americans now seeking a college education and increasing numbers of students anticipating postgraduate training, enrollments doubled their pre-war figure. With a total registration of 110,934 students, the *New York Times* reported in 1958, "the largest expansion program in the 169-year history of Jesuit colleges in America is underway."[55] By 1956, 400 years after the death of St. Ignatius, there were forty-three high schools in the United States – more than had been maintained by the entire Society when the founder died in 1556.[56] All institutions welcomed the enhanced enrollments and program development that the post-war boom brought in its wake, although few fully anticipated the long-term consequences of unprecedented growth.

The increased specialization of university administration prompted greater reliance on lay expertise. In the nineteenth century, non-clerics had not participated in a substantial way in the governance of the schools. In 1918, the progressive W. B. Rogers of St. Louis had contrasted Catholic institutions with their secular counterparts, pointing out that the latter, which had lay trustees and "who move among business men, have a manifest advantage over us." Rogers advocated the creation of advisory boards to guide institutions in fund-raising, warning, however, that the lay person must feel "that he has some interest in the institution" and that "his voice and vote count." By 1945–46, eleven Jesuit colleges and universities had created lay advisory boards and one already had laymen on its board of trustees.[57]

As colleges and universities grew in size and complexity, they relied more than ever on a non-clerical professorate, particularly in their professional schools. "We are absolutely dependent on the lay personnel," observed Albert H. Poetker, former president of the University of Detroit, in 1946. "They must develop a distinctively Jesuit spirit," he advised while confidentially predicting this could be achieved with "a very few well-selected men." Although record numbers of Jesuits would pursue the Ph.D. in the years ahead – 183 of them were enrolled in doctoral studies in 1961 – religious could no longer supply the schools' need for personnel.[58] By 1957–58, nearly 72 percent of the 5,007 faculty serving in the Society's colleges and universities were lay persons. The role of the laity in church affairs would be affirmed a few years later by the Second Vatican Council and by general congregations of the Society of Jesus. With laicization came institutional revitalization, evidenced by improvements in the caliber of both faculty and students. What one historian wrote of the College of the Holy Cross would be increasingly true of other institutions: for faculty, "scholarly excellence took precedence over Catholic distinctiveness."[59]

Changes came swiftly in the 1960s. "Catholic schools are trying to remain both Catholic and American," a Fordham University professor recounted in 1962. They want to retain "their special religious commitment, but they also want to belong, a dilemma that confronted American's immigrant groups." That predicament produced profound breaks with past practice that sounded like a death knell to some Jesuits and church bells to others. "The older generation wants to remember the old country; the new generation is in a hurry to Americanize."[60] In succeeding years, tightly structured curricula, objects of student complaints in the preceding decade and long considered excessive by accrediting committees, underwent major revision. As Catholic establishments became more and more like their secular counterparts, their curriculum became less and less a definer of institutional distinction. Required courses in philosophy and theology were reduced in order to adapt to trends in American higher education and to make way for more electives. So great was the transformation of the schools by the end of the 1960s that when Michael P. Walsh, a former president of Boston College, asked rhetorically, "Is there anything distinctive?" about his institution, he replied, "I myself cannot see it."[61]

Responding to shifts in attitudes that were reshaping American society, universities surrendered control over student lives. "We should divest ourselves of many responsibilities we have clung to in the area of student affairs," declared President Joseph Sellinger of Loyola Baltimore in 1964.[62] Authoritarianism yielded to an atmosphere of few restraints in which self-discipline played the leading role. Student bodies became more racially diversified. After restricting for decades the admission of women to graduate and professional programs, the universities joined the national movement toward undergraduate coeducation. Accompanied by a greater selectivity in admissions, coeducation marked a turning point in the history of many schools.

As Jesuit institutions assimilated to American culture and matured, they became more secular in their governance as in their curricula. In the 1950s and 1960s, a new type of president began to emerge, men who held earned doctorates and were professional academics. These leaders sought to improve their organizations by emancipating them from what they viewed as the narrow restrictions of the Jesuit Order and by finding new sources of revenue. As modern establishments with extensive graduate and professional schools, the universities' financial needs soon exceeded the capacity of the Jesuits, the Catholic community, and wealthy benefactors to sustain them. In their scramble for federal and state aid, the schools sought to reposition themselves in the public mind. In 1966, a Maryland state court ruling in the Horace Mann case raised doubts that state aid for religiously affiliated schools was constitutional, thus leading some colleges to distance themselves from explicit Catholic identification and to secularize their administration by opening their boards and administrations to more lay persons. That year, a full-page ad in the *New York Times* announced that Fordham University "will pay any price – break any mold – in order to pursue her true function as a university."[63]

In 1967, presidents of the nation's Catholic universities, meeting at Land O'Lakes, Wisconsin, defined the new autonomy sought by their establishments: "To perform its teaching and research functions effectively the Catholic university must have a true autonomy and academic freedom in the face of authority of whatever kind, lay or clerical, external to the academic community itself."[64] That same year, starting with St. Louis University, Jesuit communities and their functions began to be legally separated from the universities and their functions. Boards of trustees, on which lay persons were in the majority, assumed ownership and control. As the Jesuits embraced a largely derivative educational culture and as the schools founded by them became less distinctively Catholic, they became diversified religiously. Thus in 1966, a new president at the University of Detroit could foresee his institution "one day being a great ecumenical university."[65]

With the dissolution of oversight by religious superiors, the colleges and universities stood at the threshold of a new era. Once socially, ideologically, and institutionally isolated from American life, they were now planted clearly in the center. The institutions continued to profess a dedication to Catholic education in the Jesuit tradition, but the modes of implementing religious values had changed with the times. This was not the first occasion when Jesuit education had struggled to find new criteria and new distinctive elements. In the nineteenth century, classical literary studies had been the chief identifier. In the early twentieth century, it had been primarily philosophy and theology. After the 1960s, many schools would begin to move toward a new self-definition by educating for faith and justice in accord with the religious Order's reorientation. "For us," a Jesuit General Congregation declared, "the promotion of justice ... should be the concern of our whole life and a dimension of all our apostolic endeavors."[66] The colleges and universities would struggle to integrate the new raison d'être with their commitment to mainstream academic values. Whatever the outcome, it remained true, as one scholar observed, that they had "by choice and by design, taken on the native features of American colleges."[67]

Notes

1   James Oliver Van de Velde (Natchez) to John Ethridge, 20 June 1855, Maryland–Missouri file, BN/3/1, 2, 3, British Jesuit Province Archives, 114 Mount Street, London.

2   Philip Gleason, "American Catholic Higher Education: A Historical Perspective," in *The Shape of Catholic Higher Education*, ed. Robert Hassenger (Chicago: University of Chicago Press, 1967), 15.

3   *Catalogue of Las Vegas College, 1887–1888*, Jesuitica Collection, Regis University Archives, Denver, CO; *Santa Clara College*

Catalog, 1910–1911, Archives of Santa Clara University (hereafter ASCU).

4 *Catalogue of the Officers and Students of Boston College, 1894–1895*, Boston College Archives, Chestnut Hill, MA (hereafter BCA); Walter P. Hill, *Historical Sketch of the St. Louis University* (St. Louis: Patrick Fox, 1879), 161.

5 Gabriel Codina, "'Our Way of Proceeding' in Education: The Ratio Studiorum," *Education SJ* (May 1999), 11–12.

6 Giovanni Grassi, quoted in Robert Emmett Curran, *The Bicentennial History of Georgetown University. Volume I: From Academy to University, 1789–1889* (Washington, DC: Georgetown University Press, 1993), 192.

7 G. Marra (Pueblo, CO) to N. Mola, 30 January 1890, Archives of the Naples Province of the Society of Jesus, Gesù Nuovo, Naples, Italy.

8 [Robert Fulton], "Various Rules for the Direction of the Teachers of B. C.," in "Register of Students, 1864–1898," BCA; Thomas E. Wangler, "Religious Goals and Curriculum of Boston College, 1864–1900," in M. J. Connolly and Lawrence G. Jones, eds., *Inscape: Studies Presented to Charles F. Donovan, S. J.* (Chestnut Hill, MA: Boston College, 1977), 211–21.

9 Michele Accolti to J. L. L. Warren, 25 September 1864, J. L. L. Warren Papers, Bancroft Library, University of California, Berkeley, CA.

10 Christa Ressmeyer Klein, "The Jesuits and Catholic Boyhood in Nineteenth-Century New York City: A Study of St. John's College and the College of St. Francis Xavier, 1846–1912" (unpublished doctoral dissertation, University of Pennsylvania, 1976), 79–80.

11 *The Pilot* (Boston), 13 May 1899, quoted in David R. Dunigan, *A History of Boston College* (Milwaukee: Bruce, 1947), 168.

12 *Woodstock Letters* 9 (1880): 7.

13 A. D. Splivalo, "Corpus Christi at Santa Clara in 1853," *The Redwood* (October 1908), 4, ASCU; Gerald McKevitt, *The University of Santa Clara: A History, 1851–1977* (Stanford, CA: Stanford University Press, 1979), 39–40.

14 Annual letter of 1892–93, quoted in Donald P. Gavin, *John Carroll University: A Century of Service* (Kent, OH: Kent State University Press, 1985), 39.

15 *Woodstock Letters* 13 (1884), 424.

16 Johann Philip Roothaan to Theodore De Theaux, 10 May 1834, in Gilbert Joseph Garraghan, *Jesuits of the Middle United States*, 3 vols. (New York: America Press, 1938), III: 120; Annual Letter, St. John's College, New York, 1 October 1858 to 1 October 1859, and 1 October 1861 to 1 October 1862, in Thomas C. Hennessy, *How the Jesuits Settled in New York* (New York: Something More Publications, 2003), 92, 138.

17 *Woodstock Letters* 19 (1890), 441. The number had climbed to twelve by 1895, according to *Woodstock Letters* 24 (1895), 469.

18 Hill, *Historical Sketch*, 158–60.

19 Thomas J. Gannon, "St. John's, Fordham, a Classical College," *Woodstock Letters* 23 (1894), 126; Raymond A. Schroth, *Fordham:*

A History and Memoir (Chicago: Loyola University Press, 2002), 31; "Historia Domus, 1877," Santa Clara College, Archives of the California Province of the Society of Jesus, Jesuit Provincial Office, Los Gatos, CA.

20   Thomas H. Clancy, "Postprandial Address," *Assembly 1989: Jesuit Ministry in Higher Education; Apostolic Leadership and Jesuit Higher Education* (Washington, DC: The Jesuit Conference, 1990), 43.

21   Charles W. Eliot, "Recent Changes in Secondary Education," *Atlantic Monthly* 84 (1899), 443.

22   Richard Gilmour, quoted in Gavin, *John Carroll*, 14–24; Edward Allen (San Francisco) to L. Martín, 28 January 1896, CA. 1004-II-28, Roman Archives of the Society of Jesus, Rome, Italy (hereafter ARSI).

23   Joseph Cataldo (Spokane) to Anton Maria Anderledy, 17 January 1892, Mont. Sax. 1003-1-43, ARSI.

24   William Banks Rogers in *Report of the First Annual Meeting of the N[ational] C[atholic] E[ducation] A[ssociation] Convention* (July 1904), 80ff.; "Consultors' Minutes, St. Louis University, 1898–1921," minutes for 2 January 1899, St. Louis University Archives, St. Louis University.

25   "Missouri Province Education and Accreditation, 1917," Missouri, Record Group VI-2, Education pre-1940, Midwest Jesuit Archives, St. Louis, MO (hereafter MJA).

26   Nationwide, by 1911, 14.7 percent of the Society's courses for the B.S. degree and 20 percent for the B.A. were elective. See Wilfred Michael Mallon, "The Jesuit College: An Investigation into Factors Affecting the Educational Efficiency of the Jesuit Colleges in the Central States" (Ph.D. dissertation, St. Louis University, 1931), III: 781.

27   "Report of Committee on Studies, 1907," Missouri VI (Education pre-1940), MJA.

28   Alexander J. Burrowes, "Attitude of Catholics Towards Higher Education," *Catholic Educational Association Bulletin* 16 (1919), 167.

29   "Report of the General Committee on the Course of Studies, August 1915," Missouri VI, folder Course of Studies, 1915, MJA.

30   "Report of the Meeting of the Inter-Province Committee on Studies, 1921," JEA Collection, Burns Library, Boston College (hereafter BLBC). See also Richard M. Freeland, *Academia's Golden Age: Universities in Massachusetts, 1945–1970* (New York: Oxford University Press, 1992), 25.

31   Nicholas Varga, *Baltimore's Loyola, Loyola's Baltimore 1851–1986* (Baltimore: Maryland Historical Society, 1990), 147–49, 256.

32   James A. Reinert, "The Philosophical Curriculum in Jesuit Colleges and Universities in the United States from 1816 to 1912" (M.A. thesis, St. Louis University, 1950), 69; James T. Burtchael, *Dying of the Light: The Disengagement of Colleges and Universities from their Christian Churches* (Grand Rapids: Eerdmans, 1998), 577.

33   Joseph Havens Richards, "Georgetown College," *Woodstock Letters* 26 (1897), 183–85.

34   *Supplement . . . Report on Christian Doctrine*, 1918, MJA.

35   Wangler, "Religious Goals and Curriculum," 219; "Report of Sub-committee concerning Wilmer's 'Handbook of the Christian Religion,'" in "Minutes of the Meeting of the Central Committee on Studies," Chicago, 1893, Missouri vi-1 (Education pre-1940), folder Course of Studies, 1893, MJA.

36   Thomas J. Campbell, "Fordham," *Woodstock Letters* 27 (1898), 389; Herbert C. Noonan, "The Need of Jesuit Universities," *Woodstock Letters* 54 (1925), 244–45. See also Joseph A. Tetlow, "In Oratione Directa: Philosophy in the Jesuit Liberal Arts Curriculum in the United States," in Rolando E. Bonachea, ed., *Jesuit Higher Education: Essays on an American Tradition of Excellence* (Pittsburgh: Duquesne University Press, 1989), 105–23.

37   "St. Louis University," *Woodstock Letters* 40 (1911), 295.

38   Jesuit provincials' report, 1918, quoted in William P. Leahy, *Adapting to America: Catholics, Jesuits, and Higher Education in the Twentieth Century* (Washington, DC: Georgetown University Press, 1991), 24.

39   [Daniel M. O'Donnell], "Memorandum: Some Defects of our Educational System," *c.* 1927, Missouri vi-2 (Education pre-1940), folder Missouri Province and Education, MJA.

40   Gavin, *John Carroll*, 128.

41   President Benedict Rodman, quoted in ibid., 216.

42   "Report of the Meeting of the Inter-Province Committee on Studies, 1921," JEA Collection, BLBC.

43   "Report of the Meeting of the Inter-Province Committee on Studies, 1924," JEA Collection, BLBC; 1930 figures in Mallon, "The Jesuit College," ii: 377.

44   "Chicago Province," photostats of O'Connell Reports to Rome, O'Connell File, 1934–37, JEA Collection, BLBC.

45   "Report of the Commission on Coeducation, Feb. 12, 1940," Missouri vi-7, folder Coeducation in the Assistancy, 1938–42, MJA.

46   "The Story of Boston College," 1921 brochure, "Scrapbook, Rev. William Devlin, Nov. 5, 1920–May 19, 1921 (Campaign of May 3–12, 1921)," BCA; brochure in "The Drive, or How We Failed to Raise $500,000 in 1922" (scrapbook), E. Zeman Papers, ASCU.

47   A. C. Fox, quoted in Raphael N. Hamilton, *The Story of Marquette University* (Milwaukee: Marquette University Press, 1953), 190, n. 15; W. Ledochowski (Rome) to American provincials, 12 March 1927, Missouri vi (Education pre-1940), MJA; Leahy, *Adapting to America*, 43–44.

48   Leahy, *Adapting to America*, 40; Paul A. FitzGerald, *The Governance of Jesuit Colleges in the United States, 1920–1970* (Notre Dame: University of Notre Dame Press, 1984), 11.

49   1932 report cited in Leahy, *Adapting to America*, 42; *New York Times*, 2 April 1934; A. Schwitella (St. Louis?) to Zacheus Maher, 22 April 1937, Missouri, vi-8, file Medical School Rating, 1937, MJA.

50   Professor quoted in Mallon, "The Jesuit College," ii: 539.

51   James B. Macelwane to W. Ledochowski, 9 May 1932, Ledochowski file, Box 15, JEA Collection, BLBC.

52 W. Ledochowski, *Instructio pro Assistentia Americae*, 1934, MJA; Leahy, *Adapting to America*, 42–48.

53 Philip Gleason, *Contending with Modernity: Catholic Higher Education in the Twentieth Century* (New York: Oxford University Press, 1995), 114. See also Anthony J. Kuzniewski, *Thy Honored Name: A History of The College of the Holy Cross, 1843–1994* (Washington, DC: The Catholic University of America Press, 1999), 282.

54 *Report of the Commission on Higher Studies*, 1931–32, JEA Collection, BLBC.

55 *New York Times*, 9 February 1958.

56 John W. Donohue, *Jesuit Education: An Essay on the Foundations of Its Idea* (St. Louis: Institute of Jesuit Sources, 1970), 71–74.

57 W. B. Rogers, "A Letter of Father W. B. Rogers to Father Garesche," *Teachers' Review* 9 (October 1918), 55–56; "Lay Boards of Advisors," Box 33 ("Statistics: Various Schools"), JEA Collection, BLBC.

58 Albert H. Poetker, "The Place of the Layman in Jesuit Schools," *Jesuit Educational Quarterly* 9 (1946), 14; "Graduate Studies; Reports," Box 33 ("Statistics: Various Schools"), JEA Collection, BLBC.

59 Kuzniewski, *Thy Honored Name*, 343; FitzGerald, *Governance of Jesuit Colleges*, 279, n. 13.

60 Edward Wakin, *The Catholic Campus* (New York: Macmillan, 1963), 195.

61 Michael P. Walsh, cited in Eugene E. Grollmes, ed., *Proceedings of the JEA Denver Workshop on Jesuit Universities and Colleges: Their Commitment in a World of Change* (Washington, DC, 1969), 28, JEA Collection, BLBC.

62 Joseph Sellinger, quoted in Varga, *Baltimore's Loyola*, 449.

63 Varga, *Baltimore's Loyola*, 443; Mann case summarized in Burtchael, *Dying of the Light*, 584; Fordham declaration in *Newsweek*, 27 June 1966, 84–86.

64 Report quoted in FitzGerald, *Governance of Jesuit Colleges*, 212.

65 President Michael Carron, quoted in Herman J. Muller, *The University of Detroit, 1877–1977: A Centennial History* (Detroit: University of Detroit, 1976), 341.

66 *Documents of the Thirty-First and Thirty-Second General Congregations of the Society of Jesus* (St. Louis: Institute of Jesuit Sources, 1977), 427.

67 FitzGerald, *Governance of Jesuit Colleges*, 209.

17 Jesuit theological discourse since Vatican II

MARY ANN HINSDALE

In a 1991 essay reviewing the theological achievements of the Jesuits between the Council of Trent and Vatican II Avery Dulles, S.J., posed the question as to whether one could speak of such a thing as "Jesuit theology."[1] In response, Dulles wrote:

> If Jesuit theology is taken to mean a brand of theology distinctive and common to all Jesuits, no such thing exists. Jesuits do not follow any method proper to their Society, nor do they take any member of their own order as their theological mentor in the way that Augustinians might presumably follow St. Augustine, Dominicans might follow St. Thomas, and Franciscans might follow St. Bonaventure or Duns Scotus.[2]

However, Dulles claimed, one could speak of characteristic Jesuit concerns and themes in theology, concerns that "stem principally from the example and writings of St. Ignatius Loyola."[3] Ignatian spirituality has been and continues to be a fulcrum for the writings of Jesuit theologians; however, given the vast quantity of theological writing Jesuits have produced since Vatican II and the limited space of this essay, a narrower focus seemed warranted. Thus, I have selected three central themes from two of the post-Vatican II General Congregations of the Society of Jesus (in Jesuit parlance: "GC 32" and "GC 34") to serve as guideposts for mapping Jesuit theological discourse since the Council. Just as John XXIII's word *aggiornamento* became a byword at Vatican II, the phrases "the service of faith and the promotion of justice," "inculturation and interreligious dialogue," "cooperation with our partners in ministry" have become solidly enshrined in post-Vatican II Jesuit theological discourse.

JESUITS AT VATICAN II

Jesuit influence at Vatican II was considerable,[4] exerted certainly by the Jesuit bishops and archbishops in attendance, but especially by

Jesuit expert theologians (*periti*) who served as advisors to many bishops.[5] Such influence was no novelty, for several of the Orders' founding members had served as theological experts at the Council of Trent[6] and Jesuits from Rome's Gregorian University were "behind the scenes" at Vatican I.[7]

The election of Pedro Arrupe as Superior General of the Jesuits on 22 May 1965, during the Jesuits' Thirty-First General Congregation, meant that he, as a major superior of men, was able to participate in the Council's fourth session (14 September – 8 December 1965). Drawing upon his own missionary experience in Japan, Arrupe gave several addresses at the Council which emphasized the need for the Church to formulate a response to atheism "from within the center of world affairs, not from some intellectual ghetto."[8] He also spoke of the Church's need to become "at home in diverse cultures and learn from them."[9] As Ronald Modras notes, "two concerns – 'inculturation' and the 'integration' of faith and justice – would become hallmarks of Arrupe's tenure as superior general."[10] They would also become part of the legacy of Jesuit theological discourse.

The prominence of the Jesuit theologians Henri de Lubac and Jean Daniélou, as well as that of Pierre Teilhard de Chardin, continued to be felt well after the Council. However, it was the transcendental theology of the German Jesuit Karl Rahner and the Canadian Jesuit Bernard Lonergan, above all, that dominated the first decades of post-conciliar theology. Teaching at the universities of Innsbruck, Munich, and Münster, Rahner's transcendental Thomism and optimistic theology of grace influenced a generation of Catholic theologians world-wide. Lonergan taught for years at the Gregorian University in Rome and also at Regis College (the Jesuit theologate in Toronto), and at Boston College. Both Rahner and Lonergan make explicit reference to St. Ignatius in their theology and subsequent commentators have pointed out the strong influence of the *Spiritual Exercises* in their theological systems.[11]

Together with Yves Congar, O. P., Johann Baptist Metz, Joseph Ratzinger, Hans Küng, and other Council *periti*, Rahner founded the journal *Concilium* in order to continue theological discussion in the spirit of Vatican II. A few years later, another group of theologians, including some who had been at Vatican II, began to have second thoughts about the way the Council was being interpreted. The Swiss writer and former Jesuit Hans Urs von Balthasar, Henri de Lubac, S. J., and Vatican II *peritus* Joseph Ratzinger (who would eventually become the Prefect of the Congregation for the Doctrine of the Faith and the present Pope Benedict XVI), along with several others, founded the journal *Communio* which sought a more "orthodox" interpretation of the legacy of Vatican II. It is worth noting that, over the years, Jesuit scholars have been contributors to both journals, and that two separate volumes in the *Cambridge Companion* series have addressed the theology of von Balthasar and Rahner respectively.[12] However tempting it might be to categorize Jesuit theological discourse since Vatican II in terms of *Concilium* or *Communio* orientations, I believe it is far more instructive for the purposes of this volume to explore the impact that Pedro Arrupe and Peter-Hans Kolvenbach, and the General Congregations that took place during their terms of office, have had on the theology produced by Jesuits during this period.

PEDRO ARRUPE AND GC 32

The Thirty-First General Congregation (7 May – 15 July 1965 and 8 September –17 November 1966) followed quickly on the heels of Vatican II. As far back as 1949 Arrupe's predecessor, Jean Baptiste Janssens, had stressed that Jesuit social ministry should "provide the poor and underprivileged classes of society with the amount of temporal and spiritual goods required to lead a more human life, worthy of their vocation and dignity."[13] However, the urgency to address social injustice was not yet recognized as a priority by all Jesuits. That, however, would change when the Jesuits convened for their Thirty-Second General Congregation.

GC 32 took place from 2 December 1974 through 7 March 1975. Its "Decree Four" declared that "the service of faith, of which the promotion of justice is an absolute requirement" would become a major focus of Jesuit ministries.[14] It is important to stress that Decree Four did not appear out of the blue. Its antecedents can clearly be discerned in various addresses by Arrupe, the writings of Jesuit theologians and social scientists, and, most especially, Vatican II and its post-conciliar documents.[15] Most influential was "Justice in the World," the final document produced by the Third International Synod of Bishops in 1971. It was this document's statement regarding the relationship between Gospel faith and justice that became the decisive catalyst for Decree Four:

> Action on behalf of justice and participation in the transformation of the world fully appear to us as a constitutive dimension of the preaching of the Gospel, or, in other words, of the church's mission

for the redemption of the human race and its liberation from every oppressive situation.[16]

As Superior of the Jesuits, Arrupe, along with representative bishops from throughout the world, had attended the Synod on "Justice in the World." In a speech made that same year, he told U.S. provincial superiors: "We cannot remain silent, in certain countries, before regimes which constitute without any doubt a sort of institutionalized violence."[17] Only a few years earlier, Arrupe had urged the provincials of Latin America to put social justice at the heart of all their ministries.[18] As a result, some Jesuits in Latin America created controversy by questioning whether they should still run *colegios* for the middle and upper classes. Arrupe himself was sharply criticized for a 1973 address he gave to Jesuit alumni in Valencia, in which he asked "Have we Jesuits educated you for justice?"[19]

While Arrupe was aware that endorsing the Synod's stance on justice would have consequences, the price exacted in implementing Decree Four would be brought home starkly in Central America, with the deaths of the Salvadoran Jesuit Rutilio Grande in 1977, the American Jesuit James (Guadalupe) Carney in 1983, and the six Jesuit university professors from the University of Central America in San Salvador in 1989; and in Africa, with the assassination of the Cameroonian Jesuit Engelbert Mveng in 1995. In fact, since the time of Arrupe's tenure as Superior General, there have been forty Jesuit martyrs.[20]

In 1974 the Fourth International Synod of Bishops took up the topic of "evangelization." The significance the Synod put on the word "inculturation" also had an impact on GC 32. In the view of one commentator, by echoing the themes of "liberation" and "inculturation," the General Congregation resembled the Synod of Bishops in many respects.[21] Thus, in the wake of GC 32 "liberation" and "inculturation" became major preoccupations among Jesuit theologians writing from a variety of cultural contexts. In Latin America, the work of Juan Luis Segundo, Ignacio Ellacuría, and Jon Sobrino serve as particularly fitting examples of Jesuit theological discourse that both influenced and was influenced by GC 32.

JESUIT THEOLOGICAL DISCOURSE FROM LATIN AMERICA

Juan Luis Segundo (1925–1996)

Although Gustavo Gutiérrez is most often hailed as "the father of liberation theology," the Uruguayan Jesuit Juan Luis Segundo has been called "the most original and the most profound of Latin American theologians."[22] After theological studies in Louvain (where Gutiérrez was his classmate) and in Paris, he returned to Montevideo and worked for ten years at the Peter Faber theological and social center which he founded in 1965. Out of this experience came a five-volume series called, in Spanish, "An Open Theology for an Adult Laity."[23] Alfred T. Hennelly, S. J., once noted with irony that Segundo never taught at a university in Uruguay, even though he had an international reputation and had lectured at some of the world's most prestigious universities.

Segundo's major contribution was in the area of theological method.[24] His project concerned the circular relationship between a theologian's social context and his or her interpretation of doctrines or texts, which he called "the hermeneutical circle." Since "all ideas are always encountered in and within a social context, one cannot know God's self-revelation except as that revelation is embodied in a social context or lived experience."[25] Thus, the truth of Christian faith can never be known in a pure, ahistorical sense, but only as embodied, in particular "ideologies" that give our lives meaning and provide "the symbolic, religious, cultural, political and linguistic instruments through which to express and realize that meaning."[26]

For Segundo, the notion of "ideology" is neutral; it refers simply to the implicit and explicit explanations that give meaning to life. These may include doctrinal concepts, creeds, symbols (e.g., the cross), one's political beliefs or any other culture-bound presuppositions. Because faith is always embodied in "ideologies," our access to revelation can only be located in history, with its particular ideological structures of race, gender, class, language, etc. Failure to take account of the historical character of Christian faith "condemns the Christian faith to irrelevance" and prevents it from having an impact upon the real situation that is lived by people today.

Ignacio Ellacuría (1930–1989)

Though Ignacio Ellacuría's theological contributions were cut short by his brutal assassination (along with his five Jesuit brothers from the University of Central America in San Salvador, their housekeeper and her daughter) by an elite US-trained battalion of the Salvadoran military, his impact on Jesuit theological discourse, particularly among a new generation of Jesuit liberation theologians, has been considerable.[27]

Sent from the Basque region of Spain to El Salvador to the new novitiate the Spanish province was establishing for Central America,

Ellacuría subsequently did undergraduate studies in Ecuador. He taught philosophy at the diocesan seminary in San Salvador for three years before being sent to do theological studies in Innsbruck, where he was influenced significantly by Karl Rahner. Following ordination to the priesthood in 1961 he pursued doctoral studies in philosophy, writing on the thought of the Spanish philosopher Xavier Zubiri. Both Rahner and Zubiri profoundly affected him, but, as Robert Lassalle-Klein observes, Ellacuría moved beyond them both "precisely by grounding his philosophical and theological work in a specific historical reality, that of Latin America."[28] By making historical reality (*la realidad*) the proper object of his work in philosophy and theology, Ellacuría not only made Medellín's "option for the poor" into a "concrete universal" significant for the whole Church, but argued that "the 'crucified people' of the Third World constitute the 'principal ... sign of the times'" that must orient the Church's mission in the world today.[29]

Jon Sobrino (1938–)

Jon Sobrino was born in Barcelona and, like Ellacuría, came to El Salvador as a novice. He studied philosophy and engineering in the US and did his theological studies at the Jesuit theological faculty of Sankt Georgen in Frankfurt. Sobrino has written movingly how, upon his return from his theological studies to El Salvador in 1974, he began to awake "from the sleep of inhumanity."[30] Indebted to the theologies of Karl Rahner and Jürgen Moltmann, Sobrino was henceforth especially influenced by Ignacio Ellacuría, whose work he carries on in many ways.

As is well known, Sobrino was out of the country when his fellow Jesuits and their female co-workers were murdered. Of his many theological works, *Mysterium Liberationis: Fundamental Concepts of Liberation Theology*, a book intended to be edited with Ignacio Ellacuría, poignantly captures the "cost" that the mission of promoting justice as the absolute requirement in the service of faith would demand even of a Jesuit theologian.[31] In the Preface to the abridged paperback edition of this work, Sobrino gives a personal account of his return to El Salvador after the death of his Jesuit colleagues:

> It is only from amidst oppression, carried to its maximal expression in martyrdom, that the theology of liberation can be understood. A true theology of liberation, which would attempt to "take the crucified people down from the cross," in Ignacio Ellacuría's words,

must be prepared to share the fate of that people. This is what Ignacio Ellacuría's martyrdom, better than any theological word, expresses, and that martyrdom is the best hermeneutics for understanding this book.[32]

JESUIT THEOLOGICAL DISCOURSE FROM AFRICA

GC 32 recognized that the service of faith and the promotion of justice lay at the heart of the Jesuit mission of evangelization, the commission of Christ to spread the Gospel (cf. Decree Four, nn. 28, 30, 40). Awareness of the need for "adaptation" and "dialogue" had been a hallmark of Jesuit missionary activity ever since Matteo Ricci and Roberto de Nobili; Decree Four now stated that the "incarnation of the Gospel in the life of the church implies that the way in which Christ is preached and encountered will be different in different countries, different for people with different backgrounds."

Indigenous African Jesuit theologians had been attempting for some time to reflect theologically from within their own cultural circumstances. However, little notice of these efforts was taken until the ecumenical network of Third World theologians (now known as EATWOT) was established in the 1970s.[33] At its 1977 meeting in Accra, EATWOT gave birth to the Ecumenical Association of African Theologians (AOTA) which drew up a declaration that enumerated five characteristics of Black African Theology.[34] In the writings of francophone African Jesuits one glimpses the challenge of inculturating the Gospel in a post-colonial situation.

Engelbert Mveng (1930–1995)

Engelbert Mveng, one of the first promoters of African liberation theology, is considered by many to be a "father of the church" in Africa. This prophetic Jesuit voice at the heart of African theological research was violently assassinated in his home near Yaoundé on 23 April 1995. Throughout his life Mveng fought for the dignity of African people who had suffered so much through slavery and colonization. The multi-talented Mveng – historian, poet, artist, philosopher, and theologian – served as the founding general secretary of AOTA and directed the department of history at the University of Yaoundé for many years.

Mveng used the term "anthropological impoverishment" to describe the consequences of European enslavement and colonization. He recognized that such deprivation was not only material, but moral and spiritual, taking away from Africans "everything that makes up the foundation of their being-in-the-world" and causing them to sink into a kind of poverty that strikes at the very being, essence and dignity of the human person.[35] As this poverty becomes structural, it produces a political and economic vacuum in the State, causing people to fall into the abyss of *"anthropological annihilation* [which is] much more frightening than anthropological impoverishment."[36] No wonder that, for Mveng, "liberation" became the architectonic category for his theology.

Mveng's chief theological works have not yet been translated into English,[37] but his 1988 *Concilium* article, "African Liberation Theology," presents an important historical survey of how liberationist perspectives have operated in both anglophone and francophone Africa.[38]

PETER-HANS KOLVENBACH AND GC 34

As was the case with Vatican II, the implementation GC 32's decrees would take some time. Despite the controversy regarding the expression of Jesuit mission in terms of "the service of faith and the promotion of justice," it was clear that Decree Four had a major impact on Jesuit ministries and theology produced by Jesuits. Jean-Yves Calvez, who has served as editor of the French Jesuit journal *Etudes*, and as a professor of Social Studies at the Institut Catholique in Paris, also served as a general assistant to Pedro Arrupe, and was a delegate to GC 32. His book, *Faith and Justice: The Social Dimension of Evangelization*, not only presents a detailed study of "Decree Four," but also provides background on the events of 1980–83 that are important for understanding the controversies surrounding the implementation of this decree.[39]

Already in 1980, Arrupe, who had been Superior General since 1965, had decided to call a General Congregation and present his resignation for reasons of age. Pope John Paul II, however, was concerned about "certain aspects" of Jesuit life and did not want a General Congregation held until these matters were clarified. He met with Arrupe twice early in 1981, but due to the assassination attempt on John Paul's life that May, and the stroke suffered by Arrupe on 7 August, their discussions were interrupted. The incapacitated Arrupe had wanted to appoint his vicar, the American Jesuit Vincent O'Keefe, to take over his duties. But the pope intervened and appointed Paolo Dezza, S. J., as his personal delegate to handle the preparations for a General Congregation. Thus, GC 33 opened on 1 September 1983. Arrupe's resignation was accepted on 3 September, and Peter-Hans Kolvenbach was elected on 13 September.

When the Society of Jesus gathered for its Thirty-Fourth General Congregation in 1995 it again reaffirmed GC 32's Decree Four on faith and justice, but broadened the understanding of "mission" that lay behind these commitments. Decree Four of GC 34 emphasized dialogue with different cultures and its Decree Five emphasized dialogue with other religions. In terms of theological reflection, attending to the evangelization of culture and the dialogues with cultures and other religions involves the challenge of how to address the phenomena of theological as well as religious pluralism.

THEOLOGICAL ENGAGEMENT WITH THE THEMES OF GC 34

GC 34's Decree Five went on to state that "to be religious today is to be interreligious in the sense that a positive relationship with believers of other faiths is a requirement in a world of religious pluralism" (Decree Five, n. 130). Thus, Jesuits were urged to foster the fourfold dialogue recommended by the Church: the dialogue of life, action, religious experience, and theological exchange.[40] Regarding "the dialogue of theological exchange," Jesuit theologians from North America, Europe, and Asia have embarked upon a serious theological study of inculturation and religious pluralism.

North Atlantic Jesuit theological discourse
The U.S. Hispanic/Latino/a and Native American contexts

In North America Jesuit theologians working with indigenous peoples and immigrants marginal to the dominant culture have attempted to engage these groups in the development of their own local theologies. Two prime examples are the Jesuits engaged in US Hispanic/Latino/a theology and those promoting new understandings of "mission" among Native peoples.

Included among the first group are Alan Figueroa Deck, Director of the Loyola Institute for Spirituality in Orange, CA, Eduardo C. Fernández, Associate Professor of Pastoral Theology at the Jesuit School of Theology at Berkeley, and James Empereur, vicar and liturgist at the San Fernando Cathedral in San Antonio, TX.[41] Jesuit scholars working with Native Americans include the St. Louis University missiologist Carl Starkloff and Ray Bucko, an anthropologist at Creighton University. Bucko and John Hatcher, S. J., Director of the Inculturation Project Office and Sioux Spiritual Center for the Diocese of Rapid City, SD, were major contributors to the recent U.S. Catholic

Bishops' statement, "Native American Catholics at the Millennium," and Starkloff has worked among Native Americans in both the US and Canada for nearly thirty years.

Starkloff recounts that in his ministry with Native peoples he often experienced a "tensive interaction" which he finds characteristic of "our pilgrim condition." From the respectful conversations he has experienced with Amerindian leaders he concludes that such conversations only became true engagements of interfaith dialogue when a fundamental equality among all conversation partners was assumed. Most impressive for him in these intercultural dialogues was the testimony of Native leaders who said that "for the first time they were being listened to as representatives of an authentic religious tradition. Some even resumed their allegiance to the Church, apparently with these conversations as a starting point."[42]

Interreligious dialogue and religious pluralism
Jacques Dupuis (1923–2004)
Peter Phan has observed that "thirty years of living and teaching theology in India cannot fail to leave permanent imprints on anyone's religious outlook and theological vision."[43] This was certainly the case with the Belgian Jesuit Jacques Dupuis, who entered the novitiate in 1941 and after the requisite classical and philosophical studies went to India in 1949 to teach. He began theological studies in 1952 in Kurseong in the foothills of the Himalayas and was ordained in 1954. His doctoral dissertation from the Gregorian University in 1967 was on the religious anthropology of Origen.[44] In 1984 he left India for Rome to teach systematic theology and "other religions" at the Gregorian. The relevance of GC 34's Decree Five on "Our Mission and Interreligious Dialogue" can be seen in Dupuis's 1997 book, *Toward a Christian Theology of Religious Pluralism*,[45] which was subject to a Vatican investigation into its orthodoxy. The Congregation for the Doctrine of the Faith's (CDF) scrutiny of this work was somewhat ironic, however, given that one of Dupuis's major theological achievements was co-editorship (with J. Neuner) of the standard handbook of doctrinal orthodoxy, *The Christian Faith in the Doctrinal Documents of the Catholic Church*, first published in 1973 and updated seven times since.

Despite the "Notification" issued on Dupuis's book by the CDF in 2001, the Jesuit General, Peter-Hans Kolvenbach, immediately issued a public statement in which he positively encouraged Dupuis to continue to pursue his pioneering investigation in this field and to address the increasing pastoral challenges facing "interreligious dialogue" in the Church for its evangelizing mission. Dupuis's approach to dialogue can be described as an "inclusive pluralism" that seeks to hold together "the constitutive and universal character of the Christ-event in the order of human salvation and the salvific significance of religious traditions ... within the one manifold plan of God for humankind."[46]

Dupuis's hermeneutical method in dealing with religious pluralism is based upon an interaction among three realities: text (the data of faith), context (the total socio-cultural/political reality), and interpreter (the theologian and the community). It does not begin in the Bible or in church teaching, but in the actual praxis of dialogue with non-Christian religions in order to discover the sources of pluralism itself. Having discovered in India that to be religious is to be interreligious, and being aware of the reality of Asian poverty, an imperative of interreligious dialogue for Dupuis is that it must go hand-in-hand with actions for the liberation of the Asian poor.[47]

Francis X. Clooney (1950–)

Francis Clooney, a US Jesuit, trained in South Asian languages and civilizations at the University of Chicago, also engages the challenges posed by religious pluralism. Having taught at Boston College for over twenty years, Clooney recently assumed the Parkman Chair of Divinity and Comparative Theology at Harvard Divinity School. With primary expertise in the Sanskrit and Tamil traditions of Hindu India and the developing field of comparative theology, he is considered one of the chief architects of this relatively new discipline.

Clooney describes comparative theology as "distinguished by attentiveness to the dynamics of theological reading and writing in light of traditions other than one's own." He has written on the Jesuit missionary tradition, particularly in India,[48] and is interested in the dynamics of dialogue in a post-colonial world. Examples of his comparative work include *Theology After Vedanta: An Experiment in Comparative Theology*,[49] *Hindu Wisdom for All God's Children*,[50] *Hindu God, Christian God*,[51] and *Hindu Goddesses and the Virgin Mary*.[52] Most recently, Clooney has demonstrated his comparative method in an intriguing textual encounter between himself and the seventeenth-century Italian Jesuit missionary Roberto de Nobili as a way of problematizing contemporary Jesuit intellectual life.[53]

Michael Barnes (1947–)

The British Jesuit Michael Barnes is the Director of the De Nobili Dialogue Centre and the Centre for Christianity and Interreligious

Dialogue at Heythrop College in London. His book, *Theology and the Dialogue of Religions*, originally his doctoral thesis at Cambridge, seeks "a third way" between exclusivism and relativism. Barnes is further concerned to avoid a totalizing theory of "the other" that makes authentic dialogue impossible.[54] Using the work of Michel de Certeau, Emmanuel Lévinas, and Paul Ricoeur he seeks to avoid the theological tendency to "patronize others into a predetermined scheme of things." Without eliminating borders altogether, he wishes to explore where God may be speaking across and between those borders. For Barnes, to answer that question adequately "requires more than merely listening to the one whom Christians call the Word of God; it means attending to those complex processes which allow and sustain human relationships."[55]

In Francis Clooney's estimation, Barnes' approach "clears a new path into a world where we keep moving to different places and where we learn to honor people who are very nearby but still other to us."[56] Although the price of this endeavor may involve the loss of a single and predictable worldview, Clooney endorses Barnes' approach as essential if the Jesuits are to remain a missionary order "distinguished by encounters with people of other faith traditions whose mysteries we never finish with, and who remind us that we too are mysteries unto ourselves."[57]

Jesuit theological discourse from Asia[58]

The two major features of the Asian reality, according to the Sri Lankan Jesuit Aloysius Pieris, are its overwhelming poverty and its multi-faceted religiousness. These are the realities that have shaped the theological agenda of both Pieris and Michael Amaladoss – two of the most prolific Jesuit theologians from Asia.

Aloysius Pieris (1934–)

Aloysius Pieris is the founder and director of the Tulana Research Centre in Kelaniya, Sri Lanka. After his novitiate and philosophical studies in India, he went on to study Pali and Sanskrit and did theological studies in Naples during the time of Vatican II. Pieris was the first Christian in Sri Lanka to receive a doctorate in Buddhism. Although slated to teach at the Gregorian University in Rome, after discernment with his provincial he returned to Sri Lanka to begin working with two themes that have influenced his theology ever since: the path of *interior liberation* from greed, influenced by the Buddhist mystical tradition and experience, and the path of *social liberation* from poverty. For

Pieris, these are "the two poles of a tension that must sustain the dynamism of my apostolic life. Later they became the theme of the Asian theology I discovered within the Asian reality."[59]

Among Pieris' best-known works are *An Asian Theology of Liberation* (1988), *Fire and Water: Basic Issues in Asian Buddhism and Christianity* (1996), and *Prophetic Humour in Buddhism and Christianity: Doing Inter-religious Studies in the Reverential Mode* (2005).

Philip Endean has commented that Pieris' re-reading of the Ignatian spiritual tradition in the light of Christian–Buddhist dialogue advocates not a synthesis or syncretist spirituality, but a "symbiosis," which "enables Christians to grow within their own tradition, sharpening their awareness of inauthenticities in what they have previously taken for granted."[60]

Michael Amaladoss (1936–)

Michael Amaladoss is emeritus professor of systematic theology at Vidyajyoti College of Theology (Delhi) and Director of the Institute for Dialogue with Cultures and Religions, Chennai, India. In many ways the account of his life, "My Pilgrimage in Mission," is a microcosm of the story of Jesuit theological discourse since Vatican II.[61] Amaladoss relates how he grew up in an Indian Christian family in South India and joined the Jesuits in 1953. The "seeds of inculturation" were planted during his novitiate with Fr. Ignatius Hirudayam, an expert in Indian culture whom he still regards as his guru. In tandem with his Jesuit formational studies, he studied South Indian classical music, art, and culture. After his philosophical studies in Kurseong, during which Vatican II occurred, he made a pilgrimage to the sacred places of Hinduism and Buddhism in North India. His first published articles in English compared Gandhian and Ignatian spirituality.

Amaladoss wrote a doctoral dissertation at the Institut Catholique in Paris on the variable and invariable elements in sacramental rites, using interdisciplinary methods that became useful later for his contextual theologizing. He returned to India to teach and founded a dialogue group in collaboration with the Benedictine Bede Griffiths. From 1973 to 1983 he was at Vidyajyoti College of Theology where he was the colleague of his former teacher, Jacques Dupuis. In 1983 he became a counselor to Peter-Hans Kolvenbach with special responsibility for Jesuit missions, a position he held until 1995 and which pushed him "accidentally" into the field of missiology. Though he has held several appointments to pontifical councils and international ecumenical commissions, and helped to prepare GC 34's discussions on mission, he prefers to be known not as a missiologist, but as "an Indian theologian who is also interested in mission and dialogue, inculturation and liberation."[62]

The author of twenty-four books and hundreds of articles, Amaladoss believes that the major question raised at Vatican II – how the Catholic Church which believes it possesses the fullness of truth can tolerate others who are seen as lacking in that fullness – was "quietly side-stepped."[63] Thus, the constant aim of his own theology has been to address this topic head-on.[64] He rejects the traditional paradigms of exclusivism, inclusivism, and pluralism offered by contemporary theologians from the West, arguing that only God can be inclusive of all peoples. For Amaladoss, "each religion makes space for the others within its own view of the world."[65] In the Institute of Dialogue with Cultures and Religions, he seeks to find out the real causes of interreligious violence and to explore ways of making peace. In the process, he has found that his own self-awareness has changed: "Hinduism is no longer an 'other' religion for me. I see it as the religion of my ancestors. It is also part of my inheritance. I become a Hindu-Christian. Interreligious dialogue then becomes intrapersonal. I must integrate my multiple roots and render them transformative."[66]

Finally, two other major decrees from GC 34 bear mention here. Decree Thirteen, "Cooperation with Laity in Mission," and Decree Fourteen, "Jesuits and the Situation of Women in Church and Civil Society," are themes whose impact upon Jesuit theological discourse is still in process.

JESUIT–LAY PARTNERSHIP

Peter-Hans Kolvenbach recently admitted to a congress held at Creighton University that the initial reasons the Jesuits fostered cooperation with the laity in their apostolic works had to do with their own declining membership.[67] However, GC 34 represented "a new moment" that recognized the "reciprocity of personal presence" between laity and Jesuits as essential to Jesuit identity and ministry. Decree Thirteen mandated Jesuits to "shift the focus of our attention from the exercise of our own direct ministry to the strengthening of the laity in their mission" and acknowledged that Jesuits were not only "men for others," but also "men with others": "This basic characteristic of our way of proceeding calls for an attitude and readiness to cooperate, to listen and to learn from others, to share our spiritual and apostolic inheritance. To be 'men with others' is a central aspect of our charism and deepens our identity."[68]

The implications of Decree Thirteen for Jesuit theological discourse can best be seen in the inclusion of laity as students in Jesuit theological schools, in the hiring of lay theology professors in Jesuit theologates and university theology departments, and in the increasing presence of women as theologians, campus ministers, and spiritual directors in these institutions. In fact, in the United States, lay theology and religious studies professors currently far outnumber Jesuits in these departments at all twenty-eight Jesuit colleges and universities.

PARTNERSHIP WITH WOMEN

GC 34's Decree Fourteen, "Jesuits and the Situation of Women in Church and Civil Society," declared that solidarity with women was integral to Jesuit mission. In accepting the "challenge and our responsibility for doing what we can as men and as a male religious order" (n. 7), the Society of Jesus, as a first step, acknowledged that its members "have been part of a civil and ecclesial tradition that has offended against women." In expressing their need for the grace of conversion they asked forgiveness for a clericalism "which has reinforced male domination with an ostensibly divine sanction" (Decree Fourteen, n. 9), and committed themselves to a posture of "listening" to women's experiences.

In terms of theological discourse, it is rare today to find books or course syllabi used by Jesuit theology professors that do not include the work of women authors. Much of the involvement of women in Jesuit theological discourse has been in connection with the Ignatian charism, specifically the Spiritual Exercises of St. Ignatius. For example, Katherine Dyckman, Mary Garvin, and Elizabeth Liebert have authored *The Spiritual Exercises Reclaimed: Uncovering Liberating Possibilities for Women*,[69] and articles in the Jesuit journal *The Way* and its supplements have featured women authors on topics dealing with spirituality. Workshops on "spiritual accompaniment" for women making or guiding the Spiritual Exercises are good illustrations of how Ignatian spirituality has both influenced and been influenced by women.[70]

Yet, to my knowledge, there are only a few examples of theological "partnership" between Jesuit theologians and women theologians. Although Jesuit professors have team-taught courses with women colleagues, not many have jointly authored books with women outside of the field of Ignatian spirituality. One is hard pressed to find Jesuit theologians who explicitly self-identify as feminists, although many cite the work of feminist theologians in their writings and have directed the doctoral dissertations of women theologians.[71]

Some Jesuits are unequivocal in affirming the contributions of women to theology. Walter Burghardt, a patristic scholar and editor of *Theological Studies* from 1967 to 1990, notes with approval the number of women theologians who have contributed to this Jesuit journal.[72] Burghardt writes of his personal attraction to "reformist feminist theology," and devotes a chapter to women in the Church in his memoir.[73] Roger Haight, in a recent autobiographical reflection, includes "a feminist perspective and set of values" as one of three potential gifts that American Catholicism can offer to the universal Church.[74] An entire section of Aloysius Pieris' book, *Fire and Water: Basic Issues in Asian Buddhism and Christianity*, is devoted to the subject of women and religion, in which he discusses in personal terms several feminist issues that are significant for both Christianity and Buddhism.[75] Likewise, Michael Amaladoss devotes a chapter of his book, *Life in Freedom: Liberation Theologies from Asia*, to "The Awakening of Women in Asia."[76]

CONCLUSION

When considering the worldwide theological enterprise carried on by members of the Society of Jesus and their lay partners since Vatican II, I think of the words of Georg Evers who, in acknowledging the richness of the many new forms of contextual and inculturated theologies that have developed, also saw that this very variety poses both challenges and opportunities.[77] Whether concerning the situation of women, the crucified peoples of the Third World, or the twin realities of poverty and multi-faceted religiousness in Asia, the Jesuit theologian's "way of proceeding" must be one of both humble "listening and discernment," and courageous articulation of a Christian "faith that does justice."

Notes

1   Avery Dulles, "Jesuits and Theology: Yesterday and Today," *Theological Studies* 52 (1991), 524–38.
2   Ibid., 524.
3   Ibid.
4   Although, in Dulles' estimation, the Jesuits at Vatican II had "a significant, though not a preeminent role." See ibid., 535.

5 For further background on the Jesuits at Vatican II, see Giacomo Martina, S.J., "The Historical Context in Which the Idea of a New Ecumenical Council Was Born," in René Latourelle, S.J., ed., *Vatican II: Assessment and Perspective Twenty-five Years After (1962–1987)* (New York: Paulist Press, 1988), 1: 1–73 and Karl Heinz Neufeld, S.J., "In the Service of the Council: Bishops and Theologians at the Second Vatican Council," 74–105 in the same volume. Jared Wicks, S.J. covers the work of the theologians at Vatican II in "I teologi al Vaticano II. Momenti e modalità del loro contributo al Concilio," *Humanitas* (Brescia) 59 (2004/5), 1012–38.

6 William Rehg, S.J. names Diego Laínez, Alonso Salmerón, and Claude Jay as Jesuit experts at Trent. See "Epilogue: Do Jesuit Scholarly Endeavors Cohere?," in F.X. Clooney, S.J., ed., *Jesuit Postmodern: Scholarship, Vocation, and Identity in the 21st Century* (Lanham, MD: Rowman and Littlefield, 2006), 196.

7 John Baptist Franzelin, S.J. and Klemens Schrader, S.J. helped to draft the proposed constitutions on Catholic faith and on the Church. Joseph Kleutgen, S.J. was instrumental in drafting the definition of papal infallibility. See Dulles, "Jesuits and Theology," 530.

8 Ronald E. Modras, *Ignatian Humanism: A Dynamic Spirituality for the 21st Century* (Chicago: Loyola Press, 2004), 269.

9 Ibid.

10 Ibid.

11 In addition to Dulles, "Jesuits and Theology," 535, on Rahner, see Philip Endean, *Karl Rahner and Ignatian Spirituality* (Oxford: Oxford University Press, 2001) and Harvey Egan, *Karl Rahner: Mystic of Everyday Life* (New York: Crossroad, 1998); on Lonergan, see Robert M. Doran, "Ignatian Themes in the Thought of Bernard Lonergan," *Toronto Journal of Theology* 22/1 (2006), 39–54.

12 See Edward T. Oakes, S.J. and David Moss, eds., *The Cambridge Companion to Hans Urs von Balthasar* (Cambridge: Cambridge University Press, 2004) and Declan Marmion and Mary E. Hines, eds., *The Cambridge Companion to Karl Rahner* (Cambridge: Cambridge University Press, 2005).

13 As cited in Michael Czerny, S.J. and Paolo Foglizzo, S.J., "The Social Apostolate in the Twentieth Century," *Yearbook of the Society of Jesus* (Rome: Jesuit Curìa, 2000).

14 See John Haughey, "Foreword," in John Haughey, ed., *The Faith That Does Justice: Examining the Christian Sources for Social Change* (New York: Paulist Press, 1977), 3.

15 For example, Vatican II's *Gaudium et Spes* (1965); Paul VI's encyclical *Populorum Progressio* (1967); the documents of the Second General Assembly of the Latin American Bishops' Conference (CELAM) held in Medellín (1968); and Paul VI's Apostolic Letter, *Octogesima Adveniens* (1971).

16 "Justice in the World," in David J. O'Brien and Thomas A. Shannon, eds., *Catholic Social Thought: The Documentary Heritage* (Maryknoll, NY: Orbis, 1992), 289.

17 Pedro Arrupe, *Recollections and Reflections of Pedro Arrupe, S.J.,* trans. Yolanda T. De Mola, S.C., with an introduction by Vincent O'Keefe, S.J. (Wilmington, DE: Michael Glazier, 1986), 165. Cited in Modras, *Ignatian Humanism,* 270.

18 For a historical overview of the Jesuits in Latin America, see Jeffrey Klaiber, S.J., "The Jesuits in Latin America: Legacy and Current Emphases," *International Bulletin of Missionary Research* 28 (April 2004), 63–67.

19 This lecture, which has come to be titled "Men for Others," can be found (in more inclusive language) in Kevin Burke, S.J., ed., *Pedro Arrupe: Essential Writings* (Maryknoll, NY: Orbis, 2004), 171–87.

20 Modras, *Ignatian Humanism,* 279.

21 Jean-Yves Calvez, "General Congregations XXXI (1965–1966) and XXXII (1974–75), Their Different Times and Problems: Essential Historical Aspects," in *Conferences on the Chief Decrees of the Jesuit General Congregation XXXII. A Symposium by Some of Its Members* (St. Louis: Institute of Jesuit Resources, 1976), 8–9.

22 Alfred T. Hennelly, S.J., "Introduction," in Juan Luis Segundo, *Signs of the Times: Theological Reflections* (Maryknoll, NY: Orbis, 1993), 2. Some have argued that Segundo is actually the earliest Latin American liberation theologian, since his first book, published in 1962, was entitled *Función de la Iglesia en la realidad rioplatense.* See Roberto S. Goizueta, "Juan Luis Segundo," in *A New Handbook of Christian Theologians* (Nashville: Abingdon Press, 1996), 419–26.

23 Juan Luis Segundo, *A Theology for Artisans of a New Humanity,* 5 vols. (Maryknoll, NY: Orbis, 1973–74).

24 See, for example, *The Liberation of Theology* (Maryknoll, NY: Orbis, 1976).

25 Goizueta, "Juan Luis Segundo," 420.

26 Ibid.

27 See Kevin Burke, S.J., *The Ground Beneath the Cross: The Theology of Ignacio Ellacuría* (Washington, DC: Georgetown University Press, 2000); Kevin Burke and Robert Lassalle-Klein, eds., *Love That Produces Hope: The Thought of Ignacio Ellacuría* (Collegeville, MN: Liturgical Press, 2006). Significant Jesuit contributions in the latter volume include: Jon Sobrino, Martin Maier, Kevin Burke, and Roger Haight. J. Matthew Ashley has examined the influence of Ignatian spirituality on Ellacuría's theology: "Contemplation in the Action of Justice: Ignacio Ellacuría and Ignatian Spirituality," in Burke and Lassalle-Klein, *Love That Produces Hope,* 144–65 and "Ignacio Ellacuría and the Spiritual Exercises of St. Ignatius Loyola," *Theological Studies* 61 (2000), 16–39.

28 Robert Lassalle-Klein, "Introduction," in Burke and Lassalle-Klein, *Love That Produces Hope,* xxv.

29 Ignacio Ellacuría, "Discernir el signo de los tiempos," *Diakonia* 17 (1981), 58–59, as cited by Lassalle-Klein in *Love That Produces Hope,* xxv.

30 Jon Sobrino, "Awakening from the Sleep of Inhumanity," in *The Principle of Mercy: Taking the Crucified People from the Cross*

(Maryknoll, NY: Orbis, 1994), 1–11. This essay originally appeared in *The Christian Century*'s "How My Mind Has Changed" series in 1992.

31 "Any effort to promote justice will cost us something. Our cheerful readiness to pay the price will make our preaching of the gospel more meaningful and its acceptance easier." Decree Four, n. 46. The title of Teresa Whitfield's book, *Paying the Price: Ignacio Ellacuría and the Murdered Jesuits of El Salvador* (Philadelphia: Temple University Press, 1994), underscores this connection. Whitfield also sheds light on the internal controversies within the Central American province surrounding Ellacuría's ideas that preceded and followed GC 32.

32 Jon Sobrino, "Preface," in Jon Sobrino, S. J. and Ignacio Ellacuría, S. J., eds., *Systematic Theology: Perspectives from Liberation Theology. Readings from Mysterium Liberationis* (Maryknoll, NY: Orbis, 2000), viii.

33 The Ecumenical Association of Third World Theologians (EATWOT), which brings together theologians from Latin America, Africa, and Asia, was formed in 1976. For a concise history, see Leonardo and Clovodis Boff, *Introducing Liberation Theology* (Maryknoll, NY: Orbis, 1987).

34 The Accra Congress defined Black African theology as (1) a theology of the people, (2) contextual, (3) inculturated, (4) ecumenical, and (5) struggling for liberation. See Engelbert Mveng, "African Liberation Theology," in Leonardo Boff and Virgilio Elizondo, eds., *Convergences and Differences* (Edinburgh: Clark, 1988), 17–19.

35 Engelbert Mveng, "Impoverishment and Liberation: A Theological Approach for Africa and the Third World," in Rosino Gibellini, ed., *Paths of African Theology* (London: SCM Press, 1994), 156.

36 B. Awazi-Mbabmi-Kungua, "Les métamorphoses de la théologie négro-africaine de la libération: Quatre théologiens camerounais: Mveng, Eboussi-Boulaga, Hebga et Ela," *Nouvelle Revue Théologique* 124 (2002), 239.

37 For example, see Englebert Mveng, S. J., *L'Afrique dans l'Eglise: Paroles d'un croyant* (Paris: Editions L'Harmattan, 1985); *Spiritualité et libération en Afrique* (Paris: Editions L'Harmattan, 1987); and *Théologie, libération et cultures africaines: Dialogue sur l'anthropologie négro-africaine* (Yaoundé: C. L. E.; Paris: Présence africaine, 1996).

38 Mveng, "African Liberation Theology," 17–34. The Cameroonian former Jesuit Fabien Eboussi-Boulaga is better known in the English-speaking world, thanks to his book, *Christianity Without Fetishes: An African Critique and Recapture of Christianity* (Hamburg: LIT Verlag, 2002).

39 Jean-Yves Calvez, *Faith and Justice: The Social Dimension of Evangelization*, trans. John E. Blewett, S. J. (St. Louis: Institute of Jesuit Sources, 1991).

40 See Decree 5, n. 131 and the statement of the Pontifical Council for Interreligious Dialogue and the Congregation for the Evangelization of Peoples, "Dialogue and Proclamation: Reflections and Orientations on

Interreligious Dialogue and the Proclamation of the Gospel of Jesus Christ" (1991), n. 42.

41 Fernandez is the author of *La Cosecha: Harvesting Contemporary United States Hispanic Theology (1972–1998)* (Collegeville, MN: Liturgical Press, 2000) and co-author with James Empereur of *La Vida Sacra: Contemporary Hispanic Sacramental Theology* (Lanham, MD: Rowman and Littlefield, 2006).

42 Carl Starkloff, S. J., "After September 11, 2001: Whither Mission?," *In All Things* (Fall/Winter 2001), 4–5. Additional writings by Starkloff on Native Americans include *Common Testimony: Ethnology and Theology in the Customs of Josef Lafitau* (St. Louis: Institute of Jesuit Sources, 2002) and *A Theology of the In-Between: The Value of Syncretic Process* (Milwaukee: Marquette University Press, 2002).

43 Peter Phan, "Jacques Dupuis and Asian Theologies of Religious Pluralism," in Daniel Kendall and Gerald O'Collins, eds., *In Many and Diverse Ways: In Honor of Jacques Dupuis* (Maryknoll, NY: Orbis, 2003), 72.

44 *L'esprit de l'homme – Etude sur l'anthropologie religieuse d'Origène* (Bruges: Desclée de Brouwer, 1967).

45 Jacques Dupuis, S. J., *Toward a Christian Theology of Religious Pluralism* (Maryknoll, NY: Orbis, 1997).

46 Jacques Dupuis, S. J., cited in Terence Merrigan, "Jacques Dupuis and the Redefinition of Inclusivism," in Kendall and O'Collins, eds., *In Many and Diverse Ways*, 60. Unfortunately, the Jesuit Roger Haight, whose book *Jesus Symbol of God* also takes up the challenges of religious pluralism and inculturation of Christianity in a post-modern world, received a "Notification" from the Vatican that so far has not been rescinded.

47 Phan, "Jacques Dupuis," 73.

48 See, for example, *Preaching Wisdom to the Wise: Three Treatises by Roberto de Nobili, S. J., Missionary and Scholar in 17th Century India* (St. Louis: Institute of Jesuit Sources, 2000).

49 (Albany: SUNY Press, 1993).

50 (Maryknoll, NY: Orbis, 1998).

51 (New York: Oxford University Press, 2001).

52 (New York: Oxford University Press, 2005).

53 Francis X. Clooney, "Francis Xavier, and the World/s We (Don't Quite) Share," in Clooney, *Jesuit Postmodern*, 157–80.

54 Michael Barnes, S. J., *Theology and the Dialogue of Religions* (Cambridge: Cambridge University Press, 2002). Barnes' other works in the theology of religions include *Christian Identity and Religions in Conversation* (Nashville, TN: Abingdon Press, 1989); *God East and West* (London: SPCK, 1991); *Walking the City* (Delhi: ISPCK, 1999); and *Traces of the Other* (Chennai: Satya Nilayam, 2000).

55 Barnes, *Theology and the Dialogue of Religions*, x.

56 Clooney, "Francis Xavier," 179.

57 Ibid.

58 For a more expansive discussion of Jesuit theological discourse in Asia, see Georg Evers, "My Experiences with Asian Theology," in Leonard Fernando, S. J., ed., *Seeking New Horizons: Festschrift in Honour of*

Dr. M. Amaladoss, S.J. (Delhi: Vidyajyoti Education and Welfare Society, 2002), 107–22.

59 "Self Portrait: Religiousness and Poverty – The Collective Effort of Asian Theology. Interview with Aloysius Pieris, S. J., Sri Lanka by Georg Evers," *Yearbook of Contextual Theologies, 2001* (Frankfurt: IKO, 2001), 19.

60 Philip Endean, "The Same Spirit Is in Everything': Towards a Contemporary Theological Reading of Ignatius' Rules for Thinking with the Church," in Robert Crusz, Marshal Fernando, and Sanga Tilakaratne, eds., *Encounters with the Word: Essays to Honour Aloysius Pieris, S.J.* (Colombo, Sri Lanka: Ecumenical Institute for Study and Dialogue, 2004), 509.

61 Michael Amaladoss, S.J., "My Pilgrimage in Mission," *International Bulletin of Missionary Research* 31 (2007), 21–24.

62 Ibid., 24.

63 Michael Amaladoss, *Making Harmony: Living in a Pluralist World* (Delhi: Indian Society for Promoting Christian Knowledge, 2003).

64 The most recent example is his *The Asian Jesus* (Maryknoll, NY: Orbis, 2006).

65 Amaladoss, *Making Harmony*, 124.

66 Amaladoss, "My Pilgrimage in Mission," 24.

67 Peter-Hans Kolvenbach, S.J., "Cooperating with Each Other in Mission," Address of 7 October 2004 at Creighton University.

68 GC 34, Decree 13, n. 4.

69 (New York: Paulist Press, 2001).

70 For example, John English, S.J., Kuruvala Zachariah, and Lois Zachariah, "Twenty-four Spiritual Exercises for the New Story of Universal Communion," *Progressio*, Supplement 57 (2002).

71 On my own experiences as a theologian working in two Jesuit institutions in the USA, see my *Women Shaping Theology* (New York: Paulist Press, 2006). Boston College's Church in the 21st Century Center has recently embarked upon a publication series that involves collaboration of Jesuits with their lay colleagues on several theological issues.

72 Walter J. Burghardt, *Long Have I Loved You: A Theologian Reflects on His Church* (Maryknoll, NY: Orbis, 2000), 315–16. Burghardt's successors, Robert J. Daly, Michael A. Fahey, and David G. Schultenover, have continued this practice.

73 Ibid., 63–64; 289–327.

74 Roger Haight, "The American Jesuit Theologian," in Clooney, *Jesuit Postmodern*, 98. Haight recognized earlier than most Jesuits that "the women's issue" was not exclusively theirs at all. See his "Women in the Church: A Theological Reflection," *Toronto Journal of Theology* 2 (1986), 105–17.

75 Aloysius Pieris, *Fire and Water: Basic Issues in Asian Buddhism and Christianity* (Maryknoll, NY: Orbis, 1996).

76 Michael Amaladoss, S. J., *Life in Freedom: Liberation Theologies from Asia* (Maryknoll, NY: Orbis, 1997), 32–43.

77 Evers, "My Experiences," 122.

18 Jesuits today

THOMAS WORCESTER

In the 1960s the number of Jesuits in the world reached a peak at around 36,000; four decades later that number stood at just under 20,000. Most of the numeric decline has occurred in western Europe and in North America. In some other parts of the world, numbers have risen, and in the post-colonial era the average age of Jesuits in certain places is startlingly young when compared with that in France or Italy or the USA. India now is home to the largest group of Jesuits, a distinction that belonged for a while to the USA, and before that to various European countries. The Society of Jesus has always been international in theory and practice: a Jesuit without a passport hardly seems worthy of the company founded by Ignatius of Loyola. But how that international character is lived out has changed a great deal since 1540. And how Jesuits work with or alongside others has changed as well. Collaboration with a wide variety of people, women and men, only a few of them clerics or members of religious orders, has become the norm for Jesuit activities, in ways unimagined even a half-century ago. But adaptation to circumstances and to particular cultures in particular times and places – so central to the Jesuit way of proceeding in the sixteenth to eighteenth centuries – remains at the heart of how the Society of Jesus does whatever it does. Ignatius of Loyola wrote thousands of letters, many sent by sailing ship to Jesuits in far-flung places around the globe.[1] Today, in a culture sustained by jet travel and instantaneous electronic communication, Jesuits make abundant use of the most advanced transportation and communication technology. For example, Irish Jesuits sponsor Sacred Space, an online, multilingual service inviting computer users to ten minutes of prayer.[2]

Yet adaptation to new technologies may be a relatively easy form of accommodation to new circumstances. More difficult for the Society of Jesus was adaptation to a rapidly changing Church and religious culture after Vatican II. Some Jesuits left religious life because things were changing too fast and too much, others left because things did not

Figure 18.1. Lawrence Daka, S. J., International Visiting Scholar at the College of the Holy Cross, Massachusetts, 2006. Photo by John Buckingham.

change enough. In leaving to marry or for other reasons, many men retained strong loyalty to the Society. While some Jesuits feared that four hundred years of fidelity to the heritage of St. Ignatius had been thrown overboard, others rejoiced in the leadership of Fr. Pedro Arrupe, Superior General from 1965 to 1983. Arrupe was a man of passion, a prophet calling Jesuits to live out their vocations to intellectual, academic, and pastoral work in ways that helped to serve the poor. The Thirty-third General Congregation that elected Peter Hans Kolvenbach as Arrupe's successor issued a decree entitled

"Companions of Jesus Sent into Today's World," and it affirmed that "in all our ministries, our work will only be credible if the practice of justice is evident in our personal lives, our communities and our institutions."[3] Kolvenbach continued Arrupe's work of adaptation to the post-Vatican II and post-colonial contexts.[4]

The general congregations meet in Rome, and Rome remains Jesuit headquarters in a variety of ways, including as the residence of the Superior General and his staff, located on the Borgo Santo Spirito near St. Peter's Square. Rome is also home not only to the Pontifical Gregorian University but also to other international Jesuit educational institutions, such as the Pontifical Biblical Institute. The Vatican radio station has been staffed by Jesuits since its founding, and Jesuits from many countries play a central role in providing its multi-lingual broadcasts.[5] The Vatican Observatory, with astronomical facilities at Castel Gandolfo, the pope's summer residence south of Rome, and at Tucson, Arizona, in the United States, is also a Jesuit work.

In many parts of the world, Jesuit schools, colleges, and universities that up until the 1960s admitted only male students now admit students of both genders; in some cases, women constitute the majority of the student body. Teaching and administrative staffs have also been diversified, in gender and in other ways as well. In the United States, boards of trustees now govern Jesuit educational institutions formerly under the jurisdiction of Jesuit provincial superiors; the membership of these boards includes some Jesuits, but it is mostly made up of alumni and alumnae of each institution. Especially at the level of higher education, institutional autonomy and the academic freedom of faculty members are guaranteed. Of twenty-eight Jesuit colleges and universities in the United States, three are most frequently ranked as leading institutions of higher education: Boston College, the College of the Holy Cross, and Georgetown University. All twenty-eight embrace and foster Jesuit traditions and values. These include a commitment to academic excellence, to individual attention to the development of each student's potential, to special attention to Ignatian spirituality, and to the promotion of justice for the poor and the oppressed.[6]

Many of these institutions are especially active in promoting the arts, including theater, dance, music, as well as scholarship on the history of art. Museums with rapidly growing permanent collections as well as a full schedule of temporary exhibitions are also a prominent feature of many Jesuit colleges and universities in the United States. Boston College's McMullen Museum has drawn a great deal of praise for its innovative shows, including one focused on a long-lost

Caravaggio painting that had been discovered in a Jesuit dining room in Ireland.[7] Marquette University's Haggerty Museum, in Milwaukee, is another impressive example of priority given to the arts.[8] The performing arts prosper at Jesuit educational institutions: performances abound, and creation of new work complements innovative production of older works.

The post-Vatican II departure from Jesuit life of large numbers of men often left a void, but many of those men continued to support the work of the Society of Jesus, in various ways. Some former Jesuits work in Jesuit colleges, universities, retreat houses, parishes, and other institutions. Some may give financial support to Jesuit endeavors. Some bring Jesuit insights and traditions into places where few Jesuits normally go. One example of that is Chris Lowney's application of Jesuit principles and practices to the business world.[9] Many former Jesuits retain ties of friendship and gratitude from their years as Jesuits.[10]

A decline in the overall number of Jesuits may lead one to falsely presume a lack of spiritual or intellectual vitality. If Jesuit missionaries were once exclusively white Europeans who were sent to the rest of the world, many young Jesuits today from Asia, Africa, and Latin America travel to London, Paris, Rome, Boston, or Berkeley, to study theology prior to ordination, or to do graduate work in any number of disciplines. These young Jesuits may also engage in a variety of pastoral and other work while away from their home countries; their presence and their labors help to enrich and enliven Jesuit life and ministry, and to make it more authentically international than ever before.

One example is Lawrence Daka, a Jesuit from Zimbabwe. In Autumn term 2006, he offered a course on African philosophy at the College of the Holy Cross, an undergraduate, Jesuit, liberal arts college in Massachusetts. Holy Cross frequently hosts international Jesuit fellows, from countries as diverse as Indonesia, Australia, and Ireland. When he came to Holy Cross, Fr. Daka had completed a Ph.D. in philosophy at Boston College. Since 2007, he has taught philosophy to Jesuit students at Arrupe College in Harare, Zimbabwe.[11]

In various places in Africa what had been the mission of one or another group of European Jesuits is now an autonomous Jesuit province made up mostly of African Jesuits. Zimbabwe is one example; Zambia is another.[12] At the same time, international collaboration among Jesuits supports and staffs organizations such as the Jesuit

Refugee Service. Founded by Fr. Arrupe in 1980, and sponsored by the entire Society of Jesus, the JRS has been very active in parts of Asia (and elsewhere) providing relief and care, both physical and spiritual, to refugees.[13]

Indonesia and India are two Asian countries where Jesuit vocations have been numerous in recent decades, even though Catholics are but a small minority in each country. In Indonesia, Jesuit works include higher education; the Universitas Sanata Dharma, in Yogyakarta, offers courses and degrees in a wide variety of fields.[14] There are more than 3,000 Jesuits in India, and their influence is not confined to the subcontinent. In recent decades, Jesuits in India have done much to promote the dignity of persons considered "untouchable" or of low caste. Indian Jesuits are also writers. The works of Anthony de Mello, on Christian prayer from an Asian perspective, went through many editions in the late twentieth century, and reached a worldwide readership.[15] Saju George is another example of an Indian Jesuit; he is a professional dancer. He travels around the world performing solo a version of classical Indian dance; he draws on Hindu traditions, as he gives a bodily, artistic expression to the Hebrew psalms and to the Christian Scriptures.[16]

In Montreal, Saju George has danced before the high altar at the Church of the Gesù, a church staffed by French Canadian Jesuits since the nineteenth century.[17] In recent years, the Jesuits of French Canada have also especially turned their attention southward, to Haiti. Indeed, the French Canadian Jesuit province has become, in name and practice, the province of French Canada and Haiti. The province's Centre Justice et Foi publishes *Relations*, a magazine devoted to questions of social justice in a post-modern world. The Jesuit province of Upper Canada (English-language Canada) has also turned to the Caribbean, with a growing commitment to Jamaica.[18]

The Canadian *Relations* is but one example of a periodical published under Jesuit auspices. Scholarly journals as well as periodicals aimed at a more popular level are a principal means by which Jesuits communicate and engage in dialogue with both Catholic audiences and others. Among the more influential Jesuit periodicals, with their places of publication, are *America* (US), *Archives de Philosophie* (France), *Archivum Historicum Societatis Iesu* (Italy and US), *Christus* (France), *Civiltà Cattolica* (Italy), *Estudios Eclesiásticos* (Spain), *Etudes* (France), *Gregorianum* (Italy), *Hekima Journal* (Kenya), *Heythrop Journal* (Great Britain), *Miscelánea Comillas* (Spain), *Orientierung* (Switzerland), *Recherches de Science Religieuse* (France),

Stimmen der Zeit (Germany), *Studies: An Irish Quarterly Review* (Ireland), *Studies in the Spirituality of Jesuits* (US), *Theological Studies* (US), *Vidyajyoti Journal of Theological Studies* (India), *The Way* (Great Britain), *Zeitschrift für Katholische Theologie* (Austria).

Jesuit scholarly work takes place not only in educational institutions and through sponsorship of periodicals. As individuals, and as members of research teams, Jesuits continue a remarkable scholarly production. In France, for example, the many-volumed *Dictionnaire de spiritualité* was edited by Jesuits, from its inception in the 1930s to its completion in the 1990s. Today, the *Institut des Sources Chrétiennes* is a stellar example of a Jesuit research institute. Since the 1940s it has produced critical editions (and French translations) of patristic and early Christian texts, published in affordable volumes. There are now more than 500 tomes in this series and it continues to grow.[19]

Suspicion that Jesuit concern for justice may be at odds with – or a diversion from – Jesuit intellectual work may be dispelled by examination of actual Jesuit practices around the world. The Universidad Alberto Hurtado is a Jesuit university in Santiago, Chile, founded in 1997. Hurtado (1901–52) was a Chilean Jesuit who worked as a chaplain to university students and, especially in the last decade or so of his life, as a tireless voice for poor young people. Promoting the study and practice of Catholic social teaching, he founded a labor union as well as residences for the poor. He was canonized as a saint in 2005, and, as a role model for a university, he inspires integration of intellectual life and work for justice.[20] As Mary Ann Hinsdale pointed out in her essay, such integration can be costly. The 1989 assassination in El Salvador, of six Jesuit professors and their housekeeper and her daughter, was carried out by soldiers hired to silence those who dared to speak, and write and publish, in defense of the oppressed.[21] But martyrdom has not led to silence. In South and North America, and around the world, Jesuit educational institutions continue to help students to learn about the causes of injustice, and to think critically about solutions to global inequities.

In the past hundred years or so, many Jesuits have been imprisoned and/or killed by authoritarian regimes of the far right and the far left. In anticlerical Mexico, and in Spain at the time of the Civil War (1936–39), Jesuits were persecuted and killed. Some Jesuits paid with their lives for their opposition to Nazi policies. Some survived concentration camps and wrote about their experiences.[22] Walter Ciszek, a US Jesuit, spent many years in Soviet prisons, but was eventually released.[23] Even democratic governments have imprisoned Jesuits for their vigorous witness to a gospel of peace and in opposition to war. In the United States, Daniel Berrigan offers the best-known example of such a Jesuit.[24]

Work for justice in this world has not meant a decline in what might be considered more spiritual ministries. The Spiritual Exercises of St. Ignatius remain central to the mission and identity of Jesuits, as individuals and as members of a worldwide society committed to ministry as companions of Jesus. Jesuits do not keep the Spiritual Exercises to themselves; they "give" them to others, and they help others, in turn, to become spiritual directors. Retreat houses that were once staffed exclusively by Jesuits – houses in which the Exercises are given in eight-day, thirty-day, and other forms – now often are models of collaboration between Jesuits and other professional ministers, especially women, both women religious and, increasingly, other women. Those who come to Jesuit retreat houses to experience the Spiritual Exercises are more diverse than in the past. With their numbers down in many parts of the world, priests and religious may be less numerous among retreatants, but a variety of other people, not necessarily Catholic, are more and more numerous. Margaret Silf, a prolific British author, has written several books on Ignatian spirituality, and offers a fascinating example of how what may have seemed the proprietary domain of Jesuit priests has also been creatively appropriated by others.[25]

Jesuits today live with several tensions, tensions that include controversy and tough challenges, but tensions that at the same time offer precious opportunities for service of faith and promotion of justice, tensions that offer opportunities to live generously as Jesuits dedicated to the greater glory of God. Jesuits today retain a "modern" confidence in the possibility of human progress; they seek also to address a "postmodern" context where such confidence may seem naïve. Jesuits today are highly educated individuals,[26] often with considerable professional standing; they are also vowed members of communities with a collective identity as companions of Jesus committed to solidarity with the poor and the oppressed. Jesuits today look back to the sixteenth century for their spiritual roots; they also look to the present and future for how to live out their vocation. Jesuits today live and work in the world; they also acknowledge their need for God's grace, and cherish the Spiritual Exercises of St. Ignatius as the heart and soul of who they are. Jesuits today are proud of their accomplishments; the Spiritual Exercises place a high value on humility and detachment from honors.

Jesuits today are often on the "cutting edge" theologically and otherwise; they also commit themselves to serve the Church in the present age, an age in which the prevailing norm from Rome is one of caution rather than audacity.

What the Jesuit future will be is a matter of some speculation, but also one of choices to be made. Continued adaptation to ever-changing circumstances and contexts, together with creative appropriation of Jesuit traditions and values – by Jesuits themselves and by others – suggest something of what the future of the Society of Jesus may look like. That future is likely to be one of collaboration in ministry and in intellectual work, a collaboration that is increasingly gender-inclusive and ecumenical. It is also likely to be a future more thoroughly international, and diverse in race and culture, than ever before.

Notes

1 See the selection of letters in *Saint Ignatius of Loyola: Personal Writings*, ed. and trans. Joseph Munitiz and Philip Endean (London and New York: Penguin, 1996).

2 See www.sacredspace.ie.

3 *Documents of the 33rd General Congregation of the Society of Jesus*, ed. Donald Campion and Albert Louapre (St. Louis: Institute of Jesuit Sources, 1984), 63.

4 For Kolvenbach's understanding of the Jesuits, see his *Men of God, Men for Others*, trans. Alan Neame (New York: Alba House, 1990).

5 Vatican radio was founded in 1930 by Pius XI; see www.vaticanradio.org.

6 On Jesuit higher education in the United States, see Martin Tripole, ed., *Promise Renewed: Jesuit Higher Education for a New Millennium* (Chicago: Loyola Press, 2001). See also the US Association of Jesuit Colleges and Universities, www.ajcu.edu, and the US Jesuit Secondary Education Association, www.jsea.org. In recent decades US Jesuits have also committed major resources to the creation of Nativity schools, inner-city middle schools (for ages ten to fourteen) devoted to giving a first-rate education to those otherwise unlikely to have such an opportunity.

7 See the exhibition catalog, *Saints and Sinners: Caravaggio and the Baroque Image*, ed. Franco Mormando (Chestnut Hill: Boston College; distributed by University of Chicago Press, 1999).

8 See www. marquette.edu/haggerty.

9 Chris Lowney, *Heroic Leadership: Best Practices from a 450-Year-Old Company that Changed the World* (Chicago: Loyola Press, 2003).

10 For an extended expression of such gratitude, see F. E. Peters, *Ours: The Making and Unmaking of a Jesuit* (New York: Penguin, 1981).

11 Among Daka's publications is his essay, "Community Reconciliation and Healing among the Shona: A Reflection on the Healing Dimension

in the Sacrament of Reconciliation," *Hekima Review* 20 (December 1998), 16–25.

12 Edward P. Murphy, ed., *A History of the Jesuits in Zambia: A Mission Becomes a Province* (Nairobi: Pauline Publications, 2003).

13 See Kevin O'Brien, "Consolation in Action: The Jesuit Refugee Service and the Ministry of Accompaniment," *Studies in the Spirituality of Jesuits* 37 (Winter 2005), 1–47.

14 See www.usd.ac.id.

15 See, e.g., Anthony de Mello, *Sadhana: A Way to God: Christian Exercises in Eastern Form*, 5th printing (St. Louis: Institute of Jesuit Sources; Anand, India: Gujarat Sahitya Prakash, 1978).

16 See Brendan McCarthy, "Dancing Body, Dancing Soul," *The Tablet* (17 June 2006), 32.

17 I saw Saju George perform at the Montreal Gesù in September 2006. There, the multi-hued woods of the altar and sanctuary, drawn from the forests of Quebec, echoed in surprising ways the colors of Saju's costumes and body. For information on Jesuits of French Canada and Haiti, go to www.jesuites.org.

18 The web page for the Jesuits of Upper Canada is www.jesuits.ca.

19 For details, see www.sources-chretiennes.mom.fr.

20 See Katherine Gilfeather, *Alberto Hurtado: A Man after God's Own Heart* (Santiago, Chile: Fundación Padre Alberto Hurtado, 2004). For information on the university that bears his name, see www.uahurtado.cl.

21 See Teresa Whitfield, *Paying the Price: Ignacio Ellacuría and the Murdered Jesuits of El Salvador* (Philadelphia: Temple University Press, 1994).

22 Alfred Delp was a German Jesuit executed by the Nazis; see *Alfred Delp, S. J.: Prison Writings* (Maryknoll, NY: Orbis, 2004). See also Vincent Lapomarda, *The Jesuits and the Third Reich*, 2nd edn (Lewiston, NY: Mellen Press, 2005). Jacques Sommet is a French Jesuit who survived being sent to Dachau; see his *L'acte de mémoire: 50 ans après la déportation* (Paris: Editions de l'atelier, 1995).

23 See Ciszek's autobiographical account, *With God in Russia* (New York: McGraw-Hill, 1964).

24 Berrigan is also a prolific writer; for insight into his understanding of a prophetic vocation, see his *Isaiah: Spirit of Courage, Gift of Tears* (Minneapolis: Fortress Press, 1996).

25 See, for example, her *Companions of Christ: Ignatian Spirituality for Everyday Living* (Grand Rapids, MI: Eerdmans, 2004).

26 Readers of this *Cambridge Companion* will include Jesuits, though it is intended especially for others. Each Jesuit reader will find much that he knows well, and perhaps a few things he has forgotten or never knew. He is also very likely to be ready to offer criticism of the book, and some indications of what he might have included or excluded, or said somewhat differently.

Select bibliography

Note: Preference is given in this selection to recent works in English.

General and reference works

Bangert, William. *A History of the Society of Jesus*. 2nd edn. St. Louis: Institute of Jesuit Sources, 1986.

Begheyn, Paul. "Bibliography on the History of the Society of Jesus." *Archivum Historicum Societatis Iesu* 75 (2006), 385–528.

The Constitutions of the Society of Jesus and Their Complementary Norms. Ed. John Padberg. St. Louis: Institute of Jesuit Sources, 1996.

Diccionario histórico de la Compañía de Jesús. 4 vols. Rome: Jesuit Historical Institute; Madrid: Universidad Comillas, 2001.

Documents of the Thirty-First and Thirty-Second General Congregations of the Society of Jesus. St. Louis: Institute of Jesuit Sources, 1977.

Documents of the 33rd General Congregation of the Society of Jesus. Ed. Donald Campion and Albert Louapre. St. Louis: Institute of Jesuit Sources, 1984.

Documents of the Thirty-Fourth General Congregation of the Society of Jesus. St. Louis: Institute of Jesuit Sources, 1995.

Donnelly, John Patrick, ed. *Jesuit Writings of the Early Modern Period, 1540–1640*. Indianapolis: Hackett Publishing, 2006.

For Matters of Greater Moment: The First Thirty General Congregations. St. Louis: Institute of Jesuit Sources, 1994.

Guibert, Joseph de. *The Jesuits: Their Spiritual Doctrine and Practice*. Trans. William J. Young. St. Louis: Institute of Jesuit Sources, 1972.

Lacouture, Jean. *Jesuits: A Multibiography*. Trans. Jeremy Leggatt. Washington, DC: Counterpoint, 1995.

McCoog, Thomas. *A Guide to Jesuit Archives*. St. Louis: Institute of Jesuit Sources; Rome: Institutum Historicum Societatis Iesu, 2001.

Modras, Ronald. *Ignatian Humanism: A Dynamic Spirituality for the 21st Century*. Chicago: Loyola Press, 2004.

O'Malley, John. *The First Jesuits*. Cambridge, MA: Harvard University Press, 1993.

Sommervogel, Carlos. *Bibliothèque de la Compagnie de Jésus*. 9 vols. Brussels: Schepens, 1890–1900.

Tylenda, Joseph. *Jesuit Saints and Martyrs*. 2nd edn. Chicago: Loyola Press, 1998.

Wright, Jonathan. *God's Soldiers: Adventure, Politics, Intrigue, and Power – A History of the Jesuits*. New York: Doubleday, 2004.

Ignatius of Loyola

Begheyn, Paul. "An Unknown Illustrated Life of Ignatius of Loyola by Petrus Firens (about 1609)." *Archivum Historicum Societatis Iesu* 75 (2006), 137–57.

Bertrand, Dominique. *La politique de Saint Ignace de Loyola: L'analyse sociale*. Paris: Cerf, 1985.

Boyle, Marjorie O'Rourke. *Loyola's Acts: The Rhetoric of the Self*. Berkeley: University of California Press, 1997.

Clancy, Thomas. *The Conversational Word of God: A Commentary on the Doctrine of St. Ignatius of Loyola concerning Spiritual Conversation, with Four Early Texts*. St. Louis: Institute of Jesuit Sources, 1978.

Dalmases, Cándido de. *Ignatius of Loyola, Founder of the Jesuits: His Life and Work*. Trans. Jerome Aixalá. St. Louis: Institute of Jesuit Sources, 1985.

Donnelly, John Patrick. *Ignatius of Loyola: Founder of the Jesuits*. New York: Pearson Longman, 2004.

Gonçalves da Câmara, Luis. *Remembering Iñigo: Glimpses of the Life of Saint Ignatius of Loyola: The Memoriale of Luis Gonçalves da Câmara*. Trans. A. Eaglestone and J. Munitiz. Leominster, UK: Gracewing Publishing; St. Louis: Institute of Jesuit Sources, 2004.

Ignatius of Loyola. *Counsels for Jesuits: Selected Letters and Instructions of Saint Ignatius Loyola*. Ed. Joseph Tylenda. Chicago: Loyola University Press, 1985.

Letters and Instructions. Ed. Martin E. Palmer, John W. Padberg, and John L. McCarthy. St. Louis: Institute of Jesuit Sources, 2006.

Saint Ignatius Loyola: Letters to Women. Ed. Hugo Rahner, trans. Kathleen Pond and S. A. H. Weetman. Edinburgh and London: Nelson, 1960.

Saint Ignatius of Loyola: Personal Writings. Ed. and trans. Joseph Munitiz and Philip Endean. London and New York: Penguin, 1996.

Lonsdale, David. *Eyes to See, Ears to Hear: An Introduction to Ignatian Spirituality*. London: Darton, Longman & Todd, 1990.

Meissner, William. *Ignatius of Loyola: The Psychology of a Saint*. New Haven: Yale University Press, 1992.

Divarkar, Parmananda. "The Chivalric Inspiration of Ignatius of Loyola." *Ignis* 20 (1991), 99–106.

Padberg, John. "Ignatius, the Popes, and Realistic Reverence." *Studies in the Spirituality of Jesuits* 25 (May 1993), 1–38.

Ravier, André. *Ignatius of Loyola and the Founding of the Society of Jesus*. Trans. Maura Daly, Joan Daly, and Carson Daly. San Francisco: Ignatius Press, 1987.

Sheldrake, Philip. "The Influence of Ignatian Tradition." *The Way Supplement* 68 (1990), 74–85.

Shore, Paul. "The *Vita Christi* of Ludolph of Saxony and Its Influence on the Spiritual Exercises of Ignatius of Loyola." *Studies in the Spirituality of Jesuits* 30 (January 1998), 1–32.

Veale, Joseph. "The Unique Elements in Ignatian Spirituality." *Milltown Studies* (Autumn 1992), 97–101.
Young, William J. *Letters of St Ignatius of Loyola*. Chicago: Loyola University Press, 1959.

European foundations of the Jesuits

Bellarmine, Robert. *Spiritual Writings*. Ed. and trans. John Patrick Donnelly and Roland J. Teske. New York: Paulist Press, 1989.
Bireley, Robert. *The Jesuits and the Thirty Years War: Kings, Courts, and Confessors*. New York and Cambridge: Cambridge University Press, 2003.
  Religion and Politics in the Age of the Counterreformation: Emperor Ferdinand II, William Lamormaini, S. J., and the Formation of Imperial Policy. Chapel Hill, NC: University of North Carolina Press, 1981.
Burke, Peter. "The Black Legend of the Jesuits: An Essay in the History of Social Stereotypes." In Simon Ditchfield, ed., *Christianity and Community in the West: Essays for John Bossy*. Aldershot: Ashgate, 2001, 165–82.
  "Rome as Center of Information and Communication for the Catholic World, 1550–1650." In Pamela M. Jones and Thomas Worcester, eds., *From Rome to Eternity: Catholicism and the Arts in Italy, ca. 1550–1650*. Leiden: Brill, 2002, 253–69.
Cameron, Jennifer. *A Dangerous Innovator: Mary Ward (1585–1645)*. Strathfield, NSW: St. Paul's, 2000.
Châtellier, Louis. *The Europe of the Devout: The Catholic Reformation and the Formation of a New Society*. Trans. Jean Birrell. Paris: Editions de la Maison des Sciences de l'Homme; Cambridge: Cambridge University Press, 1989.
Christian, William A. *Local Religion in Sixteenth-Century Spain*. Princeton: Princeton University Press, 1981.
Donnelly, John Patrick. "Peter Canisius." In Jill Raitt, ed., *Shapers of Religious Traditions in Germany, Switzerland, and Poland, 1560–1600*. New Haven: Yale University Press, 1981, 141–56.
Duminuco, Vincent, ed. *The Jesuit Ratio Studiorum: 400th Anniversary Perspectives*. New York: Fordham University Press, 2000.
Favre, Pierre. *The Spiritual Writings of Pierre Favre*. Ed. and trans. Edmond C. Murphy, J. Padberg, and Martin E. Palmer. St. Louis: Institute of Jesuit Sources, 1996.
Fullam, Lisa. "Juana, S. J.: The Past (and Future?) Status of Women in the Society of Jesus." *Studies in the Spirituality of Jesuits* 31 (November 1999), 1–39.
Haskell, Yasmin Annabel. *Loyola's Bees: Ideology and Industry in Jesuit Didactic Poetry*. Oxford: Oxford University Press, 2003.
Homza, Lu Ann. *Religious Authority in the Spanish Renaissance*. Baltimore: Johns Hopkins University Press, 2000.
Höpfl, Harro. *Jesuit Political Thought: The Society of Jesus and the State, c. 1540–1630*. Cambridge: Cambridge University Press, 2004.
Hufton, Olwen. "Altruism and Reciprocity: The Early Jesuits and Their Female Patrons." *Renaissance Studies* 15 (2001), 328–53.

Kilroy, Gerard. *Edmund Campion: Memory and Transcript*. Aldershot: Ashgate, 2005.

Kloczowski, Jerzy. *A History of Polish Christianity*. Cambridge: Cambridge University Press, 2000.

Lazar, Lance. *Working in the Vineyard of the Lord: Jesuit Confraternities in Early Modern Italy*. Toronto: University of Toronto Press, 2005.

Lucas, Thomas. *Landmarking: City, Church, and Jesuit Urban Strategy*. Chicago: Loyola Press, 1997.

Lucas, Thomas, ed. *Saint, Site, and Sacred Strategy: Ignatius, Rome, and Jesuit Urbanism*. Vatican City: Biblioteca Apostolica Vaticana, 1990.

Manning, John and Van Vaeck, Marc, eds. *The Jesuits and the Emblem Tradition*. Turnhout: Brepols, 1999.

Martin, A. Lynn. *The Jesuit Mind: The Mentality of an Elite in Early Modern France*. Ithaca, NY: Cornell University Press, 1988.

  Plague! Jesuit Accounts of Epidemic Disease in the Sixteenth Century. Kirksville, MO: Sixteenth Century Journal Publishers, 1996.

McCoog, Thomas, ed. *The Mercurian Project: Forming Jesuit Culture 1573–1580*. Rome: Institum Historicum Societatis Iesu; St. Louis: Institute of Jesuit Sources, 2004.

Nadal, Jerome. *Annotations and Meditations on the Gospels*. Ed. and trans. Frederick Homann. 3 vols. Philadelphia: St. Joseph's University Press, 2003– .

Nelson, Eric. *The Jesuits and the Monarchy: Catholic Reform and Political Authority in France (1590–1615)*. Aldershot: Ashgate; Rome: Institutum Historicum Societatis Iesu, 2005.

O'Keefe, Joseph. "The Pedagogy of Persuasion: The Culture of the University of Pont-à-Mousson." *Paedagogica Historica* 34 (1998), 421–42.

Orchard, Gillian, ed. *Till God Will: Mary Ward through Her Writings*. London: Darton, Longman & Todd, 1985.

Pavone, Sabina. *The Wily Jesuits and the Monita secreta: The Forged Secret Instructions of the Jesuits, Myth and Reality*. Trans. John P. Murphy. St. Louis: Institute of Jesuit Sources, 2005.

Polanco, Juan-Alphonso de. *Chronicon: Year by Year with the Early Jesuits (1537–1556)*. Ed. and trans. John Patrick Donnelly. St. Louis: Institute of Jesuit Sources, 2004.

The Ratio Studiorum: The Official Plan of Jesuit Education. Trans. Claude Pavur. St. Louis: Institute of Jesuit Sources, 2005.

Selwyn, Jennifer. *A Paradise Inhabited by Devils: The Jesuits' Civilizing Mission in Early Modern Naples*. Aldershot: Ashgate, 2004.

Shore, Paul. *The Eagle and the Cross: Jesuits in Late Baroque Prague*. St. Louis: Institute of Jesuit Sources, 2002.

Wetter, Immolata. *Mary Ward: Under the Shadow of the Inquisition*. Trans. Bernadette Ganne and Patricia Harris. Oxford: Way Books, 2006.

Worcester, Thomas. "Defending Women and Jesuits: Marie de Gournay." *Seventeenth-Century French Studies* 18 (1996), 59–72.

  "Images of Ignatius of Loyola in the Homilies of Jean-Pierre Camus." In John C. Hawley, ed., *Reform and Counterreform: Dialectics of the Word in Western Christianity since Luther*. Berlin: Mouton de Gruyter, 1994, 31–43.

Geographic and ethnic frontiers

Alden, Dauril. *The Making of an Enterprise: The Society of Jesus in Portugal, Its Empire, and Beyond, 1540–1750*. Stanford: Stanford University Press, 1996.

Bermejo, Luis M. *Unto the Indies: Life of St. Francis Xavier*. Anand, India: Gujarat Sahitya Prakash, 2000.

Brockey, Liam Matthew. *Journey to the East: The Jesuit Mission to China, 1570–1724*. Cambridge, MA: Harvard University Press, 2007.

Burgaleta, Claudio. *José de Acosta, S. J., 1540–1600: His Life and Thought*. Chicago: Loyola Press, 1999.

Clooney, Francis X. *Fr. Bouchet's India: An 18th-Century Jesuit's Encounter with Hinduism*. Chennai, India: Satya Nilayam Publications, 2005.

Curran, Robert Emmett, ed. *American Jesuit Spirituality: The Maryland Tradition, 1634–1900*. New York: Paulist Press, 1988.

Cushner, Nicholas. *Why Have You Come Here? The Jesuits and the First Evangelization of Native America*. Oxford: Oxford University Press, 2006.

Francis Xavier. *The Letters and Instructions of Francis Xavier*. Ed. and trans. M. Joseph Costelloe. St. Louis: Institute of Jesuit Sources, 1992.

Greer, Allan. *Mohawk Saint: Catherine Tekakwitha and the Jesuits*. Oxford: Oxford University Press, 2005.

Mormando, Franco and Thomas, Jill G., eds. *Francis Xavier and the Jesuit Missions in the Far East*. Chestnut Hill, MA: The Jesuit Institute of Boston College, 2006.

Nobili, Roberto de. *Preaching Wisdom to the Wise: Three Treatises by Roberto de Nobili, S. J., Missionary and Scholar in 17th Century India*. Trans. Anand Amaladass and Francis X. Clooney. St. Louis: Institute of Jesuit Sources, 2000.

Ricci, Matteo. *China in the Sixteenth Century: The Journals of Matthew Ricci, 1583–1610*. Trans. Louis Gallagher. New York: Random House, 1953.

Ross, Andrew C. *A Vision Betrayed: The Jesuits in Japan and China, 1542–1742*. Maryknoll, NY: Orbis, 1994.

Schurhammer, Georg. *Francis Xavier: His Life, His Times*. 4 vols. Trans. M. Joseph Costelloe. 4 vols. Rome: Jesuit Historical Institute, 1973–82.

Spence, Jonathan. *The Memory Palace of Matteo Ricci*. New York: Penguin, 1985.

Standaert, Nicolas, ed. *Handbook of Christianity in China, I (635–1800)*. Leiden: Brill, 2000.

"New Trends in the Historiography of Christianity in China." *Catholic Historical Review* 83 (1997), 573–613.

"The Transmission of Renaissance Culture in Seventeenth-Century China." *Renaissance Studies* 17 (2003), 367–91.

Worcester, Thomas. "A Defensive Discourse: Jesuits on Disease in Seventeenth-Century New France." *French Colonial History* 6 (2005), 1–15.

Zupanov, Ines. *Disputed Mission: Jesuit Experiments and Brahmanical Knowledge in Seventeenth-Century India*. Oxford: Oxford University Press, 1999.

Missionary Tropics: The Catholic Frontier in India, 16th–17th Centuries. Ann Arbor: University of Michigan, 2005.

Arts and sciences

Bailey, Gauvin Alexander. *Art on the Jesuit Missions in Asia and Latin America, 1542–1773*. Toronto: University of Toronto Press, 1999.

 Between Renaissance and Baroque: Jesuit Art in Rome, 1556–1610. Toronto: University of Toronto Press, 2003.

Baroque vision jésuite. Caen: Musée des Beaux-Arts de Caen, 2003.

Dekoninck, Ralph. *Ad Imaginem: Statuts, fonctions et usages de l'image dans la littérature spirituelle jésuite du XVIIe siècle*. Geneva: Droz, 2005.

Feingold, Mordechai, ed. *Jesuit Science and the Republic of Letters*. Cambridge, MA: MIT Press, 2003.

 The New Science and Jesuit Science: Seventeenth Century Perspectives. Dordrecht and Boston: Kluwer Academic Publishers, 2003.

Findlen, Paula, ed. *Athanasius Kircher: The Last Man Who Knew Everything*. London: Routledge, 2004.

Harris, Steven J. "Transposing the Merton Thesis: Apostolic Spirituality and the Establishment of the Jesuit Scientific Tradition." *Science in Context* 3 (1989), 29–65.

Hellyer, Marcus. *Catholic Physics: Jesuit Natural Philosophy in Early Modern Germany*. Notre Dame: University of Notre Dame Press, 2005.

Kennedy, T. Frank. "Jesuit Colleges and Chapels: Motet Function in the Late Sixteenth and Early Seventeenth Centuries." *Archivum Historicum Societatis Iesu* 65 (1996), 197–213.

Lattis, James. *Between Corpernicus and Galileo: Christoph Clavius and the Collapse of Ptolemaic Cosmology*. Chicago: University of Chicago Press, 1994.

Levy, Evonne. *Propaganda and the Jesuit Baroque*. Berkeley: University of California Press, 2004.

McCabe, William. *An Introduction to the Jesuit Theater*. Ed. Louis Oldani. St. Louis: Institute of Jesuit Sources, 1983.

O'Malley, John W. and Bailey, Gauvin, eds. *The Jesuits and the Arts: 1540–1773*. Philadelphia: St. Joseph's University Press, 2005.

O'Malley, John W., Bailey, Gauvin, Harris, Steven J., and Kennedy, T. Frank, eds. *The Jesuits: Cultures, Sciences, and the Arts, 1540–1773*. Toronto: University of Toronto Press, 1999.

 The Jesuits II: Cultures, Sciences, and the Arts, 1540–1773. Toronto: University of Toronto Press, 2006.

Rock, Judith. *Terpsichore at Louis-le-Grand: Baroque Dance on the Jesuit Stage in Paris*. St. Louis: Institute of Jesuit Sources, 1996.

Rowland, Ingrid. *The Ecstatic Journey: Athanasius Kircher in Baroque Rome*. Chicago: University of Chicago Library, 2000.

Smith, Jeffrey Chipps. *Sensuous Worship: Jesuits and the Art of the Early Catholic Reformation in Germany*. Princeton: Princeton University Press, 2002.

Smolarski, Dennis. "Jesuits on the Moon: Seeking God in All Things ... Even Mathematics!" *Studies in the Spirituality of Jesuits* 37 (Spring 2005), 1–42.

Wallace, William. *Galileo and His Sources: The Heritage of the Collegio Romano in Galileo's Science*. Princeton: Princeton University Press, 1984.

Jesuits in the modern world

Arrupe, Pedro. *Essential Writings*. Ed. Kevin Burke. Maryknoll, NY: Orbis, 2004.

Barnes, Michael. *Theology and the Dialogue of Religions*. Cambridge Studies in Christian Doctrine, 8. Cambridge: Cambridge University Press, 2002.

Bea, Augustin. *The Church and the Jewish People*. Trans. Philip Loretz. New York: Harper & Row, 1966.

Berrigan, Daniel. *The Dark Night of Resistance*. New York: Bantam, 1972.

Buckley, Michael J. *The Catholic University as Promise and Project: Reflections in a Jesuit Idiom*. Washington, DC: Georgetown University Press, 1998.

Calvez, Jean-Yves. *Faith and Justice: The Social Dimension of Evangelization*. Trans. John Blewett. St. Louis: Institute of Jesuit Sources, 1991.

Ciszek, Walter. *With God in Russia*. New York: McGraw-Hill, 1964.

Clooney, Francis X., ed. *Jesuit Postmodern: Scholarship, Vocation, and Identity in the 21st Century*. Lanham, MD: Rowman and Littlefield, 2006.

Cubitt, Geoffrey. *The Jesuit Myth: Conspiracy Theory and Politics in Nineteenth-Century France*. Oxford: Clarendon Press, 1993.

Delp, Alfred. *Alfred Delp, S. J.: Prison Writings*. Maryknoll, NY: Orbis, 2004.

Dulles, Avery. *Models of the Church*. Garden City, NY: Doubleday, 1974.

Dupuis, Jacques. *Christianity and the Religions: From Confrontation to Dialogue*. Trans. Philip Berryman. Maryknoll, NY: Orbis, 2002.

Gilfeather, Katherine. *Alberto Hurtado: A Man after God's Own Heart*. Santiago, Chile: Fundación Padre Alberto Hurtado, 2004.

Hopkins, Gerard Manley. *The Poetical Works of Gerard Manley Hopkins*. Ed. Norman Mackenzie. Oxford: Clarendon Press, 1992.

Hughes, Gerard. *God in All Things*. London: Hodder & Stoughton, 2003.

Kelley, William, ed. *Theology and Discovery: Essays in Honor of Karl Rahner, S. J.* Milwaukee, WI: Marquette University Press, 1980.

Kolvenbach, Peter Hans. *Men of God, Men for Others*. Trans. Alan Neame. New York: Alba House, 1990.

Kuzniewski, Anthony. *Thy Honored Name: A History of the College of the Holy Cross, 1843–1994*. Washington, DC: The Catholic University of America Press, 1999.

Lonergan, Bernard. *Method in Theology*. New York: Herder and Herder, 1972.

Lowney, Chris. *Heroic Leadership: Best Practices from a 450-Year-Old Company that Changed the World*. Chicago: Loyola Press, 2003.

Marmion, Declan and Hines, Mary E., eds. *The Cambridge Companion to Karl Rahner*. Cambridge Companions to Religion. Cambridge: Cambridge University Press, 2005.

Martin, James. *In Good Company: The Fast Track from the Corporate World to Poverty, Chastity, and Obedience*. Franklin, WI: Sheed & Ward, 2000.

  This Our Exile: A Spiritual Journey with the Refugees of East Africa. Maryknoll, NY: Orbis, 1999.

Martini, Carlo Maria. *After Some Years: Reflections on the Ministry of the Priest*. Trans. Teresa Cadamartori. Dublin: Veritas, 1991.

McFadden, William, ed. *Georgetown at Two Hundred: Faculty Reflections on the University's Future*. Washington, DC: Georgetown University Press, 1990.

McKevitt, Gerald. *Brokers of Culture: Italian Jesuits in the American West, 1848–1919*. Stanford: Stanford University Press, 2007.

Mello, Anthony de. *Sadhana: A Way to God: Christian Exercises in Eastern Form*. St. Louis: Institute of Jesuit Sources; Anand, India: Gujarat Sahitya Prakash, 1978.

Mendonça, Delio de, ed. *Jesuits in India: Vision and Challenges*. Anand, India: Gujarat Sahitya Prakash, 2003.

Mooney, Christopher. *Teilhard de Chardin and the Mystery of Christ*. New York: Harper & Row, 1966.

O'Brien, Kevin. "Consolation in Action: The Jesuit Refugee Service and the Ministry of Accompaniment." *Studies in the Spirituality of Jesuits* 37 (Winter 2005), 1–47.

O'Collins, Gerald. *Jesus Our Redeemer: A Christian Approach to Salvation*. Oxford: Oxford University Press, 2007.

O'Hanlon, Gerard. "The Jesuits and Modern Theology: Rahner, von Balthasar, and Liberation Theology." *Irish Theological Quarterly* 58 (1991), 25–45.

Peter, F. E. *Ours: The Making and Unmaking of a Jesuit*. New York: Penguin, 1982.

Pierce, Joanne and Downey, Michael, eds. *Source and Summit: Commemorating Josef A. Jungmann, S. J.* Collegeville, MN: Liturgical Press, 1999.

Pieris, Aloysius. *An Asian Theology of Liberation*. Maryknoll, NY: Orbis, 1988.

Rahner, Karl. *Foundations of Christian Faith: An Introduction to the Idea of Christianity*. Trans. William V. Dych. New York: Seabury Press, 1978.

Schoof, T. M. *A Survey of Catholic Theology, 1800–1970*. Trans. N. D. Smith. New York: Paulist Newman Press, 1970.

Silf, Margaret. *Companions of Christ: Ignatian Spirituality for Everyday Living*. Grand Rapids, MI: Eerdmans, 2004.

Sobrino, Jon. *Christ the Liberator: A View from the Victims*. Trans. Paul Burns. Maryknoll, NY: Orbis, 2001.

Tripole, Martin, ed. *Promise Renewed: Jesuit Higher Education for a New Millennium*. Chicago: Loyola Press, 1999.

Whitfield, Teresa. *Paying the Price: Ignacio Ellacuría and the Murdered Jesuits of El Salvador*. Philadelphia: Temple University Press, 1994.

Wood, Susan K. *Spiritual Exegesis and the Church in the Theology of Henri de Lubac*. Grand Rapids, MI: Eerdmans; Edinburgh: Clark, 1998.

Index